The Striking Cabbies of Cairo and Other Stories

SUNY series in the Social and Economic History
of the Middle East
Donald Quataert, editor

The Striking Cabbies of Cairo and Other Stories

Crafts and Guilds in Egypt, 1863–1914

John T. Chalcraft

State University of New York Press

Published by
State University of New York Press, Albany

© 2004 State University of New York

For information, address State University of New York Press,
90 State Street, Suite 700, Albany, NY 12207

Production by Judith Block
Marketing by Anne Valentine

Library of Congress Cataloging-in-Publication Data

Chalcraft, John T., 1970–
　　The striking cabbies of Cairo and other stories : crafts and guilds in Egypt,
　1863–1914 / John T. Chalcraft.
　　　　p. cm. — (SUNY series in the social and economic history of the Middle
　East)
　　Includes bibliographical references and index.
　　ISBN 0-7914-6143-2
　　1. Guilds—Egypt—History. 2. Handicraft—Egypt—History. 3. Strikes and
　lockouts—Egypt—History. 4. Egypt—Economic conditions. I. Title. II. Series.

　HD6473.E3C48 2004
　338.6'32'096209034—dc22　　　　　　　　　　　　　　　　　2003061036

10　9　8　7　6　5　4　3　2　1

For Laleh

Contents

Figures

Foreword

John Chalcraft has written a wonderful book that substantially raises the level of discourse in Middle East labor, social, and political history. His study examines popular action, labor, and state formation and is important on a number of counts.

He rebuilds the bridge between nineteenth century Egyptian history and the larger field of Ottoman history. As his work demonstrates over and over again, political policies as well as economic trends in Egypt closely tracked those further north, in the lands still directly ruled by the Ottoman sultan. The many parallels between economic events, political crises, state legislation, and labor actions in the two areas remind us of the need to reintegrate the subfield of Egyptian history during the late Ottoman era back into the mainstream of Ottoman history.

Chalcraft vibrantly gives agency to subaltern groups in the Ottoman Egyptian world by persuasively illustrating that the actions of guild members determined the evolution of their organizations. He also makes a major contribution to our understanding of guilds and their evolution during this period of high capitalism. Here indeed is the world of grand economic processes, notably the threat of European industrial competitors. But Chalcraft's guildsmen are no mere passive witnesses to the great forces assailing them. In a significant set of findings, he demonstrates how journeymen skillfully used the budding language of the national state as a tool in their fight against oppression by the masters. More generally, he shows us precisely how guild members' actions determined the changing nature and fate of guilds. Guilds were not broken by European penetration nor crushed by state intervention but rather played an active role in their own reshaping.

Chalcraft also traces, in persuasive detail, the restructuring of small-scale manufacturing and the service trades and demonstrates their vitality down to World War I. He spends considerable space documenting the construction and transport sectors, a real contribution since historians often neglect the former because of source difficulties. Chalcraft demonstrates the major role they did play in the economy and in providing livelihoods to vast numbers of Egyptians. He also contributes to a growing literature both in Middle Eastern, south Asian and Asian studies that argues against the decline of local textile manufacturing in the face of competition from Europe. His story, as readers will find, is a more complicated one. For example, the number of textile workers and those in other small crafts grew dramatically in the final pre-war decades thanks to a combination of rising demand and nationalist sentiments.

This book represents the best of the new scholarship on labor and statemaking and should help us rethink the character of the Middle East just before the remapping of the region after World War I.

Donald Quataert

Acknowledgments

It is a pleasure to acknowledge and thank those whose assistance and example made this book possible. Michael Gilsenan led me from Oxford to New York University, where I completed the dissertation that formed the basis for this book. His generosity, friendship, practical help, and analytical guidance, and the inspiration of his intellect have all contributed immensely to this project and its larger positioning. Neither he nor any one else, of course, should be blamed for the analyses, judgments, and errors which follow. Zachary Lockman was my dissertation advisor and read and commented on the book manuscript. Through his clarity, integrity, assistance, and rigor he has been nothing less than a guiding light throughout. I am sure that my sometimes contrarian style has not obscured the major intellectual and vocational debts I owe to both Michael and Zach.

Donald Quataert started to read and constructively criticize manuscript drafts at an early stage. His great enthusiasm, comments, and own research have been a continuous support and source of inspiration. He has further done me the honor of editing this book and writing a foreword. Roger Owen encouraged me to pursue the research and read and commented on various drafts. I have derived considerable benefit from his quiet, powerful insight. Molly Nolan's perceptive eye showed me that my dissertation told too optimistic a story. I hope that this book goes some way to responding to her constructive critique. Khaled Fahmy, far from jealously guarding the secrets of the Egyptian archives, welcomed me and helped with the domain he knows so well, and demonstrated that research findings should be shared. His comments have always been valuable. Eugene Rogan has given great encouragement, and has long been an important interlocutor, sometimes at key moments. Juan Cole was kind enough to read and comment on the entire manuscript, catching a number of errors of transliteration, and forcing me to confront and clarify the argument in important ways. Pascale Ghazaleh constructively brought her expertise to bear on chapters 1 and 2. Amal al-Ayoubi generously helped me to decipher scribal script. Both Yasir Suleiman and Yaseen Noorani read whatever parts of the text I gave them, and suggested important improvements. Frances Lindsay spent much time carefully editing an earlier manuscript draft. I am also indebted to the two anonymous reviewers at State University of New York Press. Their close reading and constructive suggestions had a significant impact on the book.

The list of those whose insights and support contributed to this project more generally is long and justice cannot be done to them all here. Jens Hanssen has long been an important discussant, methodological inspiration, and friend. More recently, lengthy discussions with Yaseen Noorani have been enjoyable and enriching. Ariel Salzmann's ideas and suggestions were a real help in the very early stages of this work. Others whose help and ideas were important at one stage or another include Paul Amar, Fiona Arnold, Ramsey al-'Assal, Jenny Bell, Isa Blumi, Geoff Berman, Vince Darley, Lel Gillingwater, Najib Hourani, Thomas Kuhn, Jason Neidleman, Michael Rinella, Neil Sammonds, Joshua Schreier, Relli Shechter, Colin Starger, and Craig Starger.

I owe a particular debt to all the staff of the Egyptian National Archives, in particular Mme. Sawsan Abdel-Ghani, Mrs. Nadia Mostafa, Mme. Nagwa, Mme. Fatma and Ms. Afaf Ragab. A fellowship with the American Research Center in Egypt (1997–98), along with research permission from the Egyptian government, made much of this research possible, and a British Academy grant allowed me to return in 2001.

Laleh Khalili has generously read every word of the manuscript, sometimes more than once, saving me from errors large and small, making important criticisms and suggestions, and helping to clarify the argument. Her clarity, commitment, and insight have made her a touchstone for, and source of many ideas. Above all, her enthusiasm, support and love has made life worth living and books worth writing.

Introduction

T his book is about crafts and service workers in Egypt between the
cotton boom of the early 1860s and the outbreak of the First
World War. It seeks to explore and understand the ways in which
those working in small-scale, unmechanized industries survived, adapted,
evaded unwanted state intervention, and engaged in collective action during years of rapid world economic integration, state building, and colonial
rule. Using numerous new sources, the pages that follow describe and explain how crafts and service workers were radically restructured over time.
The book also traces the closely related transformation and disaggregation
of an important Ottoman institution, the guild, and the emergence of new
forms of formal and informal organisation. The idea is to bring to light
a little-known and yet important part of Egypt's popular history. Crafts and
service workers, especially those engaged in new and adapted trades, continued to employ the majority of Egypt's urban population throughout the
nineteenth and early twentieth centuries, and yet studies of such workers
are practically nonexistent. Cabdrivers, dyers, masons, tailors, and weavers
and their changing guilds, and their petitions, protests, and strikes are almost completely invisible in the existing historiography, in spite of their
importance for economy, society, and even the rise of nationalism. History
"from below" has commonly been ceded to studies of the rise of a working
class selling its labor power for wages to capital. This research breaks with
this body of literature and instead focuses on the surprisingly numerous
and expanding numbers of those working in heterogeneous forms of petty
production and service provision outside the factory gates. The aim is to
establish their place in the historiography, and provide an original account
of the dynamics of their transformation, adaptation, and political contention. In so doing I hope to shed fresh light on modern Egyptian history,
and to contribute to larger debates about uneven forms of work under capitalism and the popular history of the colonised world.

1

Popular History

The research presented here is driven by the conviction that there is much to do and much to gain from writing the popular history of the colonial world—the history, that is, of the everyday lives, practices, ideas, and struggles of poor and subordinated groups during the age of European empires and beyond. How so?

Until relatively recently, "history" *sans phrase* largely coincided with that of the imperial centers: Britain, France, Germany, Italy, and the United States. The "barbaric," "backward," or "primitive" peoples—the subjects of empire and the people without history—were studied not in the History Department, but in Oriental studies or anthropology. Hugh Trevor-Roper's dismissal of the African past in the 1960s as "the unrewarding gyrations of barbarous tribes" reflected this disciplinary division.[1] Where historians' methods were applied to the non-West, a version of the history of "Great Men" was often the result, with accounts written on the basis of colonial sources and the texts of European observers, focusing on colonial officials, diplomats, élite groups, and politicians.[2] In 1963, say, when E. P. Thompson published *The Making of the English Working Class*, the popular history of the modern non-European world barely existed.[3]

The "full retreat"[4] after 1945 of "drum and trumpet" Rankean history, and the impact of history "from below," were at first confined to the historiography of the colonizer, not the colonized. However, with national independence, and the increasing appearance of historians and social scientists in Cold War-constituted area studies, social, economic, and demographic history slowly started to make inroads into the historiography of the non-West. By the 1990s, new research from multiple sites around the world had established the place of production and exchange, social structure, demography, cities, and to some extent women, merchants, peasants, workers, and guilds within the literature.[5] Meanwhile, since at least the publication of Said's *Orientalism* in 1978, new and diverse postcolonial histories, focusing on issues of gender, power/knowledge, hegemony, and discourse have unsettled some of the categories of social and economic history, and broken new ground in writing subaltern histories.[6]

Yet, in spite of the impact of social history and the interest generated by subaltern studies, it is still the case that to a remarkable extent the voices and struggles of the majority of the world's population are excluded from the stories told by historians—whether in Cairo, Chicago, Delhi, or Paris. A recent quality, edited volume, for example, drew together thirty-eight historians "from the English-speaking world over the past fifty years to reflect the views which students today are most likely to encounter in the history they read."[7] No straw man this, but just thirteen pages touched on issues related to non-Western, grassroots history.[8] Of these pages, seven were largely devoted to minorities in the United Kingdom.

Even those who champion grassroots history in the imperial center are to be found applying different standards to the colonized world. Thus one finds Eric Hobsbawm arguing in his history of the twentieth century that "the history of the makers of the Third World transformations . . . is the history of elite minorities."[9] Here, contrary to Hobsbawm's assumptions about historical change in the West, the "backward" masses of the non-West remain but the object of élite projects. There is little or no acknowledgement, as Guha put it, of "the contribution made by the people on their own, that is, independently of the elite."[10] Instead, the majority of the population exist for power holders "to save, to capture, or to direct."[11]

Social and economic history has been effectively criticized for universalizing nineteenth century European paradigms of historical change, erasing complexity and excluding diverse subaltern voices in the process.[12] Postcolonial methodology, of course, has not necessarily generated history from below. Mitchell's groundbreaking study, *Colonising Egypt*, paid little attention to the practices and discourses of the poor and subordinate.[13] Even subaltern studies, turning to the élite production of colonial discourse by the later 1980s, had "begun to leave the subaltern out."[14] Some exaggerated the impossibility of writing any coherent subaltern history, linking the very claim of coherence to aspirations to imperial domination.[15] This antifoundational critique, however suggestive, remains methodologically underdeveloped, and misses the importance of the fact that coherence does not only erase, but can also construct resistance.[16]

Yet various currents in subaltern studies, anthropology, social history, Marxism, and social movements theory point towards a kind of history which cannot afford to ignore or misrecognize the history of the poor and the subordinate in these ways. Such work wagers that popular groups and individuals contest the terms of their integration into regimes of accumulation and domination. Slaves, workers, small proprietors, serfs, peasants, debtors, subjects, conscripts, taxpayers, and citizens do not give up their labor, resources, obedience, or loyalty without negotiation, contestation, and resistance. It is too simple to assert generally that the subaltern cannot speak.[17] Multiple and uneven processes of contestation can work to soften, and occasionally transform social relations.[18] It is crucial therefore, to study and understand these processes, an approach which has the potential to reveal much about the nature of the social relations within which popular groups and individuals are enmeshed. The point is not to exaggerate subaltern agency. Contestation is often countered by the élite construction of new forms of control or hegemonic persuasion. Indeed, *pace* James C. Scott, much élite action is incomprehensible outside of attempts to control and exploit popular activities.[19] The argument here is that open-ended and many-sided contests have an important impact on the overall reproduction and transformation of regimes of accumulation, states, and empires. To use Tilly's phrase, outcomes are often the "by-product of great struggles and provisional settlements in the course of which all parties had programs and interests but no one intended to create the political arrangements that actually emerged."[20] Popular agency is at stake, whether or not it achieves its goals. If subaltern groups were unsuccessful, it is important to understand why this was and what it meant.

Crafts, Protests, and Guilds in Egypt

In search of such a popular history, this book recovers the adaptation, accommodation, and resistance of those working as wage laborers, "disguised" wage laborers, self-employed, petty employers, and contractors in largely unmechanized and hand-powered forms of production and service provision in late-nineteenth- and early-twentieth-century Egypt.

First, this research seeks to establish the importance of crafts and service workers in Egyptian economy and society as a whole in the context of a historiography which generally underrates and often ignores them. The myth of the simple destruction and decline of Egyptian and Ottoman handicrafts and "traditional" trades at the hands of the world economy has been remarkably tenacious.[21] This book intends to show in more detail and more convincingly than before—on the basis of new or little-used sources—how wayward this notion actually is. In this respect it builds on the pioneering work of Donald Quataert and a few others regarding the larger Ottoman empire, and the handful of voices, such as those of Roger Owen and Kristin Koptiuch, that have made this point about Egypt.[22] I will show how crafts and service workers, far from simply disappearing, multiplied their numbers in line with and sometimes ahead of rapid population increase, restructured their work, and were transformed in a far-reaching way in interaction with changing times. In 1914, such workers were to be found in villages, towns, and cities throughout Egypt. They provided an extensive and indispensable range of goods and services for the population at large, and livelihoods for a significant proportion of the urban inhabitants. I hope to take the historiography forward by staking out a new position on explaining and characterizing this restructuring.

Second, the book intends to resurrect the protests of crafts and service workers from relative historiographical obscurity. Apart from a few
pioneering works, artisans and others have remained a muted or even nonexistent voice in the historiography of the nineteenth-century Middle East,
altogether overshadowed by the story of the rise of a labor movement apparently based among industrial wageworkers.[23] Sherry Vatter's innovative
work on protesting Damascene weavers in the nineteenth century showed
that it was not only industrial workers who protested pay and conditions.[24]
As for Egypt, Juan Cole's search for the social origins of the Urabi rebellion (1881–82) broached new, exciting sources, and made protesting crafts
workers and guilds key elements in his account.[25] This book has pursued
the sources used by Cole, and added many others, particularly for the later
decades. I will argue that protests and petitions by crafts and service workers in the 1860s and 1870s had an important impact on the disaggregation
of the guilds, as well as some impact on the very form of the state itself.
In bringing to light a major wave of protest in spring 1907, hitherto without its historian, I will show how these events played an important role in
the development of nationalism. I hope also to convince historians that the
mobilization of crafts and service workers must be seen as a constitutive
part of the emerging labor movement in Egypt, thus defining the limits
and nature of that movement more broadly than has been the case until
now.

Third, I provide a new account of guild transformation and disappearance during the "long" nineteenth century. Guilds have been defined
more or less adequately as "a group of town people practicing the same occupation and headed by a shaykh."[26] They were institutions which appear
to have linked urban traders to the government, protected livelihoods, and
formed communities of various kinds since at least the Ottoman conquest
of 1517, although their origins are disputed. Gabriel Baer rightly con-
vinced scholars about forty years ago that Egypt's guilds continued to exist
until the 1880s, only disappearing over the following thirty or so years.[27]
Revisionism on guilds across the Ottoman empire has largely debunked
older, negative views of guilds. Raymond's view of guilds as restrictive monopolies which stifled progress and innovation has been problematized.[28]
Baer's view of the guild as a mere "tool in the hand of the government" has
been largely overturned.[29] Ehud Toledano, for example, has argued that
guilds in mid-nineteenth-century Egypt wielded meaningful corporate autonomy.[30] Cole has gone further, speaking of guilds as involving a kind of
shop democracy, lobbying the government, and acting as a significant vehicle of protest during the 'Urabi rebellion.[31]

My contribution modifies some of this revisionism by showing how the guilds were transformed, co-opted, and increasingly disaggregated during the nineteenth century, in ways which seriously diminished their autonomy, their ability to protect members' livelihoods, or their capacity to act as vehicles for protest. This new understanding of nineteenth-century guild transformation paves the way for a new account of guild disappearance, which explains the demise of the guilds not in terms of the simple collapse of the "traditional" trades,[32] but as a consequence of restructuring, state intervention, and protest in the decades prior to 1914.

Unevenness under Capitalism

These findings should not especially surprise those debating forms of work and protest outside the factory gates more generally. For decades social scientists and historians have uncovered uneven forms of production and exchange across the capitalist world system.[33] Few would any longer argue that production is converging on the factory model.[34] Unilinear theories of industrialization, or talk of the inexorable march of capitalist relations of production, narrowly defined, have long been discredited.[35] Studies of different parts of the colonial and postcolonial world, from Trotsky to Tilly, have revealed multiple, diverse, and changing forms of work and different regimes of capital accumulation and reproduction.[36] These range from multinational corporations to insecure self-employment, and from plantation slavery to subsistence peasantry. Whole literatures have grown up around notions of the informal sector,[37] precapitalist modes of production,[38] the dual economy, partial proletarianization, casual work, and so on.[39] Different forms of work have been shown to involve different rates and forms of innovation and productivity, different rates and types of remuneration, and heavily divergent labor conditions and experiences.

Furthermore, it should be no surprise that protests were not confined to factories in Egypt. As Sewell wrote regarding western Europe and the United States, as long ago as 1980, "There is almost universal agreement on one point: that skilled artisans, not workers in the new factory industries, dominated labor movements during the first decades of industrialization."[40]

This study therefore, at this level, only confirms and extends scholarly recognition of the unevenness of work and the multiplicity of sites of worker protest in the world system, albeit with the added interest of the use of relatively rich sources from an understudied region regarding an early period, which spans both precolonial and colonial eras.

However, when it comes to putting together and explaining adaptation, protest, and guilds, the case of Egypt may have something more to offer larger debates about unevenness. For if one begins with the premise that the world economy is a coeval and interacting whole, if one abandons developmentalism and the catch-all and vague notion of backwardness, then the question of how different forms of work are generated, articulated, and distributed throughout the world system is by no means easy to solve. As my research proceeded, it became clear that few adequate explanations were readily available to comprehend the reproduction and even expansion of forms of petty production and service provision in Egypt during years of intensive world economic integration, when cheap imports and foreign investment led many to believe that such supposedly traditional forms of production would soon be destroyed.

Dual economy formulations, which posit the existence of a distinct traditional sector lagging behind a modern sector, are hardly adequate to this task. First, it quickly became clear that the term "traditional" overstates the continuity, internal coherence, and separateness of forms of petty production and service provision. Second, this theory does not explain why the traditional economy is not swept away by the more productive modern sector. If traditional producers are somehow congenitally or culturally "backward," why are they not destroyed, either by the cheap production of the modern sector, or by the modern sector takeover and transformation of their businesses?

Similar problems dog those who wish to explain uneveness in terms of the articulation of modes of production. This theory suggests that capitalism articulates with and preserves precapitalist modes of production, largely because such precapitalist modes are useful to capital. First, they are said to provide cheap goods and services, which can be used for flexible subcontracting, and more importantly drive down subsistence costs (and thus the wages) of industrial workers. Second, precapitalist modes reportedly provide a cheap safety net for a reserve army of underemployed, who can be absorbed by industry during boom periods and sacked during busts. However, "precapitalist" is far too tight, monolithic, and continuous a label for production that since the sixteenth century has been transformed in various ways through interaction with world markets, commodification, the growth of markets, the use of wage labor, and modern social and political systems. Further, this theory still does not explain why capitalism does not destroy noncapitalism in the periphery. This is because even if one allows capital's larger interest in allowing noncapitalists to subsidize industrial wages, it is still not clear how capitalism's cheap commodities do not, nonetheless, put noncapitalists out of business. This after all, was what transpired in the core economies. Why not in the periphery too? Furthermore, why do capitalists hold back from the profits to be made by taking over and reorganizing noncapitalist production? As Rey noted, "Let us cease to reproach capitalism with the one crime that it has not committed, that it could not think of committing. . . . [A]ll the bourgeoisies of the world burn with desire to develop the 'underdeveloped' countries."[41]

This puzzle appeared only soluble through a break with economism, and the pursuit of another body of literature, again reaching back to Trotsky, which has taken history, power, and culture seriously in its understandings of economic change.[42] From this diverse literature, a few ideas were particularly suggestive in showing how society and politics could be integral to the changing shape of relations of production and exchange. First of all "the economy" could only be an analytical abstraction, a moment in a set of social relations that outran it, not a prior, distinct, empirical base, juxtaposed to a superstructure of ideas and politics. As Raymond Williams has written, the base is less "a fixed economic or technological abstraction" but rather involves "the specific activities of men [and women, one must add] in real social and economic relationships, containing fundamental contradictions and variations and therefore always in a state of dynamic flux."[43] With this concept of economy, it is easier to perceive how social, political, and cultural factors might invade, intersect with, and help produce economic outcomes.[44]

How, though, to articulate politics with production? One useful answer begins with a problem within Marxian economism. As theorists of the labor process have long remarked, Marx treated labor as a commodity which once bought was effectively owned and therefore manipulated as just another factor of production, as a purely economic object, like a machine.[45] However, many have persuasively made the point that labor—consisting of human individuals—is not so easily manipulated, and constantly resists its transformation into an object.[46] In fact, labor changes its price and work rate and productivity by multiple forms of resistance and accommodation, including collective bargaining and protest, which in turn influences the rate of capital formation. As Patrick Heller has written, "The social conditions under which labor is made available to the market . . . directly shapes the logic of surplus extraction and hence accumulation."[47] In addition, the owners of capital, including masters and small proprietors, are also enmeshed in sociopolitical relations, relating to regulation, taxation, local institutions, access to markets, inputs and the state, and forms of internal competition and collaboration. Their relative success in pursuing their interests, whether through existing institutions, or through overt or covert collective action, has an impact on their accumulation strategies, access to markets and inputs, and their ability to retain profits. Hence the politics of collective action articulates with economic outcomes.

To take the analysis further, one must address the question of what drives and constrains collective action. An older, "materialist hierarchy,"[48] in which the forms of political struggle were seen as flowing—in the last instance—from larger economic structural transformation, no longer holds. From E. P. Thompson's cultural Marxism to the present, much work has pointed up the importance of neighborhood, region, race, gender, ethnicity, citizenship, nationalism, language, politics, everyday life, and so on in the making of the identities, consciousness, and protests of workers and others.[49] Anthropologists have made the same point.[50] Studies of social movements have also done much—outside of any exclusive focus on material factors—to examine how protest and political contention[51] is mobilised, culturally framed, and transformed by political opportunities.[52]

From this literature I have found most suggestive those analyses which link protest and its outcomes to the relative strength of local forms of resource mobilization—guilds, unions, and the like—the possibility of alliances between claimants and middle classes, and the form of the state. All these factors, which, as I will show, were heavily embedded within and transformed by transnational structures of power,[53] played important roles in the making and breaking of collective action and protest in Egypt.

This study hopes to contribute to the literature by using these insights to establish a connection between larger social and political factors and the form and constitution of petty commodity production in Egypt. I will argue that the political weakness of workers and masters alike constrained productivity-raising mechanization, and therefore contributed to the labor-intensive and relatively unproductive (although efficient) form of their work. The idea is to help explain the puzzle of the distribution and construction of unevenness within the world economy by drawing fresh attention to the importance of politics and struggle in the making of relations of production and exchange.

Restructuring and Political Contention, 1805–1914

It may be helpful to summarize the main lines of the argument here. During the nineteenth century, Egypt, a largely autonomous province within the Ottoman Empire, was harnessed to a world economy with its core in northwest Europe. During the early stages of this process, Mehmet Ali, an ambitious provincial ruler, seized power in 1805, and went on to establish a hereditary dynasty in Egypt, laying the foundations for a centralized state bureaucracy in the process. Mehmet Ali's progeny, especially after the cotton boom of the early 1860s, engaged in further state building in pursuit of "progress" and "civilization," incurring debts which ultimately formed the proximate cause of the British invasion of 1882 and subsequent occupation. Until 1914, as world economic integration progressed apace, the British consolidated their de facto control over the Egyptian state while holding onto the fiction of Ottoman sovereignty. From the 1890s onwards, nationalist opposition grew, putting real pressure on the British after 1906, but only fundamentally altering Egypt's relationship to the empire after the First World War.

In order to continue to pursue their livelihoods under changing conditions, crafts and service workers engaged actively in a process of restructuring, which largely began after the cotton boom of the 1860s, but which greatly accelerated during the investment boom of 1897–1907. Restructuring involved the rise of new trades and the disappearance or adaptation of old, and the far-reaching transformation of products, locations, and means and relations of production in response to deepening market relations, changing consumption tastes, and increasing competition. Crafts and service workers tapped markets where demand was weak, fluctuating, and unstandardized, a market structure which diminished the profitability of large-scale and capital intensive investment. I will be placing particular emphasis on how the drive for cheap production was secured through cutting rates and wages. Small masters and self-employed engaged in what I will call "self-exploitation," whereby they accessed inputs and sold their products at rates which did little more than permit them to reproduce their existing capital.[54] Furthermore, where labor was often cheap and abundant, and protection limited, a common result was labor squeezing, which meant extracting "absolute surplus value" from workers through diminishing wages or lengthening hours.[55] Where profits were low, machines expensive, and labor cheap and abundant, these strategies made sense, and entailed little significant productivity-raising mechanization.

Central to the argument is the proposition that these forms of restructuring did not result from purely economic factors. State building until 1881–82 co-opted guild leaderships for fiscal and regulative purposes, and undermined their autonomy and ability to act as vehicles for urban protest. Restructuring worked further to disaggregate the guilds, which were increasingly unable to protect the livelihoods of members against the ravages of competition, from both cheap imports and new forms of investment, and against intratrade competition for employment involving masters and journeymen. The failure of the guilds, alongside the lack of social leg-islation by the colonial state, accelerated and helped create forms of self-exploitation and labor squeezing. When the colonial state abandoned the guilds as units of taxation and regulation, especially in 1890, they had ceased to serve their members in political or economic terms, and were therefore increasingly by-passed from below without a struggle in their defense.

Protest was rooted in the harsh terms of restructuring, unwanted state intervention, and the failures of the guilds on the one hand, and changing political opportunities wrought from alliances with middling classes, new discourses of citizenship and nationalism, and the relative openness or closedness of the state to claim making on the other. Under Mehmet Ali, mobilization was heavily muted by the repressive powers of the state. But under Ismail, new forms of citizenship, heavy taxation, and the challenge to Isma'il's regime mounted by a rising group of provincial notables formed the basis for the increasing petitions and protests of the 1860s and 1870s, which were mobilized not by the guild as a whole, but by sub- and extraguild groupings, often in opposition to guild leaderships and forms of local ex-ploitation. After the demobilization which followed the British occupation, protests began again after the early 1900s, culminating in a major round of strikes and demonstrations in spring 1907. Crafts and service workers were reacting against unwanted state regulations and restructuring, while forging alliances with a rising nationalist middling class, the *afandiya*. These new forms of collective assertion, culminating as they did in the formation of the first syndicates and unions, were another force from below as much as from above, which by-passed and diminished the old guild structure.

Protests resulted in a number of local gains and particular successes. They also had an important impact on regulative regimes, the end of the guilds, the wider labor movement, and the growth of nationalism. Yet, they could not substantially change the harsh terms of restructuring among self-employed and wageworkers of various kinds. Political contention with the potential to overcome high rates of exploitation was stymied by the forces lined up against it: the form of world economic integration, the colonial state, and the oligarchies which had coalesced around it. As Sweezy has noted, authoritarian rule in the periphery and high rates of social exploita-tion went hand in hand "as two sides of the same coin."[56] Crafts and service workers were thus condemned to continue to engage in exploitative re-structuring, a process which was based not on productivity-raising mecha-nization and strong protections for labor, but on self-exploitation and labor squeezing, and on the malleability, cheapness, and abundance of hands and bodies.[57] Sweezy suggests that this kind of social exploitation is at the root of what he calls "underdevelopment," because it both "perpetuates poverty and at the same time prevents the growth of a mass market for consumer goods that would attract and justify investment."[58] In these ways, social, political, and economic factors intertwined to construct and reproduce a particular form of petty production and service provision in Egypt.

Structure and Scope

I trace this argument through the five chapters which follow, and provide a summary and return to wider debates in the conclusion. The first chapter sets the scene by examining crafts and guilds prior to the cotton boom of the 1860s, discussing the beginnings of changes that were to deepen during the rest of the century. The rest of the work takes up the book's main story, which unfolded during the fifty years prior to 1914 as world economic integration deepened in an unprecedented way, and as far-reaching changes were wrought in the form of the state and in social structure. Chapters 2 and 3 tackle restructuring and contentious politics under Khedive Ismail (1863–79). The final two chapters take the same themes to the period between the British invasion (1882) and the outbreak of the First World War, during which time the coming of empire ensured that collective action failed to change the terms of craft restructuring.

In principle I have sought to investigate any kind of small-scale crafts or service work, from barbering to carting, from butchery to metalwork, and from embroidery to bath keeping. In practice however, constraints of space and source material meant that I have gone into much greater detail regarding some of the most important (measured by numbers employed) trades, while referencing a wider variety of trades where useful. Regarding manufacturing, I have been chiefly concerned with textile trades (spinning, weaving, and dyeing), garment trades (tailoring, shirt making, shoemaking, dressmaking) and construction and related trades (carpentry, masonry, brick making, furniture making and the like). Thus, crafts associated with metallurgy, food production, luxury goods, art and literature, chemicals, or the transmission of power receive less attention. As for services, I am mostly interested in various new and partially new urban transport trades which appeared during the period, such as carting and donkey driving, but especially cab driving.

Documents, Newspapers, and Old Books

A growing number of social historians, using newly accessible Ottoman and Egyptian archives, have been showing the way to new sources for some years. Unsurprisingly, then, the Egyptian National Archives (*Dar al-Watha'iq al-Qawmiyya*) in Cairo provided the richest primary sources for this project.

The most important single find was a census of Cairo Governorate from 1868.[59] This hand-written, worm-nibbled document extends to seventy volumes, and lists every man, woman, child, and slave in Cairo, Bulaq, and Old Cairo, household by household. The final volume of the census divides the population of Cairo by occupation. The census helps to fill the statistical gap relating to Cairo's occupational structure stretching between the 1840s and 1897.[60] Because I am chiefly interested in the fifty years before the First World War, the census provided a useful statistical anchor (at least for Cairo) at the start of the period.

A key set of records comprises several series of petitions written to various government agencies. Two such series stand out. The first are the petitions sent to the Ministry of Interior and the police, and the correspondence between the police, the ministries, and any other relevant bodies, such as the provincial offices (*mudiriyyat*) between the late 1860s and the early 1880s. Juan Cole was the first writing in English to extensively use these petitions and correspondence in the mid-1980s in his research on the Urabi rebellion.[61] The series (containing forty boxes in chronological order) is particularly useful because the original petitions are preserved. Most of these are from landowners and officials, but petitions from artisans, service workers, and merchants also exist in smaller numbers in each box.[62] The second series, previously unused as far as I know, and consisting of petitions sent to the Khedivial Diwan (*Diwan al-Khidiwi*) between the mid-1890s and 1914, is vital in as much as it sheds light on the two decades immediately preceding the First World War.[63]

Correspondence, reports, petitions, and tax returns from and filed under different ministries (indexed under *Majlis al-Wuzara*)—Finance (*Nizarat al-Maliyya*), Interior (*Nizarat al-Dakhiliyya*), and Public Works (*Nizarat al-Ashghal*)—as well as from the Council of Ministers (*Majlis al-Nuzzar*) were also useful.[64] Other series were also used, such as research files (*Muhafiz al-Abhath*),[65] and court records where available.[66]

The Foreign Office (FO) records at the Public Record Office (PRO) in London were also employed. They contain embassy and consular correspondence internal to Egypt, the records of the Cairo British Consular Court, the Cromer Papers, and the correspondence between London and Cairo including any reports and surveys, such as the results and correspondence surrounding the Milner Mission, which was conducted by the British to ascertain the effects of the First World War on Egypt.[67]

Beyond the PRO, the Egyptian National Library (*Dar al-Kutub*) was used above all for newspapers and periodicals. The Egyptian Government statistical service in *Madinat Nasr* (CAPMAS) housed some of the censuses and external trade statistics on recently opened shelves.[68] The collection of Père Martin at the Collège de Sainte Famille in Ghamra, Cairo, was especially useful for pre-1914 writings and periodicals.[69] The Institut d'Egypte is a reorganised and recatalogued, friendly, and useful library, especially for pre-1914 books, bulletins, and statistical compendiums, mostly in French.[70] The American University in Cairo library has some useful journals (such as *al-Muqtataf*) and reference material such as the published legislation of the Egyptian government from 1876 to 1914.[71] The official publications room at the University Library in Cambridge was useful for colonial documentation—particularly Cromer's *Annual Reports*, and the *Commercial Reports* written by consuls in Alexandria, Suez, and Cairo and sent to London. It also has more occasional, unusual volumes, such as Bowring's report, or old Baedeker travel guides. The map room in the university library in Cambridge has some useful maps and compendiums.[72]

1

Crafts and Guilds
before 1863

The patterns of restructuring and collective action in which I am interested had their origins in the first half of the nineteenth century. During these decades, the projection of European power overseas, state building, and unequal world economic integration started to alter the conditions under which crafts and service workers pursued their livelihoods in Egypt's towns and cities. Market relations began to deepen, consumption tastes started to change, and certain trades in particular areas started to come under pressure from imports, prompting the beginnings of a new kind of craft restructuring in response to new opportunities and tougher competition. As for the guilds, Baer showed many years ago that these institutions survived the dynasty and empire-building policies of Mehmet Ali, Ottoman governor of Egypt (1805–1848), and continued to hold monopolies and discharge public functions until midcentury and beyond. However, as this chapter will argue, the character of the guilds was transformed in an important way during the decades that preceded the cotton boom. Under Mehmet Ali, these venerable institutions were co-opted in the name of dynasty building, and their capacity to protect the livelihoods of their members, or to act as vehicles for protest, was undermined. The weakening of the guilds, which preceded the 1860s, and continued thereafter, set the stage for crafts and service workers' search for new forms of protection and mobilization, the story of which this book picks up in detail from the 1860s onwards.

Crafts and Guilds in the Ottoman Empire

In spite of mercantilist expansion from the sixteenth to the eighteenth centuries, European influence in Ottoman lands until the early nineteenth
century remained weak relative to later years. European merchants built
far-flung mercantilist commercial networks, but these sustained a trade that
in comparison with the later nineteenth century was puny and uncertain.
Indeed, even in the later eighteenth century, the great bulk of Ottoman external commerce—perhaps six-sevenths—was carried on not with Europe,
but with Africa and Asia.[1] European merchants existed in only small numbers in Ottoman cities. The Portuguese blockade certainly cut off much of
Egypt's pepper trade during the early sixteenth century, but the irritant was
short lived, had few long-lasting or systemic effects, and was nothing like
as ruinous as some have suggested.[2] Furthermore, European military power
in the region was limited. The Portuguese and Spanish, unable to colonize
North Africa because of stiff resistance there, set sail across the Atlantic.
The balance of military power in the Balkans only started to tip towards
Russia and Austria towards the end of the eighteenth century. And until
Napoleon's short-lived invasion of Egypt in search of wealth and Empire
(1798–1801), not since the Crusades had a European military presence
been felt in the region. Thus, even as European mercantile overseas expansion took place, the Ottomans retained a substantial measure of political, economic, and social independence from external forces.

     Until the early nineteenth century, the bulk of Ottoman commerce
was in the hands of Ottoman merchants, and, notwithstanding an impres-
sive international trade, most of the crafts consumed within the empire
were made locally. Ottoman cities from Cairo to Istanbul housed numerous
crafts workers, known in Egypt as those who "possessed" a skill or a craft
(*ashab al-hiraf wa-l-sana'i'*).[3] In 1800, the savants of the French occupation
estimated that "established artisans" (including masters and journeymen)
numbered twenty-five thousand in Cairo, or a little less than a tenth of the
population of the city,[4] which was the center of manufacture and commerce
in Egypt.[5] Most produced textiles, food, furniture, and pottery in order "to
satisfy the every-day needs of the urban population."[6] A smaller group of
more specialised crafts workers made products requiring "more capital and
a greater degree of craftsmanship and skill," such as the linen weavers of
Damietta.[7] Weaving and dyeing employed about a third of all crafts workers in the eighteenth century in Cairo, and weavers left legacies that were
above the artisanal average during the eighteenth century.[8] Less well-off
leather workers, such as shoemakers, tanners, and saddlers, were the next

most numerous group of artisans in Cairo. Food trades (especially milling and baking) wood, metal, and construction work occupied most other crafts workers. Workshops tended to be small, and tools relatively simple, although in some cases larger numbers of artisans were grouped under one roof, as in a linen factory at Mansura, or a larger dyeing establishment in Cairo—with thirty or forty workers.[9] Whatever their trade, artisans were rarely wealthy. Raymond shows that during the eighteenth century the average value of the wills of 154 craftsmen was about eight times smaller than the value of the legacies of 143 regional and international merchants.[10]

A variety of service workers also plied their trades in Ottoman towns. In Cairo, most were engaged in transport, the principal trades being water carrying, camel driving, donkey driving, and porterage. Numerous water carriers, for example, carried water in leather skins from the Nile to Cairo's inhabitants from the tenth century onwards.[11] Others provided services to markets, such as weighers and measurers, worked as entertainers, or held household positions as grooms, cooks, servants, messengers, and so on. These service workers were generally of lower status and poorer even than most crafts workers. They usually possessed little or no capital of their own, and were often engaged in work considered dirty or immoral. Al-Jabarti referred to them, as well as one or two humble crafts such as blacksmithery, as the *ahl al-hiraf al-safila* (people of despicable crafts), or *arbab al-hiraf al-dani'a* (people of inferior crafts).[12]

Since at least the Ottoman conquest of 1517, most crafts and service workers in Egypt (along with merchants and retailers), whatever their wealth or status, belonged to guilds (*ta'ifa*, plural *tawa'if*).[13] In contradistinction to Massignon, who had seen the Islamic guild as above all a pact of honor between brothers, a pledge of chivalry rooted in mysticism whose origins lay among the antiauthoritarian and communally oriented Qarmatians of the seventh and eighth centuries,[14] Baer more usefully defined a guild on the basis of craft specialization: "a group of town people engaged in the same occupation and headed by a shaykh."[15] His definition has broadly stood the test of recent research, although most have stressed the flexibility of the term *ta'ifa*, which could be used to refer to other social groups, such as Copts (*ta'ifat al-aqbat*) or Armenians (*ta'ifat al-arman*). It has also been noted that some *tawa'if* appear to have gone without shaykhs, or sometimes, other aspects of guild organization.[16] In the light of these complications, the use of the term "guild" as a translation for the more generous Arabic term, *ta'ifa*, has been questioned. The term "guild" is retained here in the absence of a better alternative, and on the basis that any simple analogy to European or other non-European guilds must be avoided.

In general, guilds regulated trade life, linked trades to the government, and provided a community of some kind to members, but their practices varied by place, time, and trade. Guilds could hold the monopoly over a particular trade in a particular location, solve disputes, contract labor, distribute raw materials, levy dues, punish members, organize ceremonies for admission and promotion, remit taxes to the government, implement government regulations and requisitions, parade through the streets at certain public festivals, and organize mutual help. These many functions, however, were rarely present together in the same guild, a fact which has contributed to the controversy over the nature of the guilds. As Quataert has remarked, "[W]e do not really understand . . . the nature and functions of most Ottoman guilds. . . . [They] varied quite considerably not only over time but also contemporaneously by place. In some areas they may have been monopolistic; in others they were only loose associations of persons engaged in the same activity."[17]

Nonetheless the negative depictions of guilds by an older generation of scholars have been largely debunked by the research of recent decades.

First, Baer's view of the guild as a "tool in the hand of the government, not an independent power"[18] has been successfully challenged by subsequent work.[19] It has become increasingly clear that in the main, as long as the guilds maintained order, delivered taxes, and played their role in provisioning city and government, the authorities left them considerable room for local self-determination. As Gerber has shown convincingly, guilds were run not on the basis of either Sultanic or Sacred law, imposed from above, but on the basis of heterogeneous and locally determined customary law (*'urf*), or the "law of the trade" (*qanun al-kar*),[20] determined largely by guild members themselves, and often merely ratified in the Islamic courts.

Baer's view of guild shaykhs as government appointees is also largely mistaken. From Anatolia to Egypt, scholars have demonstrated that guild leaders were usually chosen by guild members, not the government. Usually a group of senior members gathered before the *qadi* to make their wishes known, and generally speaking, the *qadi* ratified the appointment. It has further become clear that guild leaders were usually practicing masters of the trade in question (not outsiders), and thus were intimately involved in the interests and activities of the trade itself. Shaykhs appear in many instances to have run the affairs of the guild in consultation with senior masters (*'umad*) and the experts in the trade (*ahl al-khibra*), also drawn from the ranks of senior masters.

Guilds were called on to discharge certain statelike functions, the most important of which was remitting taxes from members. Until now, historians have tended to assume that shaykhly involvement in taxation was a form of unwelcome state intervention in craft life.[21] Arguably, however, Bowring, back in the 1840s, was right to stress that it was, just as importantly, a privilege for the guild. "The sheikh becomes responsible for the payment of the tribute or poll-tax of all the members of the corporation," wrote Bowring, "who are thus released from individual responsibility to the government and protected from the exaction to which they would otherwise be exposed, from the rapacity of public functionaries."[22] The state ceded this privilege to the guilds until the later nineteenth century because of its own partial blindness regarding the wealth, premises, capital, and income of crafts and service workers.

The guilds may have become more robust in the face of state power in the larger context of Ottoman decentralization during the eighteenth century. Particularly important was that during this period the Janissaries (the professional infantry corps of the Ottoman army), garrisoned in Egypt (as elsewhere in the Ottoman Empire), entered the crafts. In some cases, members of the different military corps (*oçaks*) claimed to protect a given guild and thus demanded a share of the craft surplus—often against the wishes of existing masters and journeymen.[23] In other cases, Janissaries actually engaged in the trade in question, a factor which could work both for and against the interests of fellow crafts workers.[24] In still other cases, existing artisans managed to affiliate themselves to one or another military corps and thus received a more favourable form of protection. For example, Janissaries, in return for a down payment from the guilds, allowed tradesmen to subvert government regulations and raise wages and prices at the expense of the consumer.[25] Janissary involvement thus appears to have involved both local exploitation and the protection of guilds against outsiders. It certainly appears likely that the Janissary presence made it more difficult for higher authorities to intervene in popular craft activities.

Further, it is hard to avoid the possibility that guilds were also one of several overlapping institutions in which organizing for protest took place during the eighteenth century. Edmund Burke has identified the role of the guilds in his discussion of urban social movements in the Middle East during the period 1750–1914. He notes that at moments of urban protest "the solidarities of the urban quarter, Islamic guilds, Sufi brotherhoods (and in the Ottoman Empire, local Janissary units) provided whatever coherence the crowd had, and very often the leadership as well."[26] Raymond's examination of eighteenth century protest in Egypt exemplifies this analysis. He shows how guilds (such as those of the vegetable sellers at Rumayla or the butchers at Husayniyya) popular quarters, and Sufi orders overlapped to form a resilient organizational basis for popular protest against hoarding at moments of scarcity, and more frequently towards the end of the century, Mamluk rule. Most dramatically, he shows how various bourgeois elements, drawn from the *ulama* and the merchants, forged an alliance with artisans, guildsmen, and other townspeople against the French occupation (1798–1801). This alliance supported Mehmet Ali—an Ottoman commander sent by Istanbul to restore order—and the security his leadership promised. Raymond suggests that the guilds played a real role in the making of Mehmet Ali (Ottoman governor of Egypt, 1805–1848), noting that "the popular masses made history in Cairo." Hence both Hajjaj, the shaykh of the vegetable sellers in Rumayla, or Ibn Sham'a, the shaykh of the butchers of Husayniyya, figured in Mehmet Ali's victory cortège of 1805, where the *kapıcı* brought from the Sultan the nomination of Mehmet Ali as pasha of Cairo.[27]

Overall, Baer and others appear to have missed or mistaken a key point: the minimality and diversity of the Ottoman government.[28] As Stanford Shaw wrote almost three decades ago:

> In theory . . . the sultan had almost absolute powers. . . . In practice, however . . . [t]he nature of the Ottoman system in fact left the sultan with very limited power. . . . [S]ignificant aspects of Ottoman life were left to be dealt with autonomously, not only by the millets but also by the guilds, the corporations, the religious societies, and the other groups forming the corporative substructure of Ottoman society.[29]

This guild autonomy, more than anything else, accounts for the variegated nature of guilds in the Ottoman empire, so stressed by Quataert, for no single type of guild was imposed from above. Indeed, a problem for guild members, especially those of lower status, was not to escape the clutches of some mythically despotic state, but to persuade the state—the sultan, the provincial governor, or the qadi court—to intervene to provide justice against local exploiters.[30]

Second, the negative view that both Baer and Raymond take of guild monopolies and restrictions looks less warranted in the light of new research and changing assumptions. Baer speaks of the "economically harmful" effects of monopolistic rights and privileges.[31] Raymond supposes that monopolistic and hierarchical guild practice contributed to an absurdly fragmented division of labor and a "spirit of routine," which together resulted in the "stagnation of technique" and a hostility to progress.[32] More plausibly, however, guild monopolies positively protected the livelihoods of their members and ensured adequate provisioning of the city. Masters could only establish themselves—according to guild- and court-enforced custom and law—after acquiring a *gedik* or license.[33] The *gedik* "gave to an artisan or a trader the right to carry out his activities in a particular shop."[34] Only a limited number of such licenses were available.[35] Skilled journeymen in each trade would generally have to wait their turn for the privilege of taking one of these positions and thereby opening an independent shop. Once the elders of the guild agreed that a suitable candidate could become a master in the trade, that candidate would gain the right to one of the available positions (known in Ottoman as *gedik havai*, floating slot), sometimes the tools and equipment which went along with the position, and often the right to practice in the particular premises where the tools and equipment might be (*gedik mustakarr*).[36] Once in the hands of a master, the position became a kind of property, whereby the owner could sell it, pass it on to his heirs, and use it as collateral to guarantee his credit.[37] Guild restrictions on the number of licenses available did the crucial work of preventing too many masters from joining the trade, which could lead to glut, falling prices, internal competition, and mutual ruin for guild members. In this way guilds protected the market share of their members, as well as maintaining production to provision the city. Further, ownership of a fixed *gedik* (which gave the artisan the right to practice in particular premises) lent guild members important leverage against the landlords seeking to evict them or to raise rents.[38] Guild control over new membership was also the mechanism by which the guilds could maintain their reputation and guarantee the quality of their work, which in turn worked to ensure the livelihoods of their members.[39] This feature of craft corporate activity was only regulated by the government in exceptional cases. Raymond gives an example of where the agha "examined the workers who proposed to exercise the profession of goldsmiths, and levied a due on all those which he admitted to the mastership."[40] This unusual situation resulted from the particularly crucial role that goldsmiths played in monetary activity.

Third, although recent research has been less than clear on this point, Baer's claim that "any strong sense of belonging to a guild and being proud of it" was "more or less absent" is rather too emphatic a generalization, given the state of the evidence to which he had access, and is certainly not the last word on the subject.[41] Guilds at some level formed a community for crafts and service workers in particular professions. First, although it is not known how widespread initiation ceremonies were in the eighteenth century, descriptions of such ceremonies continue to appear for various guilds into the nineteenth century. Lane's reference to the *shadd* ceremony,[42] involving the binding of the girth of an initiate with a sash tied with knots and performed "when a son is admitted a member of some body of tradesmen or artisans," is well known. He wrote that it "is customary only among carpenters, turners, barbers, tailors, bookbinders and a few others."[43] The presence of such a ceremony, at least in certain guilds, would indicate at least the possibility of a sense of belonging, especially because the ceremony was supposed to link initiates to an unbroken chain of craft skill and virtue leading back through the generations to an original ancestor (*pir*), often a companion of the prophet. And it should be cautioned that the state-centered sources are very likely to be silent on, and thus deemphasize, ceremonies which did not bear on the essential concerns of taxation, order, and provisioning.

Second, guilds did appear in procession at numerous major public festivities and celebrations. At the marriages and circumcisions of members of the pasha's family, at the cutting of the Cairo canal (the Khalij) that allowed the flood waters of the Nile into the city, and at the festival of the *ru'ya* (the sighting of the crescent moon to begin the fasting of Ramadan), the departure of the caravan to Mecca for pilgrimage, and feast days (*mawalid*) for particular saints to mention some of the most important, representatives from different guilds appeared in floats, reenacting their crafts complete with tools and materials. "The different corporations," wrote Bowring, "have associated themselves with the religious rites and ceremonies of the country, taking part in all the great processions, such as the departure of the caravans for the holy cities, so that opinion throws round the corporations a considerable amount of protection."[44] Arguably, at least, the public appearance of crafts workers as divided into corporate entities at key religious and public festivals was a way of underlining guild membership as an important identity in a wider society. With this in mind, it does seem problematic to refuse the possibility that identification with a particular craft or guild involved some social and cultural substance.

Third, it is reasonable to suggest that in various guilds, solidarity was bolstered through common links to one or another confession (such as the Greek Orthodox), national group (such as North Africans), or Sufi order (such as the Bayumiyya). Baer's view is that most guilds were divided this way (although he did not see this as resulting in solidarity), Raymond's that only a minority of guilds were monopolized by a particular ethnic, national, or sufi group. Certainly the Cairo census of 1868 strongly supports Raymond's view, as we shall see. Nonetheless, the fact that certain guilds were monopolized by those with a strong marker of a particular identity may well have strengthened a sense of belonging to that guild.

Fourth, guilds appear to have been involved, at least in certain times and places, in organizing mutual assistance of one kind or another. Again, the claim is not that these activities were widespread—the state-centered sources do not allow one to make such an argument. But scattered references through the eighteenth century and into the nineteenth provide food for thought. Raymond reports that mutual aid had been observed by Pococke amongst the servants.[45] References to a mutual fund among shoemakers to help members in distress are several.[46] Jabarti noted how "guild members collected contributions to help arm and feed their members" prior to a battle against the French.[47] Examples of the practice of *rukiyya*, the equal distribution of guild income among members, exist, such as that involving the sugar carriers in 1720.[48] As will be discussed below, debates about the *rukiyya* flared up in Egypt the 1870s. These references do not add up to a systematic picture of mutual aid in the guilds, but they do indicate that such activities were not unknown, and where they existed, protected members and their livelihoods to some degree. Given the paucity of information on this topic, emphatic judgements one way or the other are unlikely to be persuasive, but the likelihood that in variable ways guilds formed a community of some kind for members cannot simply be dismissed.

Overall then, although the picture is not quite convincing or complete, it would appear that the guilds of the eighteenth century were more autonomous from the government, more protective of their members' livelihoods, and more likely to have involved a social community at least in certain places and trades than Baer and to some extent Raymond suppose. The argument here is that these autonomies and protections were significantly eroded by political, economic, and social change during the nineteenth century.

European Power and Egyptian Dynasty Building

During the nineteenth century, the forms of independence enjoyed by the Ottoman empire were steadily eroded. European military and economic power was projected overseas in radically new ways. There was a dizzying expansion in world trade based above all on industrial capitalism, a trade ever more systematically structured to exchange the raw materials of the periphery with the manufactured goods of the core. Egypt's trade with Europe, for example, increased between forty and sixty times.[49] European navies and armies, the products of both state building and capitalism, circled the Ottomans with increasing intent, first forcing favorable terms of trade, and then subjecting much of the region—along with most of the rest of Asia and Africa—to direct or indirect colonial rule. As Hourani has put it, "Muslim states and societies could no longer live in a stable and self-sufficient system of inherited culture; their need was now to generate the strength to survive in a world dominated by others."[50]

The beginnings of this new projection of European power overseas roughly coincided with an important political dynamic emerging from within the Ottoman empire—attempts by regional strongmen to build dynasties of their own and bolster themselves against the central control of the sultan. In this, none were as successful as Mehmet Ali, an Ottoman military leader of relatively modest Albanian origin, who seized the governorship of the Ottoman province of Egypt in July 1805. Ottoman governors, in accordance with the canons of Ottoman statecraft, were supposed to move from post to post across the empire. However, the new incumbent, building on the example of local rulers in Egypt (Ali Bey al-Kabir, 1760–1773) and Palestine (Ahmad al-Jezzar, 1775–1802), sought a hereditary dynasty in the province of Egypt.

Mehmet Ali appropriated European military and administrative practices far more extensively than his immediate forebears. Inspired by the military success of Napoleon, Mehmet Ali successfully built a European-style conscript army, in the process eliminating the rival Mamluk households that had largely controlled Egypt during the preceding century. To pay for his army, he centralized the fiscal system while abolishing the rural tax farms. To the same end, Mehmet Ali Pasha actively intervened in the economy. He tried to monopolize all trade and most production in Egypt by buying all produce at an official price and selling it at a profit. He rapidly extended the area under cultivation through dredging and building canals for irrigation, converting Lower Egypt to perennial irrigation. Significantly enough, in 1820 and 1821, the Pasha, in collaboration with a Frenchman, Jumel, introduced the cultivation of long-staple cotton for sale on foreign markets. Further, between 1816 and the late 1830s, searching for revenue and munitions, the Pasha attempted a program of industrialization. He also developed the apparatus of government, established schools to train bureaucrats and military personnel, and brought the religious establishment under state control.

On the basis of his newfound strength, Mehmet Ali launched a bid for empire which brought him into direct conflict with European power. It was a showdown he was to lose. By the late 1830s Mehmet Ali's armies had taken territory from the Sudan to Syria, and now they moved into Anatolia, threatening the Sultan himself. But the Sultan requested British assistance, and their intervention in Syria from 1839 to 1841 resulted in the withdrawal of Mehmet Ali's forces, their restriction to eighteen thousand men by the Treaty of London in 1841, and the signing of commercial treaties favoring European merchants. In recompense, however, Mehmet Ali successfully obtained the grant of a hereditary governorship from the Sultan in 1841, officially transforming Egypt into a semi-independent dynasty, while formally remaining under Ottoman sovereignty and paying a tribute to the Porte. But the meaning of 1841 was the subordination of Egypt to rapidly expanding European military and economic control. The attempt to build a relatively independent regional empire in the Levant had been crushed. From 1841 onwards Egypt's rulers had little choice but to pursue a more truncated and Egypt-centered attempt at state building— a self-strengthening movement aimed at achieving some form of autonomy in a region now clearly dominated by British and French power.

Crafts and Service Workers

The details of how crafts and guilds were transformed by interaction with these changes during the first half of the nineteenth century remain somewhat obscure. In particular, the forms of craft adaptation and collective action in which I am interested, and about which this book tells a detailed story from the 1860s onwards, can only be partially inferred from rather fragmentary and sometimes contradictory evidence. Nonetheless, recent research has indicated that an older view, which consigned the handicrafts to stagnation and decline during these years, and simply ignored service workers (not to mention most Ottoman merchants and retailers), is problematic.

Statistics are few, but those which exist for employment indicate a broad continuity rather than any sudden diminution in numbers employed in crafts and trades. Mehmet Ali's urban tax census of 1821 to 1823 listed 186 guilds with about 26,000 members between them, while enumerating a further 7,000 workers in forty-two government-run establishments.[51] Susan Staffa estimated that as many as 30,000 merchants and artisans worked in Cairo in 1839.[52] The census of 1846 enumerated around 27,000 artisans and industrial workers in Cairo.[53] None of these figures compare unfavorably with the 25,000 "established artisans, masters and journeymen" listed by the French savants, and in fact consistently show continuity rather than decline. It would appear reasonable to suggest that as far as the evidence goes, at a time when Cairo's population remained relatively stable, so did the proportion of those working in crafts and trades.

For all the ever-earlier back projection of a world system that one encounters in the literature, it is perhaps surprising to discover that only in the 1830s did manufactured imports from Europe start to increase in a way

which had little precedent. During the eighteenth century, although specific crafts were under pressure from certain manufactured imports from
Europe, notably French woollens, the impact of such pressures was limited,
sectoral, and reversible, and cannot be said to have caused any universal or
far-reaching transformation.[54] As Roger Owen has written, "[European im-
ports] affected only some aspects of economic activity in some areas, and
then often only for a short space of time."[55] Indeed, British trade with the
Ottoman Empire actually declined during the eighteenth century, only
reestablishing itself after 1801 following improved relations with the Sultan after the British assisted in the repulsion of the French from Egypt.
Furthermore, French trade practically disappeared from the Eastern
Mediterranean in the 1790s because of the Napoleonic wars, and did not
recover until the 1840s. In short, as Şevket Pamuk recently remarked,
"[T]he volume of trade with Europe remained limited, and Ottoman manufactures were not subjected to any serious competition from European industry, until the nineteenth century."[56]

The 1820s saw the beginnings of a relatively modest trade exchang-
ing long-staple Egyptian cotton for the machine-made and increasingly
cheap cotton fabric of Manchester, as well as a much smaller value of European luxury goods in demand among Egypt's Turco-Circassian rulers for
conspicuous display. But only in the 1830s, with the development of steam
shipping, increasing tonnages and speeds, and deepening and bigger har-
bors in the Mediterranean did this commerce start to increase rapidly.[57]
Egypt imported about six times more cotton fabric in exchange for currency earned from ginned and pressed cotton at the end of the 1830s than
it had in the later 1820s. Then, in the wake of the Commercial Treaties of
1838 to 1840, which imposed a low external tariff of 5 percent on European imports, Egypt's purchases of British cotton goods doubled again between the later 1830s and the later 1840s to reach a value of about 300,000
LE. With cotton production and prices rising, Egypt's total external trade
came to be worth around 4 million LE in the later 1850s. Thus it was probably only from around the mid-1830s that imports started to have an impact of any significant kind on artisans in Egypt.

The assumption must be that from that time, pressure was brought to
bear by these imports on particular crafts. Those who produced certain luxury items for the upper classes, who now turned, if modestly at this stage, to
certain European products, must have been hit. Above all cotton weavers
were now encountering unprecedented competition in the shape of rising
imports of machine-made cotton. Nonetheless, the impact of these changes
on local crafts should not be exaggerated. Even by midcentury, Egypt's

external trade with Europe remained less than half of its total trade. Commercial increases were accompanied by local population expansion and new wealth acquired through the agricultural production of cotton. The absolute level of imports at this stage, especially compared to later in the century, remained relatively small. The absence of case studies means that it is not definitively established that even cotton weavers were thrown out of work by the rapid increase in Manchester's market share. It is hardly likely that local cotton weavers were actually flourishing under new conditions, but there are no adequate statistics to allow one to pronounce the death of cotton weaving during these years, and reports from later in the century certainly affirm that cotton weaving was a vital and in some cases expanding industry in Egypt.

Quataert argues that in Anatolia urban and workshop weavers were hit quite hard by the initial wave of imports (but were able to recover later in the century), an argument echoed by Reilly and to some extent Chevallier for Syria.[58] These analyses are plausible, but it must be pointed out that to a considerable extent they remain based on deductions, and relatively firm statistical evidence has only been discovered respecting particular trades. If the initial wave of imports was purchased with the increased wealth which came from growing cotton, which it inevitably was (because such imports could only be bought with hard currency—excepting a drain on specie), then the impact of such a growing commerce on local weaving production must have been diminished.[59]

It is important to note also that cotton weaving was not by any means the only textile production in Egypt, let alone the only handicraft production. As for textiles, silk, wool, and flax were spun and woven, dyers worked with either imported or locally woven cloth, and weavers of straw baskets, reed mats, rope, and twine, and braiders and trimmers of various kinds were not directly affected by the import of cotton cloth. Quataert has also made the important argument that Anatolian countryside and household weavers were in a relatively strong position (compared to their urban counterparts) to expand production for growing markets because of low production costs and proximity to markets.[60] He has also showed that textile production migrated in some measure to the countryside in Anatolia in response to imports. Tucker suggests that putting-out systems may have multiplied during these years, although Cuno sees no substantial evidence of this, noting only that women appeared to work independently as spinners in the textile industry.[61]

With regard to other handicrafts, tailoring and shoemaking were hardly affected negatively by imports until the 1860s, along with construction, carpentry and related trades, metallurgy, food production, and a number of luxury trades such as work in precious metals. Cuno's examination of the land tax registers of two villages in Lower Egypt in the 1840s revealed the presence of a "significant number of households engaged in non-agricultural pursuits," including millers, builders, carpenters, blacksmiths, boatmen, and jewellers.[62] These findings prompted Cuno to propose discussion of transformation rather than simple deindustrialization. Very few persons in Egypt could afford to import consumer goods (other than cotton cloth) from Europe during the first half of the nineteenth century. In other words, the majority of Egypt's handicrafts were probably not dramatically affected by the increases in external trade, rapid though they were, between the 1830s and the 1850s. Although European capitalism had now encountered Egypt's crafts and trades, more far-reaching transformation was to wait for the deeper world economic integration that accompanied the cotton boom of 1861 to 1864.

The impact of Mehmet Ali's program of import substitution was also somewhat mixed, and older views which asserted the destruction of handicrafts in this context have long been discredited. It is certainly the case that a number of weaving workshops were mandatorily closed, and their masters and journeymen forced to work in the Pasha's establishments. It was in this context that al-Jabarti reported the abolition of the *tara'iq* (customs) of the weavers' guild. Further, the textile trades found themselves (at least for a time) in stiff competition with the Pasha's establishments. There are also a number of bloodcurdling tales of the punishment meted out to crafts workers, such as weavers, who violated Mehmet Ali's monopolies or contravened his regulations.[63]

However, as early as 1964, Baer usefully pointed out that Mehmet Ali's industrialization drive of approximately 1815 through the 1840s did not affect all handicrafts by any means and was in any case short-lived.[64] Certainly, the majority of artisans worked outside of textiles, and so suffered little direct competition from the factories. Owen's work has underlined these points through a relatively sober analysis of the extent of Mehmet Ali's import substitution projects, even at their peak in the 1830s: Mehmet Ali's experiments probably employed only about thirty to forty thousand workers, rather fewer than the one or two hundred thousand suggested by earlier historians. And even then, not all workers were employed all the time, because factories were often not running at full capacity because of operational problems relating to placement, machinery (and its maintenance), and fuel costs. Further, a certain proportion of even these workers were recruited from the *fallahin*, and not just from urban crafts workers. Finally, most of Mehmet Ali's factories were destined to close during the 1840s, which meant that weavers and others were now able to return to their workshops. In certain instances they took with them training in European-style skills, methods, and the use of machinery. Clerget gives an example of a family of weavers who successfully weathered the transformations of import substitution. The son of a weaver of fine lingerie was employed in one of Mehmet Ali's factories, Khurunfish at Cairo, but after it closed, the son set up a silk-weaving establishment of his own, along with a shop from which to sell its produce. His sons in turn went on to produce new products, making striped silk for headgear and sashes for luxury robes.[65]

A further point, which has not received sufficient emphasis, is that when one examines the factories themselves, one finds not wage labor subject to a single productive discipline and a significant degree of mechanization, but instead aggregates of artisans organized under one roof. At the arsenal at Alexandria, for example, according to Bowring, one found hundreds of carpenters and joiners, and scores of borers, caulkers, rope makers, smiths, filers, turners, coppersmiths, sailmakers, block makers, tailors, shoemakers, painters, plumbers, coopers, sawyers, and others. In all, three thousand artisans who possessed a craft skill of one kind or another were employed in the arsenal. Bowring also mentions the Coptic handloom weavers in the textile factories, an indication that one should not assume in advance that "factory" meant mechanization and power-driven machinery. Khurunfish brought together numerous different trades: more than a hundred fitters (*barradin*), more than ninety local carpenters (*najjarin baladi*), more than fifty ironsmiths (*haddadin*), forty iron turners (*kharratin hadid*), and so on.[66] The very limited deployment of steam power—"at most . . . seven or eight steam engines" across the country—gains fresh significance in this context.[67] In other words, import substitution and its factories did not simply displace or work to destroy artisans, even where it was relatively successful, but employed them and to some extent provided training in the use of new equipment. The sheer variety of trades present in the factories is striking. Further, apart from one or two European-made machines brought over to serve as models, most factory equipment in the 1820s and 1830s was actually constructed—under the supervision of the French advisor Jumel and his assistants—by Egyptian carpenters, smiths, and turners using improved lathes and tools.[68]

Thus, although the details remain largely unknown, it seems most likely that the economic activities of crafts and service workers were not radically transformed during the first half of the nineteenth century. Artisans continued to work in numbers up and down Egypt. Most still plied their trades in Cairo, which remained the center of production, although this distribution was probably starting to change with the growth of cities connected to the export economy, most dramatically Alexandria, but also other towns in Lower Egypt, such as Mansura. In spite of new pressures, textiles probably continued to be the largest sector of production. Moreover, there is no reason to suggest the general extinction or decline of Egypt's numerous service trades. Indeed the expansion of trade probably provided new employment for weighers, measurers of grain, porters, and so on.

Guilds

Baer showed long ago that contrary to the conventional wisdom, which suggested that Mehmet Ali had destroyed the guilds, a "ramified system" of guilds survived in Egypt until the 1880s.[69] Baer's point that the economic basis of the guilds in the handicrafts was not destroyed by economic or political change prior to the 1850s is only echoed here. And he rightly pointed out that Mehmet Ali's state—for all its newfound reach and strength—could not yet do without the fiscal and administrative link to the urban populace that was provided by the guilds, and even added new functions to existing ones. With one or two possible exceptions, Mehmet Ali's regime and those of his successors continued to appoint guild shaykhs and use guilds as units of urban administration, taxation, and requisition in the towns.[70] Indeed, especially in the light of recent research, it would appear that the guilds were actively brought to heel by Mehmet Ali's regime, and co-opted in the service of dynasty building and revenue raising. They were not destroyed like the Mamluk households and the rural tax farms, but pressed into service like the heads of the urban quarters and the shaykhs of the villages. Baer already assumed that guilds were supine before the government, and thus saw this process as quite unremarkable. The argument here, however, is that Mehmet Ali's regime actively subordinated the hitherto partly autonomous guilds. In other words, the heavy use of the guild by the state in the nineteenth century, and the guild's subsequent inability to protect its members, were not the timeless outgrowth of a mythical Oriental depotism, but the result of dynasty building under nineteenth-century conditions.

Local *ulama*, merchants, and popular groups may have been instrumental in the accession of the Ottoman governor, but they were soon neutralized, or eliminated. Mehmet Ali "gradually turned his back on the native bourgeoisie and popular forces that had brought him to power," writes Nazih Ayubi, "preferring instead to rely on the familiar Turco-Circassian elite for matters related to the army and administration and on the European bourgeoisie for matters of commerce and transportation."[71] Much of the independent wealth of the religious establishment was brought under state control, and the positions of the *ulama* gradually sidelined anyway with the spread of European-style education and law. Furthermore, the alliance that had at least temporarily bound middling strata to popular groups, and which had formed an important part of the basis for the collective action of crafts and service workers was slowly dissolved. According to André Raymond,

> The alliance forged [during the early 1800s] between popular elements and the Egyptian bourgeoisie, which had been for Muhammad Ali a stepping stone towards power, did not survive the victory. Their aspiration for political stability satisfied, the ulama only desired to return to 'normal,' which conformed to the wishes of Muhammad Ali. Willingly or unwillingly the *ra'iyya* became resigned to disarm; their chiefs, 'Umar Makram and Hajjaj, were progressively neutralised and eliminated. The heavy weight of the authority of Muhammad Ali fell on Egypt, and the popular masses of Cairo returned to their age-old obscurity.[72]

Moreover, the privileges and position of the Janissaries within the crafts and guilds were progressively sidelined as Mehmet Ali's new army took shape, and then abolished after 1826 with the empire-wide elimination of the Janissary corps under Sultan Mahmud II (1808–1839). As Quataert has noted, an important barrier to state intervention in the guilds and crafts had been removed.[73] Finally, the sufi orders, which had overlapped with guilds to provide another organizational bulwark against state intervention were gradually brought more closely under the control of the central institutions of the state.[74] With these changes, popular forces were isolated, and the door to state intervention in guild and craft affairs lay open.

The government now used the existing shaykhs of the trades to levy new and increased taxes on the crafts and trades, as well as to requisition an apparently increasing number of goods and services. Mehmet Ali's income tax—the *firda*—was imposed anew and reorganized in respect of the guilds after an extensive survey of guild members in the cities.[75] According to Edwin Lane, the *firda* amounted to approximately a twelfth of a man's annual income, the maximum being a fixed rate of five hundred piastres per annum.[76] The shaykhs of the trades were responsible for assessing this tax on guild members, as state institutions still had very little information on the income of individual guild members. In 1842, the *firda* seems to have been replaced by another tax assessed also by the guild shaykh, the *wirku*, which became over time the key income and professional tax paid by crafts and guilds until its abolition in 1890.[77] The institution of the *wirku* may have coincided with the abolition of the role of the *qadi* and his court in ratifying the selection of a guild shaykh by the senior members of a guild. This long established practice, whereby senior guild members went to court in order to declare their wishes regarding guild leadership, a symbol of the partially independent role of the religious establishment, and of the links between the guilds and *ulama*, was now abolished and the selection of the guild shaykh was now ratified by those salaried officials responsible for administering the *wirku* in the new tax bureaus. This move simultaneously symbolized and actualized state building, the secularization of the guilds, and where appointment ratification was now in the hands of tax officials, the clear predominance of taxation in state/guild relations.

Ghazaleh's work, which provides the most important recent account of guild transformation in the early nineteenth century, draws a nuanced picture of an ascendant state which both co-opted and worked with the guilds while simultaneously transforming them. In her argument, the state attempted to "enframe the guilds within another hierarchy" controlled principally by the *dabtiyya* (the reorganized police) at the local level and the nascent Interior Ministry at the central level. She notes the prime concern of the state "to benefit from the existing guild framework, while using it for the state's ends."[78] She notes that "a few of the orders sent by Muhammad Ali to his supervisors and directors in Cairo or the provinces contain references to the removal of certain shaykhs and their actual replacement by government personnel." This was a considerable intervention into a previously more autonomous domain, but it also meant a "strengthening in the role of the shaykh, who was simultaneously drawn into closer cooperation with state authorities." However, the state was not immediately in full control, for "orders sent to shaykhs to locate missing guild members and send them to the relevant authority were often repeated several times before being either obeyed or dropped."[79]

Customary practice, long the dominant basis for trade regulation, and a key basis of guild autonomy, was in various cases deemed inadequate by government officials for the new concerns of organization (*tanzim*), order and discipline (*dabt wa rabt*).[80] Thus codified regulations were drafted for trades of strategic or public importance, such as pharmacists, butchers,[81] couriers (*sa'is*), brokers (*simsar*), engravers of seals (*hakkakin al-ahkam*), real estate brokers (*dallalin al-'aqarat*), and weighers (*qabbani*). In the case of couriers, limits were placed on the sum that could be put in couriers' care, safeguards established where couriers carried government documents, a scale of punishments for infringements was drawn up, and the regulations also required the recording of the courier's departure and arrival and the use of receipts.[82] As Ghazaleh notes, "[N]o reference . . . [was] made to previous practice or to old laws and common usage which were so frequently mentioned in the *mahkama* guild documents [of the eighteenth century]."[83] The idea that only the centralizing state could deliver order, discipline and organization worked to delegitimate customary practice and erode local autonomies based on it. Government policy, although involved in an overall project to subordinate the guilds, operated in part to "strengthen the shaykhs of the guilds" in order to deliver revenues and provisions and "simultaneously to integrate them into the growing bureaucracy."[84]

Guild organization—the means by which crafts and service workers had been able to resist the French and the Mamluk Beys—was now co-opted to enforce taxation of all kinds, the very task which was putting crafts and services under new pressure. In this context, especially where craft and service workers had been isolated from middle-class allies (who were weakened in any case), organization for protest and evasion was severely restricted, and collective action was apparently sporadic, and subject to repression. Reports of punishments meted out to artisans who produced illegally indicate that artisans clearly did attempt to evade new regulations and forms of extraction.[85] Al-Jabarti chronicled an incident where Cairo's butchers, being forced to sell to the government at low prices, mounted a collective protest by shutting their shops, although it does not appear that their action was successful.[86] Bowring mentions in passing that the lower classes of Cairo were involved in an attempt to "combine and resist the authorities" who were trying to count and register the population.[87] (The connections between information and power were apparently not lost on Egypt's urban crafts and service workers in the early nineteenth century). Yet, Mehmet Ali's censuses went ahead, and protests, at least at the level of changing overall policy, were not successful. (This is not to suggest that "weapons of the weak" could not have been deployed in the encounter with the census takers). But even informal protest, when discovered, was severely punished, Mehmet Ali—in the context of widespread and heavy-handed conscription—going so far as to form a corps of the very soldiers who had mutilated themselves in order to avoid conscription.[88] Further, during the 1820s in Upper Egypt, rebellions which broke out among the peasantry in the name of Mahdist and millennarian savior leaders battling conscription and exaction were ruthlessly crushed.[89] Had such state actions become known in the towns, as they may have through Upper Egyptian migration to Cairo and the Delta, they must have acted to discourage thoughts of rebellion in the cities.

Thus, whereas the Mamluk beys had faced significant and sometimes effective popular resistance to their extractive policies from popular constituencies in the towns, Mehmet Ali's state, in the main, seems to have preempted even the possibility of such protest.[90] Indeed, the urban guilds, which had wielded a certain corporate autonomy and had proved able to robustly defend their interests in the last days of the Mamluks, were largely co-opted in the service of the new state. Mehmet Ali's "state machine," to use Hunter's language, like analogous states emerging in Anatolia after 1826 and after the 1860s in Tunisia, "greatly augmented the power of autocratic rulers over their subjects, who became increasingly subordinated to the demands of the central administration."[91] Notions of Turkish superiority over local Egyptians—often contemptuously dubbed *fallahin* (peasants)—ideologically reinforced these state institutions.[92]

Conclusion

While the story of craft adaptation and guild transformation during the first half of the nineteenth century remains rather obscure, this chapter has attempted to draw out some important points in order to set the stage for the post-1860 period. Economic change in the crafts was far less dramatic than some of the older accounts would have us believe. Where world economic integration based on the new forces of industrial capitalism remained in its early stages, the impact of imports remained sectoral and worked against the fortunes of only certain specific trades. It is likely that in the face of Manchester, textiles—especially cotton weaving—started to employ a smaller proportion of the urban workforce. On the other hand, it is quite possible that, in a process that was to become more marked as the century wore on, weavers and others started to migrate from town to country in search of lower costs. Mehmet Ali's import substitution projects probably employed just as many artisans as they suppressed, and from 1840 onwards, crafts workers were able to return to their workshops in any case. Instead of destruction or dislocation, the available statistics indicate that crafts workers continued to employ a roughly similar proportion of Cairo's population as they had in the later eighteenth century. Further research is needed before the details of how relations of production may or may not have been restructured, but it would appear that more far-reaching transformation awaited the cotton boom of the early 1860s.

Mehmet Ali's state—for all its newfound strength—did not sweep away the existing guild structure, preferring to co-opt and subordinate the guilds in pursuit of fiscal and administrative objectives. The abolition of the Janissaries and the marginalization of the religious establishment brought the guilds closer to emerging bureaucratic institutions. Guild leaders were used as intermediaries to increase taxes and to regulate their members in new kinds of ways. It would appear that the development of Mehmet Ali's state machine began to seriously undermine the customary and institutional autonomies of the guilds. Again, further research is required before stronger conclusions can be drawn as to how guild members responded to this situation. Nonetheless, it would appear that organization and collective action remained but sporadic and weak in the face of an autonomous state, which was willing to deploy heavy repression in search of dynasty and empire.

2

Restructuring after the Cotton Boom

O my eye, why do you out of all eyes suffer—ha allah!
All the eyes of the people see you—ha allah.
I am calling out—o eye—complaining to Malik—ha allah.
And Abu Hanifa will be our rightful judge—ha allah.
And if I am wrong, love will chastise me—ha allah.
And if you are wrong God will punish you—ha allah!
(Boatman's song, Egypt, 1900s)
　　　　　　　—N.G. Mavris, *Contribution à l'étude*
　　　　　　　　　de la chanson populaire Egyptienne

*I*n the wake of the cotton boom of the early 1860s, and after the accession of Khedive Ismail Pasha (1863–1879), the forms of restructuring and collective action among crafts and service workers under study here started to take definite shape. World economic integration was deepened and transformed by rapid commercial expansion and the galloping increases in Egypt's foreign debt. After the 1860s, more than half of Egypt's external trade started to be with Europe, and the transnational economy became for the first time an important overall force in shaping Egypt's polity, economy, and society. British and French power, built on the economic strength of world capitalism, was increasingly projected into the region. And local self-strengthening entered a new phase with the vigorous efforts of the new Isma'il Pasha (1863–1879) to overcome Egypt's increasingly evident subordination. Heavy taxation and deepening competition from imports and southern European migrant labor forced crafts and service workers to adapt and restructure in new ways in order to survive. This chapter analyzes this restructuring, with particular reference to construction, garment making, textiles, and urban transport.

Unequal World Economic Integration

The early 1860s witnessed a wave of economic expansion which greatly increased Egypt's commerce with Europe. The American civil war of the early 1860s drastically reduced supplies of New World cotton on international markets and thus drove up cotton prices. Egypt's cotton growers were ready to take advantage of this development. Domestic political security was largely guaranteed. Cotton was already grown in some quantities, assisted by government canal dredging and irrigation schemes. Financial and commercial institutions were expanding in Alexandria and had appeared in Cairo by the 1860s. And Egypt's communications infrastructure was developing with the arrival of the railway in 1856 and the expansion of harbor facilities in Alexandria from the 1830s onwards. Thus, with rising prices, the value of Egypt's exports of ginned and pressed cotton roughly quadrupled during the early 1860s, and large-scale cotton ginning and pressing was rapidly developed in Lower Egypt. The nominal value of imports, purchased with cotton revenue, increased by about a factor of four during the early years of the 1860s and then fluctuated around an only slightly rising average value over the next two decades. Imports were valued at between one and two million LE in the 1850s, but in the 1860s and early 1870s were worth between five and six million LE, and thus came to be worth about one LE per head of population.[1] Whereas imports in the pre-1860 period had been dominated by cotton cloth, a more diversified array of manufactured goods were purchased in Egypt from abroad after the cotton boom of 1861–65, although cotton cloth remained the single largest category of import by far.[2] Arguably for the first time, the exchange of raw materials for manufactured goods became a genuinely important factor in shaping the economy. Cotton prices certainly went up and down, but without significant increases in productivity, the value added to the economies of northwest Europe from manufactured products was starting to outstrip the value added in Egypt's economy from raw materials, for all the wealth that cotton brought to a small minority in that country.[3]

Commercial integration had an important impact on the composition of the ruling strata in Egypt. Members of the pasha's family and their allies had received land grants from Mehmet Ali from the 1840s onwards. These grants seem to have been related to Mehmet Ali's attempts to continue to secure his monopolies in agricultural production after they were officially outlawed in 1840. Hence the fact that "for most officeholders, Muhammad Ali's land grants were a punishment, not a privilege."[4] However, from the later 1840s onwards, rising cotton and grain prices (the latter during the Crimean War of 1854 to 1856) started to make land into an economic asset and a privilege of high office for the first time.[5] The khedivial family itself and a class of predominantly Turkish-speaking *dhawat* (literally, persons of high state rank) were able to consolidate and expand their landholdings (often in absentia), particularly in the wake of Sa'id's Land Law of 1858, which established de jure private property in land for the first time. Further, Ismail's lavish land grants of the 1860s and 1870s continued to bolster this form of class formation, and for the first time close links were forged between land ownership and power.[6]

From the 1850s onwards, a qualitatively new form of world economic integration took place as Sa'id Pasha (1854–63), but especially Ismail, contracted ever larger debts to European financiers in order to fund their state-building projects and their search for 'progress.' Mehmet Ali had always refused to borrow a penny from Europe, just as he had refused to allow the construction of any canal linking the Gulf of Suez with the Mediterranean, seeing in such moves a problematic slide towards European domination. However, by the later 1870s, Egypt's debts ran to around 100 million LE, absorbed more than half of state revenue in interest alone, and from 1876 effectively bankrupted Isma'il's state. From around 1870 onwards Egypt was effectively mortgaged to British and French finance capital.

Imperialism

In fact, both commercial and financial integration did draw in European power, as especially did the opening of the French-built Suez Canal in 1869, which put Egypt at the center of British imperial thinking by placing it astride a vital communications and trade route to India. European military expansionism in fact needed no invitation from capital, as Napoleon's short-lived invasion, not to mention the state-led commercial treaties of 1838 to 1840 demonstrated. Guns and capitalist expansion worked together and shaped each other, and were especially potent in Egypt whose army had not only been defeated (1839–41), but was now restricted to eighteen thousand men by the Treaty of London (1841).

This coercive asymmetry made already unequal economic exchange even more asymmetrical. European subject merchants,[7] whose numbers now expanded because they controlled the growing import/export trade, continued to trade under the Capitulations, which exempted them from local taxation and regulation, and enabled them, through the intermediary of the consuls, to escape unscathed from many a legal conflict with local subject merchants. The numerous indemnities paid to European merchants for more or less spurious reasons resulted effectively from the military imbalance, mediated to the khedives by the threats of the consuls—these "wolves" as Sa'id Pasha is reported to have called them.[8] Certainly everyone knew that behind the consuls stood the armies and navies of a Britain or a France. Nor were debt relations contracted on anything like an equal basis. For financiers, Egypt was "the great land of 12 and 20 percent."[9] Here, in the words of Landes, they could "exploit the needs of Egypt and the weakness and ignorance of the Egyptian government . . . imposing one-sided conditions and charging exhorbitant fees."[10] Hence, imperialism reinforced and compounded unequal world economic integration. Those who benefited most were the metropolitan (colonial) financial and industrial bourgeoisie, and an emerging commercial "comprador" bourgeoisie resident in Egypt.

Self-Strengthening

Isma'il Pasha, grandson of Mehmet Ali, inherited the state apparatus built up by his grandfather, and sought to use it to counteract Egypt's increasingly subordinate position in a world more and more dominated by European economic and military power. Ismail's ambition was to take Egypt to what he saw as its rightful place as an equal among the European monarchies, and use his power to further what he took to be progress and civilization. He thus sought to build up the central state, extend the cultivated area, dredge canals, lengthen the railway network, develop Egypt's ports, build the secular judiciary, greatly develop Egypt's education system in the European style, and construct an entirely new khedivial Cairo according to a French plan with palaces for the royal family, an opera house, boulevards, gardens, and imposing squares.

The implementation of these projects involved the further growth and functional differentiation of the secular and centralized bureaucracy. The Ministry of the Interior had been established in 1857, but after a period of redundancy now rapidly expanded to become one of the most important bureaucratic agencies in the land. The Ministry of Public Works was established in 1864, particularly to oversee the transformation of Cairo. The Ministry of Finance multiplied its tax bureaus (*qalam*) throughout the country during the 1860s and 1870s. To direct these and various other bureaucratic agencies, an administrative code on the French model began to emerge: written regulations which competed with and often replaced both Islamic and customary law.

To finance his projects, Ismail set in motion an "active search for every possible subject of taxation"[11] in order to both obtain the maximum amount of revenue in the shortest possible space of time, and eventually stave off bankruptcy and ensure the very survival of his regime. By 1872, the overall tax burden in Egypt was nearly twice what it had been in 1852.[12] But Ismail worked under heavier constraints than his grandfather had done. He could not touch a key source of revenue, the wealth of the European subject merchants who dominated the growing import/export trade, and since more powerful landed classes were becoming intimately connected with the regime, and thus harder to tax, Ismail looked to initially expansive European financiers to make up the difference.[13]

Ismail also extracted revenue from weaker and poorer groups across the country, and the requisition of goods and services, forced labor, and taxation of urban crafts and service workers was taken to new heights. As Cromer remarked in 1880,

> [T]here was scarcely an industry or occupation, however humble, there was not an article of food or of household use, however necessary, there was scarcely an act in life in which the poorest part of the population could engage, which was not liable to the payment of some special tax. Donkey-boys, porters, carters, gipsies, public scribes, jewellers, market-gardeners, and many others, all paid some special tax apart from the tax levied on their special trade or calling.[14]

Cromer, of course, had every reason to emphasize such bad fiscal policy—to justify the activities of the Debt Commissioners (of whom he was one) in changing Egypt's fiscal system to suit their interests. Furthermore, the Debt Commissioners had little to boast about in regard to high taxes—at least in the late 1870s—for even as petitions and deputations of shaykhs arrived in Cairo to urge tax relief, Rivers Wilson was "authorizing tax-collecting forays into the countryside without regard to the means used."[15] But whether or not Cromer's statements were born of a later phase in colonial politics, they also reflected in some measure another political project—heavy taxation to fund self-strengthening.

Direct taxes on business substantially increased during these years. The income-related professional tax (*wirku*), levied on all local subject merchants, shopkeepers, manufacturers, service workers and laborers, was raised significantly. For example, the provincial governor of Daqahliyya received an order in the mid-1860s which instructed that in view of the recent gains made by the people of Mansura in industry and trade the "professional tax should be raised until it corresponds to this increase in their wealth."[16] Such ad hoc directives gave way to more systematic legislation raising the lowest tax bracket to 50 piastres per year and the highest to 750 piastres.[17] This probably meant a significant rise in tax, since the average tax paid by members of the trades (*arbab al-karat*) in Mansura in the early 1860s was 40 piastres per annum. The new legislation meant that the lowest tax bracket was higher than this, at 50 piastres per annum. A number of petitions registered the complaints of those who were hit. Muhammad Mahmud Mawsi of Fayum, for example, a merchant in grains and other goods, complained in 1872 to the provincial offices of the recent doubling in his professional tax.[18] In a further indication of tax rises, arrears in the professional tax mounted fast.

A plethora of levies hit businesses and business transactions. New direct taxes were introduced during these years on the licenses of weighers, porters, tax collectors, and the certificates of construction workers. An oil-pressing tax already existed (established in 1853), as did a market tax (*hamla*) (1857)—a levy of 2 percent on all transactions in the markets. A new tax on carts and livestock appeared under Isma'il; a sheep and goat tax was raised after 1867. The octroi—a tax of 9 percent ad valorem on goods entering towns—was reestablished in 1866.[19] Weighing tax, navigation taxes, and slaughter taxes were a familiar feature of the 1860s and 1870s. A variety of special dues proliferated during these years, including a stamp tax on precious metals, the tax on selling animals in Cairo, Alexandria, and Suez, a special food-weighing tax, taxes on petitions and guarantees, the auction tax, the sale of precious metals tax, the tax on the verification of seals on guarantees, the tax on estate agents, the special tax on humus, the leather skin tax, the Alexandria meat-weighing tax, the tax on sand cargo boats in Alexandria, the cereals-measuring tax in Qaliubiyya and Bahira, the fields tax in Damietta, the tax on loads of pottery in Damietta, the Alexandria wood-weighing tax, taxes on bills of exchange, and so on.[20] Just one of these many taxes, such as the tax on reeds (used in building) entering Alexandria, had led to diverse inconveniences, a slackening in building activity, and generated piles of useless straw standing outside the town.[21]

Traders had to contend not only with higher taxes, but with a mode of collection that Riad Pasha, the President of the Council of Ministers, was later to call "pernicious."[22] Tax collectors of all kinds were able to follow their own interest, to engage in corruption, to overtax and cream off the difference. The complaints of a merchant of building materials went to the prime minister (Nubar Pasha) himself in the mid-1880s. The merchant spoke of the "ruinous and vexatory inconveniences in existence" in respect of the octroi duties levied on goods entering towns. He said that the estimation of the value of products passing through the octroi station was "fantastic," and elevated to absurd heights. He described how one of his carts laden with plaster was sold wholesale in the market for 12 LE, and how the octroi taxed the cart at 8.10 LE. "That's to say," he wrote, "that the duty took about 75 percent from me." He claimed that such "abuses that are authoritarian, vexatious, and illegal in every respect . . . go on every day" according to "fantastical" evaluations, which "no decree has sanctioned."[23]

His story is familiar from a number of reports and communications. Take for example, the complaints of thirty-one landowners of Alexandria: they stated that the octroi "is so ruinous that it makes entirely impossible and derisory our works and exploitation of the soil." Instead of the levy being 9 percent, they went on, it was usually 20 to 30 percent, and often 50 percent. The percentage was, furthermore, taken on a price which had not "the least basis in reality."[24] Nor, apparently, were adequate safeguards in place to deter officials from taking their cut. As a report stated, the fines for tax officials in contravention of regulations were "derisory," and across the board legal and disciplinary measures were inadequate.[25]

The burden of the forced requisition of the labor, goods, and services of the crafts and trades by the state most likely increased under Isma'il. In the 1870s, the owners of "carts, carriages, horses, camels, mules and donkeys"[26] were regularly forced to transport materials without pay for government construction work in Cairo. Water carriers were routinely dragooned into manning the capital's fire stations without wages.[27] However, it should be noted that some trades, such as dyers or jewellers, did remain largely unscathed.

Another form of indirect taxation was underpayment on government contracts. Not all labor or contracts for the government were forced (*sukhra*) or unpaid. Much of it was paid on contract. For example, in 1872, the government contracted for the leather drive belts for the steam engines in use on the rafts on the Ibrahimiyya canal from one 'Abd al-Qatar 'Abd al-Rahman for four piastres and thirty silver per Ratl (0.44 kg). Paper, bricks, steel basins, oil, copper vessels, cartridge wool, steel wire, donkeys, building materials of all kinds, and construction labor, among other things, were also bought on contract for the artillery, Interior, and Ministry of Public Works.[28] Borg describes how construction labor contracted by the government, however, was often underpaid. He wrote that the government "profess to pay them wages in accordance with the amount named in the certificates," but instead it paid them in three ways: first, in copper coins, which led to a loss of 50 percent "because their market rate is reckoned in full tariff value;" second, by "Promissory Notes" for the sum due, which, when discounted led to a loss of 60 to 70 percent; third, the delivery of salt, butter, sugar, or treacle according to the stock in hand of each article. These commodities were given at above market prices, leading to the loss at times of up to 65 percent. These methods, in addition to the "loss of work for many days until a payment of some sort is obtained," meant that workmen would be only too glad to give work to the government for 20 percent of the certificate rate if payment were certain and immediate.[29]

As Isma'il's regime came close to bankruptcy, its attitude towards tax defaulters became increasingly severe. When low floods and famine adversely affected revenues from 1875 to 1878, governmental resolve to collect at any cost rose to new heights—as it became clear that the very survival of Isma'il's government had started to depend on staving off bankruptcy. In such a context, even as the controller of indirect taxes insisted that "it is useless to foist on the provinces—to their detriment—sums which are in my opinion absolutely unrecoverable," the Council of Ministers responded, "The State in fact, has obligations which do not vary with the product of the harvest. . . . The only excuse for not paying is the absolute inability to do so. . . . To the extent that a due does not amount to what was predicted, the state may be obliged to raise the tariff of certain others or to create new ones."[30]

Thus Isma'il launched an assault on the subaltern population in order to pay for his Europeanizing schemes, and finally to shore up his tottering regime.[31] It was said that the *fallah* "only knew that if he had more than he required to keep body and soul together, the tax-gatherer appeared, and he was beaten till he gave it up."[32] Local subject craftsmen may have felt practically the same way. Vallet, for example, who conducted considerable research among workers and artisans in 1910, wrote that the "terror of taxation" had not entirely disappeared, even after thirty years of respite.[33]

Restructuring

Unequal world economic integration, imperialism, and self-strengthening accelerated the transformations in urban economy and society which had begun earlier in the century, forcing crafts and service workers to engage in more far-reaching restructuring in order to survive, and driving them to find new ways to organize in defense of their interests.

Contrary to the views of much of the older historiography, Egypt's artisans were not simply destroyed under the weight of imports and taxes. In regard to employment, the evidence available tells a story not of simple decline, but of restructuring, whereby certain trades employed more, some held their own, and others employed fewer or even disappeared over time. Ismail's census of Cairo Governorate of 1868, taken after the cotton boom, lists 31,316 persons as employed in textiles, garment trades, construction, food, metallurgy, and various other artisanal crafts.[34] This total is slightly higher than the average of the numbers known for employment in crafts for the first half of the nineteenth century, which in turn is higher than the figures listed by the French around 1800. Granted, Cairo's population had grown from around 300,000 persons (circa 1800) to 331,279 (in 1868), but it would nonetheless appear that crafts workers, far from being wiped out, were more or less holding their own as a proportion of the expanding population, in spite of their relatively diminished share of the overall wealth. Further, if Ismail's tax return of 1863 be believed, the delta town of Mansura, which was emerging as a node of trade and transport in connection with the cotton economy, was also home to a substantial population of 1,137 artisans. Hence, in spite of a wider range of imports than before, and the impact of Ismail's taxation, crafts were able, through adaptation and re-structuring in an expanding market, even to expand (in absolute terms) numbers in employment.[35]

Part of the reason for this was that the impact of imports, even in the 1860s and 1870s, was not as comprehensive as was once thought. Although in some ways system changing, imports had not yet expanded in the way they did after around 1890. Increases in imports should be understood in the context of an expanding economy and growing population. In this context, imported products did not invade Egypt and devastate her local producers, but were purchased by Egyptians as foreign currency was earned and wealth based on the export economy increased, and had a more complicated and sectorally specific impact on local manufacturers than proponents of the invasion theory suggest.[36] It is important to note that even in the 1860s and 1870s, beyond cotton cloth, the purchase of luxury consumer goods from Europe was still something that could only be afforded by a tiny élite. These groups—a model set for them by Isma'il's Europhilia—became more interested in various luxury items imported from Europe during these years for conspicuous consumption and display. French shirts, European-made shoes, canes, parasols, some ready-made clothes, and occasionally furniture and some domestic utensils—crockery and glassware—were imported by a wealthy few. Retail outlets were established in Alexandria and in the

Isma'iliyya quarter in Cairo. But such consumption patterns were still only the preserve of a rich minority. With respect to the overwhelming majority of the population, the only significant import consumed was probably cotton cloth (and some yarn). European luxury goods were in the main beyond their reach. Inflation during the cotton boom also meant that the real value of imports increased by less than is reflected in the crude prices given in the external trade statistics. Imports therefore had a more sectoral and specific impact during these years than for the period after 1890.

More importantly, crafts and service workers continued to employ so many workers because they started to find a place in the new system. Masters and workers in construction, textiles, garment making, transport, and beyond adapted their skills and products, forged new relations of production, changed jobs, drove down costs of production in an increasingly competitive market, engaged in self-exploitation, and squeezed labor that was abundant and cheap in order to survive. In what follows, I trace some of the themes of this restructuring through an examination of four of the most important (judged by numbers employed) sectors of artisanal and service activity: construction, textiles, garment making, and transport.

Construction

According to the census of 1868, construction and carpentry in Cairo held a considerably greater place in terms of employment than that accorded them in eighteenth century Cairo by Raymond. The census suggests that construction and related trades (chiefly those for supplying building sites and fitting finished buildings) occupied towards one-third of the artisanal workforce, and made up the largest sector by employment of artisanal activity in 1868.[37] Isma'il's grand projects for the transformation of Cairo in time for the opening of the Suez canal extensively employed Cairo's construction guilds—a practice signaled by 'Ali Mubarak's construction law of 1868 which attempted to regulate the building trades to this end.[38] Urbanization and infrastructural works in Suez, Port Sa'id, and Alexandria also meant work in construction.[39] Further, construction workers attracted élite consumption expenditure. Landowners made wealthy during the cotton boom looked to build and purchase town houses built in new European styles in the prestigious new streets of Cairo and Alexandria in the 1860s and 1870s. Such houses were built by, fitted, and partly stocked with the products of artisans in construction and carpentry. Finally, construction work was sheltered to some extent from the competition of imports. Buildings could not of course be imported ready-made, and bricks, cement, tiling, roofing materials, furniture, and so on were weighty and expensive to import also. For example, even a comparatively well-off English judge, as late as the 1890s in Alexandria, found it prohibitively expensive to import furniture from Europe.[40] Moreover, construction and carpentry trades came to use and benefit from imports. Marble and stone was the second largest category of imports in the 1860s and 1870s,[41] all of which material was transformed by masons in Egypt. Wood for construction was also worth about 120,000 LE per annum between 1874 and 1878.[42]

Local subjects had to compete, however, with migrant construction workers from southern Europe. Stone workers, plasterers, decorators, and builders from Malta, Italy and Greece had skills which in many cases made their labor attractive to elite consumers who sought work in European styles. European artisans also benefited from the protection of their consuls and the Capitulations. They paid no professional taxes prior to 1891, and were less subject to various regulative restrictions than their local subject counterparts, especially prior to the 1880s and 1890s.[43] In some cases, therefore such migrant labor dominated. In construction at Suez in the 1870s, for example, European artisans were employed for work requiring skill, locals being employed for more menial tasks. Here is West on the matter:

> In the excavation and rough work near Suez, as well as in other parts of the Maritime Canal, people flocked in considerable numbers from the villages and towns of Egypt; but for all work requiring . . . skill, labour was imported and invited by the Canal Company from the south of Europe. Messrs. Dussaud frères, in building the dock, new port, government house, and other works at Suez, have also considered it advantageous to employ chiefly European labour. The Messageries Impériales and the Peninsular and Oriental Companies have mostly employed European artificers, and only availed themselves of the labour of the country for work not handicraft, as porterage and coaling ships.[44]

A small town such as Suez could hardly be expected to provide the numbers of skilled labor required to dress stone and raise warehouses—particularly as the style of building and planning was European.

Nonetheless, migrant labor appears more generally to have taken a relatively small proportion of the overall work available. The first document to count European subject employment in the construction trades (the census of 1897) put their participation at only 3 percent of the total numbers employed.[45] Further, in spite of West's observations above, in the table he gives for skilled labor in Suez, local subjects outnumber European subjects in all categories—carpenters, "boat builders and caulkers," "smiths and boiler-makers," "smiths and rivetters," bricklayers, and stone masons.[46] Thus, even in a small town in the early 1870s, where much labor was imported, it is clear that local subjects participated, and even more than this, were often in the majority, and by hook or by crook picked up new skills and adapted in order to maintain their position.

Better-off elements in the construction trades were more strongly placed to compete. As Borg wrote, certain local subjects could be depended on for work, "for, *being in better circumstances* they have a sense of honour in executing the work they undertake. Such workmen, though limited in their number, can be met with in almost all trades. They would not allow a piece of work to leave their shop until they are themselves satisfied of its thorough finish, and from the skill they possess in the . . . craft, they can be relied upon as being fair judges."[47] Local subjects could also make use of the fact that, if Borg is to be believed, "natives and Levantines as a rule prefer [to employ] their fellow inhabitants to foreigners."

Others in construction were able to seize available opportunities and compete with European subjects by picking up the European-style skills so much in demand. As early as 1870, Borg spoke of "the practical progress which the native is daily making in the principal trades," and listed a number of construction trades in which local subjects imitated European styles: carpentry, masonry, stone sculpting, marble paving, gilding, plumbing, and shipbuilding. In this context, Borg maintained that the "competition carried on by the natives to secure [work]" was an important reason for the "impoverishment" of European subject builders in Cairo.[48] And partly for this reason, Borg was not all that optimistic for the prospects of European migrant labor in Egypt, stating that "[t]heir condition . . . cannot be said to be flourishing." As West wrote respecting Suez, "Since the influx of Europeans, and the great demand for skilled labour, caused by the works completed and still in progress, the native skilled labour has somewhat improved."[49] "Improved" in this context surely meant "became increasingly able to produce work according to European designs." Stanley, while holding that "Egyptians are inferior workmen in every industry," did qualify this in regard to masons, who were "much helped by the excellent material of the country."[50] In other words, it would appear that local subjects in certain construction trades were relatively quick to obtain the skills necessary to tender for more highly paid European-style work in Egypt's growing cities.

Adaptation to changing times certainly enabled certain larger masters and contractors to expand their operations, even to flourish during these years. To pick an example, Ahmad Abu Bakr was a master building engineer, age fifty-five, and the head of a substantial household in Bulaq in 1868 according to the census. His home boasted ten men and nineteen women including two slaves. His brother, one Suleyman Abu Bakr was a builder (*banna*), and of three nephews, two were builders and the third was a *fiqi* (someone who performed religious services of various kinds). Both sons were traders in lime (*tajir jir*).[51] The presence of the slaves, a privately owned house, which must have been of a certain size to accommodate the extended family, as well as the presence of large numbers of women (whose occupations are not stated, as was the norm for the census of 1868) indicates that the family was relatively well off. Family ties in merchant trades related to construction must have bolstered Ahmad's overall position in the business. Other relatively wealthy figures involved in construction crop up in the sources. 'Abd al-Baqi 'Ali, shaykh of the guild of limekiln workers in the 1870s, appears to have owned premises and capital goods worked by him and probably others in the trade. His legacy included three boats, limekiln buildings, and livestock.[52] Disputes in his family involved large sums, amounting to around one thousand LE. The legacy of al-Hajj 'Ali Salim, chief of the guild of marble tilers (*murakhkhimatiya*), was sufficiently substantial as to provoke a lengthy court battle in 1890.[53] His title also indicated that he had enough wealth to make the pilgrimage to Mecca during the decades prior to his death. Master workmen of this kind, according to Borg, could often afford to rent apartments in large buildings (*rab'*), at twenty to sixty piastres per month.

But the majority of those in construction were not so well off. In fact, beyond the sometime and not always valued provision of quality work and the ability to pick up European-style skills, perhaps the most important reason for local subjects' ability to obtain work and compete with migrant labor was that they were willing, or had little choice but to offer themselves to building entrepreneurs and contractors at lower rates.[54] According to Borg, local subject workmen, who spent less on accommodation, clothes, and food could offer lower rates than European workmen.[55] This was part of the reason why "the inhabitants give [the local subject] preference" for hiring.[56] According to Borg, a European master artisan was typically paid 45–50 piastres per day, and skilled labor 18–25 piastres per day, or, if employed by the government 25–35 piastres per day. But rates paid to local subjects were considerably lower: those working in European styles earned 10–20 piastres per day, and those in local styles 6–15 piastres per day.[57] Given that Borg estimated that a working man and his family required 16.5 piastres a day to survive, one catches a glimpse of some of the hardship involved. Borg stated that most local artisans lived in huts, paid 10–15 piastres per month in rent, ate "coarse broad beans and vegetables," purchased only one suit of clothes every six months, had one change of clothes for holidays, and afforded the "family a trifle from miserable earnings." Nor was this battle for subsistence getting any easier, because, according to Borg, the price of food was increasing because of taxation. As Dr. Mackie, who reportedly had "ten years' experience in extensive medical practice in Egypt and a long and intimate acquaintance with the class of artizans here," wrote in 1870, "For the price that an ordinary artizan is able to pay for lodgings it is all but impossible to find dwelling rooms ventilated, premises drained free from miasmatic dirt, over-crowding, and air-poisoning. Although the rate of wages he receives may seem to strangers to be high, the rate for board and lodgings is also high, out of proportion to his wages; the consequence is, that he has to take the cheapest place he can find, which, of course, is in the filthiest and most unhealthy parts of the town."[58] For such workers, the major luxuries were tobacco, coffee—at 10 paras a cup (one quarter of a piastre) in cafés "frequented by the lower classes exclusively"—and other beverages, the most popular being *buza*, "an intoxicating liquor made of barley bread."[59] One can see that where the cost of living was so high in comparison to the price of adult male labor, wives and children would be expected to contribute to the family economy, making education a distant luxury.

Thus, local subjects had to push their rates down in order to compete with European subjects, a process which inaugurated more intense competition between local subjects themselves. Both factors—the unregulated appearance of European subjects, and intense competition between local subjects—appear to have heavily undermined the ability of the construction guilds to protect members through meaningful monopolies or minimum prices. And the guilds were weak not just because of economic factors. The *gedik* system, whereby only a limited number of slots were available in a trade, had long been determined by the guild and not the government (although different degrees of government intervention there were). Moreover, Mehmet Ali and his successors, as far as is known, did not in any substantial way seek to support these restrictions. And, where guild monopolies were in the de facto sense partially redundant (because of the presence of Europeans), and where individual masters were under pressure to work at lower rates, and where the guild leadership had an interest in admitting more and more members into the trade, on account of the dues and fees they could collect on admission and promotion, restrictions on numbers in individual trades were extremely difficult to organize. With the relaxation of such restrictions went the protections held by artisans. A passage published in *al-Tabkit wa al-Tankit*—one of Egypt's first opinion-based journals devoted to discussing political and social issues—is suggestive in this regard:

> If certain proprietors wanted to build a building, for example, they would consult the building guild . . . and if the work was worth 1000 LE one [member of the guild] would say to [the proprietor], [that he would take it on for] 700 LE, thereby provoking a reduction [in the price] and then [another builder] offers 500 LE, thus provoking a second reduction, and [another builder] offers 300 LE, and [the process continues] likewise until the price is established at 200 LE. The proprietor supposes that [even] the 1000 LE is insufficient to undertake the work, let alone the 200 LE, but rejoices in this reduction and demands security and a signed guarantee from the worker (*'amil*), and then he leaves him without paying out any advance. Thus, the unfortunate man starts by selling his wife's gold and finery, and pawns his house. When the work ends, the proprietor faces one of the masters and starts to curse his brother and insult him, saying that the work is badly done, the stone is too rough, the marble is weak . . . the plaster is insufficient . . . the whitewashing has [only] one coat, the gypsum cold . . . the roof bent . . . the wall lacks 10 cm and all of this prevents me from approving the quality of your work.

In the end the proprietor says "it will be alright if you concede 10 percent from the original demand." Thus the "unfortunate [builder] . . . leaves the work without a home and with many debts, angry, mutually envious, in poverty and without security and trust."[60] Although the author of this passage wants to ascribe this situation to the psychological failings of local subject guild members,[61] it is more plausible to suggest that intense competition in construction, and the weakness of the construction guilds, meant that small masters had little choice but to offer lower and lower rates in order to obtain work. Masters' response to this cutthroat competition is here conceived as self-exploitation, wherein those owning some means of production sold their work for cheaper than that which would realize a profit above what was necessary for their reproduction. Under conditions of self-exploitation there was little or no profit to the master, only enough to reproduce his livelihood, and thus there was no surplus left over for productivity-raising investment. In the case cited, as elsewhere, the surplus accrued not to the master, who owned most of the means of production, but to the proprietor, who could then spend it on conspicuous consumption, or reinvest it, not in crafts and service work, but in the export economy.

Where possible, masters tried to recoup what they lost in self-exploitation to journeymen or assistants by squeezing their labor through longer hours, cheap and sometimes dangerous conditions, lower wages, and extraeconomic coercion. According to Borg, those working in European styles paid their assistants 5 to 10 piastres per day, and those in local styles, 2.5–7.5 piastres per day. And Borg's estimates here may have been on the high side. Cairo's box makers mentioned that their shops (*dukkan*) generally employed two apprentices (*sunna'in ashraq*), who were paid 1.5 piastres per day.[62] Further, the bargaining power of labor may have been diminishing as unskilled hands became ever more abundant, and as changing conditions made wage labor increasingly available. Although the pressures of conscription and the corvée were not forcing peasants from the land to the same extent as they had been under Mehmet Ali, large-estate formation and peasant dispossession were having a similar effect, and urbanization and rapid population expansion were increasing the reserve army of the underemployed.[63] Moreover, the obsolescence of certain crafts and services because of imports or investment increasingly produced workers such as water carriers who had effectively been deskilled, and were now forced into searching for manual labor. The 1868 Cairo census lists as many as 5,160 "laborers, foremen, and unskilled workers" (*fa'ala, muqaddimin, fazama*), and 401 diggers (*tarrasin*).[64] At Suez, West estimated that about 400 "ordinary labourers" were present.[65] In the growing but still relatively small provincial town of Mansura in the early 1860s, we hear that the "unemployed of the merchants quarter—i.e. [mostly construction] laborers" (*battalin harat al-tujjar–ay fa'ala*)—numbered fifty-nine persons and the "unemployed of the Rihan quarter" thirty-three persons. In as much as these groups increased in size, their ability to withhold their labor in the hope of higher wages must have decreased. Consul Stanley recorded that "a good Egyptian laborer" excavating three cubic yards per day was paid 12.5 piastres. He noted, however, that it was "usual to employ boys and girls of from 12 to 18" who were paid from 4 to 7 piastres per day.[66] And labor squeezing did not just mean low wages, but the withholding of those wages. Those contracted to man Cairo's fire depots in the 1870s—"poor people like us without means of subsistence"—petitioned the Interior Ministry suggesting that their contractors might be keeping back their wages, which meant that "we have become in the last stage of need."[67]

A highly unusual account of the experience of contracting and of child labor exists. This story is a near firsthand narration by a certain Hajj Ahmad, a mason, who started out in life in the 1830s as a boy laborer contracted to work on a building site. We have the tale because Artin Pasha—an Armenian and major figure in literary and scientific circles by the turn of the century, and minister for education, among other things—met the elderly Hajj Ahmad when Artin was having his house built in the 1860s in Cairo. Ahmad had retired from the guild of masons, but came every day to pick up his hard-working son from the construction site (Artin Pasha's house-to-be). Warming to Ahmad's "good sense" and "intelligence superior to his rank," Artin invited the old mason in, and "many times" sat with him listening to his stories. Artin then put the mason's narrations "in order" so he could present a kind of brief autobiography of the man. Artin's rendering lends an insight into increasingly widespread forms of contracting and ever more precariously protected child labor, in addition to the glimpse it gives of a subjective world about which historians know almost nothing.

Hajj Ahmad said his father came from Sharqiyya, and had been a little boy when the French came to Egypt. A "good fellah," the father enrolled in the army. Then, "misfortunes" were "heaped on" Ahmad's mother's head. She went to Cairo to be close to a brother who was a merchant at Hasaniya, but was full of tears and anger against the Pasha [Mehmet Ali] when she learned of the death of Ahmad's father. Ahmad recounted:

She eventually married a copper merchant in order to defray the expenses that her brother had put out for us.

He was excellent for her but would not suffer me. She sent me to school in order to become a fiki, this was her ambition for me. But, the copper merchant was illiterate and did not want to spend the small fees due each week to the mistress of the school. Therefore my mother was obliged to send me to work. She sent me out in my worst clothes, keeping my pretty red Tarbush for Friday and a new blue shirt. She gave me bread—made by her—and I went off with Shaykh Hasan. We called him Uncle Hasan. He was a great strapping man (un grand gaillard) and cut a frightening figure. He had a long baton in his hand and walked so quickly that I was obliged to run around him.

When we arrived at the work site he motioned for me to start lifting earth. I began to cry and call my mother. He took me by the ears, and almost lifting me off the ground shouted at me as if to make me deaf: "Today, this is your work. Like it. Tomorrow when you are Qadi you will get yourself a bellyfull of fish if you like!" The singing of young girls, the noise and movement of the work site soon made me forget everything. I ate my bread heartily at midday. Shaykh Hasan was a good man. Everyone liked him. He was the supervisor of the workers. When the master came and a few of the children were slacking, whether due to tiredness or laziness, to show his zeal he struck the basket—but never the body—with his baton. Everyone knew these ways of Shaykh Hasan, and when he struck we screamed like the deaf. On one occasion a young girl who was too feeble to carry the earth was brought to him. He did not refuse because the poor grandmother who brought her needed bread, was infirm and without resources. . . . During eight days while I was working in the ditch next to her I was sure that this poor girl had not even carried eight full baskets, and at the end of the week she received just as much money as the best and strongest of the children thanks to the . . . charity of Uncle Hasan.

Uncle Hasan was friends with me and often sent me to buy him bread, conserves for his lunch, and sometimes beans—he would give me some of it—which we would eat with our bread. These little kindnesses and our friendship were especially precious because poor Mother had been obliged to send me out of the house, and her husband did not allow her to go out. So we stole some meetings at prayer time on Friday, or sometimes during lunches . . . [although I] could be beaten myself by my chiefs for being absent from the building site. . . . This miserable life lasted a few years.[68]

The tale gives a glimpse above all of how the charity and paternalism of a particular contractor mitigated a boy laborer's otherwise harsh experience of coercive-intensive relations of production and forms of labor squeezing on a building site, albeit thirty years before the cotton boom. Aside from the charity of Uncle Hasan (along with the fleeting meetings with mother and the singing), work was "miserable." Ahmad had been driven to manual labor by the death of his conscript father and the difficult-to-oppose actions of his stepfather. Education of any kind in this context was a distant dream. Once on site, the threat of force was constantly present, whether from the master or from the chiefs (presumably the more important contractors). In a vivid metaphor, the children "screamed like the deaf" in order to fool the more powerful contractors that they were being adequately beaten. In other words, paternalism may have mitigated this larger picture in some cases, but the larger impression is one of coercion-intensive relations of production, where cheap and abundant child labor had little formal redress against exploitation and the sanctions of contractors and masters.

Interestingly enough, however, once Hajj Ahmad was taken on by a master mason, rather than a labor contractor, he began to experience more cooperative and protective relations of production. He notes that he had the "good fortune to meet a master mason, who, liking me, taught me his art and what is more, my religious duties and the holy practices according to the sunna of the prophet." This mason "was the most expert and skilful in his trade" but was "humble and patient," did not "neglect advice," and "everyone respected him." He gained the "favor" of his employers and had a "good reputation" among his fellows. The master then took his apprentice to Tanta for a year, and initiated him there into the Sufi order of Sayyid Badawi. As Ahmad recalled "I tasted ineffable delight being devoted to this great Saint." He added, "Since then I have succeeded." Certainly Ahmad was able to mount a superb marriage and then realize his ambition of making the pilgrimage to Mecca. Hajj Ahmad was also evidently solicitous of his son, training him to be a mason in his turn. We hear from Artin that Ahmad's son was pious and hard working. He clearly had a better-paid job working in the European-style on Artin Pasha's house.[69] One might note that these more cooperative relations are redolent of Borg's discussion of the better off and more honorable crafts workers, who "select the best workmen to assist them," and "allow them better wages," thus ensuring that they are "gradually trained to put their character into the work." Clearly experiences of relations of production were highly uneven, even within professions and within single biographies.

Textiles and Garment Trades

Whereas employment increased in the construction trades, it seems likely that textiles were losing their predominant place, at least in the city. Raymond argues that textiles employed between one-quarter and one-third of the artisanal workforce in Cairo in the eighteenth century, but by 1868 (according to the census) they now employed less than one-sixth of the artisanal population.[70] Weaving and dyeing of all kinds employed 4,406 artisans in Cairo in 1868, or only about 14 percent of the total numbers in manufacturing. This development was above all traceable to imports. Cotton cloth remained the single most valuable import by far, rapidly increasing its value to a worth of around 1.3 million LE by the later 1870s.[71] In other words, imported cotton cloth continued to take market share from local cotton weavers. The decreasing proportion of textile workers was vivid testimony to the fact that artisans in Egypt worked successfully where they did not duplicate products made more efficiently and quickly elsewhere.

Competition from imports, however, was uneven. Silk textile imports were relatively unimportant in the 1860s and silk weavers could thus continue to work in numbers where markets and population were growing.

The old port of Damietta, on the Mediterranean on the eastern branch of the Nile, long known for its textiles, was a major producer of silk during these years. The census of 1872 noted that its 166 workshops produced twenty thousand pieces of silk valued at 21,000 LE per annum, much of the produce being sold in sixty-five shops in the town.[72] Further, in Mansura in the early 1860s, where silk textiles was dominant, weaving and dyeing employed 448 persons, or around 40 percent of the artisanal work force. Self-exploitation may have been the only way to continue to make such operations viable, for as the tax return shows, these silk weavers were among the poorest artisans in Mansura, paying 18–19 piastres per year in professional tax.[73] Where much cloth was imported into Egypt undyed, dyeing, using natural indigo imported from India and other dyestuffs, continued to be practiced and perhaps even expanded with the increase in markets and population. According to the available figures, more than a third of those working in textiles in Cairo were dyers (*ta'ifat al-sabbaghin*), who numbered 1,703 persons in 1868. Ali Mubarak recorded that these artisans worked in 441 dye houses.[74] Beyond this, where flax and linen were not imported in any quantities, both household and workshop production of these cloths must have been widespread. Accordingly, flax and linen producers in Cairo imported over two hundred tons of unworked flax and linen into Cairo from the countryside in 1883.[75] Thus, unsurprisingly, artisans were comparatively successful in textiles where they encountered less imported competition.

Artisans could adapt further by lowering production costs and avoiding taxes. As in Ottoman Anatolia, it is quite possible that textile production fared better in the Egyptian countryside than in the towns during the 1860s and 1870s.[76] The 1872 census lists as many as 16,997 weavers outside of Cairo and Alexandria (where only 685 weavers were recorded). Sharif Pasha's return of 1870, which appears to have been an underestimate for most categories, listed 5,109 dyers in Egypt as a whole, which would indicate an extensive rural dying industry.[77] And certainly, the statistics given in the *Statistique de l'Egypte* of 1873 argue for a substantial rural-urban textile trade. According to this source, 33,066 locally woven linen pieces and 21,219 silk veils for women were imported into Cairo in 1871, and 3,780 silk and cotton veils for women and 14,400 cotton pieces arrived in Alexandria from the surrounding hinterland in the same year. Minufiya apparently bought up 124,352 pieces of cotton cloth woven locally. Damiat purchased 21,623 pieces of butter muslin, and 6,269 female veils. Hundreds of thousands of mats, baskets, and items of straw and palm-leaf work also arrived in Egypt's cities and towns in 1871. These figures include, for example,

179,747 mats of red reed imported into Cairo, over 400,000 locally made mats imported into Minuf, and 211,800 baskets into Alexandria.[78] Ali Mubarak noted that around ten tons of flax and linen weave (finished goods) was imported into Cairo from the contryside in 1883.[79] Rural production can only have benefited from the dismantling of Mehmet Ali's monopoly system, which bought their products at below market price. Also, such producers went unmolested by the urban guilds in as much as there is no evidence that town-based guilds attempted to shut down such rural producers.[80] Further, the appearance of cheap standardized thread imported from Manchester may have helped weavers lower production costs, as well as providing a vehicle by which town-based merchants extended their activities into the countryside through the supply of this key raw material at low prices. More importantly, household textile production, whether for the market or not, was likely able to escape to some extent the heavy taxes which were imposed on city-based guild production under Isma'il. Finally, and above all, production costs were cheaper in the country where wages, premises and other costs were lower, especially where gender categories and family ties meant that labor could be squeezed. While figures are largely lacking, Tucker has given us a glimpse of the important contribution that rural women and children made—all at low rates of remuneration—to spinning cotton, the cleaning, spinning and even weaving of wool, and as "own-account producers of textiles for home use and exchange."[81]

Whereas the textile industry was migrating to the countryside and losing out in terms of relative numbers employed in the city, garment trades—tailoring, shoemaking, seamstressing, shirt making, and the like—were probably employing more over time in both absolute and relative terms, especially in Egypt's cities. Indeed, according to the census, such industries employed as many as 4,874 persons in Cairo in 1868 (around 16 percent of all artisans), which meant they had come to absorb more workers than textiles—quite unlike the proportions described by Raymond for the end of the eighteenth century. This transformation can be traced to low levels of imported competition, commercialization in the economy as a whole, and restructuring by garment makers.

In the 1860s and 1870s, very few ready-made clothes were actually imported from abroad.[82] On the one hand, imported French shirts, parasols, canes, European hats, and so on were a luxury that was the preserve of a very narrow and wealthy elite, and on the other, local tailors, seamstresses, and shoemakers, particularly those who adapted to work in the European style, were a customizable and cheap alternative to imports for many. Europe-leaning consumers could purchase European-style shoes and clothes from local workshops. Tailors were able to tap into some of this expenditure. In Mansura, for example, they were of above average wealth for crafts and service workers, paying about forty-nine piastres per annum in professional tax.[83] Imports acted in another kind of way, as in the textile industry, by providing the cheap semifinished or intermediary goods such as cotton cloth which were then used by tailors and others to produce their wares. In this way the garment trades could benefit from, but also became more vulnerable to and dependent on, technological change and forms of production in the core economies. Beyond imports, it appears that increasing employment in industries of clothing and dress was also linked to urbanization and commercialization in the economy as a whole. That there were so few workers in garment trades in Mansura (just seventy) as compared to Cairo indicates that commercialization and concentrations of wealth were crucial in taking the production of clothing out of the home and into the workshop or boutique. In Cairo this process had progressed further than in Mansura. A statistic which brings this out even more decisively is provided by the 1872 census, which suggests that there were 1,648 tailors in Cairo and Alexandria, but only 840 in the whole of the rest of Egypt.[84] Finally, as with other trades, cheap labor likely played an important role in the ability of tailors and shoemakers to obtain employment. West noted that at Suez these groups "work at a lower rate of wages" than those working in trades related to construction—carpenters, smiths, bricklayers, and stonemasons.[85]

Restructuring among Cairo's shoemakers illustrates some of these patterns. The census of 1868 indicates that by the later 1860s, Cairo already had a substantial number of shoemakers making shoes in European styles (*jazmajiya*). Whereas there had been few or no such artisans in Egypt in the eighteenth century, by 1868 there were 307 such persons, or around 13 percent of the total numbers of shoemakers listed, that is, 2,361, consisting of, in addition to the *jazmajiya*, 1,751 makers of red or yellow leather shoes (*sarmatiyya*), 298 makers of yellow leather slippers (*bulghatiyya*), and five makers of wooden clogs (*qabaqiybiy*). These shoemakers were presumably responding to Europe-leaning consumption patterns, especially on the part of those who could not afford to import European shoes. Even for critical, high-status Europeans, the efforts of Egyptian shoemakers in this regard were not completely dismissed. As Consul Stanley wrote in 1870, the Egyptians are "fair rough shoemakers. . . . They do their work conscientiously, and take a certain pride in it, firmly believing that no work can surpass theirs."[86] A key point is that in this case, a Europe-leaning consumption pattern did not necessarily mean importation. One suspects that European-style shoes brought greater wealth to their producers in as much as they were increasingly in demand among wealthier strata—this seems to have been the case in Cairo.[87] However, those working in the local style, such as the *saramatiyya* in Mansura, appear to have survived by working for lower rates: their annual tax was well below the mean, at about twenty-five piastres per year.[88] Shoemakers were thus among those who could attempt to tap into changing consumption patterns during these years by adapting to produce a new product, and by self-exploitation. That they had little choice in the matter was testament to their vulnerability in the changing economy.

Urban Transport

One of the most dramatic examples of restructuring relates to transformation among the cluster of service and transport trades moving goods and persons around the city.

The piecemeal introduction of piped water in Cairo from the 1860s onwards threatened the livelihoods of the city's water carriers, who were still very numerous (employing more than three thousand in 1868), and who had carried water from the Nile to the inhabitants of Cairo for many centuries.[89] These lowly and impoverished figures—they paid a lower annual tax than anyone in Mansura, for example—did what they could to adapt.[90] At some point they started to use carts and metal containers of various kinds to transport their water more efficiently, a development which was especially possible with improvements in the transport infrastructure, and desireable where Cairo's built area was starting to expand more rapidly.[91] They also started to work transporting water from newly built public fountains to households. In addition, they took alternative professions such as water bearers for public consumption on the streets, or began to carry tamarind juice, aniseed, or sherbet for public consumption, where their cries were a favorite among tourists and travelers.[92] Or, they worked cheaply for government departments or at cotton gins in the countryside.[93] Thus, during the 1860s and 1870s, while the piped water network remained incomplete in Alexandria, limited in Cairo, and practically nonexistent elsewhere in Egypt, water carriers were still numerous, although transformed and increasingly vulnerable in the face of new kinds of investment in infrastructure.

Just as water carriers were being threatened or were diversifying their activities, carting and cab driving started to employ more, especially after mid-century, as road surfaces, shapes and widths in major towns began to make wheels and carriages more practicable.[94] At midcentury carriages were rare in Cairo and Alexandria, and largely absent elsewhere. As St. John noted of Cairo, "[T]here is no rumbling of carriage-wheels to deafen the ear. Now and then, it is true, a crazy vehicle, imported by some bey or effendi . . . comes jolting over the mud pavement of the great streets, preceded by a running footman. . . . But this is a rare occurrence; and camels, which are the wagons, and donkeys, which are the cabs of the country, alone mingle with the mass of human beings."[95] Indeed, at midcentury, the governor of Asyut still rode around the town on horseback "preceded by two men carrying torches."[96] But during the 1860s and 1870s carriages brought in from Europe became increasingly common and work was increasingly available for coachmen working in private service. By the late 1860s, as consumption patterns started to copy European styles, officials in Isma'il's government "preferred to ride in expensive carriages rather than on horseback."[97] The grooms and horsemen (sing. *sa'is*, pl. *suwwas*, Fr. *palefrenier*) of eighteenth-century Cairo gradually became coachmen in the private service of the khedivial family, newly wealthy landowners, leading government officials, and merchant elites. In Cairo, carriages started to appear above all in the new streets laid out by Isma'il between the Nile and the Ottoman city. By 1887, according to 'Ali Mubarak, there were four hundred private carriages in Cairo alone.[98]

It was not very long after the introduction of private carriages into Egypt that some enterprising individual or individuals in either Cairo or Alexandria decided that similar carriages could be hired to richer elements within the urban population seeking to take short journeys around the city in this prestigious and new form of transportation. Public cabs were probably quite self-consciously modeled after their private service counterparts: it was said (somewhat later) that "the usual shape . . . [of the public cabs followed] that of the private carriages, viz., a one-horse or pair victoria with hood. Both classes are built for two persons, with a small let down seat capable of holding, with some discomfort, two more passengers."[99] By 1878, according to Karl Baedeker, public passenger cabs existed in some numbers in Cairo. As he wrote in 1878, "Carriages, generally good, and with two horses, abound at Cairo. The principal stand is to the right of the entrance to the Muski, and there are others in the Ezbekiyeh, near the Hotel d'Orient, and in the Place 'Abidin, near the offices of the Minister of Finance."[100] The census of Cairo Governorate of 1868 lists 1,470 coachmen and carters (*'arbajiya wa qumashjiya*),[101] although this category appears to include coachmen in public and private service, carters of all kinds (who were also called *arbajiya*) including those of refuse (*qumashjiya*). The first definite indication of numbers of public cabs in Cairo is given by 'Ali Mubarak, who drew on the local authority records from 1887. He wrote that there were 486 such vehicles in Cairo, Bulaq, and Old Cairo.[102] Baedeker indicates the infra- structural changes which assisted the multiplication of carriages: "[m]ost of the streets in the old part of the town are still unpaved and inaccessible to carriages. . . . The khedive, however, is annually increasing the number of carriage-ways by the demolition of old streets and the erection of buildings in the modern style."[103] Public cabs started to be distinguished from private under the style 'arbajiya al-rukub (literally, carts for passengers).[104]

There is some evidence to suggest that those who managed to secure employment in both public and private cab driving were from Upper Egypt and the Sudan. As many as seventy-seven "Nubian and Sudanese cab- drivers" of Cairo ('arbajiya barabira wa sudaniyya) sent a petition to the in- terior minister in 1871.[105] The vast majority of these were working as pub- lic cab drivers, and a minority—ten of those who signed their names and stamped their seals on the back of this petition—specifically indicated that they were in private service. Of the latter, we find master (al-usta) Husayn Ahmad in the service of Shilan Bek or master Khalil in the service of al- khawaja Kahin.[106] Indeed, this group included some of the most prestigious (at least by association) coachmen in town, as master 'Awwad Allah was working in the service of his excellency Nubar Basha—a leading statesman, foreign minister, several times president of the Council of Ministers, and key financial and political negotiator under Isma'il. It is quite likely that these coachmen came north alongside other Nubians and Sudanese who were contracted to work in transport, domestic service and security, and various other occupations. Demand for their services in private households was in the ascendant as slavery was gradually abolished.

As migrants they may have been willing to accept lower wages than their local counterparts, and without substantial links to the local commu- nity, it may have been easier for patrons to squeeze their labor.[107] Cab driv- ers hired themselves and their carriages out for up to 12 piastres per hour. A short ride might cost 8 piastres, and a whole day 80 piastres. Cabbies could obtain more (up to 100 piastres per day) if they improved their carriages. They were also able to charge more on Sundays and holidays, according to Baedeker, when "fares rise considerably, and it is often difficult to get a good vehicle." The boy who ran before the carriage to clear the way, which still seems to have been standard practice in the 1870s, was cheap and earned unpredictable wages, requiring but "a small additional fee."[108]

Carting, like cab driving, was another small, low-wage transport in- dustry which appeared in Cairo around midcentury and started to expand quite rapidly in the 1860s and 1870s.[109] When paved roads started to appear in Cairo and Alexandria, those transporting goods found it practicable and convenient to start putting their construction materials, refuse, and other heavy items on one- and two-axle wooden carts behind either one or two horses or mules (rather than on camel and mule back). Small-scale local entrepreneurs started hiring out carting services on their own account, or renting carts to drivers. By 1868 there were probably several hundred carters of all kinds in Cairo.[110] In the mid-1860s the health board had mentioned that the removal of around six hundred tons a day of human and animal excrement from the houses, streets, stables, and barns of the city of Cairo to prevent "foul and noxious vapours" required the labor of about four hundred carts, making two runs a day.[111] The census of 1868 suggests that most carters in Cairo were from the capital and the provinces (*al-aqalim*), but their number included a dozen or so Turks, North Africans, and Syrians. The growth of this trade was uneven by region. It varied in relation to road paving and urbanization. Ali Mubarak's list of trades states that there were eighty-two carters (*'arbajiya jarr*) in Alexandria in 1877. There were apparently no carters in Mansura in 1863.[112]

Something of the expansion of Cairo's guild of carters (*ta'ifat 'arba-jiya karu*)[113] in the 1870s can be traced through a letter written by the Cairo police commissioner to the Ministry of Interior in 1879.[114] The police reported that a certain Ahmad Muhammad, shaykh of the guild, "deposed that the deputyship (*mukhatiriya*) of Bulaq [had become] extensive and 'Ali al-'Ajuz, the deputy in this region wants to appoint a colleague as deputy for the sake of collecting the taxes (*amwal al-miri*) and carrying out the [government's] orders. An explanation from the Governorate arrived . . . that after taking the necessary statement from 'Ali 'Ajuz the necessary [procedures] for an election will be implemented. . . . 'Ali was instructed as to what the shaykh petitioned. He responded that the deputyship is extensive and includes many individuals, so it is necessary to appoint a deputy to help 'Ali regarding those works connected to the deputyship." 'Ali 'Ajuz was to get his assistant in the election which followed. On the face of it, the guild of carters was expanding in the deputyship of Bulaq, a fact which required the appointment of two deputies to levy the tax and channel the orders of the government. Indeed, such expansion made sense in as much as the short journey from the trading center of Bulaq to the central districts of Cairo with an improved road running between the two was a prime stretch for the activities of carters, especially those carrying construction materials from the sahels (ports) of Bulaq to the now rapidly expanding city. Further, Bulaq was home to by far the largest proportion of Cairo's *cochers* and *char-retiers* according to the 1897 census.[115]

Donkeys and asses had long been a popular means of transportation in Cairo. A fairly extensive system of hiring donkeys (as well as camels) for transporting merchandise in Cairo and surrounds existed before and during the eighteenth and nineteenth centuries.[116] The popular classes also rode donkeys, whether hired or owned, in order to move around the city, although women riders were sometimes liable to elicit moral sanction or outright prohibition. Mules were more prestigious, and sometimes forbidden to religious minorities and native Egyptians.[117] Donkeys had lost none of their popularity in the 1860s, and one of the commonest single professions in the 1868 census of Cairo was donkey driving, which employed more than three thousand people. One suspects that the systematic hiring of donkeys for cash to the general public was even expanding with urbanization and a growing tourist industry. Certainly, Baedeker evinced marked enthusiasm for the use of the services of donkey boys in 1878, particularly recommending them for those seeking to explore the narrow streets of the older parts of Cairo. As he wrote, "Lovers of the picturesque will find such [donkey] rides very enjoyable."[118] In his view, donkeys "form the best means of conveyance both in the narrow streets of the towns and on the bridle paths in the country. They are of a much finer, swifter, and more spirited race than the European, and at the same time patient and persevering. Those in the towns are generally well-saddled and bridled in Oriental style. The attendants are either men or boys, who contrive to keep up with their beasts at whatever pace they are going, and often address long sentences to them in their Arabic *patois*." Baedeker continued, "The boys are preferable to the men, as the latter are generally more exorbitant in their demands and less obliging, and even their donkeys appear to partake of their unpleasant disposition." "The donkey-boys," on the other hand, "especially at Cairo, are generally remarkably active, intelligent and obliging."[119] One notes here that, unsurprisingly, widespread child labor in donkey driving was cheaper and more malleable than that of adults, and must have played an important role in the continuing viability of this trade.[120] Adults tried to improve their subsistence wages, but obviously met with difficulty where this was framed (by wealthy Europeans) as their making "exhorbitant demands." Although by ensuring that their donkeys were "well saddled and bridled" in an "Oriental" (i.e., tourist-pleasing) style, such workers could enhance the value of their product. The boys may have had some slight success, however, using whatever cultural resources they had to bargain up their wages. They were not only "remarkably active, intelligent and obliging," but, as Baedeker noted, "they often possess a considerable fund of humour, which they show most readily when well-paid."[121]

Conclusion

Unequal world economic integration in the 1860s and 1870s and state building under Ismail did not destroy the crafts and trades, but it also did not allow them to continue in their previous form. Crafts and service trades neither collapsed nor underwent rapid factor accumulation on the basis of productivity-raising investment. Instead, they combined with the dynamics of a rapidly changing economy and polity, and restructured in order to survive.

Where crafts and service workers came into direct competition with the products of industrial capitalism, and in particular where demand was strong, continuous, and standardized, they were not able to compete, and trades such as water carrying and cotton weaving lost out. Where there was some shelter from imports because of transport costs (such as in the construction trades) or perishability (such as in food production), and especially where demand was customized, fluctuating, local, or weak new small-scale trades appeared, such as shoemaking in the European style; Italian and French-style construction work; and public cab driving. Where there was real shelter from imports, such as in silk weaving, a certain accumulation was possible among wealthier masters, especially those with connections to merchant capital.

Increasingly competitive conditions, resulting from unequal world economic integration, the spread of market relations, population expansion, the weakness of the guilds, and speedier communications, meant that crafts and services were engaged more urgently than before in a drive for cheap production. This involved the restructuring of productive relations: textiles started to migrate more rapidly to the countryside, where production costs were lower, and contracting became more extensive in the construction trades. Restructuring also meant switching to purchase cheaper raw materials, such as industrially produced yarn for weavers, or Manchester cloth for tailors. The drive for cheap production also involved reducing the cost of labor. First, this meant the intensification of self-exploitation among those possessing skills and tools in a trade, which effectively wiped out profits above what masters required to subsist and reproduce the small capital they owned. Self-exploitation was arguably compounded by guild weakness in enforcing minimum prices for masters. Guild monopolies were broken up by the arrival of unregulated European migrant workers, and by the fact that the labor market was increasingly competitive, the state was indifferent, and guild leaderships had every interest in expanding membership in order to levy higher dues and control more taxes, thus reducing the incentive to protect members by restricting numbers in the trade. In search of lower costs, masters and contractors also engaged in labor squeezing—the extraction of absolute surplus value through lower wages, longer hours, tough conditions, and extraeconomic coercion. Again, the weakness of the guilds in protecting workers, and the problems faced by extra- and subguild organization, which will be analyzed in more detail in the following chapter, made it easier for masters and others to squeeze the labor they controlled.

Both self-exploitation and labor squeezing, it is argued here, combined to constrain productivity-raising mechanization. The former wiped out profits which might otherwise have been reinvested in tools and skills, and the latter increased the competitiveness of hands vis-à-vis the machine, and thus made labor-intensive production strategies more successful. Heavy taxation for self-strengthening further wiped out any surplus that might otherwise have been available for productive reinvestment. As the extension of market relations and the growth of wage labor actually fed into these patterns of restructuring, these factors coincided with and even reinforced labor-intensive production.

Overall, crafts and service workers' vigorous attempts to adapt to changing circumstances secured many of them their livelihoods and provided much needed goods and services to the wider population, but did not enable most of them to break from economic subordination, vulnerability, and a continuous and often harsh struggle for survival.

3

Petitions and Protests under Isma'il

Hey! Hey! Pasha of Pashas! Our Pasha has gone to the north and is never coming back.
                    —Construction workers' song, Upper Egypt, 1900s

*R*estructuring of productive relations was only the economic dimension of crafts and service workers' response to the pressures of the 1860s and 1870s. Urban workers also reorganized and engaged in new forms of collective action in defense of their interests. Where guilds were becoming increasingly incapable of defending members collectively against higher taxes, economic change, and local exploitation, crafts and service workers sought alternatives. In particular, they tried to draw in state intervention in attempts to change the terms of their restructuring. They wrote petitions to the authorities, brought court cases, and mobilized resources collectively in sub- and extraguild networks. They appealed to government regulations, and less frequently, customary practice. They often depicted themselves as loyal subjects in search of the mercy of a just ruler, but increasingly asserted a kind of citizenship. Where attempts to engage the state officially through formal and collective claim making failed, guild members and crafts workers often resorted to more illicit "weapons of the weak," dodging taxes, subverting regulations, creating unofficial networks, and bribing officials. Crafts workers' mobilization played a significant role in bringing down their guilds, and had some impact on shaping the form of state intervention in craft affairs, but was largely unable to change the terms of restructuring.

Co-opting the Guilds

Like his grandfather, Ismail did not see the need to abolish the guilds, but
again sought to use them in the service of state building. Most importantly,
guild shaykhs were used to assess and collect existing, increased, and new
taxes. As West, reporting on Suez in 1870, wrote, "all taxes" were collected
by the guild shaykh.[1] Ali Mubarak agreed.[2] The rising professional tax
(*wirku*) levied on the profits of all merchants, artisans, and service workers
in Egypt (*arbab al-karat*) continued to be assessed and collected by the guild
shaykh in the 1860s and 1870s. When the octroi returned under Isma'il in
the 1860s (it had been abolished under Sa'id), the guild shaykh was to assist
in its assessment.[3] The government also used shaykhs to collect many of the
smaller dues which proliferated during these years. In 1878, for example,
the head of the expanding guild of boatmen (*murakibiyya*) in Alexandria was
instructed to levy a tax on every 198 litres of dry goods transported by his
boatmen.[4] After 1868, the heads of the construction guilds were supposed to
sign a statement on appointment affirming, among other things, that they
would do what is necessary "in the assessment of [the guild members'] tax
bracket and what is fixed for them."[5] Further, the close link between guild
activity and taxation is continuously underlined in the hundreds of petitions
sent by guild members on guild-related matters to the government, where
the majority of such petitions during the 1860s and 1870s were connected
in one way or another with taxation. Overall it was not without some justi-
fication that in 1870 Borg wrote, "[The guilds'] object at the present time is
to facilitate the levying of the capitation and other taxes, and to secure the
due execution of the works required by Government."[6] Under Ismail, it
would appear that the character of the guild as a unit of taxation became
more marked than ever before.[7]

These policies heavily compromised the ability of the guilds to protect their members in the face of what were becoming punitive fiscal demands, for the guilds, of course, were the very instrument through which
the government raised such taxes. Guild leaders thus found themselves in a
precarious situation, for they were supposed to deliver higher taxes to the
government, while simultaneously maintaining support within the guild.[8]
For although the government expected more from guild shaykhs, seeking
to make them fulfil statelike functions, it did not propose to pay them a
salary or to subsume them into the bureaucracy. Indeed, most shaykhs remained practising masters of their trades, and effectively received monies
in return for their duties—not from the government, but from customary
dues owed them by guild members. Responsibility for taxation certainly in

some sense bolstered the shaykh's position at the local level (it turned the shaykh into a key figure in the craft and gave him access to a significant resource flow), but the government was also seeking to tighten up on the activities of figures responsible for tax, thus putting additional pressure on them from above. According to Lady Duff Gordon, the prisons of Upper Egypt in March 1867 were "overflowing" with village shaykhs who had exacted too little in taxes.[9] In other words, shaykhs—and probably not just those of the countryside—were caught between the rock of government demands and the hard place of maintaining support from within the guild. As we shall see in more detail below, their intermediary position between government and craft—a key basis of guild functioning—was stretched to breaking point during the tax hikes that accompanied the last days of Ismail.

Where the government increasingly saw the guild as an extension of its urban network of control, and a tool for a new interventionism, guild shaykhs were used for new regulative tasks and expected to fall in line behind government policy. Their customary and local jurisdictions were increasingly ignored in favor of newly codified regulations, which were more and more thought to be the only adequate basis for order and progress. The process which began under Mehmet Ali, where various trades, especially those which raised health concerns or public regulation issues, came under closer government regulation, continued, in particular with weighers, retailers of various kinds, butchers, barbers, and the construction trades.[10]

The Ministry of Public Works, for example, drew up a law in the late 1860s to regulate the construction trades, with a view to the more efficient implementation of the grandly conceived khedivial schemes for the Europeanisation of Cairo. The government publications also contain a pledge (ta'ahhud) which shaykhs in the construction trades had to sign on their appointment, the content of which is revealing. The shaykh was supposed to undertake "a continual supervision of all the workers." He was "responsible for their work and their regulation (dabt)."[11] This word dabt, often in conjunction with the word rabt (roughly, order and discipline, regulation), combined with another term, nizam (order), were key words in the texts of regulations and the urgings of anxious government officials during these years. Order and discipline were to be judged not against custom but by regulations issued in written form by the relevant ministry or governorate. Hence the shaykh had to "undertake to execute all that . . . occurs in orders and regulations regarding these issues." He had not so much to prohibit evil and enjoin the good (as in the old formula impressed upon the old market inspector through centuries of Ottoman rule), but to "guard against all con-

traventions in the town planning measures" and to "follow the fundamen-
tals of reform in all building procedures, and likewise follow the fundamen-
tals of building whether in the [strength of the materials] . . . or the excel-
lence of the mortar, and in ensuring the adequacy [of materials] and
avoiding adulteration . . . and not to appoint any [person] . . . in any work
unless he is suitable and prepared."[12] The drafters of this legislation—in this
case Ali Mubarak—sought efficacy, regulation, and work according to new
government regulations.

To give one more example, the Health Board used the heads of the
guilds in connection with urban sanitation and sewerage. In a report to the
Majlis al-Khasusi, health officials described the problem of the removal of
human and animal excrement from the houses, streets, stables, and barns of
the city of Cairo as "very pressing, and damaging to public health." Inadequate removal had led to "vile winds," especially in the intense heat of the
summer. The Health Board urged that "this matter cannot, according to the
principles, be allowed to continue. Rather, it is necessary to totally prevent it
by the government, meaning that strong pledges (*ta'ahhudat*) must be taken
from the senior members and the heads of those *tawa'if* [to the effect that]
that they do not leave the droppings of animals and pile them up against
walls or on roof tops, but rather that it must be taken out of the city.[13]

Here again the government tried to use guild shaykhs in the service of
state building. There was ever less room in this equation for guild autonomy, especially on the basis of customary law. Shaykhs were again caught
between the bidding of the government and the interests and concerns of
guild members. It would appear that often enough, the shaykh had little
choice but to fall in with government demands, and thus put the guild at the
disposal of the state.

In the case of a certain merchant called al-Ghardani, the shaykh
could only stand by to affirm a heavy-handed intervention by the government. In the Spring of 1888, the subgovernor of Damietta conducted a
domiciliary requisition of some sacks of beans from the house of Khalil al-
Ghardani, a merchant from Damietta. The subgovernor stated that he had
suspected that al-Ghardani was harboring smuggled tobacco and thus had
conducted a lawful domiciliary visit. When he found no tobacco but instead beans, which he suspected of having evaded local octroi duties, he
impounded them. The investigation concluded that it was lawful to search
for tobacco which had evaded customs, but not lawful to seize the beans,
whether or not they had evaded local octroi dues. The police therefore invited the Governor to return the sacks. The committee went on to argue,
"It seems to us that the suspicions of existence of fraudulent tobacco in the

house of the merchant do not appear to us to have been sufficiently well founded to justify a domiciliary requisition, something always delicate; in fact, the indication given on the existence of tobacco at the house of Ghardani came from a young ambulant seller retailing beans . . . and who, moreover, on questioning, denied the fact."

In view of this, the role in this case of the head of the guild of merchants in Damietta is worth noting. Notwithstanding the committees findings, al-Ghardani wrote, "The Governor invited me to present myself in front of him and in the presence of the head of the guild of merchants and several notables, he said to me, even while expressing his regrets, that he had perfect knowledge of the requisition . . . by the subgovernor and his entourage, [and] that he sought to gain entry into my house again to proceed with a second requisition, and that to this end he requested my consent."[14]

In the most benign interpretation, it was a compromising scene for the head of the guild. Far from joining with al-Ghardani in the mobilization of his apparently legitimate grievances, the head of the *ta'ifa* appears to have had little choice in the context of local power relations than to stand by while the governor proposed a second, even more questionable, requisition. The shaykhly presence can only have legitimized the governor's demands and isolated al-Ghardani further.

It is worth noting that Baer originally formulated his thesis that the guilds were tools in the hands of the government on the basis, above all, of evidence culled from nineteenth-century Egypt, when, as I have argued here, in strong contrast with the eighteenth century, guild autonomy was indeed seriously undermined by a new process of self-strengthening, and guilds found it increasingly difficult to protect their members against unwanted government intervention.

Weapons of the Weak

Yet, one should not exaggerate the attrition of guild autonomy and local protection, particularly because the state-centered sources systematically obscure guild independence, for autonomies of the official variety were rarely recorded, and those of the unofficial variety tended to be hidden from the eyes of the state. Shaykhs, it should be recalled, were not subsumed into the government apparatus: they did not become government officials, nor were they paid a salary; they were chosen by guild members themselves, and dismissed in large measure according to legal procedure, not according to government whim, as will be shown below. Some measure of guild autonomy was retained until the end, and, as we shall see, was part of the very reason for the abolition of the guilds, because of the way such remnants of guild power interfered with tax 'reform' in the 1880s. During the final years of self-strengthening in Egypt, guild shaykhs were able to act as a significant buffer between guild members and the grasping hands of tax collectors. The key tactic, revealed again and again in the petitions and government correspondence of the 1860s and 1870s, involved guild shaykhs illicitly sheltering their allies in the guild from the full burden of taxes, hiding them completely, or reducing their tax burden.[15]

In a case involving the boatmen and brokers of Alexandria, for example, Ahmad Ali, a senior member of the guild, accused the newly elected shaykh of "hiding a number of people from the professional tax (*wirku*)." A subsequent investigation revealed that his accusations were well-founded, and that among those whom the shaykh had hidden from the tax collector were his own sons.[16] In another case, six individuals from the guild of Nubian servants, who presumably were losing out in the new situation, brought allegations before the Cairo Appeals Court in 1880 against their shaykh 'Imran Qurni:

> He [they claimed] has been responsible for corruption (*al-'ass*) and treachery [in connection with] the dues of the government and the guild, in that, [whereas] previously all the individuals of the guild appeared on the professional tax, [now, some appear, but others are hidden] . . . and he currently collects from some people who are not taxpayers. . . . And they requested that he be prevented from [raising] the tax for 1294 and that the tax be levied by the Nubian shaykh *al-'umum* in conjunction with the senior members [of the guild] by means of the tax bureau, and they offered a clear statement of the professional tax which included fifty names which were not present on the taxation for 1293.[17]

In this case the shaykh was apparently defending fifty servants from government exactions.

One of the most dramatic cases of this illicit tactic involved the Cairo bakers. Successive investigations by the local authority in 1880 eventually revealed that no less than 545 bakers had managed to avoid the levy in 1878. The local authority was moved to warn "all the masters in the district," and request that all master bakers tender statements concerning the numbers of those who were working with them. Furthermore, it was stated that "because they are masters, they are required therefore to pledge upon the tax register that were it made clear afterwards that persons existed who were profiting from the guild and yet did not pay the *wirku*, then [the masters] will be held responsible."[18] The success of the bakers was so far-reaching that the authority took the unusual step of reaching beyond the shaykh to the master bakers themselves in an attempt to deal with this form of resistance.

Al-Ahram—one of Egypt's major new newspapers, founded by Christian Syrian émigrés in 1876 and published in Alexandria—took a dim view of tax evasion. They spoke of how the shaykhs of the guild distributed the professional tax among craftsmen (*ashab al-hiraf*) without justice (*'adala*). As *Al-Ahram* wrote, "For example, they impose on the metalworker (*al-haddad*) and the haircutter (*al-muzayyin*) whose profit had not exceeded one pound every month, 20 piastres or 30 per month. [But they imposed] on those whose monthly profit exceeded 10 pounds, [only] 2 or 3 pounds [in tax] in an [entire] year." But this writer, working in a largely prenationalist context, saw nothing of the difficult situation which punitive taxes had placed the shaykhs, did not appreciate that the shaykh was simultaneously sheltering a certain group from taxation, and assumed that unfair taxation resulted from the personal malignancy of the shaykhs. As the journalist wrote, "and this [injustice was] because of the tyranny (*istibdad*) of the shaykhs of the trades in distributing this tax, in as much as they were distributing it for their own profit from it, big or small."[19] But such a strategy was pursued, one might wager, not because shaykhs were somehow by nature tyrannical or backward, but because it was extremely difficult for them to complain about the level of taxation per se. And this difficulty sprang at least in part from the fact that hegemonic discourse did not admit the culpability of the state on this matter. In fact, where the identity was made among elites between state centralization, regulation, and progress the state appeared blameless and the agent of beneficial transformation, and those outside of its ambit backward and inimical to the modernizing projects of elites. But illicit tax evasion, based on the remnants of guild power, yet also signifying the breakdown of the corporate solidarity of the guilds, defended significant numbers of crafts and service workers against punitive taxation.[20]

New Avenues of Participation

State intervention, just as it was breaking old autonomies and protections, albeit unevenly, opened the door, in some measure, to new forms of participation and mobilization. The increasing prominence of state agencies and regulations, the assault on customary law, the association of centralization with progress, and the various constitutional concessions made by Ismail to a rising class of Egyptian provincial notables seeking inclusion within the power elite resulted in a political opportunity for new claims and new forms of mobilization. Crafts and service workers were quick to seize such opportunities, organizing informal networks which did not coincide with guilds, writing petitions, and articulating new (and old) discourses of protest, particularly in the struggle against local forms of exploitation: unfair taxes, contracts, guild dues, wages, conditions at work, coercion, and so on. In the process, crafts and service workers went beyond the discourse of the loyal subject, and started to assert a version of citizenship.

One of the few means of legitimate protest available to lowly crafts and service workers had long been the petition, an accepted element of Ottoman statecraft. If the sultan's justice was to be upheld, the population to flourish, the treasury to be replenished, and the army to be funded, in turn to uphold the sultan's justice, then it was imperative that the sultan's slaves—the military and administrative class—be prevented from either oppressing the population or robbing the treasury of revenue. In theory then (and often in practice), the sultan needed to know of the activities of rapacious officials. One means to this knowledge was to accept the petitions of the *reaya*—the flock. Such acceptance had the additional effect of enhancing the image of the sultan as that of the merciful ruler who dispensed justice over and above the conniving and oppressive activities of his officials.

Even while Mehmet Ali's dynasty radically changed the institutions of governance—as a by-product of dynasty building—it continued to admit petitions on similar grounds, although their scope was now enlarged. With the multiplication of officials and departments, the higher echelons of the state wanted to know if lowlier officials were diminishing revenue by waywardly oppressing the population or fleecing the treasury. This thinking formed a kind of kernel of citizenship which the new system contained: the merest foot in the door, as it were, for those seeking to assert themselves within the new khedivial state machine, even at its most autonomous. As early as 1829, Mehmet Ali published a codified law providing for the punishment of wayward officials responsible for "neglect of duties in connection with taxes . . . offences by village shaykhs, injury to persons, and damage to property." In addition, penal codes of 1840s, in Baer's words, "tried for the first time to guard the rights of the citizen vis-à-vis the government and to prevent arbitrary punishment."[21] Under Said's penal code of 1851, "village shaykhs who forced fellahs to work without compensation were to be punished . . . with up to 45 days imprisonment."[22] In other words, the complaints of the people were to be harnessed to the state-building project, where they could reveal treachery by lesser officials in the matter of illicitly appropriating tax revenues, or overtaxing the population, both of which practices would rob the treasury of much sought after funds. Such legislation was all about effective state building and revenue extraction, but it provided a crucial handle which popular elements could use to try to drag in state intervention—and in fact take the state in directions that it might not have initially planned to go.

The populace—crafts and service workers included—were not slow to seize on this handle and use it for all its (often limited) worth. During the third quarter of the nineteenth century, with government ministries expanding, with police reorganization, with increases in bureaucratic efficiency, and with state intervention becoming more widespread, lowly urban workers, among others, using the services of professional Arabic language petition writers (*'ardhaljiyya*), and purchasing official government paper on which to write their screed, began to send more and more petitions to the authorities: the police, the governorates, the provincial governors, and the Ministries of Finance and Public Works (established in 1864), and above all, the minister of the interior (established 1857). Meanwhile, government agencies became better organized to process petitions. For instance, Cairo Governorate was established in 1854, replacing a *katkhuda* (an official in the pasha's household), and its work was "facilitated by the establishment of police departments with boards to hear complaints and receive cases."[23] Such departments also began to take on more authority to act in response to the complaints of the people. For whereas, as Hunter explains, under Mehmet Ali the executive departments (excepting Finance and Education) took "few responsibilities" and "passed on nearly every problem, great or small, to the central diwans," after 1849, this situation started to change, whereby government agencies acquired the authority to act more independently.[24] As Hunter explains, by April 1859, "this department [Interior] was [among other things] receiving petitions and complaints from Egyptian subjects and officials in Cairo and the provinces . . . and deciding which of the material it received should be sent to the Khedive."[25]

Certainly, the Egyptian National Archives bulge with petitions and registers summarizing such documents for these years. To pick just one example, the index for the Provincial Offices of Bani Suwaif, a medium-sized province some way south of Cairo, lists 150 registers of petitions for the years 1854 to 1879. Each register has about 140 pages and includes about four petitions per page. In other words, over this quarter century, the inhabitants of Bani Suwaif produced as many as 84,000 petitions. And, if the "Arabic Correspondence" petitions (sent to the interior minister) are anything to go by, the number of petitions sent was increasing over time. In this series, for example, during the 1860s, one box was sufficient for up to two years of petitions, but by the end of the 1870s, up to eight boxes were required for just one year of petitions (a sixteenfold increase).

The logic of state building was intertwined with another avenue of participation which opened for crafts and service workers in the late 1860s. In an important move, a formal election process was established for the heads and deputies of guilds in 1869.[26] Their appointment now required "an election (*intikhab*) of whoever commands consent and approval (*al-rada wa al-tasdiq*)."[27] In practice this meant that guild members would have to assemble in the police station or at some other suitable location and cast their vote for their favored candidate by stamping their seals on a ballot. On one typical occasion, an assistant of the police was to "go to the place . . . and . . . hold a meeting of its people and by means of those who have the right to elect, carry out an election of whoever obtains consent."[28] The candidate with the most votes took the post, provided that he was a man of probity (*istiqama*) and had the capacity to execute guild affairs, a guarantor, someone to verify the guarantor, no criminal record, and no reasons for suspicion. The police would report to the Interior enclosing supporting documentation. In a typical example, the police reported that "the election of whoever is worthy [was carried out] . . . with the consent of whoever has the right to elect from the people of the guild."[29] The Ministry of the Interior then ratified the appointment as long as all the documentation was in order.

This legislation was not the sudden invasion of a previously unknown democracy into guild affairs. In the Ottoman empire at large, senior guild members had for centuries nominated their preferred candidate to the *qadi* in court, who was then usually appointed guild head—with the approval of the *qadi* and sometimes with the ratification of one or another military or administrative official. Between 1842 and 1869 in Egypt it would appear that various senior members of the trade nominated their shaykhs to the local tax office, who then ratified the appointment. Moreover, the new procedures do not seem to have secured a secret ballot. But the new legislation did replace nomination with a formal voting procedure, where votes were actually counted. Further, the police were supposed to verify the ballot. Significantly, in the new procedures, every vote was theoretically equal; the seal of the most senior members counted for no more than the lowliest seal. Also, in practice, more guild members seem to have had the right to choose their leaders. Shaykhs were not simply nominated by a small clique of senior masters. The majority of the guild, one can tentatively suggest, were now involved in the voting, although it remains a little unclear as to who exactly had the right to vote in these elections. In large guilds, hundreds voted, and sometimes it is made clear in the police records that everyone voted. With the new legislation, election procedures were at least now clearly defined and recognized by the new order, and as we shall see, guild members could repeatedly insist on the proper implementation of the rules.

The new legislation also related to dismissal. It stipulated in reference to heads and deputies of guilds that "not one of the [above] mentioned can be dismissed without a misdemeanor (*junha*) established in the Courts and a [statement] about it issued from the police according to the law."[30]

The legislation of 1869 was linked to the logic of state building and revenue extraction. Where the government sought to raise higher taxes, it had to try to ensure the probity of those it called upon to do the job, to prevent treachery (*ghadr*) to the people and above all to the Treasury. It seems that the authorities were unhappy with the way the tax offices were behaving—one suspects that such tax offices were often working in cahoots with guild shaykhs or cliques of masters seeking to defend themselves against taxes—and by formalizing procedures and involving the police, the government hoped to regulate more tightly the links between tax base and treasury. And if the government suspected that contested elections would subsequently reveal information about tax fraud, they turned out to be right. The legislation on dismissal, furthermore, involved granting jurisdiction to the spreading network of secular courts—the Tribunals of the First Instance (*ibtida'i*) in Cairo, Alexandria, and Mansura, and the courts of appeal (*Majalis al-Isti'naf*)—whose new functions were steadily ousting those of the religious courts, whose potential autonomy for action was being increasingly curtailed. Such legislation was a state-building measure, but it simultaneously gave shaykhs some defense against both calumny from below and arbitrary dismissal from above. In addition, it underpinned an increasingly accessible forum to which crafts and service had growing recourse. As Hunter noted, by the late 1860s, "petitions alleging violations of the law were to be sent to the proper court without even a preliminary investigation, unless they contained charges against government officials."[31]

Partly because the legislation was bound up with state-building goals, the government appears to have been serious about implementing the new procedures. The ministries and the police reacted swiftly when dissenting voices were raised to one or other appointment. They were willing to respond to accusations of tyranny or corruption once levelled against a particular candidate for the shaykhate. At least, this is the impression one has from the documents, where dates of correspondence sent backwards and forwards between departments are close together, where questions are raised internally when any documents or facts are missing, where police become suspicious when there are too many or too few names on the ballot sheet, where the criminal record of persons is attended to with some care, when there are those voting who are apparently not involved in the trade, where outside character witnesses are brought in in some cases, and so on.

The legislation was also a constitutional concession by Ismail's regime and the *dhawat* to the rising provincial notable class of Egyptian landowners, who staffed the newly established (in 1866) Consultative Chamber of Deputies (*Majlis al-Shura al-Nawwab*) on the one hand, and a newly educated class of constitutionally minded reformers on the other. These groups—some local Egyptians graduating from new schools (previously only open to Ottoman Turks) and attaining positions of administrative power for the first time, and provincial notables who had benefitted from Mehmet Ali's land policies, as Cuno demonstrated, and then made substantial sums during the cotton boom—sought ways to convert their newfound ideas and wealth into political power.[32] Constitutionalism was one avenue of participation, and constitutional ideas were present across the empire during these years in any case—during the *nahda* in Syria, amongst the Young Ottomans in Istanbul, and to some extent among reformers and others in Egypt, especially those who believed that European political (and not just military) models should be duplicated in the East.[33] For Ismail, the Consultative Chamber of Deputies worked to legitimate his revenue-raising projects, as he could now start to claim that the assembly held responsibility for higher taxes rather than the khedive himself.[34] He could, further, use examples of Egyptian constitutionalism to try to support loan-raising activities from European financiers. Thus, instituting guild elections was very much bound up with the logic of revenue raising and state building, but it was also in part a concession, and indeed an attempt, to incorporate rising groups in Egyptian society, especially where such concessions could come as a quid pro quo for the increasing burden of taxation.[35] As we shall see in the cases below, crafts and service workers seized on this constitutional legislation and its practices and languages—whether or not this had been intended by either Ismail or the provincial notables to whom Ismail was making concessions—in order to fight forms of local exploitation.[36]

A final point—perhaps obvious but in need of clear articulation—on the political opportunities of the 1860s and 1870s: it was far more

straightforward for humble crafts and service workers to protest the activities of local exploiters than it was to take on the powerful. In fact, it
remained extremely difficult for crafts and service workers of any stripe
to complain directly about government policies or senior government officials, on taxation, economic policy, or otherwise. This came too close to
a direct challenge to the powers-that-be. Lady Duff Gordon's remark, although possibly an exaggeration, sheds some light on this. "Who is
there" she asked, "on the banks of the Nile who can say anything but
'hader' (ready), with both hands on the heads and a salaam to the ground
even to a Mudir; and thou talkest of speaking before Effendina!"[37] Only a
few discourses of official complaint were open to those who sought to alter directly the behavior of the powerful. Relatively high-status figures
could claim tax exemption on the basis of some customary privilege or
other. The Cairo *sartujjar*—the head of all the merchants in Cairo, and
major figure in the newly convened Consultative Chamber of Deputies—
clearly felt he had sufficient clout and prestige to demand on the basis of
customary practice exemption from his one thousand piastres per annum
professional tax (*wirku*) in the late 1870s. He claimed that "from past
agreements and past times whoever takes up the position of Sartujjar of
the capital is exempted from the professional tax . . . and this practice is
one of the fundamental rules followed from the past." The investigation
revealed that in fact the exemption had been granted in 1874 and not before, but nonetheless, the wish of Mahmud al-'Attar (the Sartujjar) was
granted.[38]

For those without such privileges, complaints which affected government policy itself could be made by humble subjects seeking royal mercy in
times of distress. For example, the craftsmen of Halfa district (*qism*) (deep
in Upper Egypt) wrote to the provincial offices at Esna in early 1864 claiming that Sa'id Basha (deceased) had previously forgiven them their professional tax on account of the "weakness" of the people of the district, and
the fact that some of them were linked to traders in the Sudan. They
sought the continuation of this special dispensation. Esna then communicated with the Ministry of Finance, and the upshot was a decree forgiving
them the tax in keeping with the practice under Sa'id.[39] Here customary
practice added weight to their claim. But these forms of complaint were
only possible in a limited number of cases, and granted their protagonists
but narrow leverage before power holders, factors which likely account for
their infrequency.

On other hand, it was easier to take on the corruption and tyranny of
local shaykhs and contractors. These were acceptable grievances to the

powers-that-be, perhaps partly because of the negative attitude held by élites to the tyrannies of guild shaykhs, and hence an upper-class predisposition to believe the complaints of the people in this regard. The government was certainly ready to take action against shaykhs it suspected of treachery, for tax fraud was precisely the practice that government actively wanted its subjects to mobilize against. Crafts and service workers understood this, and thus to get their voice heard laid endless stress on tax issues. By insisting on their status as taxpayers, furthermore, crafts and service workers were underlining the asymmetric bargain that existed between them and power holders—something like "we loyally remit taxes, you govern justly"—and were indeed trying to improve its terms. They also held a certain, if limited, power of institutional disruption in this area, under a régime increasingly desperate to tap all sources of revenue.[40] The key point here is that political opportunities for protesting the actions of local (as opposed to more distant and more powerful) exploiters were far more extensive, and it was here that the weight of mobilization appears to have been focused. The rest of the chapter examines some of these varied forms of mobilization and their highly uneven success during the 1860s and 1870s.

The Box Makers of Cairo and Taxation

This examination can begin with a group of box makers—styling themselves the "people of the al-Khidr box makers' guild" (*ahali ta'ifat al-sanadiqiyya al-khidr*)—who attempted to bring their guild leadership to book for overtaxing them in December 1868. These artisans made furniture of some kind, either ornamental boxes (inlaid with mother-of-pearl) or small cabinets. It would appear that under pressure from Isma'il's tax-raising policies, the leaders and senior members of the box makers' guild were trying to foist most of the tax burden onto poorer and weaker members—a scam in which the local tax office was also involved. Such practices may have been fairly widespread in Egypt as taxes rose.[41] In this case, the weaker members were able to petition the Interior Ministry on the basis of regulations which were continually being restated by a tax-hungry government. These exploited box makers enunciated to the "high and merciful [Minister]" (*li-l-marahim al-'aliyya*) at the outset of their petition the basic regulation that they knew was supposed to govern the taxation of their trade: "The assessment of the professional tax is according to the level of income and taxation raised from craftsworkers (*arbab al-sanay'*) is according to the tax brackets fixed by the Government bureaus." Thus the box makers sought mercy and affirmed their loyalty to government regulations, whereby taxation was levied on income, according to a sliding scale of tax brackets. After this affirmation they went on to claim that such regulations were in force everywhere "except in our guild, whose condition has deteriorated, and whose poverty is evil and which [now suffers from] incapacity."[42]

They explained that the brackets fixed by the government bureaus were ignored in their case. The tax office had decided different rates of taxation, with the guild leadership collaborating with them by fraudulently sealing the register affirming that the tax had been according to the official tax brackets. One notes that the register, which was supposed to be the written technology which would guarantee the probity of the system, was being subverted by guild leaderships pursuing their own interests. The box makers went on to claim that his honor the Sar Mi'mar, the "head of construction", had investigated the matter and found that the truth was at variance with what the guild leaders claimed. It is interesting that the guild members had had recourse to the Sar Mi'mar, who earlier in the century had been a notable and tax farmer and possibly a member of the pasha's household or of a particular Janissary corps.[43] By the 1860s, his position may have been merely ceremonial, or he may have still held the tax farms in certain construction levies which had not yet been centralized. In appealing to his authority, the lowly box makers were in part harking back to an older political pattern, when guild members had regular recourse to different elite figures from the *askeri* (military) class.[44] State building had marginalized such figures and the decentralized political negotiation they represented. Appeals like this were in part therefore the last of a kind. But they were also part of a new kind of politics oriented towards the emerging institutions of the state.

In the light of the Sar Mi'mar's findings the box makers claimed that they had sent a petition to the Privy Council which had in turn issued an order to the Governorate, which in its turn demanded that the tax office send it a statement explaining the situation. (Perhaps the box makers were able to obtain all this information from the Sar Mi'mar, or perhaps they had gone to the governorate to find out for themselves). Meanwhile, however, the tax office had closed the box makers' workshops in order to force them to pay the disputed taxes, which, as the box makers explained, they simply were unable to pay. They said that 125 piastres (per year) was being levied on eight-year-old apprentices who were only themselves paid one and a quarter piastres per day, and that all the shops had two such journeymen-apprentices (*sunna'in ashraq sic.*), the professional tax being levied on both of them. In this regard, the box makers said that the *ma'mur* (a police official) and various notables had permitted them to get their tax assessment changed.

Nonetheless, claimed the box makers, the tax office continued to demand from them the payment according to the first assessment. The box makers then heighten the urgency and personal tone of the petition and ask, "But with our inability to pay, from where can [the money] be obtained? [Even] if we sell all our capital (*rasmalana*) then this would not come to half of the assessment [that we have to pay]." The "people of the box makers' guild" continue, "In accordance with the justice of the government ('*adl al-hukuma*) and the mercy of the benefactor and the justice of your excellency (*haqqaniyat sa'adatkum*), who does not permit tyranny over slaves (*al-'ibad*), particularly the poor like us, our guild is committed to requesting the issue of a decree directing that the professional tax is levied on us according to the rightful fixed brackets." Thus it is emphasized that because of the subjects loyalty, and because of their unshakeable faith in the beneficence and justice of the powers-that-be, they are bound to request justice in this matter. They further press their case by invoking their status as members of a guild, even though, of course, they are seeking to attack the activities of their guild leadership in this case.

A deputy in the Interior Ministry then forwarded this petition back to Cairo Governorate requesting that a statement be made explaining the situation. The reply was swift (as so often during these years), and came from the governorate deputy on 13 Ramadan 1285/27 December 1868. It was to be bad news for the poorer members of the box makers' guild. The governorate reported that it had asked the tax office about the situation. The tax office affirmed that it had a statement listing the names of the box makers (*najjarin al-sanadiq*) and that during the last tax collection these names had been read out to the shaykh and the senior members, who then determined the tax of each individual. The tax office considered the guild leadership's activities trustworthy because there were nineteen of them who had carried out the enumeration and taxation, and that they had all sealed the register in the presence of the notable merchants, and that the tax distribution thus arrived at was the same as in previous years. As far as the governorate was concerned, the complaints of the box makers therefore could not be pursued any further.

It would appear overall that the guild leadership, probably pressed to deliver more and higher taxes, was working to shift the tax burden onto poorer members of their trade. Exploited carpenters were then able to respond on the basis of government regulations and interventionism. In this case they were thwarted when they faced what was on the face of it a complicit tax office, the solidarity of a large number of senior guild figures, and the presence of the notable merchants, who were willing to support, ignore, or be fooled by the tax scam instituted by the guild leadership.

Thus were the limits of both popular protest and state intervention in the 1860s, and in this case, as in others, government officials, through struggles and petitions such as these, probably became aware that tax was not being levied in the way they sought, and that guild leaderships, among others, were subverting the process.

A Stone Mason and Guild Dues

Others in the construction trades protested the unjust extraction associated with guild leaderships' levies of customary dues. Guild leaders in the construction trades as elsewhere clearly profited from the customary dues owed them by members. Borg mentioned that new entrants paid substantial sums to guild shaykhs: apprentices (*ashraq*) paid 20 piastres, journeymen (*sani'*; Borg called them "Foremen") 40–75 piastres, and masters 150–250 piastres.[45] Hence, the shaykh of an expanding guild of several hundred members—such as the carters of Cairo, or the boatmen of Alexandria, or the warehouse workers of Bulaq—stood to make significant sums from new members. Other kinds of guild dues were not insignificant. Ali Mubarak, minister of public works in the 1860s, mentioned that in the construction trades, masters received various dues known as the *ghada'* and the *taba'* from builders and unskilled construction workers (*fa'ala*). He noted similar practices amongst carpenters, carvers and sculptors, glass crystal makers (*qamaratiyya*), and marble workers.[46] In a case mentioned in more detail directly below, it would appear that dues taken by the guild shaykh from guild members amounted to half their daily wages. Such levies represented a selective use of custom, in an ever more market-dominated age, by more powerful members of the trade who, struggling to secure their own livelihoods under more vulnerable circumstances, attempted to extract resources from workers and masters under their control. Instead of protecting members, the guild—where dues were raised artificially high and where workers received no real monopoly protection in return—became in some cases a form of local exploitation.

As elsewhere, guild members were not slow to protest, especially where the political opportunity presented by new forms of state intervention encouraged some to take action. Particularly suggestive is the summary of a petition of one Husayn Muhammad, a Cairean stone mason. It runs as follows:

A deposition offered by Hussayn Muhammad a stone mason of the capital in which he explains that because he stopped giving half of his daily wage to the shaykh of the guild in accordance with the deal in force between the masters and the above-mentioned shaykh without the knowledge of the government, that shaykh has attacked him with blows (*ta'adda 'alihi bi-al-darb*). So he demands an investigation in as much as this is [a matter] related to the supervision (*ru'ya*) of the Diwan of Public Works because the building guilds are attached to it.[47]

It appears that in this case the master stone masons negotiated with the shaykh of the guild to reduce the level of dues owed, and the shaykh is here depicted as breaking the bargain and physically attacking Husayn when he refused to give up half his daily wage. This proceeding had gone on, of course, without the knowledge of the government, this being an area of trade life which was customarily the preserve of guild determination. The interest for my argument here is that Husayn Muhammad took the initiative, in the context of increased regulative intervention by Public Works into the Cairean construction trades, to appeal to Public Works to intervene or to investigate the situation, which he regarded as unjust. Although the outcome of the case is unknown, it would seem likely that Public Works would not want to get involved, for this would require potentially problematic intervention in what was still regarded as an internal guild matter. If Husayn Muhammad wanted to bring a case against his shaykh, he would probably have been directed to do so before the courts.

Contracting, Labor Relations, and Merchants

Where market relations deepened, the scale and volume of contracts increased, such as in domestic service (especially with the abolition of slavery), construction, and porterage, and where competition intensified, contractors—guild heads, deputies, and contractors (*muqaddimin, muqawilin*)—may have pushed further the exploitation of labor under their control. Those who suffered were not slow to protest on the basis of new political opportunities, dragging the state into guild affairs—albeit unevenly and not always successfully—in the process.

In a case from 1880, domestic servants from Alexandria (*ta'ifat khaddamin al-barabira*) took their shaykh to court when he started to contract outsiders, abandoning members in the process. As these Nubian servants alleged in the case, which went all the way to the Cairo Appeals Court, "The shaykh, by his contracting, has prevented some of the men of the guild from making a living . . . [and has employed] people other than guild members in domestic service."[48]

On another occasion, a number of impoverished water carriers started to suspect those who had contracted them to work for the government at the fire stations in the capital. As they wrote to the interior minister:

> We have become in the last stage of need, and . . . it was not thought that the Ministry would order the service of poor people like us [who are] without means of subsistence, and perhaps the contractors take wages . . . from the Ministry for us. . . . And so we have had the audacity to request that an enquiry be made, and if it were made clear that the truth is as mentioned [that is, that the contractors do take wages from the Ministry for us], then [there can] be payment of our due from [the contractors], and if not . . . and the Ministry employs us as forced labor (*sukhra*) then we have served for this long period and others can enter and undertake [the work] instead of us . . . and the government does not consent to tyranny like [that existing over] us.[49]

In this petition, even while presenting themselves as loyal subjects, imputing good intentions to the government and, in their impoverished state, throwing themselves on the government's mercy, the water carriers still underline that it cannot be right that poor people are forced to work for such a period in this way, and that a benevolent government knows this. They manage to convey this "tyranny" without of course impugning the government's motives. Unfortunately the success or failure of their plea is unknown.

One can also briefly illustrate how in 1869, a master mason seeking a more equitable division of contracts challenged a well-placed figure in the guild leadership who sought to monopolize construction work in Ezbekiyya. In this case, the mason complained about a certain Faraj Badawi, who was deputy (*wakil*) of the mason's guild. Badawi, using his position as deputy, had allegedly "taken all the government contracts . . . for the buildings in Ezbekiyya."[50] Faraj Badawi may have felt that he was entitled to monopolize contracts in one or another area of the city, but the police would have none of it. Following the complaint, the police moved quickly to interview the deputy in order to get to the bottom of his illegal monopolization of these contracts.

Guild members also petitioned, sometimes successfully, against exploitative labor relations. In the late 1870s, for example, a certain Ahmad Allabsi was put up as a candidate for the post of shaykh for the guild of farriers in Cairo. It would appear that his candidacy was based on his kinship with the outgoing shaykh, also called Allabsi. Certain rank and file may have been opposed to this situation, however, for it came to be an issue that at a certain point in the past the aspirant shaykh, Ahmad Allabsi, had offended against the "law of the trade" (*qanun al-kar*). He had, it was said, permitted a young assistant (*ghulama*) to wash a horse at the "waterwheels"—possibly at the mouth of Khalij just north of Old Cairo. The young assistant or apprentice had drowned and Ahmad Allabsi was held responsible at least to a degree. This fact was represented to the police in the run up to the election by a number of farriers who took this grievance out of the guild possibly in part in order to undermine the authority of an established family in the guild.[51] Whatever the case, the police deemed this offence against the law of the trade sufficient to bar Ahmad Allabsi from running for the post. On the one hand custom had played a role in defining the terms of the case, but on the other, this was yet another example in which guild members had attempted to bring in state powers to unseat the more powerful members of the guild. In this instance it curbed the powers of kinship ties at the top of the guild hierarchy.

Small masters also attempted to tackle exploitative merchants through petitioning the authorities. In 1873, for example, an indigo dyer from Alexandria, one 'Abd al-'Al al-Shafa'i, was taken to court (the recently established *Majlis al-Tujjar*, or merchants' tribunal of Alexandria) by his supplier, an indigo merchant called Hasan al-Sukri. The merchant claimed that al-Shafa'i owed him 5,355 piastres for indigo which he had supplied. The dyer had refused to pay the sum in full, according to a later petition from the dyer himself, on the basis that the indigo was overpriced, and had not been of high quality. According to al-Shafa'i, the merchant had refused to come to any kind of understanding with him over this, and the two had therefore ended up in litigation.[52] The court judgement came down in favor of the merchant, who shortly afterwards appeared at an Alexandria police station holding a summary of the court judgement and demanding that al-Shafa'i be made to pay up. Al-Shafa'i then, as a last resort, threw himself on the mercy of the police and said that he was incapable of paying. At this point, the intervention (*wasita*) of the shaykh and senior members of the guild was required to establish whether or not the dyer was telling the truth about his financial status. In other words, at this key interface between emerging government institutions and crafts and service workers—at the point at which police registers and other stored information was inadequate, the police, at the urging of the merchant, sought the relevant information from the shaykh and senior members of his trade (*kar*). The shaykh was supposed to tell the truth in this matter, without favoring one side over the other. In the event, the guild leadership stated that the dyer was capable of paying. Al-Shafa'i, having been let down by his local leaders, and as a last resort, petitioned the interior minister, laying out his case in some detail.[53] When the deputy of the Alexandria police then explained the facts of the case to the deputy of the interior just over a month later, Interior regarded the case as closed, taking no further action.[54]

Strikingly enough, al-Shafa'i the dyer could not persuade his own shaykh to provide a statement showing that he was unable to pay. Indeed, al-Shafa'i even hoped that the ministry might turn out to be more sympathetic than his own guild leader. This would seem to imply that the pressures of restructuring were again dividing rank and file from guild leadership. If the truth was that al-Shafa'i could pay, the shaykh may have been under pressure to declare this in this case from police and others, in view of the penalties of being found to have acted treacherously. On the other hand, the shaykh and the merchant may have been linked in some way, particularly if the shaykh was a wealthier dyer who also engaged in the indigo trade, or ran a version of a putting-out system. Such linkages seem more likely inasmuch as the police were harsher on shaykhs over taxation than over private transactions. It is certainly possible to see in this case some of the pressures of the new political economy. It would appear that merchants and guild leaders seeking to bolster their own position under more vulnerable conditions tended to work against and put pressure on lowlier figures in the trade, who in turn protested as best they could. In this case, al-Shafa'i's protests were unsuccessful.

Seeking Mercy: The Cabdrivers of Cairo

In one or two cases, ethnicity played a role in facilitating resource mobilization among guild members who faced discrimination at the hands of their leadership. In a case involving a dispute between the Arab head of the cabdrivers' guild and newly enrolled and exploited migrant labor from Upper Egypt, it would appear that the old guild leadership was effectively challenged by the newcomers. During October, November, and December 1871, up to seventy-seven Sudanese and "berber" cabbies of Cairo, working for private patrons and selling rides to the public, sent a series of petitions to the police and to the minister of the interior, protesting the activities of the Arab shaykh of their guild. As they wrote on 4 October 1871,

> We the berber and Sudanese cabdrivers petition to your esteemed Excellency (sa'adatkum afandim) that now we cannot find rest (laisa hasil lina raha) with the shaykh of the guild of cabdrivers present here. In view of this, we dared to petition your Excellency requesting

the issue of a decree to whoever is necessary to detach us [under a separate] shaykhate [so that our shaykh will be] one of us. For there is no rest for our race (*abna jinsna*) or agreement with the shaykh mentioned. [This is] leaving aside the fact that in Alexandria there was previously no agreement for something like this and the Arabs (*abna al-arab*) had a shaykh who was one of them, and the berbers had a shaykh independently established to prevent burdens and difficulties (*al-ta'b wa al-mushaqq*). And your Excellency is most beloved of the comfort of [your] slaves (*rahat al-'ibad*), the prevention of tyranny, and the affairs of justice, and we wish for your Excellency enduring might and glory. The list stamped with our names and our seals is attached and with that the ruling is entrusted to [your] honor.[55]

This would appear to be a case of tension within one guild (which included both public and private coachmen), between the arriving migrant Nubians and Sudanese on the one hand, and the Arab leadership on the other. It would seem likely, although the details are not specified, that the Arab shaykh was using his position to favor Arabs over the migrants in the labor market and possibly in the pressured politics of taxation. Thus the Nubians could find no "rest" and claimed that the situation meant burdens and difficulties. Using the precedent (but no "custom from old times," partly because these Nubian migrations were likely of relatively recent origin) of what had happened in Alexandria, where both Arabs and *barabira* had separate, independent shaykhs, the Nubians demanded their own shaykh. They were effectively thereby demanding their own guild—a radical enough solution to the tyrannies that they claimed to face.

In this case as in many others, even though the protagonists sought a new guild, the dispute was not solved through guild mechanisms or the customs of the trade alone. The Nubians engaged in collective claim making before the higher and increasingly interventionist authorities of Isma'il's state. In order to do the work of organizing seventy-seven individuals to stamp the petition with their seals they presumably used the interpersonal networks established through both their two trades and their common ethnic origins. In one of the several petitions they sign themselves as the "guild of berber and Sudanese coachmen in Cairo" (*ta'ifat al-arbajiya barabira wa sudaniyya bi-misr*). In other words, they used the corporate designation "guild" to refer to themselves as a legitimate category of persons before the government. This was an affirmation of a still authorized form of social organization, and it facilitated the legitimate claims of the coachmen. There was some useful sleight of hand here also, for the cabdrivers quite adventurously constituted themselves as a *ta'ifa* in advance of any official recognition of this fact, as officially of course their *ta'ifa* still included Arabs.

The cabdrivers appealed also to the justice and glory of the ruler: "your Excellency is most beloved of the comfort of [your] slaves, the prevention of tyranny, and the affairs of justice, and we wish for your Excellency enduring might and glory." This appeal was probably in part one of the necessary formulas impressed upon the petitioners by the professional petition writers themselves, who were familiar with the necessary protocol in these matters. But their appeal was not merely formula or flattery. It was a way of saying, "Because you are just, you must want what we want."[56] This insistence on the justice of the ruler was also a way of reminding the powers-that-be of the way they publicly legitimated their rule in the first place, and thus a way of holding them to their promises regarding the "prevention of tyranny and the affairs of justice."[57] It reinstated and reiterated the putative and publicly declared bargain between ruler and ruled. It stated that "we are loyal subjects on the basis that you are beloved of justice." In this context, "just and glorious ruler" and "loyal subject" were two sides of the same coin. Buried in this petition as in many others is the hidden threat that if this understanding, this asymmetrical bargain between ruler and ruled, were in some way shattered, that is, if the ruler were not just and glorious, then the loyal subject might also become rebellious. Although there was no discourse of citizenship here, there is no reason to be too dismissive about the utility of this potentially effective subaltern assertion before the powers-that-be.[58]

Claiming Citizenship: The Carters of Bulaq

During the 1860s and 1870s, however, crafts and service workers did go some way beyond the language of humble and loyal subjects beseeching the mercy of a just ruler. In collectively organized petitions, often tackling forms of local exploitation, crafts and service workers made vigorous use of new electoral procedures, and constantly asserted their dues or rights (*huquq*), especially in connection with taxation.[59] Through such mobilization crafts and service workers brought new constitutional legislation and the forms of citizenship it involved into guild practice in a significant way.

In the case of a protracted struggle for guild leadership among the carters of Bulaq, which is examined here in some detail, the majority of guild members were successful in retaining the leader they favored, a certain Ahmad Muhammad (shaykh of the Cairo carters at least from 1874 to

1878), and ousting the one they considered to be a tyrant, a success which owed considerably to the constitutionalism and political opportunities of the post-1869 years.

When the existing deputy of the carters in Bulaq, 'Abd al-'Al Salih died (probably in early 1874), a struggle for succession developed. Ahmad Muhammad wanted to nominate 'Ali 'Ajuz for the post, and had offered the necessary approval (*tasdiq*) and guarantees (*damanat*) to the police. But, another candidate, Muhammad 'Alaywa, had been nominated for the position by Hasan Abu Shabika, who was not from the carters of Cairo, but the head of the guild of donkey drivers, carters of commodities, and the cameliers of Shughriyya. Hasan Abu Shabika and his allies, who had positions in the livestock and transport trades, were trying to take over the Cairo carters' guild and its future revenues. The struggle went on from August 1874 until at least February 1875 and involved a number of petitions, police and ministerial correspondence, and at least one court judgement from the Cairo Tribunal of the First Instance. Ahmad Muhammad and his protégés, with the backing of the great majority of carters, were to emerge triumphant, but only after a considerable battle.

The challengers put forward Muhammad Alaywa for election to the empty post of deputy, and an election by all the carters in Bulaq was held in the presence of Hasan Abu Shabika and Ahmad Muhammad in March 1874 at the police station. As Ahmad Muhammad later claimed in a petition, "Most of them wanted [the candidate of] your slave, and about 100 individuals sealed [their names on the ballot] for me."[60] Following this, an election was held among "all the people of the guild from Cairo." As Ahmad Muhammad was to argue, at this election 'Ali 'Ajuz was victorious by sixty-six votes,[61] a result which was communicated to the governorate in a police statement.

A number of carters had good reason to vote against Hasan Abu Shabika and his candidate. If Ahmad Muhammad is to be believed, certain Bulaq carters had originally been under Abu Shabika in the guild of cameliers, carters, and donkey drivers at Shughriyya. But because of Abu Shabika's "tyranny" (probably overtaxation), they had been forced to sell off their livestock and had fled to join the carters of Bulaq (under Ahmad Muhammad).[62] Further, Ahmad Muhammad himself appears to have had some popularity in the earlier 1870s. In a later court judgement it was revealed that he had tried to resign from an earlier position as deputy of the carters of Lukaf (a smaller carters' guild in Cairo) after coming to blows with the shaykh of the Lukaf carters, 'Abd al-Fattah 'Abd al-Wahhab, but the people of the guild had not consented to this.[63] In other words, the carters of Lukaf were already favorably disposed towards Ahmad Muhammad from an earlier period. This might explain why when escaping the "tyranny" of Abu Shabika various transport workers had turned to Ahmad Muhammad's guild.

Nonetheless, although these facts were later recognized, in March 1874 those who were challenging Ahmad Muhammad and his protégé, 'Ali 'Ajuz, were not to be defeated by an adverse election result. Partly working in cahoots with Isma'il Effendi, head of the Bureau of Police Administration and Shaykh Mahmud, an official in the governorate, Abu Shabika and his allies brought a number of more or less dubious accusations against Ahmad Muhammad. Abu Shabika and the aforementioned 'Abd al-Fattah 'Abd al-Wahhab now appear to have been working together.

Abu Shabika actually had some clout among the carters of Cairo and in the deputyship of Bulaq already, not just because of his position as head of the cameliers, carters, and donkey drivers at Shughriyya, but because he had become responsible for collecting Isma'il's new livestock tax over the donkeys of Lukaf, camels of Shughriyya and, more importantly, the horses of Bulaq.[64] This last aspect of the job gave him an in on the affairs of the carters in the deputyship of Bulaq, especially those who used horses.

From this position, and hoping to disqualify Ahmad Muhammad from his post as shaykh, Abu Shabika then claimed that Ahmad Muhammad had actually been culpable in a fight with 'Abd al-Wahhab, and had gone to prison for twenty days. (This accusation later turned out to be false). Another more damning accusation was raised by Sultan Makawi, a disaffected deputy of the carters of Cairo, who had previously lost his post as deputy when the court judged him guilty of meddling in the taxation process, and Ahmad Muhammad therefore pledged not to use him as a deputy. Sultan Makawi, dislodged from his position, then accused Ahmad Muhammad of using seven unregistered deputies, appointed illegally by his own authority and not according to due procedures (recently established in the regulations of 1869).

On this basis, and because of various other unproven accusations which had been made against Ahmad Muhammad, the challengers got their way, the police dismissed Ahmad Muhammad, and 'Abd al-Fattah 'Abd al-Wahhab was appointed shaykh of the Cairo carters (it seems without an election). It is not clear whether or not Muhammad Alaywa was installed as deputy in place of the duly elected 'Ali 'Ajuz, but this seems likely. In ousting Ahmad Muhammad, Abu Shabika, al-Wahhab, and others had managed to subvert the regulations. Ahmad Muhammad had not, in fact, been convicted of any misdemeanor, which was required for his dismissal, nor had a new election been held for the new shaykh. That the regulations could have been subverted seems to be due to the unofficial activities of Isma'il Effendi and Shaykh Mahmud, who were in cahoots with Abu Shabika, presumably in return for kickbacks, although this is unclear.

But Ahmad Muhammad was not to be defeated, and he was able to muster considerable support among the carters of Cairo against the usurpers. In early 1875, no fewer than ninety-one carters put their seals on a petition to the interior minister opposing the incomers and urging an investigation. Ahmad Muhammad had the law on his side, as was finally recognized by the judgement of the Cairo Tribunal of the First Instance in February 1875. Having reviewed the various accusations against Ahmad Muhammad, and the various occasions when he had been guilty of infractions of regulation, the court still decided that "Ahmad Muhammad was not convicted in the way that would entail a dismissal and thus Ahmad Muhammad should be returned to the post [of shaykh]." We know that this judgement was implemented because Ahmad Muhammad, alongside his deputy 'Ali 'Ajuz, appears in 1878 seeking to increase the number of deputies in Bulaq.

In this case, we see the prominent use of growing state agencies—the courts, the bureaucracy, and new regulations—by the parties to the dispute. Those better placed in the livestock trades attempted to use regulations and government intervention where they could in order to extend their own clout and their own networks, which nonetheless still depended on a corporate structure, however transformed, in as much as these groups were struggling for guild positions which would give them some status and control over the urban surplus. Unofficial linkages to government figures, such as those between Hasan Abu Shabika and Isma'il Effendi, also played a part in these conflicts, and the importance of these linkages was only diminished when official practice and discourse prevailed, as it did in this case through the court judgement. In an expanding trade like carting, conflicts over the surplus were an urgent matter among those struggling to make a living during the rapid transformations of these years.

The principal point here is that the rules on elections and dismissal and the democratic procedures instituted in 1869 meant that the more popular and less exploitative leader, Ahmad Muhammad, triumphed in the end. As the balance of forces was not in his favor at all stages, this was a precious victory, one which without the petitions and the procedures could hardly have been won. Of course it was only when Ahmad Muhammad lost his position that he sought to use his popularity through petitions and an election to regain it. But here it would appear from the petitions that the

carters of Bulaq genuinely did not want Hasan Abu Shabika, who had tyr-
annized many of them previously, and were able to make their voice heard
and improve their situation through a form of democratic procedure, bal-
lots and petitions. This may have owed much to new state intervention. It
certainly represented a move beyond the localism of the guild. Where
guilds were internally conflicted, the state was dragged in to settle the dispute. But where the state could be corrupted, through bribery, then it
ceased to serve this liberatory function, and a locally exploitative network
could be secured. As the example shows, formal election procedures involving vote counting and police supervision were central to guild succession, if their practical effect depended on a constellation of other forces.
The government took the electoral consent of guild members seriously, in
as much as these were very much included in claims emanating from below.
Thus those who put their signatures on the petitions, further, were not
simply being used by those with more clout in the trade, but presumably,
in the new climate, had some capacity to give or withhold votes, or to swap
sides, or to bargain with their deputies and shaykhs. In this sense, they too
were looking to government agencies to express their wishes. As Ahmad
Muhammad stressed in his above mentioned petition, of early 1875 to the
interior minister, "The appointment (*tansib*) [of the shaykh] . . . is according to the wish of the people (*raghbat al-ahali*) as stipulated in the regulation and as has been carried out [in this case] by his excellency Afandim
'Abd al-Qadir Basha. And if [on the other hand] it were according to the
will of Isma'il Effendi and Shaykh Mahmud then this is something under-
handed (*mustatir*) only to be understood properly by intelligent men (*la tu-
drikuhu illa al-'aqul al-zakiyya*)."

Here of course, Ahmad Muhammad is implying that the interior
minister is just such an intelligent man who should step in to provide justice according to the regulations. The "wish of the people" had now become an important legitimating principle in these struggles, accepted by all
sides as part of the debate.

This quite dramatic idea and form of constitutional practice—the
outcome of state formation, concessions to the provincial notables, and
popular struggle—is in evidence in many other cases during these years.
For example, in a similar, lengthy struggle for control of the boatmen's
guild in Alexandria, another expanding transport trade, the same languages
and practices were deployed by different parties to the dispute. Ahmad Ali
was a senior boatman and deputy in the guild who wanted to see his guild
shaykh dismissed, ostensibly on the basis of the shaykh's tyrannies and in
view of the fact that the people of the guild had not voted for him. As he

boldly began his petition to the Interior Minister in 1878, "[I]t is not hidden from Your Excellency that the decrees issued in the right of the appointment of the heads of the guild require that the people consent to whoever is appointed for them, and this decree is known and famous among the general public in accordance with the regulations and publications abiding in all the Courts and Ministries, and this rule (*qa'ida*) is the current basis for legal judgements."[65]

Ahmad Ali was not afraid to remind the minister of the law, indeed reinforcing his reminder with the information that these decrees were "known and famous among the general public" in spite of their recent origin. And here, where the public, rather than some notable or other is invoked, one might even detect a whiff of popular sovereignty. And however much Ahmad Ali called the minister "Your Excellency," he was also willing to assert that regardless of the minister's wishes, in effect, these decrees required a certain set of actions. Indeed, what they required was the consent of the people to their leader. It was at points like these that guild members were shifting the discourse, as and how they dared, from that of humble and loyal subjects throwing themselves on the mercy of the just king, and towards that of citizens with rights.

Of course such incipient constitutionalism was sometimes subverted by guild leaders opposing legal electoral challenges to their position. Everything depended on whether electoral regulations could be enforced, by both state and society in interaction. The struggle for guild leadership in the case of workers in the grain warehouses (*musa'idin*) in Bulaq port was a case in point. For reasons which we cannot necessarily know from the public claims made in the sources, a certain Ta'lib Salih was in conflict with the guild shaykh. Thus, when the former stood for election as deputy to the guild in early 1879, the shaykh did his best to subvert the electoral process by harassing those who had voted for Salih by deliberately overtaxing them subsequent to the election. As the police suspiciously noted after investigation, "The reality is that . . . those who put their seals [on the ballot paper] for [Ta'lib Salih] in the past election have seen an increase in their professional tax (*wirku*) such as has not appeared for them in the past."[66] Meanwhile, the shaykh appears to have rigged the ballot in support of his favored deputy by bringing in an extraordinary 213 people to vote who very likely did not belong to the guild. For as the police discovered, following a tip-off from an aggrieved Talib Salih, who was apparently trying to play by the rules, of the 347 voters in the election for the new deputy, only 134 of them appeared on the guild taxation records for 1878. The rather flimsy defence of the guild shaykh when challenged by the police, who were mainly concerned about taxation, was that most of the persons who voted were new to the guild in 1879, and furthermore, that some had appeared in the 1878 tax records under different names. These arguments could hardly be considered wholly convincing. Nonetheless, the shaykh managed to escape a court case and for the time being, Salih's constitutionalism had been subverted.[67] Here the subversion was possible partly because the state was not able to gainsay the claims of the shaykh. Neither the registration of guild members nor the fixity of their names was sufficiently established for the shaykh's word to be adequately questioned.

As with electoral practice, the new legal procedures on dismissal were dragged into guild life by those struggling over guild leadership. Crafts and service workers appear to have become rapidly aware of their rights in this regard, and pressured the state to deliver on its legislation. For instance, Bayumi Hijris, the deputy of the guild of oil dealers from Old Cairo, claimed that he had been unfairly dismissed and cited the fact that no misdemeanor had been judged against him. He stated that the "decrees and publications issued regarding the right of office holders [meant that there was to be] no preventing or dismissing anyone from his post except when a misdemeanor [had been proved] by a process in the courts" and when the ruling had been "published by the police."[68] It is interesting that he added even this last detail, that the police should publish the ruling made by the court, which as we note from above is indeed specified in the regulation. It would appear that copies of the legislation were available or some source of information, most likely the professional petition writers, was actively operative in transmitting the details of the new legislation. Certainly the faithfulness to the wording of the regulation and the clarity with which their implications were understood is remarkable.

In numerous other cases, claim makers referred to the presence or absence of a proven misdemeanor in order to strengthen their case in support of or in opposition to a particular leader. For example, Ahmad Ali, a boatman of Alexandria, complained to the tyranny "stemming from the fact that Muhammad Sha't, head of the boatmen, and Ibrahim Sha't, head of the dealers and brokers have not been dismissed from their posts even though a previous judgement from Alexandria Tribunal [of the First Instance], [stated that] they should be dismissed from the headship." Ahmad Ali's grievance as certainly recognised as valid by the governor of Alexandria.[69] Or, witness this claim on unfair dismissal: "your servant 'Abd al-Samad al-Jabri was one of the heads of the guards (*ghafarat*) of the pyramids of Giza and was dismissed from this headship without a misdemeanor."[70] Al-Jabri, like Hijris above, was a member of the guild hierarchy who sought to use the legislation of 1869.

In other words, in an interesting contradiction, the shaykhs and deputies whose very independence was threatened by the arrival of new codes used certain of them nonetheless to bolster their positions before their rank and file. This was not an isolated phenomenon.[71] The different strands of centralization did not all point in the same direction.

Again, the government often appears to have worked to respond to complaints. Guildsmen were not gesturing at nothing when they mobilized petitions and complaints, a fact which in turn probably generated more such grievances, which in turn led to more state intervention.[72] The police nearly always made reference to the presence or nonpresence of the judgement of "misdemeanor" when deliberating the question of dismissal. In one police investigation, the assistant was able to confirm that "the sentence from *ahkam* [the high court] has confirmed the invectives of the measurers from Giza in the right of their head (*shaykh*) Hassan Niqah."[73] The shaykh was then dismissed from his post.

The case of the weighers of Daqahliyya offers a more nuanced example of the process of dismissal, the role therein of the misdemeanor, and the activities of the various parties involved. Al-Jawhiri al-Sini, backed by a local coalition, was returned to the shaykhate despite the existence of a previous ruling against him in a court. However, the existence of the prior ruling severely damaged his chances of remaining in the post. As the local authority noted, he was now shaykh "despite the existence of a ruling against him." The authority also mentioned that letters had been sent to the provincial authorities regarding the unlawful nature of his return to the post, and requesting his dismissal and the appointment of a temporary deputy. Further, it was known that the inspector "could not decide whether or not to return [al-Jawhiri] to the office of shaykh because of the previous ruling issued against him." A succession crisis was reached when the court ruled that Amin Ibrahim should be returned to the post, whereas the "merchants only accept al-Jawhiri." A further petition from Amin Ibrahim revealed that despite the fact that he had been returned to the post by the ruling of the court, his rival al-Jawhiri "is still at the weigh station, carrying out the work of shaykh with the foreigner Angelo, who is zealously in league with him, and I was prevented from working by force. . . . I told him of the folly of his opposition and his resistance to the orders of the government [but] he remained at the station by force." The deputy of the province came and "instructed [Angelo] not to get involved in the appointment and dismissal of government employees." Nonetheless, claimed Amin Ibrahim, "Al-Jawhiri is still there [taking] the name shaykh despite all orders from the government dismissing him." It seems, in this case, that al-Jawhiri was finally ousted, and Amin Ibrahim invested as shaykh, in spite of the "zealous" activities of the foreigner Angelo.[74] Clearly, then, the new legislation did not light a match on a new era. The opinions of merchants were important, coalition building was part of the picture, and the misdemeanor stipulation was not always enforced. The important thing to note is that the legislation was a, if not the, central issue in the struggle in Daqahliyya.

Thus, new legislation in 1869 put consent in relations between guild hierarchy and rank and file at play. It provided a way for different factions to contest the leadership within a framework sanctioned by the state and by the police. This process certainly brought the illicit activities of certain leaders to the attention of police and others, who could use them as a lever for further intervention. All struggles were conducted in terms and the language of the new order, and less in terms of the customs of old. The fact that the legislation on dismissal gave deputies and shaykhs a handle against rank and file in a sense made intraguild conflicts even more intense, for it gave ammunition, as it were, to both sides. Cole was right that this legislation represented something of a "democratic moment" in the trades, but it did not unleash guild assertion against a predatory state as Cole argues.[75] Instead the legislation formed part of the background to usually intraguild contestation which brought the new codes and institutions of the centralizing state into guild practice, and undermined the customary autonomy previously granted to the guild by the state.[76] Through contestation a certain practice of citizenship was instated among crafts and service workers.

Bidding for Redistribution: The Porters of Alexandria

At the limits of popular claim making, guild members dared to move beyond claims to liberal rights and went so far as to petition the state in support of more radical measures of wealth redistribution within the guild. One such series of petitions was mobilized by members of the guild of porters at weigh stations (ta'ifat 'attalin qabbaniyya) in Alexandria between 1871 and 1872. These low-status and poor workers carried coal and other goods to and from the port weigh stations, where goods were given an official weight to avoid disputes between merchants and buyers, in return for which the state levied a tax. The porters were opposed to the weighers employing men from outside the porters' guild to carry goods. As a number of porters were reported to have claimed in a petition to Alexandria Governorate, "[S]ome persons are not able to subsist because the weighers are bringing whoever they need from outside, and not bringing individuals (al-anfar) from this guild."[77] One suspects that the weighers were bypassing the guild and employing those who had no publicly recognized claim to be porters in order to obtain cheaper, untaxed, and unregulated labor. By using nonguild porterage they may have been able to avoid registering their use of the labor with their own guild, and thereby avoid taxation and regulation at home. It is interesting that the porters felt able to make this claim before the state: they clearly, and in this case correctly, believed that the state still recognized that only guild members were allowed to practice a particular trade, the state's interest at this point being above all in ensuring taxation.

The porters who wrote the petition, however, unusually enough, requested that in order to compensate those who had lost out, a communal division of income (*al-rukiyya*) should be carried out within the porters' guild. The police, always much closer to the life of the urban trades than other government institutions, explained to the governorate, who were apparently unclear on the matter, that the "communal division of income (*al-tarwik*) required the division of all the income (*taqsim jami'a al-irad*) among the rank and file of the workers ('*ala 'umum al-anfar*),"[78] a radical request indeed.

The request, however, implied that those who demanded the *rukiyya* could not persuade the guild leadership or more senior members to divide their income willingly, perhaps not surprisingly. The increasing opportunities for certain guild members for accumulation which commercialization provided meshed with a guild structure already transformed by state building in such a way as to undermine the corporate bargain and cause the impoverished members of the guild to turn, daringly, to the increasingly interventionist agencies of the state in order to deal with local exploiters, via the implementation of a long-known but probably not often implemented customary practice.

Indeed, the Alexandria police themselves, in an effort to clarify whether or not the *rukiyya* existed during the 1870s, had this to report: "[A]s for the existence or nonexistence of similar *rukiyyat* in other guilds the situation is not devoid of that; in some of the guilds the workers equalize with each other (*yatasawi al-anfar ma' ba'daha*) outside of government intervention (*barraniyan*) and it is known officially by the police that the guild of brokers and agents agreed on this *rukiyya*."[79] In other words, the *rukiyya* was probably not general practice, but undoubtedly still existed in various guilds. Importantly enough, this kind of mutual aid was practiced "outside of government intervention," meaning that it was neither endorsed nor enforced by the government. Here we catch a rare glimpse of an aspect of corporate life that the state-centered sources typically miss.[80]

According to Borg, a different kind of mutual help existed among the shoemakers (*saramatiyya*), who possessed a fund for the relief of distressed members. On entry into the trade, each member presented five copper vessels worth from forty to hundred piastres to the society in addition to paying a fee to the shaykh for his own use. The guild then hired out these copper vessels and pooled the proceeds in a fund. From this fund, every year a member in distress was entitled to a dinner, a suit of working clothes, and five piastres.[81] In other words, the guilds were not completely without welfare functions, even in the later nineteenth century. The fact that much of this activity was very much outside of government intervention makes it hardly surprising that very little information about it is available.

However, guild welfare provision under harsh conditions of restructuring and co-optation should not be exaggerated. Borg mentioned that the shoemakers formed the only guild where such practices existed, and noted more generally that the object of the guild was "not benevolence."[82] Furthermore, Martin's fieldwork of the early 1900s suggests that mutual assistance and help for widows and orphans or for needy or sick workers did not leave any recollection in the minds of old members of guilds,[83] whose principal recollection, it should be noted, was of "all these abuses which were committed [by the shaykhs of the trades]" and of a past which appeared "black with vexations and rough jokes."[84]

The porters of Alexandria, then, were involved in a daring attempt to get the state to compel redistribution in the guild, where the guild itself no longer pursued such a radically redistributive policy. In some measure, arguably, the claimant porters were aggrieved because they considered it their right, as members of the porters' guild, to be hired by the weighers. Outsiders did not have this privilege. Such a sense of guild privilege may have even been heightened where guild-organized porters paid heavier taxes than ever, and outsiders could escape such taxation. As taxpayers, furthermore, perhaps the porters felt that the government should respect their privileges in this regard all the more. They also knew that the government would pay some attention to this demand as it continued to recognize the guild as a legitimate category of social organization. Some of this information could have been conveyed to them by the scribes who wrote their petitions.

Nonetheless, one suspects that the grievance against the weighers was in some sense just the occasion for the porters' demand. This is because a more obvious and familiar solution (and indeed the one eventually adopted) would have been to prevent the weighers hiring outsiders, not to undertake a communal division of income among the porters. In other words, the porters' claim was probably above all about asserting the claims of the poorer members of the guild against the richer.

Neither the police nor the governorate knew exactly what to do. Should they intervene and regulate this aspect of guild practice, so long outside of government intervention, or should they eschew this role for the government and try an alternative solution? At one level, they recognized a degree of corporate autonomy for the guild itself. As the governor explained to the interior minister, the request "required the presence of the shaykh of the *ta'ifa* and the persons claiming the *rukiyya* [so that the police] could find out from them what was necessary [regarding this practice]."[85] This indicates that the authorities felt that proper procedure required that the guild, as represented by the shaykh alongside the claimants, should at least explain the relevant custom in this matter. That there was to be no direct and immediate intervention except through the intermediary and corporate bargain still instantiated in the guild. Nonetheless, the police (and higher authorities if necessary) should in some way have deciding power over what was desireable, and should oversee any implementation.

After consulting the guild, however, the police were opposed to the *rukiyya* (it is not clear what the shaykh and claimants had told them at the meeting). The police argued that "some [of the porters] are weak and unable to earn, and some have not worked at all or their work is very slack. Given this it is not permitted that [a man] dedicated to work (*al-munhamik fi al-shughl*) should pay his income [to others] as *al-ruk*. And whoever does not work enters into [receiving communal income] step-by-step, and the results of this in respect to [having to give] charity and the multiplicity of complaints is not hidden."[86] Hence the police argued that those who worked hard should not have to give up their income to those did not work or who did not try to work, especially in view of deleterious social consequences on a population who would then be tempted not to work, which would lead to more complaints and alms giving. Clearly this social vision stressed individual responsibility above communal obligation, and emphasized the importance of productive work. Additionally, one senses police pragmatism in the desire to avoid complaints from the population or from senior guild members. What we do not know is what the shaykh had said to the police, for there is no reason to suppose in advance that the guild leadership would have been in favor of redistribution, and a number of reasons (economic self-interest, for one) to suspect that they would not. Further, it is hard to imagine the claimants telling the police that they were "slack" at their work, which means that unless this was direct police observation, it would have been information given by their shaykh. Finally, the police may have been skeptical about getting involved in the rather un-usual, interventionist, and perhaps difficult task of persuading guild leaders and senior porters to part with their income. What is relatively clear is that it was the police, rather than the Governorate or Interior, who in the first instance "did not approve the *rukiyya*."[87]

In response to this, the governorate used a solution which was much more familiar and which would not run up against vested interests among the porters. They "clarified to the police what was necessary with regard to taking a pledge (*ta'ahhud*) from the shaykh of the weighers [to the effect] that [the weighers] will only take the individuals (*anfar*) that they need from the shaykh of the *ta'ifa* of porters."[88] The shaykh of the weighers was duly sum-moned to the police and "a pledge taken from him and he guaranteed that he will now take pledges from the weighers on this and keep [the pledges] with him (*taht yadihi*)."[89] On the one hand, the corporate status of the guild was reaffirmed in that the shaykhs were to contract labor from each other and to oversee the process of ensuring that outsiders were not hired. This solution, far from upsetting guild leaderships, reaffirmed their importance and powers in front of their members. On the other hand, the semiauton-omy of the guild was diminished in as much as it was seen not to be func-tioning effectively on its own but only after pledges by somewhat errant shaykhs to the police. Invoking the *rukiyya* seems to have been above all an attempt by the poorer and weaker members of the trade to gain more equal-ity within the guild. But the guild leadership, the police, and a social vision which stressed individual obligation and hard work foiled their attempt. The limits of petitioning had again been underlined.

Conclusion

This chapter has examined the ways in which crafts and service workers—under heavy pressure from taxation, economic change, the co-optation of their guilds, and local exploitation—vigorously attempted to both secure and subvert state intervention in the 1860s and 1870s. The key to popular mobilization lay in the political opportunities provided by the interaction between state formation and the rise of the provincial notables. The logic of revenue raising and state building and the constitutional concessions made by Ismail's regime to rising groups in Egyptian society worked to in-state electoral practices among the guilds and to promulgate regulations that crafts and service workers could subsequently seize upon to try and de-fend themselves. As elsewhere, elites did not voluntarily concede anything. And crafts and service workers had actively to make use of and partially redefine new forms of regulation and intervention in order to be able to begin to make these practices conform to their interests.

As we have seen, crafts and service workers were able to petition, and they were especially able to complain on certain specific issues, above all tax fraud. Grievances of many other kinds were probably subsumed to this language on numerous occasions, although of course this is impossible to verify on the basis of the source material. And after electoral practice was instated in the guilds after 1869, lowly workers went beyond the discourse of the loyal subject and the merciful ruler (which itself should not be entirely dismissed) and added to it a more assertive language of citizenship, appealing to law, due process, electoral practice, and popular consent. On a number of occasions, those mobilizing in terms of this practice and language were successful, such as in the case of Ahmad Muhammad's bid for leadership of the carters' guild. Such outcomes cannot simply be attributed to the purely monolithic and coordinated interests of state builders, landowners, and the colonial bourgeoisie. They owed something to the way elite interests accommodated and clashed with each other, and the ways in which crafts and service workers seized whatever crumbs fell from the table.

When formal mobilisation was inadequate, crafts and service workers could resort to the weapons of the weak: subverting regulations, bribing officials, persuading local notables to mislead the government, and above all hiding themselves from punitive taxation in one way or another. Indeed, one of the most effective defenses that guild members had against taxation was to form an illicit alliance with the guild shaykh and thereby drop off the tax rolls or receive a favourable (that is, low) income assessment. This form of evasion appears to have been widespread, involving thousands in Egypt's towns up and down the country. It was perhaps the only form of crafts resistance which genuinely put a dent in a key policy emanating from the highest echelons of power.

Thus, through their resistance, crafts and service workers made some limited impact on the terms of their restructuring: masters were able to hold onto wealth in a way they might otherwise not have been able to do, and some workers were able to protect themselves against exploitation.

Contrary to the conventional view, it would therefore appear that collective action from below played an important role in the attrition of the guilds. Where guild structures were co-opted or unable to protect their members' livelihoods, crafts and service workers banded together in informal networks that were either subguild, or extended beyond guild boundaries. Guild members, in the search for more adequate protection, were to some extent rejecting their guilds and forging informal networks in order to pursue their interests. Had guild members remained passive, the government might have retained guilds intact for the purposes of regulation and taxation. But the very resistance of guild members, on a variety of fronts, led to state intervention, which furthered the attrition of guild autonomy.

But both official and unofficial mobilization were drastically limited in spite of the best efforts of crafts and service workers. Informal practice was at best a short term measure, and was unable to change structural relations during these years, and often involved more individualistic acts which exploited other workers, often the poorer members of the guild. Trying to avoid taxation often led to even more invasive state regulation, as in the case of the bakers. Official mobilisation, for its part, was by no means always successful, even in the short term. The box makers of Cairo failed to bring their leadership to book for unfair fiscal practice; the porters of Alexandria, for all the radical daring of their proposal, probably never stood a chance of persuading the state to get involved in wealth redistribution in their guild. On other occasions, elections could be rigged, voters bought off, and officials bribed. Partly because the interests of masters and journeymen were often opposed, the success of one often came at the other's expense, rather than resulting in the redistribution of resources in their collective direction.

Further, one notes the resounding absence of complaints about the negative effects of imports. Only further research can resolve the explanation for this silence, although one can hypothesize that guild members were aware of how such complaints were entirely out of bounds and would not be countenanced by the authorities, whose policies were closely linked to the export economy. It is clear that world economic integration, which ultimately set the terms of restructuring, went ahead unhindered by any protests from those whose livelihoods were eroded as a direct result.

Finally, crafts and service workers may have been partially able to escape their failing guilds, but what were they getting themselves into? Where they petitioned loyally and in terms faithful to new discourses, working to root out local tax fraud and expose illicit practice, they were actually dragging a practically unimpeachable and ever more centralized state machine into their affairs. For it was all very well to complain about local exploiters, but, for all the beginnings of a discourse of citizenship, to raise questions about Ismail's policies remained almost impossible. Yet it was Ismail's very policies that collective action was drawing more minutely to bear on craft activity. The negative consequences of this were to become far clearer after 1882, when the Egyptian state was captured by the British and subordinated to the workings of a vast Empire.

4

Restructuring under Colonial Rule

After the midday meal, the work begins again, God help us to the end of
the labor.
The day will last a long time yet, God help us to the end of the labor.
—Construction workers' song, Upper Egypt, 1900s

smail's regime was plunged into crisis between 1876 and 1879 because
it could no longer meet all interest payments on the debt to European
financiers. Egypt's economy had not been able to deliver the resources
which could have saved self-strengthening projects, which as a result not
only failed to deliver independence, but even acted as a beachhead for European imperialism by plunging Egypt into debt. Ismail was too independent
for the European Debt Commission, which was convened in 1876 to take
charge of Egypt's finances, and pressure from Britain and France led to Ismail's replacement by his son, the more pliable Tawfiq (1879–1892). At this
point, in a bid to save Egypt from European control and khedivial autocracy,
elements from the army, the constitutionalist provincial notables, certain
merchants, ulama, and popular groups combined to mount a major rebellion, led by Ahmad 'Urabi, a colonel of peasant origins.[1] While Tawfiq attempted to hang on to his battered authority from his refuge on a British
frigate off the coast at Alexandria, 'Urabi's forces controlled much of the
Egyptian government and territory during 1881 and 1882. The British could
not tolerate the threat they perceived to bondholders' interests, and invaded
the country in the fall of 1882, crushing 'Urabi's forces at Tal al-Kabir.

With these events, the looming asymmetries that imperialism had imposed on Egypt from at least 1840 onwards were written into the local government itself with the construction of a colonial state which seized de facto control of the centralized bureaucracy built up by Ismail and his predecessors, while continuing the fiction of Ottoman sovereignty. State building, which had sought to strengthen Egypt in the face of European military and economic power, was now replaced by a colonial program directly serving that power, and seeking not to strengthen Egyptian society and economy against Europe, but to parsimoniously secure her territory and population for the bondholders and the British Empire. Under this kind of rule, world economic integration deepened radically, particularly during the boom years of 1897–1907, when direct investment was added to existing financial and growing commercial ties.

During these decades of rapid change, crafts and service workers continued to multiply their numbers at least in line with rapid population growth. In order to forge livelihoods under conditions which were now remote from those of even the early nineteenth century, they had little choice but to restructure in ever more far-reaching ways, and the patterns of adaptation, self-exploitation, and labor squeezing which had become visible after the cotton boom were deepened. Although crafts and service workers continued vigorously to engage in collective action to protect themselves, and although substantial strikes were joined in 1907 and afterwards, and new organizations such as syndicates and unions were formed with the abandoning of the guilds and the rise of nationalism, crafts and service workers were still unable to substantially change the terms of their restructuring or achieve anything close to popular participation in the colonial state.

The Colonial State and World Economic Integration

Whether or not the British remained vague in defining their presence in Egypt, only abrogating Ottoman sovereignty in 1914, and whether or not colonial officials, with an eye on French opposition, continued to give the impression that Britain was about to leave at any moment, the first two decades of British policy in Egypt were dominated by the mantra of "sound finance." The invasion had been in the interests of metropolitan bondholders, who owned approximately 100 million LE in Egyptian government bonds; and under Lord Cromer (1883–1907), "sound finance" was about effectively repaying the debt to this colonial bourgeoisie. As Cromer himself put it in one of his annual reports, it is "incumbent on those who are responsible for the administration of Egyptian finance to bear constantly in mind that the secure maintenance of financial equilibrium constitutes *the first and most important interest of the country*, and that both the execution of fiscal reforms, however desireable, as well as the expenditure of money on the most praiseworthy objects, must be subordinated to this primary consideration."[2]

Revenue raising for debt repayment meant the austerities of fiscal reform and balancing the budget. But, just as in India (although not yet in Britain), it also meant state intervention in the economy to try to boost revenues.[3] Accordingly, significant sums of taxpayers' money were ploughed into agricultural irrigation schemes. Particularly notable was the conversion of Upper Egypt to perennial irrigation and the completion of the Aswan dam in 1903. The British were willing, against the canons of metropolitan Treasury orthodoxy, to add to Egypt's already heavy debts in order to invest in agriculture.[4] By the 1890s, this policy started to bring returns, as the growth of the cotton trade raised customs revenues and land taxes.

Investment in agriculture was not just about revenue raising for the bondholders, but also a key move in securing an alliance between the colonial state and on the one hand the ruling dynasty, the largest landowner in Egypt, and on the other the increasingly wealthy landed classes, from the Turco-Circassian aristocracy to the provincial notables, whose fragile constitutionalism and patriotism was now exchanged for the increasingly lucrative cultivation of their estates.[5] All such large landowners had the capital and connections to take over recently irrigated and ever more valuable land, especially after 1890, when price rises started to make cotton and land more of a boon than ever before. Much of Egypt was converted into a cotton farm: more than a quarter of the total cultivated area was planted with cotton in the early 1900s. More than 90 percent of Egypt's export earnings were in cotton by 1913. Favorable movements in the cotton terms of trade during these years only increased the real levels of wealth that cotton, purchased above all by Manchester's textile mills, could bring to those who controlled it.[6] Under these conditions, estates grew and landlessness increased. With peasants unable to force the colonial state to intervene, landowners were increasingly able to "eat" the lands of surrounding small holders, who labored under taxes, usurious debts, rent increases, insecurity of tenure, and extraeconomic coercion.[7] These labor-squeezing tactics were sufficient for the profits of landowners, who under such protected and uncompetitive conditions had little impetus to improve the productivity of their estates through mechanization.

As uncertainties among investors over the status and continuation of the British occupation were slowly allayed, and as Egypt's commercial success became apparent during the 1890s, more and more investment from external, foreign residents and local landowning and merchant sources went into land and mortgage companies, banking, insurance, shipping, utilities, import/export commerce, transportation, and construction. World economic integration entered a new phase. Water piping, gas lighting, paving, and sanitation appeared in the cities, as did tramways after 1896 in Cairo, Alexandria, and Port Sa'id. Heliopolis, the city in the desert, was built in the early 1900s by the Baron Empain. The Anglo-French agreement of 1904 put an end to the overt diplomatic friction between Britain and France over the British presence in Egypt, and increased confidence in political stability further. This factor contributed to a speculative boom which only burst in mid-1907. While less than 7 million LE was held in capital in large-scale and capital-intensive banking, commerce, and industry in 1883, this figure had doubled by 1897, doubled again by 1902, and then tripled before the slump of 1907, before adding a few more million to attain about 100 million LE in 1914.[8] For the comprador bourgeoisie, who invested in the growing infrastructure of this export economy, and exploited the labor power of a growing class of wageworkers, who were only just starting to be able to protect themselves by changing the terms of their exploitation, Egypt was a land of riches. As Pierre Arminjon remarked, "For a number of years leading up to the middle of 1907, Egypt had acquired in the mind of its inhabitants . . . the reputation of an El Dorado, the fabulous prosperity of which was truly something supernatural."[9]

During the same period, comparatively little was invested in the large-scale industrial production of tradable goods. By the early 1900s, large-scale industry probably only employed 2–3 percent of those listed in the 1907 census as employed in manufacturing.[10] Any new ventures had to face the intense competition of metropolitan industry. And industrial investment was not in the interest of already established and lucrative banking, commerce, transportation, or land. Agriculturalists, for example, felt that attention to industry might diminish their own wealth by undermining their supply of cheap and abundant labor.[11] Cromer applied the same argument even to education, which he branded a "national evil."[12] Import merchants saw in the promotion of local industry a threat to their trade. Many, especially prior to the mid-1900s, were happy to fall in with the British insistence that Egypt was by nature, and even by divine will, an agricultural country. Above all, colonial control meant favoring the supply of raw materials to core industries, not the encouragement of peripheral industrial competitors. Indeed, industry was hardly mentioned in a quarter of a century of official reports, commissions, and official correspondence.

Cromer's *Annual Reports* contained no category "industry." Moreover, when industrial ventures appeared, the colonial state moved against them, the most famous example being the duty applied to a recently established, large-scale cotton weaving factory in 1901.[13] Such a policy, of course, was a reversal of that pursued, albeit with limited success, by both Ismail and Mehmet Ali. It was now left to less powerful groups developing anticolonial nationalism to champion the idea that Egypt's future prosperity depended on a revival of her industries.

Crafts and Service Workers and Restructuring

The "fabulous prosperity" of the Egyptian "El Dorado" only applied to a relatively tiny elite, comprising mainly the colonial and comprador bourgeoisie and large landowners. Radically deepening world economic integration put crafts and service workers, on whose livelihoods and products the majority of the urban population continued to depend, under tremendous pressure. Never before had Egypt's crafts been exposed to competition on such a scale from a broad range of European machine-made goods purchased by nearly all strata of the population. The consumption of European goods broadened from cotton cloth and luxury items consumed by a narrow elite to a more everyday basket of consumption goods: cotton cloth continued to lead the way with an import worth over 3 million LE, but silks, woollens, and linens were also purchased, as were, on a grander scale than before, dyed fabrics, clothes of various descriptions, furnishings, domestic utensils, and so on.[14] Furthermore, new investments in municipal utilities and transport came into direct competition with small-scale service providers of various kinds, from water carriers to cabdrivers, as well as having downstream effects on artisans who served those industries. Further, the spread of market relations, the development of transport infrastructure, rapid population expansion, and overall urbanization which appear to have set in from the 1890s onwards brought crafts and service workers, searching for livelihoods and incomes, into sharper competition with each other.

But it is important to emphasize, contrary to the claims of the older historiography, that crafts and service workers—in construction, furnishing, garment making, weaving, dyeing, urban transport, metallurgy, ironwork, carpentry, tannery, milling, butchery, patisserie making, chemical industries such as oil, soap, candlemaking, and artistic trades such as jewellry, fine carpentry, and embossing—continued to find work in significant numbers and continued to deliver much needed cheap goods and services to large sections of the population. Although these workers were put under considerable pressure and relatively impoverished, the available statistics indicate that numbers in employment steadily increased in absolute terms, and even advanced slightly as a proportion of Egypt's fast growing population. According to the census of 1897, for example, about 260,000 worked in manufacturing of all kinds in Egypt, all but a tiny proportion of this total being employed in small locally run workshops. By 1907 this figure had risen to around 380,000, and by 1917 to around 490,000. Such totals represented a steady advance on the proportion of the population employed in Egypt in industry, from 2.7 percent to 3.9 percent over the period.[15] The statistics for Cairo tend to confirm this picture. In 1897 around 53,000 worked in manufacturing, and by 1917 around 84,000, totals which advanced the proportion of the population working in industry from 9.3 percent to 10.6 percent. Again, the overwhelming majority, perhaps more than 97 percent, of these workers were employed in largely unmechanized small enterprises. In an indication of this, employers and self-employed outnumber workers in the 1917 census.[16] As the Commission on Commerce and Industry—commissioned to enquire into the state of Egyptian industry during the First World War, when local production suddenly became an issue for British rulers now interested in wartime provisioning—noted, "[I]n reality, and despite its appellation, ["small-industry" is] the most important because it occupies the greatest number of workers and extends its network in all towns and farmsteads of Egypt."[17] Only where crafts and services faced direct competition from large-scale industry duplicating the exact product or service to meet strong and standardizable demand were they steadily destroyed. Where demand was weak, fluctuating, or customized in one way or another, crafts and service workers could continue to make a living.[18]

The availability of such low-profit areas in the economy was only the prerequisite for crafts' survival in a new age. Increasingly competitive conditions forced crafts and service workers to restructure their production. New trades appeared, older trades adapted or were abandoned, and larger workshops and putting-out networks were built. Production costs were lowered by the use of cheaper premises and the widespread purchase of cheaper and more convenient raw materials, often produced by factory industry. Productivity was improved to some degree in various cases by piecemeal mechanization. The key to cheap production, however, was reductions in the cost of labor, both skilled and unskilled. In competition with large-scale production and with each other, crafts and service workers owning some means of production engaged in self-exploitation, lowering their rates to the extent that their profits only sufficed for their own subsistence and the reproduction of their existing fixed and working capital. And where labor was cheap, abundant, and largely unprotected, masters squeezed the semiskilled and unskilled workers under their control, lengthening hours, lowering wages, raising the intensity of work, and allowing conditions to deteriorate. This chapter examines these processes of restructuring with reference to some of the most numerous and rapidly changing sectors of craft and service employment: garment making, textiles, construction work, and urban transport.

Garment Making

New and adapted garment trades—seamstressing, tailoring, shirt making and shoemaking—appear to have comprised the fastest growing sector of artisanal activity in terms of employment during these years. From apparently employing about 10 percent of crafts workers in Egypt in 1897, these trades employed around 30 percent of such workers in all Egypt by 1917. In Cairo, a similar trend increased the employment proportion of clothing and dress from about 15 percent in 1868 to about 30 percent of all artisans in 1917. In Mansura such crafts expanded from making up about 6 percent of all manufacturers in 1863 to about 32 percent in 1917.

The most dramatic development was the ballooning of the category of "sewers, dressmakers, ladies' shawl and veil manufacture, and makers of other articles of women's dress." Numbers recorded under this heading show increases by a factor of about nine in Egypt between 1897 and 1917, and even steeper increases were recorded for Cairo during the half-century preceding 1914. These producers, mostly women, came to account for between a third and a half of all those working in this increasingly important manufacturing sector. Arguably the key to this employment, in an age where hands and bodies were forced to compete against machines and technical capacity, was that women's work was cheap, both in absolute terms and in comparison to the activities of men.

One expanding and well-known trade, "entirely carried on by women and girls working in their own homes" was shawl making based in and around Asyut in Upper Egypt.[19] These workers combined a certain kind of metal strip with mosquito netting in a distinctive way to create a product that was much in demand as a veil or shawl in Egypt's towns. It was also in demand among tourists, being mentioned by the Commission on Commerce and Industry as one of the trades which suffered when tourist demand fell off during the war.[20] Merchants imported the raw materials from Austria and elsewhere and provided them to the women working in their houses—not only to those in Asyut but also to the women "of the fellahin" in the surrounding villages such as Bajur in *markaz* Asyut and Nakhila in *markaz* Abu Tij. It would appear that the women paid for these raw materials at the point of delivery, and then sold the finished product, probably to the merchants who organized the provision of raw materials.

The success of this trade rested on the cheapness and availability of female labor. Sidney Wells's team recorded that the price obtained from the Cairean merchants for Asyut shawls was apparently only a "very little more" than the price the women had paid for the raw materials, meaning that the women worked for tiny returns.[21] This was partly possible because women's wages were defined as supplemental to the household income: in this context, women had little choice but to accept less than a bread-winning wage. Further, female workers were not severed from the means of subsistence—especially those living in the villages surrounding Asyut—and thus could be paid below subsistence rates. Moreover, geographical dispersement and gender norms constraining women to the domestic realm operated as an obstacle to women's organizing in defense of wage rates, and made women easier targets for exploitation. Finally, neither women nor merchants had to make capital outlays to train female workers, whose skills had often already been learned in domestic settings and thus could be transferred cheaply and rapidly to more commercial activities. Women thus constituted an available, ready-trained, and above all extremely cheap workforce whose products cost little more to the wholesale merchants than did the raw materials. Where labor was so cheap, such industries could survive and employ more workers over time.

Home workers in the villages surrounding Asyut also produced tulle, a delicate, netlike fabric for use principally in veils. According to an industrial survey undertaken in the mid-1920s, output was greatest between 1908 and 1912.[22] This trade was organized by twelve clothes and fabric merchants based in Asyut who distributed white tulle and tulle thread (via intermediaries) to workers in the surrounding villages. Three metres of white tulle (costing 10 piastres) and about a kilo and a half of thread (costing about 70 piastres) were required for each veil. When the work was completed the producers themselves transported the finished garments to the merchants and took payment for what they had done. The veils were sold by the women to the merchants by weight, one dirham (3.12g) costing 3–3.5 millimes, which meant, in the early 1920s, about 2 piastres for heavy veils and 1 piastre for light veils. Production costs were kept low in part by the purchase of cheap machine-made thread imported from France and

Germany, but above all, inputs were inexpensive because female labor was extremely cheap, evidently adding only very slightly to the cost of the raw materials. Between 1 and 2 piastres for what was likely at least a day's work in the early 1920s was nowhere near a living wage, but at best a small supplement to household income.

Male tailors working independently in small boutiques in the cities were also able to respond to available demands and significantly multiply their numbers by offering cheap customized goods in new European styles, and working for low returns and low wages. Whereas the census of 1897 listed around 9,000 tailors in Egypt, the census of 1917 recorded around 29,000 "tailors, clothiers and costumiers." In Cairo numbers increased from around 2,400 tailors to around 5,900. This expanding trade more and more produced the European styles so much in demand among the new *afandiya* and elite groups, eschewing the flowing robes and turbans which had dominated even upper-class tastes as recently as the 1830s.[23] Tailors found work in part because importing competition—where machine-made, mass-produced clothing was still to come—was nothing like as intense as in other trades, such as cotton weaving. Indeed, the external trade statistics show no great rises in the per capita nominal value of imported ready-made clothes during the period, and inflation meant that the real value of these imports may even have been falling.[24] Most of the British imports appear to have consisted of government orders for uniforms. Little came from Germany, and the principal imports from France were "the more expensive clothes for ladies," although France also exported some of "the very cheapest form of workmen's clothing, such as smocks etc.," although, not the ubiquitous *jallabiya* (long shirt). Austria reportedly had more success, selling long overcoats for men at 24 to 80 francs (that is, about 1–3 LE). As the British Chamber of Commerce reported, "[T]he cheapest imported goods, made without much regard for cut, workmanship and materials employed, come from Turkey. . . . It is stated that the cloth used for the goods in question is mainly supplied by England, but the fact remains that clothes can be sent to Egypt at such a price that even Austria cannot compete on point of actual £. s. d."[25]

Tailors further secured their markets, even in the face of competition from Austria and especially Anatolia, by lowering their costs, especially in competition with each other, which above all meant having to accept low rates and pay low wages. The article in the Egyptian Gazette just quoted continued as follows, "[T]he remarks last made apply with even greater force to the goods turned out by the numerous small tailors who abound in Alexandria and Cairo. These men, for example, can turn out a full length overcoat at about 8/- [about 40 piastres] and sell it in their shops for 10/- [about 50 piastres]." In other words, Egyptian tailors could produce overcoats more cheaply and effectively than Egypt's sternest overseas competitors. Such garments were 50 percent cheaper than even the cheapest of the Austrian products. These tailors relied, in certain measure, on cheap imports of English cloth, the 2 1/2 yards necessary for an overcoat being obtainable for 4/7 (about 23 piastres). Linings and buttons, which were probably also imported, cost tailors a further 1/5 (7 piastres). Here as elsewhere crafts workers combined with factory industry. But the key to cheap production was not cheap raw materials, which were available to overseas competitors, but the cheapness of local labor. The labor component of the overcoat considered here amounted to 10 piastres, minus other outlays on tools, premises, and overheads. Thus, although tailors appear to have been able to earn a living wage, unlike women working from their homes outside of Asyut, they were nonetheless working at subsistence rates, amounting to self-exploitation where so little was left over for reinvestment.[26]

Finally, certain kinds of shoemakers were able to capture changing consumption tastes and find livelihoods by producing cheaper European-style shoes for Egyptians and faux-traditional slippers for tourists. On this basis their numbers expanded ahead of the rate of population increase during these years. In all Egypt, numbers rose from around 12,700 shoemakers of all kinds to around 21,600 between 1897 and 1917. In Cairo, numbers grew from 2,361 in 1868 to 5,682 in 1917. In 1868, as we saw, those making European-style shoes were decidedly in the minority.[27] But by 1917 all this had changed. We find in Cairo 4,209 "manufacturers of European footwear" (*jazmaji*) and just 1,441 "manufacturers of native footwear" (*marakib*, and so on). Thus, Cairo's European-style shoemakers had multiplied their numbers more than thirteen times, whereas makers of old-style shoes had lost out both relatively and even absolutely. Almost three-quarters of Cairo's shoemakers were now makers of Western-style shoes. The same pattern is visible (inasmuch as statistics exist) in the figures for Egypt as a whole, although older styles appear to have continued to appeal to those in the provinces for longer than in Cairo. Makers of European-style shoes had become a substantial majority by 1917 at 64 percent of the total. In addition, old-style shoemakers adapted their products for tourists. By the turn of the century, some of the major guidebooks pointed tourists towards the "Arab" shoes available in Khan al-Khalili, a fair indication that such shoes were in demand among visitors. For example, in the Baedeker of 1908 we hear of "the bazaar of the shoemakers, in which the pretty red shoes of the Arabs may be purchased."[28]

Shoemakers of all kinds reduced costs by obtaining cheap tanned leather and other raw materials from Europe.[29] Makers of traditional slippers for tourists were able to diminish production costs by "dumbing down" their product. As Cromer noted, such shoes were not made with all the traditional materials.[30] For Cromer this was a sign of decadence, but it was more plausibly a way in which cobblers could lower costs by using cheaper raw materials, while continuing to sell to a tourist market which still saw such shoes as the authentic "pretty red shoes of the Arabs."[31] Capital costs were kept low. Martin estimated that the total equipment utilized by a maker of Turkish slippers in Cairo in 1909 was worth 8 to 10 francs (that is, about 30–40 piastres).[32] Thus the labor value accumulated in this cobbler's capital stock was but the worth of three or four days' wages. Labor was also cheap. A shoemaker working for the prisons department in the Ministry of Interior was paid from 15 to 19 piastres per day in 1919,[33] a wage which would probably have represented the high end of what shoemakers could hope to earn.

On this basis, shoemakers, like tailors, were able to mount real competition against imports. Whereas the value of imported shoes increased nominally to some degree between the 1880s and 1913, the actual number of pairs of shoes imported did not increase overall (it rose until 1907 and then diminished thereafter). In fact, the number of shoes per capita imported into Egypt was substantially less in 1913 than it had been in the 1880s. By producing a cheaper alternative through lowering their own costs, above all their labor costs, Egyptian shoemakers continued, under heavy pressure, to compete against imports.

Textiles

Unlike the garment trades, spinning, weaving, and dyeing encountered far more intense competition from imports. Textiles were by far the largest category of manufactured imports (by value and volume) into Egypt. The average annual value of textiles imported into Egypt from 1885 to 1888 was about 2.7 million LE. This figure rose to 6.9 million LE from 1909 to 1912. Manchester cotton cloth alone made up around half of this category, putting cotton weavers under particular pressure.[34] In this context, employment in textiles diminished relative to employment in other sectors of artisanal activity. Whereas textiles employed 30 percent of Egypt's artisanal workforce in 1897 (engaging around 75,000 workers), by 1917 this proportion had apparently dropped to 15 percent (while numbers employed remained at around 75,000). The same pattern is apparent in the figures for Cairo, where although around 5,000 remained employed, their place as a proportion of all artisans slipped from around 15 percent to around 6 percent of the workforce. In Mansura, whereas about 40 percent of all manufacturers had worked in textiles (mostly silk weaving) in 1863, by 1917 this proportion had shrunk to 6.5 percent. Under such pressures, the battle for survival in textiles was quite possibly more acute than in any other sector of the craft economy.

But spinners, dyers, and silk, wool, flax, and even cotton weavers managed to adapt their products, force down production costs, self-exploit, and squeeze their labor in ways which permitted them to survive and even expand in some cases. Sidney Wells's survey of 1910 revealed the presence of thousands of looms up and down the country, from Mahallat al-Kubra in Gharbiyya to Akhmim (the 'Manchester of Egypt') and from Naqada in Qena province in Upper Egypt to Idku near Rosetta on the Mediterranean coast.[35] The value of local cotton-weaving production by itself had to amount to well over 300,000 LE per annum in 1913, in as much as cotton yarn imports alone (transformed by cotton weavers) were valued at this figure in that year. Up to one thousand were engaged in spinning and washing raw silk at Manzala alone in Lower Egypt. The censuses of 1907 and 1917 record more than 10,000 wool weavers up and down the country. Mat making was widespread, the production of *samar baladi* (a mat made of a particular kind of reed) in Zaqaziq alone being worth around 100,000 LE per annum.[36] As for dyeing, the Commission on Commerce and Industry noted that it "is one of the most important industries of Egypt and one of the most widespread."[37] According to the censuses of 1897 and 1907 dyeing employed around 18,000 persons in Egypt, making it one of the most numerous nonagricultural occupations in the country, and the largest employer in the textile trades.

Textiles masters and workers continued to find markets for old, adapted, and new products. Demand for *ghazli*, a common quality cotton weave used in making *jallabiya* remained widespread, especially in the countryside, and weavers also produced a slightly finer quality version of the same cloth known as *ghazli mazwi*. As the 1916 Commission remarked, "[I]f people turned away from making their clothes with the Egyptian fabric which is so common 'el-Ghozlia' [sic] the great part of the weaving industry would be paralysed."[38] Cotton weavers also produced *milaya* (a cotton wrap worn by women), *futa* (napkins, towels, handkerchiefs, and so on), and to a lesser extent *dammur* (a fairly coarse, white cotton shift).[39] Wells's team found a range of silk weaves in Damietta: expensive silk cloth at 40 piastres per meter was produced for men's clothing;[40] a relatively inferior silk for the black dresses of women at 20 piastres per meter; an even more inferior silk for the less fortunate classes sold in 23 meter pieces for 180 piastres, that is, 7.8 piastres per meter. Finally, there was a coarse white silk which was sold at 6 1/2 piastres per meter.[41] Wool weavers produced a number of cloaks, garments wraps, blankets, and drapes. The *bishta* was a fairly rudimentary, short woolen cloak worn by Egyptian agricultural workers. The *za'abut* referred to both a popular woolen fabric as well as a woolen garment. The *hiram* was a woolen blanket which was usually worn as a garment around head and body. The *firash* was a woolen blanket in use among the *fallahin*. Wool was sometimes used for *jallabiya* also, and indeed the 1910 survey praised it for its quality in this regard.[42] The *'aba'* was another kind of cloaklike woolen wrap, occasionally striped. Such products were long-lasting, strong, and warm. Beyond these cheap and functional items, a certain prestige could be conferred by the finer versions of Egypt's famous woolen cloak, the *diffiya*. Those in the villages with a certain wealth might aspire to the purchase and display of well-made black or brown *diffiya* (costing up to 300 piastres).[43] Cheaper *diffiya* (as little as 60 piastres) were also available for those with less means. Among tourists and certain sections of Egypt's upper classes, the *mashshaya* (a long, narrow carpet), and the *kilim* (a rug), were increasingly in demand.[44] Further, wool products were made to take advantage of new, more bourgeois furnishing tastes and forms of interior decoration: by the early 1900s, furniture coverings were sometimes made of wool, as were cushions, curtains, and drapes of various kinds.[45]

The search for cheaper production costs, and above all cheap labor, transformed the textile industry, in the space of several decades, from a largely urban to a predominantly rural trade. The ruralization of textiles, already visible in the 1860s and 1870s, now accelerated greatly. In the cities, according to the available figures, employment in textiles barely increased, and sometimes diminished between the 1860s and 1914. Whereas textile manufacturing had accounted for around a third of artisans in Cairo in the early 1800s, by 1907 it only employed around 7 percent of the industrial population. In Mansura, numbers engaged in textiles declined quite markedly even in absolute terms. Moreover, Egypt's new towns—Suez, Port Sa'id, Isma'iliya, and Zaqaziq, for example—did not become home to substantial textile manufacturing. The same could not be said, for instance, of garment or construction trades. Wells's industrial survey of 1910 makes clear that textiles had become a predominantly rural activity.[46] We hear, for example, that almost all of the 6,000 weavers in al-Mahallat al-Kubra— Egypt's principal textiles center—worked in their own homes "scattered all over the town and surrounding district."[47] The same was true of the numerous weavers of Qalyubiya, where there was "usually not more than one loom per house in a small and badly lit room."[48]

The organization of production varied from largely independent producers who obtained raw materials from nearby and manufactured for individual orders locally, to household workers who were more or less entirely subordinated within putting-out systems—involving raw materials, credit and markets—controlled by merchants from Cairo or other cities. As an example of the former, it was reported in 1910 that weaves from Asyut and other locations in Upper Egypt were mostly made on order by local clients and sold locally.[49] But at the other extreme, one of Wells's team noted that "big Cairo merchants" imported raw silk from Syria, cleaned and colored it by machines in special workshops and sent it ready to be woven to weavers in the provinces.[50] In such cases, putting-out systems linked rural manufacturers to the extensive markets of the cities.

In all cases, production was competitive because of the low costs obtainable in rural areas. Home working reduced overheads, because it meant that no commercial premises had to be maintained and no additional rent paid. In some cases, textile production avoided the need for built premises entirely, by using public space to manufacture goods. An example comes from an important center of wool production, Abu Qurqas, a relatively small town of only 7,000 inhabitants (in 1907) in al-Minya province in Upper Egypt. In 1910, there were reputedly 400 looms scattered in houses around the town and in the vicinity. In order to supply the demands of these weavers, 750 persons were at work continuously spinning wool thread for use in local weaving. In 1910 it was said that "one meets a large number of persons sitting along the length of the roadside spinning wool just shorn from sheep."[51]

Another factor, particularly important in the wool industry, was the availability and proximity of cheap, quality raw materials.[52] Wool weavers, who were concentrated in Upper Egypt, lived in proximity to the sheep, goats, and camels maintained by local pastoralists in the arid zones adjacent to the Nile. The 1925 survey suggested that the increase in sheep raising under Mehmet Ali and Isma'il had led to a great quantity of wool becoming available for needs of many wool workshops that were established in Egypt at that time.[53] Where inexpensive materials were unavailable locally, merchants provided rural producers with the cheap and standardized yarns of Manchester or Lyon. Yarn imports averaged almost 600,000 LE per annum from 1909 to 1913, a fivefold increase on the 1870s, most of this total being divided between cotton and silk threads. The dyers of Asyut also imported cotton yarn for dyeing from abroad via Alexandria.[54] Asyut weavers got their cotton thread spun and dyed partly by locals and partly by European factories.[55] In al-Mahallat al-Kubra most of the cotton threads came from Manchester.[56] Qalyubiya weavers used much American cotton, bought from dealers in Cairo. In Daqahliyya cotton threads were also bought from big city merchants who imported threads from India and England.[57] Mat makers used imported flax threads, and the industry suffered in 1914 and 1915 when the price of this material increased because of the war.[58] After 1901, dyers purchased imported German synthetic indigo, which was cheaper by a factor of three than natural indigo (grown on colonial plantations in India) as well as being more convenient to use.[59]

Most importantly, however, in the countryside labor was cheap, flexible, and abundant. Male wages in wool weaving, at 4–6 piastres per day, were quite close to the bottom of the barrel for any male wage anywhere in Egypt at that time.[60] Wells noted that flax weavers in Qalyubiya earned even less, at 3–4 piastres per day.[61] Moore Gordon recorded that silk and cotton weavers in Mahallat al-Kubra made 3–5 piastres per day.[62] Such rates may have been below subsistence levels, even in the countryside. A male adult earning 5 piastres per day and even working six days a week throughout the year would fall 440 piastres short of the 2,000 piastres per annum estimated by a commentator in *al-Muqtataf* to be enough to suffice a farmer and his wife and children for food and clothing. Furthermore, this same author estimated that with inflation and increases in the cost of living, such *fallahin* would soon require nearly 3,000 piastres for mere subsistence.[63] Such evidence suggests that not only were these weaving wages extremely low, but they may have been falling in real terms over time. These wages and returns were additionally in no way guaranteed, but dependent on orders, and thus intermittent and insecure. For instance, in Fudamin in Fayum province, as elsewhere, journeymen were paid by the piece, in this case earning 5 piastres for a piece five meters long and seventy centimeters wide.[64]

Moreover, hardship may have been exacerbated by rising expectations about consumption. As the writer mentioned above wrote in *al-Muqtataf*:

> Whoever casts a reflective view on the condition of the land of Egypt will be apprehensive of a calamity in the future condition of the population, for the expenses of the fellahin . . . increase year on year, and their incomes increase likewise. But, their income is restricted because it is tied to tilling the land. . . . [B]ut as for expenses, these are not restricted because they will increase with the increase in

population, the arrival of European commodities, and the return of people to luxury after the spread of learning and the ease of communications. In this way, the man who was living on his ezba . . . content with a woollen shirt—he and his wife and children—[content] with seed bread and barley and a little . . . whey, is not expected to be content with this after his children are educated and sit on one seat— they and the children of the *'umda* and the children of the *ma'mur al-markaz*—or after the railway has reached his town and he sees his peers wearing what he does not wear, and eating what he does not eat.[65]

Of course the author here is concerned about social instability, and the continued supply of cheap labor on which large estates rested. But, from a less elitist perspective, one can note the sense of economic exclusion that comparatively diminishing earnings must have fostered among nonagricultural specialists (as well as land-poor *fallahin*) in the countryside.

Adult male masters and journeymen were wealthy compared to the women, children, apprentices, and assistants who also worked in the textile industry in large numbers, who ranged from occasional assistants working in auxiliary roles without pay, to those engaged for long periods at particular tasks for tiny remuneration. In Fayyum province as many as 2,083 women were listed in the 1907 census as being employed in the textile trades, of a total of only 4,882 persons employed.[66] Cheap female labor was particularly in demand in the silk industry, where the preparation of the threads required so much more labor time than the same activities in wool, cotton, or flax production. Silk cocoons in Daqahliyya were washed by women, who were paid at a rate of 5 piastres per kilogram, or 1 piastre per day—three to eight times less than a male weaving wage. At Al-Manzala, a "great quantity of raw silk" was spun on local spindles and mostly sent on to Mahallat al-Kubra. Wells suggested that around a thousand persons were at work there, more than half (500–600) being women, the rest (400–500) being men and children. He estimated their production at 50,000 okes (sing. *uqqa*) per annum, that is, a substantial 62,400 kg.[67] Women were also involved in the production of wool. Wives and children raised sheep for the provision of cheap raw wool.[68] Yarn was spun cheaply by family members, women, children, and the old: of the town of Ashmum in Minufiyya the industrial survey stated that "many of its people work in spinning wool in their homes and in their spare time."[69] The numerous women who spun wool in Daqahliyya were apparently paid 1/2 piastre per *ratl*, which also meant they earned about 1 piastre a day. With labor as cheap as this, locally spun wool was significantly cheaper than imported thread: in 1910, for example, indigenous wool in wads was three to five times cheaper than imported, spun, and dyed thread.[70] The relatively small, but well-known and expanding carpet weaving industry in Beni Adi was unusual in that the weavers were women. Such women could weave a 1 1/2 by 1/2 meter carpet in ten hours (one day), which then sold at the quite high price of more than 2 LE. Such carpets were mostly made on order and were sent to Asyut, Beni Suef, Minya, and Jirja, but also as far afield as Lower Egypt.[71]

Children also worked for minimal pay in significant numbers in rural textiles. Among all kinds of weavers in Daqahliyya, Wilson noted that "one generally sees a large number of children amongst the weaving journeymen."[72] As noted above, children were present in large numbers assisting the silk spinners at al-Manzala. It was said that boys helped prepare the threads for wool weavers at Abu Qurqas in al-Minya, rolling the thread for the weft onto the bobbin. Up to 2 piastres a day could be earned for this work.[73] At Asyut, Shearer noted that for the first six years, child assistants in the weaving workshops earned nothing more than a nominal wage—up to 1 piastre per day—while they picked up the trade as best they could.[74] Boy assistants in silk and cotton weaving at Mahallat al-Kubra earned between 1 and 3 piastres per day for preparing the bobbins for the weft.[75]

In these circumstances, where labor reserves were vast and cheap and largely unprotected by guild or other forms of organization, labor-squeezing production strategies made as much if not more economic sense than productivity-raising mechanization, which would have required risky capital investment, expertise which was scarce, costly maintenance, and expensive fuel, or power sources which were not present. In one of the few cases where large-scale mechanization was attempted in the textile trades, the colonial state moved against it in order to prevent competition against European industry by the promulgation of a countervailing duty. Significantly, labor-intensive production was exempted from this tax: in article 4 of the decree one finds that "[a]ll small local workshops (al-ma'amil al-mahalliya al-saghira) using hand-powered looms only . . . are forgiven the duty fixed in Article 1."[76] Under these conditions, mechanization was limited. The looms in use in the weaving trades were mostly made locally and could be repaired locally and at a minimum of expense.[77] In the wool trades we hear that mostly handlooms and spindles were in operation.[78] It was said that most of the looms in al-Mahalla al-Kubra were very old and out of repair.[79] The cost of a loom was on the order of tens of piastres—little more than the price of a day's production.[80] Thus even as putting-out systems developed, and as wage labor became abundant, and as market relations thoroughly penetrated textiles, labor squeezing rather than mechanization prevailed.

Productive relations remained labor intensive even where certain entrepreneurs, seeking to rationalize and coordinate production, grouped numerous looms under one roof, or brought together in one location different stages of the productive process. An Egyptian government report of 1919 suggested that in all the major centers of textiles production—Mahallat al-Kubra in the Delta, Akhmim, Damietta, Qalyub, and Cairo—were "workshops containing as many as 100 looms" worked by hand and foot.[81] Martin described workshops for weavers, dyers, mat makers, and coppersmiths in Cairo where up to thirty workers worked under the orders of a few overseers. Some such establishments "cluster all the tasks necessary for the production of finished cloth ready for sale in one place." These tasks included spinning, dyeing, drying of the skeins, weaving, mangling the woven cloth, and then hammering the silk or wool cloth for lustre. As Martin wrote, "[T]his is Cairo's big industry."[82] In Damietta, the largest workshops belonged to 'Abd al-Fattah Bey al-Lozy who in 1910 owned thirty-seven looms (of the two hundred present in the town). Al-Lozy's looms produced about 170,000 meters of silk fabric per annum.[83] Such aggregations of handlooms did not attract colonial taxation.

Like their rural competitors, these largely urban enterprises bore the marks of the drive for cheap production. They were set up not where rents were high but, as Martin wrote, "in the quarters where most of the buildings are ramshackle, at the back of courtyards, in sheds deprived of their rooves" and in "long, narrow and badly lit spaces," in rooms which were "sombre and dark."[84] The Committee on Industry reported that larger weaving establishments were to be found in tumbledown quarters occupying "shanties" half in ruins, open to the winds, with dirty walls and dusty floors. As the commission noted, the "preoccupation of locals with very great economy displaces all other considerations."[85] Other premises were cramped and had no ventilation, endangering the health of the workers "who pass there the biggest part of their existence." The commission went on: "[I]n another more prosperous workshop for the production of braiding and trimmings, a manufactury in which the mechanism is moved by cattle, the locals are so pressed that men and beasts work in some way, side by side, and in the very worst conditions of hygiene and lack of space."[86] Underlining the tough conditions of these larger workshops, Clerget noted that an official enquiry before the war in Kirdasa (a suburb of Cairo in Imbaba, Giza Governorate, on the west bank of the Nile) revealed that nearly all the weavers had eye diseases because the workshops were so unhealthy.[87]

The search for lower production costs created not only abusive conditions for workers, but longer hours, monotonous work, and low wages. In such workshops, hours were long and work was said (by Martin) to be more "regular" than in the smaller workshops. Martin mentioned that weavers and spinners in Cairo were among those who took night work during one third of the year, which lasted until midnight or one o'clock in the morning.[88] Indeed, Martin reported that the adults and numerous children working in Cairo's larger workshops were "tireless." He spoke of the "major resistance on the part of the workers" which was necessitated by the "deplorable hygienic conditions" and the "very long time it takes to accomplish a task." Their activities, he reported, were kept up sometimes by a rhythmic chant, and sometimes by the extremely regular cadence of the wood mallets which lustred cloth.[89] Workers learned to produce quality work without the benefit of expensive equipment. As Martin continued, "To understand how good delicate work can come from defective tools, one must know the essential qualities that the . . . worker proves himself to have. These correspond to an ability of sense, eye, hands, and feet which are infinitely more developed amongst them than amongst European workers."[90] Such skills and physical contortions were available at cheap prices. Wages for male journeymen, although slightly higher than in the countryside, where life was cheaper, cannot be said to have risen above subsistence levels. Wells noted that silk weavers in Damietta earned from 6 to 10 piastres per diem.[91]

Owing to the cheapness, stamina and efforts of labor, technical and mechanical innovations only occurred where there was some profit in substituting machines for bodies. There were mechanical workshops for silk weaving in Abu Tig by the end of the First World War. The weavers there apparently constructed "wooden machines . . . on the lines of the ones imported from Manchester."[92] This development was probably related to the Industrial School which had been established on private initiative in Abu Tig in 1903. It is noteworthy that the weavers avoided the cost of importing and running a foreign loom by imitating and manufacturing one themselves. The weaving looms of Cairo, Beni-Suef, Akhmim, Qalyub, and Mahallat al-Kubra, where trade was more vigorous and markets larger, were more developed in different ways than most of the looms in operation in the rest of the country. For example, in some cases the shuttle was moved by the loom itself.[93] In Fayum in 1911, we hear that weavers used "more complicated" looms, which were brought from Cairo.[94] In sum, as one author put it, "for the most part the looms are of crude construction, but here and there machines of European origin have been introduced."[95] Where there was some profit to be made through mechanization, then such innovations were made, provided a surplus was available. In the main, however, the exploitation of cheap and abundant hands and bodies was a less risky route to cheaper production costs and competitive goods, and labor-intensive production prevailed.

Construction

During the 1890s and early 1900s, Egypt witnessed an overall expansion in construction the like of which had not been seen there for centuries. Investment in land and real estate companies soared as confidence increased following the success of Egypt's cotton economy and the Anglo-French agreement of 1904, fuelling a speculative boom that was only to collapse in the summer of 1907.[96] The constructed area of Cairo and Alexandria increased by a factor of between 1.5 and 2,[97] and urbanization of a significant order got underway in Egypt's twenty-three largest towns.[98] The central districts of provincial towns such as Zaqaziq or Mansura were built up.[99] Tens of thousands of buildings of all kinds—warehouses, train stations, business premises, hotels, consulates, and private homes among others—were erected in the principal towns. Public gardens and imposing squares were laid out in Cairo and Alexandria, canals were dredged or filled in, roads were paved, and dams and bridges were built.[100] In Cairo, "the speed of building, their dimensions, the multiplication of building sites astonished the Europeans themselves," who "watched the last [market] gardens devastated."[101] In the "European town"—Ezbekiya, 'Abdin, and areas bordering the Nile—"all non-constructed earth" was the object of intense battles between speculators and real estate companies.[102] In the years leading up to 1907, land values spiralled upwards: ten times, forty times, and even more in some areas. The value of imported building materials multiplied almost twenty times between the mid-1870s and 1914, coming to be worth around 2 million LE, almost 10 percent of all imports in 1913.[103] In 1900, construction materials vied with cotton as the most important commodity traded through railway and boat-landing stations in the provinces.[104]

The census data regarding numbers of crafts workers engaged in Cairo in the trades relating to construction—brick makers, lime and plaster kiln workers, masons, roofers, tilers, carpenters, zinc workers, bricklayers, glaziers, electricians, painters, plumbers, furniture makers, upholsterers, manual laborers, and so on—are difficult to use. Categories are vague and change from one census to the next; women and children are often excluded. Numbers of laborers recorded fluctuate disconcertingly. But adding together all trades related to construction and fitting in an inclusive way (while excluding the wildly fluctuating category of laborers), the censuses indicate that around 82,000 were employed in Egypt in 1897, approximately 112,000 in 1907, and roughly 100,000 in 1917. As for Cairo, approximately 8,500 were employed in 1868, roughly 16,500 in 1897, around 24,000 in 1907, and about 18,500 in 1917.[105] Such numbers certainly trace the impact of the boom of 1907 and the slump which followed. And although these figures include a small proportion of European subjects on the one hand, and of those working in more capital-intensive industry (such as Sornaga's brick works) on the other, the majority of such persons were local subjects working in hand-powered and labor-intensive production.

The fact that construction materials, fittings, and furnishings were often bulky, heavy, and expensive to transport gave those producing bricks, tiles, cement, fittings, and furnishings, some shelter from imports. A successful cement factory making high quality Portland cement was established at al-Ma'sara in 1900. Operations also benefited from the proximity of the raw material and an abundant labor supply. Several hundred workers were employed. Their produce was used in bridges over the Nile at Cairo.[106] A brick factory was established in 'Abbasiya in 1910, powered by two steam engines, employing three or four hundred workers, and turning out one hundred thousand bricks per day.[107] Clerget spoke of the slow, painful and "friendless" evolution of Sornaga's factory for making household pottery, construction materials, fireproof material, sanitation installations, pipes, and even artistic potteries. Sornaga's works was originally founded in Tura (south of Cairo) in 1884, but finally became successful after a move to Rod al-Farag in 1902.[108]

Small, low-capital, and locally run workshops also manufactured and supplied construction materials and fittings, found their own markets, and restructured in order to compete. Clerget mentioned "native ovens" making bricks in both Old Cairo and just north of the Citadel. These bricks (sing. *tub*) were made of Nile clay which was mixed with straw or reed (also found locally) and then baked for twenty-four hours in ovens at a rate of four to five thousand bricks a time. Brick making located in Old Cairo was mentioned by Raymond, but the brick works north of the citadel appears to have been newly established: one can suggest that as Cairo expanded towards the Nile, brick-making ovens, which in the eighteenth century were situated between Cairo and the Nile in order to be close to raw materials, were then relocated north of the citadel.[109] Bricks made from Nile clay were often thought unsuitable and insufficiently solid for pricier constructions, but there is little doubt that these bricks continued to be in demand where purchasers could not afford factory-produced or imported products. The compendium of industry in Lower Egypt, for example, of 1899, mentions brick making as a common industry of the provinces in Egypt at the turn of the century. Beyond this, Chenouda reported tile makers in Asyut, for example, who kept down production costs by importing cement and colors from France.[110] Limekilns had produced lime (*jir*) at Bab al-Nasr and Bab al-Sha'riya in the eighteenth century,[111] and were still to be found there in the years before the First World War. The ovens were built in brick and used stone and sand particles from stone quarries south of the citadel, a firing of two days and one night producing 150 qantars of lime per oven.[112]

Furniture making—often low capital, small scale, and labor intensive—started to employ more after the turn of the century, when its products began to compete seriously with European imports, which were expensive to transport and more expensive to manufacture. During the nineteenth century, consumption tastes had been completely transformed. By the early 1900s, it was said that the only buyers of traditional Arab furniture were local eccentrics, foreign collectors, and tourists. In this context, local makers adapted their products and started to reproduce the Louis XV chairs and divans so much in demand among the wealthy. On this new basis, employment in Egypt in upholstery rose from 3,000 in 1897, to 4,000 in 1907, to 5,000 in 1917.[113] During the first decade of the twentieth century, the value of furniture imports started to diminish significantly for the first time, while the value of wood imports for cabinetmakers increased rapidly.[114] As Marshall, a British resident and judge, wrote, implicitly contrasting the 1890s with the 1920s, "[I]n the autumn of 1891 . . . [f]urnishing was very difficult. There were very few if any sales of furniture at that time. . . . Indeed there was no good furniture then in the country. If people wanted good furniture they had to bring it from Europe."[115] This situation began to change during the early 1900s. Clerget noted that local makers during the first decades of the twentieth century were able to make use of better-seasoned wood as well as plentiful and inexpensive labor, which made their products considerably cheaper than those made in Europe.[116] Certain furniture makers were able to publicize their wares through industrial exhibitions which were organized by nationalists for the first time in 1907 and after.[117] Others touted their goods by lugging them through crowded public squares, such as 'Ataba al-Khadra in Cairo.[118]

Furniture makers were not always in direct competition with European goods, which were far too expensive for the great majority of the population. For most, "real" Louis XV was also not an option, and for such consumers furniture makers turned out cheaper and more rudimentary work, and lowered production costs greatly in order to do so. Hence, workmanship in Asyut was said to be "very rough." The undersides of tables and divans were not planed. All joints were nailed—there was little or no dovetailing. The use of unseasoned wood meant that it soon split: "[C]heapness and not quality dominates."[119] Such furniture seems to have found its way up and down the country and even into the houses of the rich, who appear to have been all too familiar with such work, and complained loudly. The following anecdote appeared in al-Muqtataf in 1911:

[B]uy a wardrobe from a European carpenter or import it from Europe and you will pass years [with it] in [unchanged] condition. Buy it from a local carpenter and the wood will warp and its paint will peel off and its drawers will stick. Get a chair upholstered by a European upholsterer and it will last years in [good] condition, but [buy it] locally and you will see it very soon become rigid as wood and after a while the threads will escape from their settings and be ruined.[120]

This kind of anecdote indicated that these kinds of lower-value furnishings, however notorious, had a certain ubiquity and were in demand, not only among poorer classes.[121]

Although transport costs gave many producers some shelter from imports, neither furniture makers nor others in crafts related to construction and fitting were sheltered from the competition of migrant labor from southern Europe, especially Italy. Quite the contrary: under the Capitulations, European subjects were still privileged to escape local laws and taxes, which gave them a systematic advantage over their local subject counterparts. This brought local crafts workers under great pressure. Competition was intense, and pitted those who already, by and large, possessed the skills so much in demand, and who benefited from an asymmetrical legal system and a colonial perception of their superiority, against those who did much to pick up those skills, but who above all had little choice but to compete by cheapening the price of their hands and bodies.

In this context, European subjects continued to hold in general the better paid and more highly skilled positions. In certain areas, foreign artisans were still imported en masse for major contracts. In Aswan, for example, during the building of the dam in the early 1900s, most masons were imported from Italy. Again, for the construction of the barrage at Esna between 1907 and 1908, the principal contractor was an English company, Aird and Co., which supplied the engineers, the plans, and the overall direction. The bulk of the skilled labor was provided by Italians, housed close to the site in bungalows, and the unskilled labor was provided by local workmen and laborers.[122] In the cities, these hierarchies were still present, although less marked. According to Vallet, a French resident who wrote his doctoral thesis on workers in Cairo, one found about four Europeans for every one indigenous worker among skilled mechanics and electricians. Among zinc workers and plumbers, numbers of Europeans and indigenous workers were about equal, but in Cairo construction overall, according to Vallet, local subjects tended to outnumber Europeans by about four to one.[123]

However, tax reductions on local subjects in the 1880s and 1890s, resulting from the dismantling of Ismail's self-strengthening, reduced the salience of the tax-free status of European workers. And local subjects did manage to adapt and pick up new skills over time: local subject presence of any kind, as exemplified in Vallet's proportions given above, in trades which in many cases were entirely new in Egypt gives an indication of this. Glaziers, electricians, painters, plumbers, and workers with steel and iron building material, for instance, emerged from practically nowhere in the 1860s to occupy about 11,000 jobs—around 10 percent of all those involved in construction—by 1907 in Egypt.[124] Even if Europeans dominated these trades at the outset, local subjects started to acquire the necessary skills, often while working in teams of contracted labor on site.[125] After the turn of the century, nationalist and state-sponsored industrial education was also starting to have an impact on some. Painting and decorating, for example, was taught in the newly established model workshop in Cairo in the early 1900s.[126] While Cromer's reports give the impression that all such new trades were entirely dominated by Europeans, more detailed studies, such as that of Clerget, suggested that after about 1900, the leading specialities in Egypt's building trades generally witnessed steady indigenization.[127] Vallet argued the same, noting in 1911 that whereas European subject labor had been very much in demand "five or six years ago," times were changing.[128] Vallet's figures suggest that such trades offered comparatively high wages. Electricians, mechanics, ironsmiths, zinc workers, tilers, masons, and plumbers made from 20 to 40 piastres per day. Other skilled trades, such as glaziers, brick and plaster workers, carpenters, and joiners also earned more than other craftsworkers, taking home between 15 and 30 piastres per day.[129]

In all trades, and more especially where less skilled work in carpentry, masonry, and earthworks was in demand, local subjects' principal weapon in competition with more skilled and privileged European subjects was self-exploitation. They had little choice but to offer themselves to contractors and subcontractors cheaply in order to survive. As Martin wrote, "[M]ost salaries are slender compared to European workers."[130] Martin's wage figures regarding the construction trades, possibly simply because of local variation, are lower than Vallet's in any case. He suggested that an excellent turner could earn 15 piastres per day, whereas carpenters and masons earned from 8 to 10 piastres per day.[131] Vallet's work on family budgets in Cairo in the early 1900s indicates that for a breadwinner, wages of 14 piastres a day were at the "minimum necessary for existence."[132] Especially because of periodic unemployment (particularly after the slump of 1907), and usurious money lending practices in the towns, poverty was the norm, and families were regularly trapped in debt. Vallet details the family budget of a carpenter with a wife and four children who was earning 14 piastres a day. The family could afford two rooms and some oil for lighting. They had one or two pieces of furniture, and a few pots and pans. They took a change of clothes every few years, and had one spare set of clothes, kept carefully in a box, for celebrations. They ate bread and vegetables, but almost never meat. Major luxuries in this context were tobacco and coffee, which were mostly the preserve of the male breadwinner. Vallet's carpenter's wife underpinned the family economy through child rearing and food and clothes production. But even thrift, sobriety, and careful organization could not save the family described by Vallet from chronic insecurity and debt. Unemployment after 1907 (and sometimes before it), and the high interest rates of the local Greek pawnbroker trapped them into a debt which was extremely difficult to shake.

There were many who earned less than even this subsistence minimum. Local construction workers competed with European subjects and continued to produce cheaply through female, child, and cheap unskilled labor. Women and children were a cheap recourse for either contractors or subcontractors who had to shift considerable amounts of earth or materials. The census is a poor document of their participation: that of 1907 only recorded three women in the building trades. Further, the contractors interviewed by Vallet claimed not to have employed women on their sites. Nonetheless, Vallet's evidence especially, but other indications too suggest the quite widespread use of women on building sites. As Vallet wrote, in spite of what census and employers said, "a large number of women are used as laborers on building sites." He noted that their main function was to transport material such as bricks, lime, and sand from ground to upper floors of a building under construction. They climb the scaffolding, he wrote, in long lines carrying loads in round panniers. Vallet suggested that he found 27 women for every 150 carpenters and masons.[133] In other words, women were the heavy lifters of Egypt's construction boom. It appears to have been cheaper and more convenient to recruit women for heaving earth upwards than it was to install mechanical hoists, or sometimes even to put up more rudimentary block and tackle type equipment to raise the materials. Martin suggests that these women were desirable labor on the one hand, and suited to the task on the other, in as much as they were used to carrying great weights on their heads, such as pots of water, and thus they were employed in construction carrying earth in baskets.[134] They were also cheaper to employ: whereas male laborers could earn 6 piastres per day, females earned just 4 piastres per diem.[135] Cheaper still were the relatively small numbers of boys and girls that Vallet witnessed working as laborers.[136] On some such sites it seems that adults did the heavy digging, and boys and girls carried the earth away in baskets. According to Vallet, boys were also used as laborers and assistants to mechanics and electricians.[137]

Local subjects not only competed with European subjects in point of price, but also by forgoing forms of protection, which were in any case difficult to assert where cheap and abundant labor urgently sought subsistence and even below-subsistence wages. As Clerget noted, by the 1900s, contractors were more and more heard to complain that European subject workers could be difficult to employ. Such workers had certain forms of relative legal immunity under the Capitulations, and were thought to be more demanding over contracts and more recalcitrant on labor issues. Vallet mentions that employers had to insure European subject workers against accidents, and indemnities had to be paid if the master was found to be at fault. No such provisions protected local labor. European subjects required a written contract specifying the duration of employment; local subjects did not.[138] Labor legislation did not exist for local subjects in Egypt in any sense prior to 1909, when a law was passed prohibiting the labor of minors in cotton gins and various other factories. Practically no government regulations existed to regulate hiring and firing, pay, hours, conditions, female labor, child labor, holidays, and so on, let alone benefits or insurances.[139] As a reform-minded lawyer put it in 1910, "There is no social or worker's legislation in Egypt, and, except for a law on the work of minors in factories, nothing has been done till today to protect workers against accidents at work."[140] Guild protections had largely disappeared, and as we shall see in detail in the following chapter, crafts workers could not, in spite of their best efforts, significantly change the terms of restructuring through collective action.

In this context, workers had little choice but to insert themselves into exploitative contracting networks. According to Vallet, the "numerous abuses" of construction subcontracting were so thoroughgoing that the only solution was outright suppression of the institution. He argued that workers were at the mercy of these "entrepreneurs of work." The proprietors (those who originally ordered the work) had hardly any contact with their workforce and did not even know their salaries. Worse, there was never a written contract between workers and the subcontractor.[141] Clerget noted that the "moazen" (*mu'adhdhin*, labor contractor) "abuses his powers."[142] For those living on wages that kept them close to the minimum necessary for existence, abuses in contracting must have been particularly hard to bear. One summarized petition sent to the Khedivial Diwan in June 1907 affords us the briefest of glimpses of this. A certain Marzuq Ibrahim and a group of fellow construction workers stated that they were poor and had been working on earth works under Ahmad Mahmud, a contractor. They claimed that they had worked for 2,083 piastres, according to a receipt which was in their possession. The contractor, however, sold the work to another, making a small profit, and then fired the workers, promising to pay up on the following day. At the time of writing, the workers had gone twelve days without payment, and were, they claimed, along with their families "in the most intense need."[143]

In this context, labor squeezing—involving long hours, short and uncertain breaks, night work, and dangerous conditions—was common. Twelve hour days were said to be the norm. When deadlines approached, women (as well as children) were also used in night work, which stretched up to eight hours a night.[144] In winter, a morning break of a quarter of an hour and a one-hour lunch break was taken, whereas in summer the lunch break was extended to two hours on account of the extreme heat of the early afternoon, particularly for those engaged in manual labor. Workers were apparently not allowed to go far from the site during breaks. For lunch they ate bread, cheese, and olives purchased from nearby sellers. Fridays were usually free although there was no legislation on this point, and when deadlines approached, work could continue for four or five weeks uninterrupted for no extra compensation and without any kind of holiday. Some remissions existed: Vallet wrote that "in the small enterprises directed by a Muslim businessman and where only Muslim workers are employed, there is, however, [always] a holiday on Friday." Hours were reduced during the religious festivals also: during Ramadan, afternoons were cut short by a half. Apparently, 50 percent extra was paid out for night work, although again no legislation existed in this regard: it was decidedly difficult for

workers to hold their employers to account on this point. Work on building sites was also physically dangerous. A familiar short item in the Egyptian Gazette ran as follows: "On Monday morning a workman fell from the
scaffolding of a building in construction near the Théâtre des Nouveautés,
Cairo. He fell from a height of 14 metres and broke his leg. The victim was
conveyed to hospital in a dangerous state."[145] It was above all through offering themselves as cheap and unprotected labor that local subjects could
compete with European subjects and imports, and thereby obtain the overwhelming majority—according to the censuses around 97 percent—of the
jobs available in construction.[146] Under such conditions, songs such as the
following offer a glimpse of how workers resisted:

> God is with us! God is God!
> They say that I am ill/ But no, but no. God is God!
> We have not got a conveyor belt/ Instead we must walk,
> Keep apart your sick camel/ Because it will contaminate its neighbour.
> I swear by my right hand that my camel and I/ Are the bravest of the
>   band.
> God is with us. God is God![147]

Urban Transport

Patterns of restructuring were by no means restricted to manufacturing,
but, especially by the 1900s, were to be found among small-scale service industries of all kinds. Trades engaged in urban transport came to employ
many thousands in Egypt's cities, even as large-scale transport infrastructure, such as the tram, appeared and increased levels of competition.

Public cabs had started to outnumber private carriages in Cairo by the
1880s, and for at least twenty-five years thereafter, cab driving underwent
rapid expansion, leaving private carriages in the shade. No less than 6,156
Cairean cab drivers are listed in the census of 1917, which meant that cab
driving had become the single commonest occupation in the capital. From
their original concentration among the newly constructed streets between
the Ottoman city and the Nile to the West (the Isma'iliya Quarter), cabs
spread in all directions: westwards to Bulaq, making an important stop at
the Gare Centrale,[148] southwest over the Qasr al-Nil bridge towards Giza,[149]
and south to Old Cairo.[150] From their center of gravity, which became above
all 'Ataba al-Khadra Square, they also moved south towards 'Abdin on 'Abd
al-Aziz Street, southeast towards the citadel on the newly cut Muhammad
Ali Street, east on *al-Sikka al-Jadida*, and in the early 1900s, appeared on

routes headed north towards Wayly, Shubra, 'Abbasiya and Heliopolis.[151] Coachmen became even more numerous than Cairo's ubiquitous tailors (5,880 strong), shoemakers (5,682 persons), carters of goods (5,195 persons), and bakers (4,449 persons). According to the 1917 census, they were only outnumbered by such inclusive categories as public administration (9,451 persons) and trades in alimentary products (17,598 persons), for example.[152] Thus during twenty-five years or so, public coachmen emerged from relative obscurity to become one of Cairo's commonest and most visible urban occupations.[153] A broadly similar development took place in Alexandria. Whereas Ali Mubarak listed 409 passenger cab drivers (*'arbajiya rukub*) there in 1877,[154] the census of 1917 recorded 5,179 cab drivers, an increase of more than ten times.[155] Ilbert published a postcard showing a view of Alexandria's Gare du Caire in the 1930s, and apart from the station building itself, the most striking thing about the picture are the extensive ranks of carriages awaiting fares.[156] In 1908, Lamplough's guidebook noted that arriving on the quay in Alexandria, "there are always plenty of cabs."[157]

Outside of Cairo and Alexandria, cabs appeared in smaller numbers in the major and not so major towns, their passage facilitated by the laying of paved streets and wider roads. Almost 16,000 cabbies are recorded as working in Egypt as a whole in 1917.[158] In the 1900s, cabs were noted in Port Sa'id,[159] al-Fayum,[160] and Luxor.[161] By 1917, 238 coachmen were recorded in Mansura.[162]

Coachmen were in demand among Cairo's new wealthy classes, the beneficiaries of Egypt's 'El Dorado.' Colonial officials, civil servants, bankers, merchants, landowners who did not own private carriages, and the *afandiya* made up the bulk of Egypt's new carriage passengers, often preferring cabs to omnibuses, donkey drivers, and the tram. For example, the route to Lord Cromer's residence was so familiar to cabbies that even years after his departure, it remained engrained in their minds. A foreign resident judge wrote, "I found that even eighteen years after Lord Cromer had left Egypt to tell a cabman to go to the Dar al-Himaiya or the Wokala-al-Britannia was quite hopeless. He simply stared in blank ignorance. One had to say: 'Go to Lord Cromer's!' Then he knew at once."[163] Tourists were also an important market. As Baedeker's guide made clear, carriages and donkeys were a staple of the traveller's day, and apparently added about 20 percent to tourists' travelling costs.[164] Cabs were also to be recommended: "[I]n the large towns [cabs] are generally very good. . . . The cabs usually drive rapidly so that their use saves time and strength."[165] Another guide suggested that in Egypt "visitors can, if they wish, hire very good private carriages for the whole or part of their stay."[166]

Carting was another labor-intensive trade which rapidly employed more during these decades.[167] By the late 1870s, carts bearing stone, earth, bricks, and sand for construction and other materials were increasingly common, but over the next three decades, carters multiplied their numbers almost as dramatically as the cab drivers had done. In Egypt as a whole, the 1917 census recorded almost 12,000 carters. In Alexandria there were about 1,700 and in Cairo just over 5,000, especially plying routes west to Bulaq port and south and east to al-Khalifa and Old Cairo, transporting to the lime and brick kilns there, and the quarries south of the citadel.[168] By 1917, about 135 carters worked in Mansura. Wherever paved roads spread, carts followed.[169] Carters above all transported the construction materials so much in demand during the construction boom. Demand for rubbish disposal also increased with urbanization. Further, the forced requisition of carts and livestock ceased with the abolition of forced labor (*sukhra*) everywhere in 1892, and Cairo carters benefitted beyond this to the tune of about 5,000 LE per annum from the abolition of the Cairo carts and livestock tax in 1899.

A trade which had been very numerous in the 1860s started to employ fewer in the 1890s and 1900s. For all Baedeker's keenness on Egypt's donkey drivers, and despite the increasing numbers of tourists, donkey driving in Cairo absorbed fewer workers over time, apparently losing out wherever paved streets came to dominate, for when this was the case, legs could not compete with wheels. Thus, although almost 5,500 were employed in the country at large in 1917, Alexandria had only a very few donkey drivers by 1917 (at 49 persons), and in Cairo numbers fell many times over to 417 in 1917. An additional factor was that riding mules, now considered unhygienic and relatively uncomfortable, was becoming less a sign of status, and more a mark of low class, and even social backwardness. Even Baedeker had to admit in 1908 that "[a]s at Alexandria, donkeys are becoming less and less fashionable in Cairo."[170] Finally, in the larger cities, especially after the 1890s, trams and horse-drawn omnibuses offered alternatives, probably especially for lower middle classes, who could not afford a cab. Martin, for example, mentioned that petty traders and artisans in Cairo started to use buses and trams to get to work rather than mules in the early 1900s.[171]

Cab drivers and donkey drivers had to compete not only with each other to find livelihoods, but also with trams after the 1890s, and motor cars shortly after the turn of the century.[172] The first tramline appeared in Cairo in 1896, and by 1914, electric trams carried quite large numbers of passengers in Cairo, Alexandria, and Port Sa'id.[173] In Cairo, at least five lines,

owned by Belgian interests, converged on 'Ataba al-Khadra: they led from
Bulaq via the Gare Centrale, from the Citadel, from Isma'iliya Square via
Bab al-Luq, from the mouth of the Khalij, and from Heliopolis via 'Abbasiya. To add insult to injury, in order to permit the speedy running of the
tram, a government order was issued in 1901 banning cabbies and others
from the filled-in canal bed of the old Khalij, the site of a major tramline
since 1898.[174] In a single decree, the government both favored a foreign-
owned competitor and closed off a major thoroughfare—one of the few
which cut directly through the older neighborhoods—to local transporters.

Local transporters adapted and forced down costs in order to compete. They turned tram, rail, and shipping termini to their advantage by
appearing in large numbers at points of embarkation and exit where mass
flows of passengers were guaranteed.[175] They drove on routes where trams
were yet to be found,[176] and as the following incident related by Marshall
shows, cabbies worked at night: "My daughter was born at the end of July
[in Ramleh in the 1890s], and I well remember having to go for Dr. Mor-
rison at Alexandria about one o'clock in the morning on a donkey. The last
train had gone, and we had no telephone, and I do not know whether Mor-
rison had one either. I roused him, and we came back in a street carriage,
which I found prowling about."[177]

Others did their best to acquire useful language skills: as one guide
wrote, visitors "can almost always find a coachman who knows some English."[178] They improved their cabs, as we hear from one Abd Allah Faqr, who
improved the condition of his vehicle until it became "the best of cabs."[179]
Cabbies obtained cheap credit from family sources. Abd Allah Faqr purchased his cab with the help of his niece. Cab drivers obtained their cabs
from local workshops, and cheap whips, in one example, from whipmakers
and sellers who plaited and hung their wares on the railings and newly
planted trees which surrounded Ezbekiyya gardens.[180] Fodder for horses
was supplied by a stream of cameliers and donkey drivers, whose presence
was especially noted on the new Qasr al-Nile bridge.[181] Horses, which were
squeezed in terms of health, nutrition, and workload, as we shall see, were
probably both owned and rented from dealers,[182] shod by local blacksmiths,
and housed in stables (probably rented)[183] and in the open air around the
city. The cabbies themselves ate from pavement restaurants and bread sellers, or slaked their thirst from zirs (earthenware jugs which cooled water)
set up on public thoroughfares.

Cab drivers ranged from owner-operators to wageworkers.[184] Abd
Allah Faqr was an example of the former: he wrote in a petition that both
he and his niece "profited" from his cab.[185] But at a time when the carriages

themselves were quite expensive (relative to the fixed capitals owned by, say, a tailor or a weaver), plenty of cabbies did not own their carriages, but drove for wages; these were always low, and sometimes extremely low. Some of the better paid worked for the government. For example, a coachman working for a government hospital was paid 10–13 piastres per day for his services in 1919.[186] Other wage-earning cabbies probably included those working for the big hotels, some of which controlled carriages for patrons.[187] But wages could go far lower than this. A certain Ali Zayyid, for example, declared himself to be a coachman "at the Hackney stand by the side of the Ezbekiyya Gardens opposite the New Hotel." He said that "the carriage is not my property," "my wages are PT [Piastres Tariff] 5 per diem," and "I do not pocket any portion of the hire [fare] paid me [by passengers] for my master."[188] Once again, in competition with new and capital-intensive business, local workers in small operations had to sell their hands and bodies at subsistence or below-subsistence rates in order to compete.

Figure 4.1. Cabdrivers lunching in 'Ataba al-Khadra Square, at the convergence of Cairo's trams

Figure 4.2. Donkey boys waiting for customers outside Cairo Railway Station

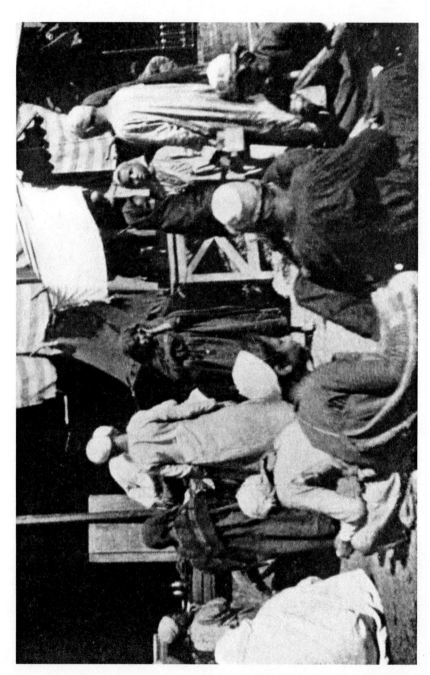

Figure 4.3. A food stall for donkey boys just south of 'Ataba al-Khadra Square, Cairo

Figure 4.4. Transporting bread and fodder for livestock in the Suq al-Nahhasin in Cairo

Figure 4.5. An omnibus in 'Ataba al-Khadra Square, Cairo

Figure 4.6. Three modes of transport: steamships, cabs, and women

Figure 4.7. An itinerant draper and shoeblacks at the top of Musky Street, Cairo

Figure 4.8. Vendors at a market in Giza

Conclusion

This chapter has attempted to trace the more far-reaching processes of restructuring among crafts and service workers that accompanied colonial rule after 1882 and the investment boom of 1897 to 1907. Growing imports and investment, changing consumption tastes, deepening market relations, and the final attrition of the guilds intensified competition, both among crafts and service workers on the one hand, and between them and their large-scale competitors on the other. In the search for livelihoods, new products were brought in, older products were adapted, and new markets were tapped. Crafts and service workers engaged in a drive for cheap production involving new kinds of productive organization, new raw materials, and piecemeal mechanization. Most importantly, labor costs were reduced by self-exploitation, whereby masters sold their work so cheaply that they were only able to reproduce their existing capital, on the one hand, and labor squeezing, whereby masters increased their absolute surplus value at the expense of labor, on the other. As we shall see in the following chapter, neither masters nor journeymen were able to substantially change the terms of this restructuring through collective action. Their route to modernity was above all labor intensive.

On these bases, numerous crafts and service workers continued to make up a very substantial proportion of Egypt's rapidly expanding urban population. They were never destroyed as an older conventional narrative suggested, but because of their efforts, continued to supply an array of cheap goods and services to all social strata. Indeed, during the First World War, the Commission on Commerce and Industry spoke of an "infinity of small workshops" in Egypt.[189] Particularly where trades were sheltered from imports, or where demand was not constant, strong, and standardized, such as in cab driving, crafts and service trades multiplied their numbers rapidly and dominated particular sectors.

Crafts and service workers were unable to escape the chronic vulnerability that resulted from labor-intensive production and lack of factor accumulation. Masters had little surplus to reinvest in productivity-raising mechanization because of self-exploitation. Moreover, where hands and bodies of journeymen and laborers were so cheap and unprotected, labor-squeezing strategies were chosen in preference to the risks and expenses of mechanization. Whatever its costs, this was a rational, and not a "backward", response to conditions stemming from colonial rule and unequal world economic integration. As Patrick Heller has argued regarding the "informal sector" in Kerala, India, in the later twentieth century, "[T]he predominance of labor-squeezing has less to do with the forms of direct coercion that characterize precapitalist economies than with the social vulnerability of labour [under new conditions]."[190] As Martin wrote regarding the lack of mechanization in Egypt, "[T]hese procedures are only comprehensible in our age in a country where labour is cheap in a way which has no analogue in Europe."[191] Such labor-intensive production was not undergoing transition to some form of more full-blown capitalism, but, being thoroughly the product of market relations, the spread of wage labor, and the larger conditions of empire, represented another form of work within the capitalist world system.

5

Strikes and Protests under Colonial Rule

Eh! Eh! Eh! Quick, quick, quick!/ O my eyes, why do you cry?
Eh! Eh! Eh! Quick!/ To find money!
O my eyes, it's useless/ No son, no money.
Eh! Eh! Eh! Quick, quick, quick!/ It is in my eyes
That we will see a king one day.
Eh! Eh! Eh! Quick, quick, quick!/ At the gate of Paradise
Is found one who pardons faults./ At the gate of Hell
There is money.
    —Construction workers' song, Upper Egypt, 1900s

*C*rafts and service workers did not engage in the economic processes of restructuring without entering into, affecting, and being impacted by social and political relations. In particular, after 1882, just as during the 1860s and 1870s, they attempted to associate, organize, and act collectively in order to change the terms of restructuring in ways which conformed to their perceived interests. They tried to cooperate with one another and to some degree with outsiders in order to protect themselves against unwanted state intervention, competition, self-exploitation, and labor squeezing. This chapter examines first a period of demobilization during the 1880s and 1890s which accompanied the dismantling of Ismail's self-strengthening, tax remissions, the abandoning of the guilds, and the construction of the colonial state. It then goes on to discuss how crafts and service workers, faced with heavy-handed colonial intervention and intensified restructuring during the boom of 1897 to 1907, and inspired by the political opportunities presented by middle-class nationalism, found new ways to organize and protest. In one of the most widespread cycles of collective action prior to the 1919 rebellion, and in the wake of a mass strike by Cairo's cab drivers, crafts and service workers came out onto the streets in their thousands during the spring of 1907. These protests were linked to the subsequent formation of new kinds of organization, syndicates and unions, which began to replace the long co-opted and now largely disaggregated guilds. Protests joined by crafts and service workers also had an important impact on an emerging activism among industrial workers, and even shaped the larger construction of Egyptian nationalism itself.

Demobilization

As we have seen, the colonial state was assembled in Egypt above all in the interests of bondholders and empire. The British retained and worked through the state apparatus inherited from Ismail, while establishing a modus vivendi with the Turco-Circassian aristocracy and the Egyptian provincial notables. As for the rebels, the constitutionalist and popular forces of the Urabiyyin were crushed by force, 'Urabi himself being exiled to Ceylon. But newly mobilized crafts and service workers in the cities, who through the 1860s and 1870s had started to develop a language and practice of citizenship, and who, during the sociopolitical crisis of 1878 to 1882 had marched in the streets in the name of 'Urabi's patriotism, were far too numerous to be similarly exiled.[1] Nor could they simply be thrown into prison by the notorious Brigandage Commissions of the 1880s, which were principally used by the British for imposing order in the countryside.[2] Furthermore, although strikes and demonstrations in the cities did come to an end after the British broke the 'Urabiyyin, crafts and service workers continued to complain through petitions in a newly unleashed protonationalist discourse about the privileged situation of European subjects who engaged in the crafts and trades.

The local subject weighers of Alexandria, for example, complained vigorously in collectively organized petitions during the mid-1880s about the fact that they were hit by the weighing tax which their European counterparts could get away without paying by simply refusing to do so. These complaints were not simply dismissed by prominent Egyptian politicians whose sensitivities to European privilege may have been reinforced by the British invasion on the one hand, and protonationalist sentiment on the other. The minister of finance argued to the president of the Council of Ministers that the complaints of the local subjects were "fully justified," and that "it has long been remarked that regarding the weighing tax, Europeans are placed in a privileged situation." Petitioners also argued that European subjects could refuse to have their weights checked and their registers examined, and could "know nothing of the trade of weighing" and have no proper authorization to practice without the government having the teeth to reign them in owing to their protected status.[3] In another example, complaints were raised by oil pressers regarding European-owned oil presses, which were exempt from the oil-pressing tax. A memorandum on the subject in 1886 noted that the oil-pressers "do not cease to formulate complaints."[4] The note went on to acknowledge the damage to the local-subject oil-pressing industry occasioned by this tax, and mentioned that unequal levies had forced some local-subject oil presses to close.[5]

Faced with potentially problematic protonationalist complaints from below and to some degree within the corridors of power, at a time when the financial and economic situation was not secure, the British found a way to deal with the situation without in any way jeopardizing what they saw as the vital interests of the bondholders. It would have been politically difficult to start taxing European subjects in Egypt, as this would have involved the lengthy and delicate process of obtaining consent to change the Capitulations from the Great Powers—not easy when Britain's position in Egypt was neither thoroughly defined nor fully accepted, least of all by France. The British therefore endorsed steady tax reductions on local-subject urban crafts and service workers. Remissions of arrears were repeatedly granted in the 1880s, and then in 1890 the professional tax was abolished entirely and a licenses tax (*'awa'id al-rukhas*) set up in its place.[6] This abolition meant a major reduction in taxation and was probably worth 120,000 LE to traders as a whole per annum.[7] In 1892, however, even the smaller licenses tax was abolished, and another 30,000 LE was handed back to crafts workers and traders.[8] By 1892, direct tax was reduced on almost the entire body of crafts and service workers (not to mention merchants, traders, and retailers of all kinds) to zero. Most of the remaining direct taxes on business, furthermore, such as the tax on weighers' licenses, the oil-pressers' tax,[9] the Cairo carts and livestock tax, and various boat taxes paid by fishermen were abolished by the early 1900s, remitting another 50,000 LE from the yearly tax burden of traders. As for indirect taxes on business, the market tax, various dues on navigation, railway rates, taxes on those using bridges over railways, customs tariffs on various raw materials, and most importantly, the octroi duties were lowered or abolished by 1906. These indirect taxes amounted, according to Artin, to a remission of about 750,000 LE.[10]

Colonial policy in this regard was possible in large measure because the British only sought to pay back the debt.[11] They were not engaged, whatever their rhetoric about a "civilizing mission," in making Egypt strong in the face of European expansion as Mehmet Ali's dynasty, for all the contradictions and set backs, had been. All expenditures unrelated to debt repayment were therefore reduced or haggled over minutely, one of the most notable examples being the budget for education. Reductions here had the further advantage for the authorities of reducing levels of politicization in the country at large. The key point is that the colonial state was no longer taking on the burden of self-strengthening intervention, but was instead merely holding the territory and resources of Egypt for colonial exploitation.[12] This logic began to take hold in 1879, shortly after the bankruptcy of Ismail's administration, when the minimum professional tax (*wirku*) was reduced from 50 piastres to 20 piastres,[13] a remission which Artin estimated to be worth 85,599 LE per annum.[14] Although bankrupt, the state was not looking any longer to squeeze every penny from the population for the purpose of further self-strengthening. It now sought only to manage and pay back the debt. Within this framework, previous policies were condemned, and tax reform and remissions in specific areas, especially for political purposes, were permissible.[15]

During the 1880s, furthermore, it was increasingly evident to the Debt Commissioners that revenues raised on the export economy—the customs duties, land tax, and revenue raised from the state monopolies (chiefly in railway and salt)—were more lucrative and easier to extract than the relatively small-scale and so-called vexatious taxes on crafts, which sometimes cost more to levy than they were actually worth. In other words, the relative economic weakness of urban crafts and service workers in a changing economy, coupled with their own ability to subvert tax-raising policies which still used guild heads in the collection and assessment process (although this was changing, as we shall see), was a force operating to drive the colonial state to seek taxes from the export economy.

If the policy was intended in part to demobilize an urban population organizing on the anticolonial and protonationalist issue of European subject privilege, at a time when the colonial state was trying to consolidate its position, it was a success. Remissions were celebrated across urban Egypt. "Their honours 'Abd al-Salam Bek Badr al-Din Sartujjar of [Rosetta] Port and Muhammad Bek 'Alwan and other notables and prominent persons (*al-'ayan wa al-wujuha*)," reported *Al-Ahram* on 26 November 1889, "have left us for the capital to present their obligation of gratitude to his highness the great Khedive for his mercy in issuing a decree forgiving the towns the professional tax and the weighing [tax] and other [taxes]. The populace here had received [the news of] this decree with the greatest happiness (*bi-ghayya al-ibtihaj*) and they hailed the Khedive to live long and always be powerful."[16] *Al-Ahram* reported a similar reception from merchant notables in Cairo to the remission of the professional tax, and reported that this "reduction in the burdens of the people" to the tune of 150,000 LE per year was a "tremendous service to the country" (*khidma jalila li-l-bilad*).[17] Celebrations were not surprising. By the later 1890s, artisans, service workers, and merchants were paying over one million LE less to the treasury every year in direct and indirect taxes. In addition, forced labour (*sukhra*) was also finally abolished in 1892 across the country.[18] And these tax breaks were also significant because, by all accounts, rather more was paid to government officials in taxation than reached the coffers of the Ministry of Finance, owing to corruption in many forms. Abolishing the octroi, for example, prevented a whole battery of state employees from lucrative modes of unofficial extraction from those importing goods into towns and cities.[19] Although the remissions were framed as emanating from the mercy of the Khedive, the colonial state, which in reality was using the khedive as a proxy (whatever comforts the population obtained by believing that this was not so), reaped the political benefits of this, at least in the short term, as it consolidated the overall system of power. Even in the later 1900s, when new forms of anticolonialism and nationalism were on the rise, Martin found that the worker in Cairo's workshops, in the context of the new tax regime, made a certain play "of being content with his daily lot," because "the time is not so distant when all work, all gathering of taxes, was only effected after a considerable distribution of blows with the whip. Today, now that the courbash no longer lacerates the 'chairs' of the workers, they appear to live in a golden age of work."[20]

Although a "golden age" is almost certainly too rosy a view, Martin, a French subject, was no propagandist for the British, and crafts and service workers reaped the economic benefits of tax remissions occasioned by the dismantling of self-strengthening. Crafts workers' multiplication after the 1890s must have owed something to the significant fiscal benefits of this colonial conjuncture, and in this sense their existence was underpinned by colonial policy. Not that crafts and service workers had been passive in this regard by any means: fiscal change was in part a response to their own formal and informal mobilization in defense of their interests.

Abandoning the Guilds

The guilds, which were increasingly a network of shaykhs and deputies who levied taxes for the government, and whose monopolies were not protecting the livelihoods of members in the way they once had, were abandoned by the state as part and parcel of this fiscal transformation and the larger dismantling of self-strengthening. We have already seen how guild shaykhs, struggling to protect certain guild members in the face of tax increases, had resorted to informal strategies of hiding allies from taxation, which in turn had attracted state intervention following protests from guild members who lost out. The attempt by the government to use shaykhs as state officials but without actually turning them into bureaucrats and paying them a salary was reaching its limits by the late 1870s, and after bankruptcy in 1879, policy changes to make fiscal extraction more effective was high on the agenda. Cases like that of the Cairo bakers, where hundreds were found to be dodging taxes because of the treachery of the guild leadership, would no longer be tolerated, and the state was in any case being dragged into guild affairs by the protests of guild members who were overtaxed.

In the late 1870s and in 1880, various ad hoc measures were taken by the expanding Ministry of Finance to get closer to taxpayers in the guilds and bypass the apparently unreliable—from the government's perspective—shaykh. Already in the 1860s and 1870s police had access to records of what individuals in guilds had paid each year, and by comparing year-to-year results could make some headway in tracking down treachery (*ghadr*) or embezzlement. Directives from Ismail's regime insisted that shaykhs tax members in accordance with the level of profit. We recall that in the extreme case of the Cairo bakers in 1880, the local authority went as far as getting masters to sign pledges to this effect.[21] But in the wake of the debt crisis, policy changed more systematically. Shaykhly activities in collecting (but not in assessing) the professional tax were abolished by new procedures instituted in 1881.[22] Early in that year, the Ministry of Finance sent out a publication demanding that appointments be made from among the various district officials (*ma'murin*) for the annual levy of the professional tax on artisans and traders (*arbab al-karat wa al-hiraf*). It reminded officials that the khedivial decree of January 1880 had reduced the lowest tax bracket to twenty piastres. It stated that appointments were to be made to the many professional tax offices in order to prevent treachery against the government (*maghduriya*) on the one hand, and injury to the people on the other (in the matter of the levy). The ministry specified that the tax registers (presumably in the hands of the local tax bureaux) must be kept in duplicate. During collection, one copy was taken to a particular location, its contents verified, and then the tax collection effected "according to what is suitable for the condition of the artisans." Afterwards, a schedule was to be sent to the Ministry of Finance with a statement "clarifying the details" of the collection. The tax collectors had to make it known that the artisan would face responsibility and the courts for any arrears. The ministry attempted also to impose a strict timetable: the schedules were to be completed by November, the collection by the following March.[23] The Ministry of Finance had to repeat its regulations of January 1881 in January 1882.[24]

These regulations replaced the tax collecting activities of the shaykh with those of the officials of the local authorities. As a Ministry of Public Works commission affirmed in 1888 in respect of the building guilds, "[T]he collection of the professional tax is not the responsibility of heads, but is undertaken by delegates of the local authority."[25] Nonetheless, the process of assessing the level of profit of each worker in the guilds still remained largely within the shaykh's sphere of influence. The only way the collectors could confirm that they were assessing the right amount of tax from any given individual was by consulting the shaykh or comparing the tax with the previous year. Thus the 1881 regulations instituted a period of dual control of the levy, whereby bureaucrats collected and the shaykh assessed the professional tax.

Throughout the 1880s, the government made moves which steadily undercut even this diminished role for the head of the guild. In January 1885, a Ministry of Finance publication emphasized that the professional tax be collected according to the level of profit again without betrayal of the taxpayers or the government. It also stated that local tax officials must draw up a clear schedule breaking down the guilds into the different tax brackets and showing how many members were in each bracket, and that the Ministry of Finance required a statement showing clearly "the divisions of payment." Government agencies were gradually acquiring the information and control which could hold the shaykh to account, diminish his local powers, and reduce his ability to protect certain members from taxes.

But Finance remained unhappy. On the 25 September 1886 a publication was issued declaring that attempts by the bureaus of the professional tax to chase up arrears had been "entirely inadequate."[26] It would appear that by one informal means or another, traces of which are barely visible in the written sources largely because of their very nature, crafts and service workers were able to resist and subvert the activities of the government tax collectors. Their advantage of course, was that government officials had nowhere registered their income, the size of their capital, their place of work, the nature of their premises, or even their fixed and official name. In order to overcome such difficulties, Finance reminded its minions what measures they were permitted to take in the case of default. They could confiscate the possessions of the taxpayer in arrears and his furnishings and moveable property. They could even confiscate his real estate and land "if the situation demands it," although it was cautioned that zealous officials were not to confiscate furnishings and clothes necessary for life, nor books or machines necessary for trade. The results were still inadequate for the ministry, which prepared a more complete policy change.

On 9 January 1890, a decree was announced which abolished the professional tax (*wirku*), and with it the shaykh's role in assessing taxation on guild members. This was the first time the bureaucracy had attempted to get the whole of the taxation process squarely in its hands. A new license tax (*'awa'id al-rukhas*) was now levied on two categories of trade. The first category had a fixed rate of tax to pay as shown in a schedule attached to the decree. The second category, which included most crafts workers, was a sliding tax assessed yearly: traders were to pay 5 percent per annum on the value of the hire of their premises in which they practiced a trade, although the minimum tax was established at twelve piastres a year (reduced from twenty piastres). To assess this rate, fixed machines and such things as carpentry equipment were also to be taken into account. To this end, all taxed persons would have to publish in the tax collectors' official journal a statement including their name, title, the name of their father, their trade, the street where the trade was, the number of their house, the value of their capital, and the amount of rent paid on their premises.[27] The gaze of the state was penetrating the lives of the population.

The key result for the shaykh was that he was no longer involved in assessment of the tax. Of course, it had been the case, during the 1880s, that documents were being used by tax offices and sent up to the Ministry of Finance which showed the numbers of artisans and in which tax bracket they were placed, and the assessment and suitability of these tax brackets was meant to be checked, even carefully, by the officials annually appointed for this job, but nonetheless, the information necessary for a realistic assessment remained in the hands of the shaykh. The officials had been merely yearly appointees: the shaykh of the guild, on the other hand, was present all the year round, and had access to information generated by face-to-face contact which was nowhere written down. Now, for the first time, the information necessary for a complete assessment was, at least in theory, to be in the hands of the local authorities and the Ministry of Finance.

Such a registration was no mean procedure. For example, on 24 January 1890, in the wake of the 1890 law, the Financial Council granted Alexandria local authority 500 LE "necessary for the registration of the members of trades and crafts (*arbab al-hiraf wa al-sana'i'*) . . . [because] the required process of registration is a necessary and considerable task, which must be completed by the end of March." It was deemed necessary to appoint fifteen officials and fifteen secretaries to do the work in Alexandria.[28] These bureaucratic apparatuses were a new political technology which substituted for the old fiscal powers of the shaykh.

But not entirely. The draftees of the law of 1890 had not forgotten about the shaykh of the guild. They directed that consultative councils be established which would sit when necessary to hear complaints connected to the new license tax. The shaykhs of all the *tawa'if* within each province or governorate were instructed to elect the ten members of this council. The governor or mudir (of the province) would then appoint someone to lead the council. This council would convene to hear complaints. So in the last gasp of the tax role of the shaykh, a few elected shaykhs would sit and hear complaints about tax evaluations conducted by bureaucrats.

However, this cadre of local trade notables were not to hold even an attenuated fiscal role for long. On 28 January 1892 a decree declared, "In force from 1 January 1892 the tax of the trade licences (*rukhsnamat al-sana'i'*) is annulled."[29] In these few words, in article 6 of a decree which also annulled forced labor and reduced the price of salt, the principal direct tax on artisans, service workers, and most traders was abolished. The *wirku* which had weighed on the workers for decades, and had recently been transformed into a license tax, had disappeared. This put a definitive end to the newly organized consultative councils, filled with the various chiefs, deputies, and adjuncts of the old guild hierarchy. It concluded the role of any guild officials in taxation in Egypt, and brought to a decisive end the steady annulment of their fiscal powers which had begun in the wake of the debt crisis of 1876 to 1879.

The tax reform was inextricably linked to the ultimate attrition of the official powers of the guild shaykh before his rank and file. For the decree of 1890 permitted traders to practice outside of the jurisdiction of their shaykh: "It is permitted for any person living in Egypt to practice any craft (*sina'a*) or profession (*hirfa*) or art (*fann*) or trade (*tijara*)."[30] Arminjon took this to mean the "tacit abrogation" of the guilds.[31] It certainly seems plausible that it referred to the fact that traders were now free to practice outside the jurisdiction of the shaykh. It was only when the state could keep fiscal track of traders without the intermediary of the shaykh, of course, that it could deny him jurisdiction over all those in a particular trade, and thus announce the "freedom of the trades." For the state no longer needed or thought it desirable to continue to make crafts and service workers practice under shaykhly authority. Under conditions of self-strengthening, his position had come to depend on his services to the state, especially his fiscal activities, and once they were no longer required, his jurisdiction was abrogated. Thus, during the fiscal changes linked to the dismantling of self-strengthening and the construction of the new colonial state that followed the debt crisis, what remained of the guilds in Egypt was quietly abandoned.

Guild members likely had few reasons to lament the official demise of the guilds, which had been heavily co-opted during the nineteenth century, and were no longer by any means unproblematically protecting members. Their role as a buffer against the extraction of the state was now irrelevant as tax cuts proceeded. Crafts and service workers more likely welcomed tax cuts and the attrition of shaykhly powers, which had become above all powers to tax, especially in the later nineteenth century. In any case, there is practically no evidence of protest or petition against these measures.

Informalism

It is important to point out, however, that superficially guildlike activities did not simply disappear overnight. As Baer and others have underlined, guilds were abandoned, but not actively suppressed. Moreover, guild leaderships had never come to rely exclusively on the government for their local positions, and thus retained for some time and in different ways unofficial powers in allocation and decision making. As Vallet pointed out, de facto guilds still existed in Cairo in 1911. He wrote that everywhere between the citadel and Kalaoun mosque among the "armourers, saddlers, carpenters, tentmakers, slipper makers, silk-weavers, perfume merchants, copper beaters," and others, one might find discussions among rivals appeased by the oldest in the trade. Or, when a dispute arose regarding the price of an object between seller and buyer, the matter would go to the arbitration of the old man. As Vallet noted, recourse to this arbitration was not mandatory and wielded no sanction, but still such practices survived, as a continuation in some measure of the old powers of the heads of the *tawa'if* under new conditions. Martin found similar practices in Cairo in 1909. He wrote, "[O]ne must . . . note the existence of individuals who take the name of shaykhs and to whom the members of a few professions submit their differences."[32] Ibrahim Siyan, for instance, identified himself as the shaykh of the guild of builders in al-Minya in 1902, and stated that he had been elected in 1878.[33]

Other shaykhs, or would-be shaykhs, continued to attempt to regulate their trades in the early twentieth century. A series of petitions by the head of the guild of Cairo brokers were an attempt to buttress his move to eject a corrupt broker from the trade in the early 1900s. He complained of corruption (*al-'ashsh*) in the practice of one of his brokers, Hassan al-Jawkhi, who was in league with a wood merchant. The wood merchant was selling wood at an inflated price via the broker, who the buyer thought was impartial, as brokers were supposed to be. In this case, the broker took a 10 percent cut of the transaction—considerably more than the standard 1 percent—owing to his willingness to participate in this dishonest practice. The head of the guild sought inspection and the issue of an order from the the Diwan al-Ma'iyya preventing al-Jawkhi from continuing to practice the trade.[34] Probably the very fact that the boss of the trade could not dismiss the offender from the trade on his own indicated a waning in his powers. Nonetheless, such a case allows a glimpse of a shaykh continuing to regulate the activities of those in the trade.

Whereas the chief of the Cairo brokers apparently sought the right regulation of the trade, other shaykhs continued to assert their powers in other ways. Here is a summary of a petition from 1902:

> Ibrahim 'Abd al-Rahman Halal from Giza deposes that the shaykh of the weighers and two others stole his wages and . . . other things, damaging the affairs of the guild. He raised complaints against them in Giza District and after establishing their validity they were transferred to the Provincial [offices] where they were held without being passed on to the magistrate (*niyaba*).[35]

Such a claim may have meant that the shaykh was still trying to collect customary dues from his weighers, and Halal now defined this as stealing. Or, it could have been a matter of outright theft. Or, it may have been, especially because of the reference to the "affairs of the guild," a matter of the shaykh withholding wages from a contract secured by him. Whatever the case, it is clear from such a petition that even in the early twentieth century shaykhs were still part of the everyday life of certain traders, and that patterns of local conflict and accommodation continued.

In certain trades, shaykhs appear to have retained much of their former power as labor contractors in the decade preceding the First World War. Metin noted, "[T]he shaykhs have lost their official authority and those who subsist do so only as foremen and labour contractors."[36] The Nubian domestic servants are a case in point. Arminjon wrote that Nubian domestics still "depended narrowly" on someone who called himself a shaykh, "who answered to their probity, to whom they pay a fairly heavy monthly fee, of which the police do not disdain to take a cut, and who are, to speak more exactly, employment agents."[37] Martin made exactly the same point in his work, adding that the shaykh makes "plenty of money by the taxes which he imposes on the occasion of every placement."[38] Complaints were raised in the English press concerning the activities of the shaykhs of the unofficial registry offices. Employers claimed that "frequently, if one [a servant] is obtained who can fulfil his duties in a possibly satisfactory manner, the sheikh of the registry office trades on him by inducing him to leave one place to go to another, and so increase his registration fees." What this and other correspondents sought was "the establishment of an official Government registry office properly organized for native servants."[39] These complaints suggest that it was impossible to find a servant except through these shaykhs-cum-employment agents. Thus, in some cases, despite the attrition of their official powers, the old transformed hierarchy was able to maintain its grip on the flow of trade and contracts, and act as a kind of mandatory employment agent where lack of effective regulation, ethnicity, migration patterns, and kickbacks to police shored up their position.

To give one more example, among the fishermen, the shaykhs and concessionary tax farmers of yesteryear became the racketeers and local bosses of the early twentieth century. Levi's investigation of the Qulali fish market in Cairo revealed that despite the fact that fish tax farms had been definitively abolished by 1903, and fishing had been made free, it was "very interesting that in the actual organisation of fish commerce one still finds vestiges of the *ancien régime* and the guilds."[40] Prior to 1903, the Ministry of Finance had granted concessions in return for a fee to what were effectively tax farmers in each province. These tax farmers were entitled to some percentage of the catch of the fishermen who fell within their tax farm, whether one third, one half, and possibly more in certain circumstances. These percentages were extracted at the point of sale, the tax farmers controlling the local fish markets. The tax farmers collaborated with the shaykhs of the fishing guilds to regulate traders and in various ways to extract surplus from those under their jurisdiction. In such ways the fish farmers and shaykhs took on statelike functions and operated as semiautonomous intermediaries between the government and the fishermen.

In 1903, however, fishing was declared free on the Nile, the sea, the lakes, and tributaries of the Nile. (This reform, incidentally, represented the abolition of the last of the tax farms in Egypt). This meant an enumeration of all the boats in operation, a statistical exercise in part, and a due on a sliding scale on each boat paid directly to the government. In other words, centralized and direct taxation was introduced. The tax farms were abolished. Nonetheless, as Levi explained, the old tax farmers still played an important role due to their experience, their financial clout, their prestige among the fishermen, and the "ignorance" of the fishermen. The market at Qulali certainly did not conform to Levi's notions of sanitation and order. It was "very unsanitary," served by a dirt road, stank, was crowded, and consisted of five narrow dirty shacks for sales. These shacks belonged to the old tax farmers who were entitled to a commission of 5 percent on sales, although the "poor fisherman usually pays a great deal more." The merchandise was sold at auction by a weigher who was an agent or associate of the owner of the outlet. The weigher wrote in a register the price and quantity of the sale. "In fact, he writes what he wants—no one controls him." It is interesting to note further that a system of "useless intermediaries" connected this market to hotels and restaurants, who could not buy directly. Thus in a sense the old hierarchies retained their prestige. The fishermen remained in "ignorance."[41] Intermediaries, ex-shaykhs and ex-tax farmers maintained their networks and resource bases as far as they could, and kept the ministries and provincial authorities as much as possible at bay.[42]

For all the superficial continuities, the old established guilds had gone forever, the result of processes of change that reached back into the nineteenth century, and it is highly problematic to see the activities undertaken by unofficial figures in the trades after 1890 in terms of some traditional continuity. For ongoing authority among the post-1892 ex-guild hierarchy was not based on time-honored custom, the autonomies and local jurisdictions of which had carried the sanction of the state, at least until centralization in the nineteenth century started to undermine this sanction. No longer did official discourse recognize and approve the local autonomies of shaykhlike activities in the trades, which were now deemed "tyrannical," "malignant," and "backward," as they escaped state regulation and the progress such regulation supposedly guaranteed. Indeed, such local figures were not sanctioned by state regulations, which they often sought to undermine or transform in one way or another. In addition, the crafts and service trades were undergoing rapid sociological change. The speedy growth of completely new trades such as cab driving and the attrition of others, the drift to the countryside of textiles on the one hand, and significant rural-urban migration on the other, and the increased participation of women meant that many in the trades in the early 1900s had no established links to a prior tradition of shaykhly authority in a trade. Small wonder that many of those questioned by Martin in the 1900s were vague about the old guild regime. In other words the forms of "informalism"[43] among the crafts and service trades after the 1890s were distinctively new: an outgrowth of modern social relations under colonial rule.[44]

Out of the Frying Pan, into the Fire

The benefits of tax remission and the attrition of the guilds notwithstanding, crafts and service workers were in some sense moving out of the frying pan of self-strengthening and into the fire of the colonial state. As Tilly has written with striking aptness in a different context,

> [A]s a result of exploitation by middlemen, an alliance with a distant king or his agents often seemed an attractive alternative to exploitation close at hand; villagers then appealed to royal agents, took their cases against landlords to royal courts, and cheered the curtailment of urban privileges. In the short run, they sometimes gained by these choices. But in the long run, the destruction of intermediate barriers made them more vulnerable to the state's next round of war-generated demands.[45]

The construction of the colonial state left crafts and service workers politically weaker than before, although this fact was shielded by the short-term benefits of tax remission.

The "freedom" of the trades meant nothing of the sort. It meant that instead of being subject to the local jurisdiction of shaykhs, crafts and service workers were now subject to the decision-making and regulative powers of a growing bureaucracy and the expanding secular judiciary, the whole apparatus being harnessed to the interests of a vast empire based in London.

Regulative power now accrued to the bureaucracy as codified regulations multiplied. The Code Administratif Egyptien, published in 1911 and including "all general decrees and decisions for magistrates, lawyers, students, civil servants, administrators, etc." expressed and articulated the power of the new bureaucracy, expanded by self-strengthening, and now deepened (albeit selectively) by the colonial state in the name of order, method, clarity, publicity, and regularity. In particular, trades that raised public health and environmental concerns—from butchers to purveyors of "alcohol and spiritous drinks," from street vendors to fishermen using fine-mesh nets, to tanners and their "noxious" emissions, to the chimneys of metal workers, to weighers and measurers, to the health and hygiene of the livestock of cab drivers and carters—were subject to new kinds of written regulation.[46] The sphere of official determination for local custom decided by guild leaders, long battered by Mehmet Ali's *dabt wa rabt* and Ismail's "known legal means," was now attenuated further, and simultaneously delegitimized. With it went the electoral practices of guilds instated after 1869, not to be replaced, in the colonial context, by any kind of binding consultation with new bureaucratic powers. And even where certain regulations delineated a role for shaykhs, as in the case of the donkey drivers, where shaykhs were supposed to negotiate with passengers, settle disputes, fix prices, check registers, and supervise salaries, the shaykh was very much subordinated, officially at least, to bureaucratic regulations.

The new secular *majalis* of the Mehmet Ali dynasty had already begun to make inroads into shaykhly jurisdictions, and this process took a decisive step with the establishment of the National Courts in 1883. Vallet cited this legislation as a major reason for the demise of the local jurisdiction of the head of the trades.[47] Arminjon wrote that "the institution of the indigenous tribunals in 1883 has stripped them [the shaykhs] of their jurisdiction," and argued that the new judges put in place by the law of 1883 "ignored" the shaykhs of the trades.[48] Metin made more or less the same assertion, that after the application of the Napoleonic Code in 1883, contracts were to be made between individuals without the intermediary of the shaykh and thus courts no longer called on the shaykh to witness in the legal process.[49] The construction commission affirmed in 1888 that shaykhs should no longer get involved in disputes over contracts: "[I]f problems arise from [a contract] then the issue goes to the courts."[50] The reorganized courts no longer recognized the customary status of the shaykh or the old *ahl al-khibra* as expert witnesses. This was because new experts had to have received a diploma or similar qualification from a professional or technical college in the relevant trade before they could be considered such. This provision excluded the overwhelming majority of traders and craftsmen from witnessing as experts in court, the shaykhs and deputies no less than anyone else.[51] Customary determination of this legal status was now replaced by qualifications guaranteed by new, and highly exclusive, educational institutions.

Crafts and service workers were now entirely without official collective institutions—neither old-style guilds, nor new-style charities, syndicates, or unions—to articulate their interests or to act as a protective form of organizational density against the actions of the state or against economic threats. Moreover, resources for mobilization were relatively diminished as crafts and service workers became increasingly poor, for even as their numbers multiplied, and in spite of tax cuts, incomes diminished relative to the economy as a whole. Little surplus for organization was left over. Without collective organization or social legislation, masters would continue to self-exploit, and patterns of labor squeezing and labor-intensive accumulation would continue.

Further, workers had few powers of institutional disruption where production was scattered in small units up and down the country, and where revenues from crafts and service production were increasingly unnecessary to the tax base of the colonial state. Indeed, the economic benefits of tax remission did not come without a political cost. For how could crafts and service workers now assert their citizenship, in the way they had done in very close association with taxation during the 1870s, if they no longer paid these taxes, and thus no longer made a contribution to the government which dominated their affairs? Arguably, whereas political representation historically has often been granted or squeezed from power holders in exchange for the payment of taxes—in Europe and elsewhere,[52] in Egypt, the British reversed this principle, and essentially instated the regressive bargain: "no representation without taxation." Nontaxpayers had few weapons in this situation to combat a discourse identifying them as backward, economically weak, and in need of tutelage and the light of new civilization. The colonial state was not any longer engaged in expensive self-strengthening, under which subjects were beaten and impoverished, but subaltern groups could at least assert their rights in the matter of taxation, and possessed some power of institutional disruption in terms of their ability to stall the tax flow. Under the British, who instated a new fiscality, these (slight) political advantages were neutralized. In part, citizenship was exchanged for tax remission.

Finally, the fragile constitutionalists of yesteryear, the provincial notables, had now thrown in their lot with the British, while the intelligentsia remained too small, weak, and ideologically conservative to provide leadership or support for popular groups. Crafts and service workers therefore had few organizational or ideological means to break the patterns of self-exploitation and labor squeezing that survival in the changing economy entailed. And with the end of the guilds, subaltern crafts and service workers now faced directly a colonial state with significant autonomy from a newly precipitated society. Where political opportunity was so constrained, and where the colonial state had made concessions over taxation in any case, it is hardly surprising that protests were few and far between for the years between the late 1880s and the early 1900s.

The Rise of Nationalism

Times changed. Political opportunities started to be transformed in the late 1890s and early 1900s with the rise of nationalism. By the 1870s, educational change in Egypt had already brought into being a relatively small group educated in the European style and articulating notions of patriotism—"love of the fatherland"—in part as a challenge to the autocracy of the khedive and as a source of strength and solidarity in the face of the growing influence of Europe. After the British invasion, and especially during the early 1900s, nationalist ideas were more and more widely articulated. The development of secular law, bureaucracy, medicine, engineering, architecture, and journalism, and the growth of secular, Western-style education, contributed to the expansion of a previously embryonic "middling" strata, who came to be known as the *afandiya*, wore Western-style clothes, worked in the liberal professions, and read and published in an emerging print media. Such groups had considerable exposure to and interest in the ideas elaborated in European nationalism, which was often viewed as a force for strength, unity, and progress. Although the *afandiya* remained numerically small, their influence, owing partly to their weight in the emerging media, was disproportionately large.[53] The material interests of these professions were less directly tied to both land and the export economy than the aristocracy or the colonial bourgeoisie. Furthermore, their aspirations to political power and status, at least in a collective sense, were often frustrated by the domination of the British and the landed classes. The ideas they developed started to challenge the imperial system established by the British in the 1880s and 1890s. For these rising middle classes increasingly articulated the idea that there was a nation called Egypt, with a common history, language and culture, whose destiny was independence and freedom from colonial rule, and whose powers, resources, and culture should be developed to this end. Crucially, as Yaseen Noorani argues, the nascent nationalist bourgeoisie depicted *themselves* as the leaders and standard bearers of this rising Egyptian nation—an Egypt of progress, independence, learning, industry, military strength, parliament, building, steam, and electricity.[54] Abbas II (1892–1914) was at least outwardly more sympathetic to nationalism than his predecessor; the victory of the Japanese in the Russo-Japanese force gave confidence to those who sought to challenge Europe. And nationalist ideas received wide publicity following the notorious Dinshaway incident of June 1906, when a number of villagers, seen as guilty of little more than defending themselves against the aggression of a number of British officers out shooting, were punished by hanging, flogging, and imprisonment. Literate urban opinion was outraged and sympathized with these villagers against British tyranny as sons of a rising nation, rather than despising them as an illiterate, heterodox, rural rabble. "For the first time," wrote Jacques Berque, "the opposition of educated Egyptians made common cause with peasant violence."[55]

Nationalists discussing the "backwardness" (*takhalluf*) and weakness of Egyptian industry,[56] increasingly paid attention to the fate of Egypt's crafts workers, who, it was argued, had too long suffered from the "contempt of notables," lack of education, or the application of science, and their own tendency to "sloppy" and "unpersevering" work.[57] Artisanal education, it was thought, could enable crafts workers to respond to new demands, increase the prosperity of the country, contribute to the well-being of its inhabitants, and bolster Egypt's position in the face of colonial rule. Some looked back to a putative bygone age when Damascene textiles or Cairean artisans had been the pride of the region, lamented decline over the centuries or through more recent years, and in this way bolstered the urgency of their call to action. Others spoke of the talents, energies, skills, and creativity which continued to exist among artisans.[58] This argument defended artisans against those who claimed that it was not worth diverting resources to "backward" and "improvident" craftsworkers,[59] but it also carried the message that such persons should be cultivated lest their talents and skills be lost to the nation forever.[60] Such thinking gave the emerging national bourgeoisie a leadership role in a project to educate and revive artisans and their industry. And whereas landowners were often opposed to large-scale industrial ventures, on the basis that these would divert resources from Egypt's vocation as an agricultural country and generate a perceived threat to their own wealth and power rooted in agriculture and cheap labor, they were more susceptible to the argument that small-scale industry could be materially developed in a way which did not threaten agriculture. Thus landowners could make some concessions to the nationalist cause and find an outlet for nationalist sentiments on this question by supporting assistance to small-scale manufacturing.[61] Some recommended that more should be done by merchants to organize putting-out systems to activate further the "spinning, weaving, tailoring, carpentry and sandal-making (*al-sakkafa*), embroidery and the fattening of goats and calves" which one found all over the countryside: to "buy raw materials, provide a master to teach them weaving, and hire them for weaving."[62] Overall, nationalist thinking started to see artisans as having a real role in developing the powers and resources of an emerging Egyptian nation.

Schools for the technical instruction of artisans started to be founded on private initiative from the early 1900s. In 1903, Mahmud Sulayman Pasha, a landowner from Asyut province, founded an industrial school at Abu Tij entirely at his own cost for teaching artisans, who required only a *kuttab* education to enter, basic reading, writing, and arithmetic as well the practical skills of weaving, carpentry, turning, blacksmithery, and one or two other trades, free of charge. By 1907, ninety-two pupils were enrolled. In 1904, the Tawfiq Coptic Society, a nongovernmental charitable organization, founded an industrial school for carpentry and smithery in the Faggala quarter of Cairo. At the same time, some funding was even wrung from the Debt Commission for artisanal education. The workshops attached to the School of Arts and Crafts in Bulaq were established in 1904 independently by the Department of Public Instruction as a model workshop performing the same teaching functions as Sulayman Pasha's new school.[63]

Both government and private intervention accelerated in 1906. The (nongovernmental) Coptic Patriarchate decided to fund a second industrial school in Bulaq. Further, a charitable organization, *al-'Urwa al-Wuthqa*, began funding and planning the construction of a large industrial school (intended for about 550 pupils) in Alexandria. The government responded further by founding a new model worskhop along the same lines as that of Bulaq in Asyut in 1906, and then took the interesting step of granting exemption from military service for those attending the model workshops at Bulaq, Asyut, and Mansura, and the School of Arts and Crafts at Bulaq. This was a clear indication to humble artisans from government that the cause of crafts development and education was an important one. As Wells wrote,

> [I]t was therefore evident that the public in general was interested in the question of technical education and was clearly showing its desire to see it progress. . . . [T]he foundation through private initiative of the four [private] schools [mentioned above] . . . was the best proof that this interest truly existed, and the success of the model workshops also showed quite clearly the necessity of this instruction and was a gauge that it would give satisfaction to a real need.[64]

During the course of 1906, committees were also formed (on private initiative) in al-Fayum and Bani Suwaif for gathering subscriptions for industrial schools. These committees turned to the government for funds and organizational support. As Wells wrote, "Soon, similar demands arrived from other parts of the country, and it became clear that the moment had come [for the government] to do something." Further, the economic boom and increasing demand for skilled artisans had its own impact under new and more nationalist conditions. As Wells continued, "It was a time of great financial prosperity, commercial and industrial activity as everyone can remember, and the need for skilled and trained artisans was becoming more and more clear." In this context, "[t]he Government quickly understood the necessities of the situation and decided to put to study the elaboration of a plan for the development of technical education in general."[65] A Khedivial decree of December 1906 created a new subdepartment attached to the Department of Public Instruction for technical, industrial, and commercial education." In practice the subdepartment was up and running by the end of 1907 under the direction of Sidney Wells, who was recruited from England. The British were here making a concession to nationalist pressure on an issue which they did not feel threatened their vital interests. Artisanal education was desireable, for as Cromer wrote, "[T]here is a rapidly growing need for skilled labour of various kinds, and scope for the development of many useful industries,"[66] but more importantly, such a project would not threaten the transnational or local structure of power, would not cost very much, and could serve as a legitimating example of the way Britain was assisting in the "civilization" of the country.

The Advent of Mass Popular Protest

By 1907, nationalist thinking was beginning to provide a new way of framing social order in Egypt, pitting a struggling Egyptian nation against an alien and oppressive colonial regime. Further, middle-class nationalists, in the wake of Dinshaway, had started to regard the "lower orders" as legitimate political subjects, at least to a limited degree. Nationalist ideas were beginning to be transmitted to crafts workers, both in a diffuse way through the growing print media, and in a more direct way by the organization of industrial education, in which nationalists were sometimes directly involved. Such new forms of framing and the political opportunities they suggested coincided with two new developments. First, the boom of 1897 to 1907 significantly increased the pressures of restructuring. And second, the colonial state, in a reversal of its own hands-off approach to subaltern groups, made several insupportably heavy regulative interventions into particular trades. These factors formed the background to what was surely the most significant wave of popular protest prior to the 1919 rebellion in Egypt.

The cycle of contention began with the mass strike of Cairo's cab drivers, upwards of two thousand strong, in April 1907, which brought Cairo to a standstill, generated something approaching hysteria in the colonial press, and prompted new thinking among nationalists.

Just when numbers working in carting and cab driving in Cairo were increasing as never before, a new threat to their livelihoods emerged, far more problematic than the tram, and far less amorphous than the pressures of restructuring: the British-run Society for the Prevention of Cruelty to Animals. A branch of the British RSPCA[67] was set up in Cairo in the 1890s and, after one or two false starts, appears to have attracted the support of Lord Cromer (and possibly Lady Cromer). As Marshall put it,

> [T]he first attempt to start a Society for the Prevention of Cruelty to Animals in Egypt was made by an Army Chaplain. His efforts were not very successful, and culminated in his being charged before the Consular Court for thrashing a camel-driver who had ill-treated his animal. However, small beginnings have notoriously great endings, and at length the society was started with the encouragement and support of Lord Cromer, and has been, for many years, doing great work.[68]

Around the turn of the century, an animal hospital was built on Shari'a al-Sahel between Bulaq and the Gare Centrale.[69] It was not long before the society turned its attention to the health and safety of the livestock being used by cabbies and carters around the city. The SPCA and its supporters lamented the lameness, emaciation, and beating of "dumb animals," which in its view resulted from the cruel and wanton behavior of cab drivers and others. They spoke of "animals with sore backs, shoulders, legs," "sores and swellings," and of "overloading, underfeeding, cruelty, [and] beating."[70] The Society combined favorable British opinion[71] and a certain political clout[72] to enforce existing regulations relating to the health and well-being of horses.[73] They worked with police and even secured the appointment of one of their own, Major Jarvis, as a special inspector with powers to impound animals and arrest offenders himself. Hence, in the early 1900s, thousands of arrests were made, licenses withdrawn, animals ordered rest or forcibly hospitalized, prosecutions pursued, and convictions obtained. The SPCA celebrated over five thousand convictions in 1906, which was declared a record year.[74] Just as nationalist ideas were more widely disseminated, a British institution associated with the colonial state was behind a severe intervention, which struck at the heart of the livelihoods of Cairean transport workers, who, in addition to squeezing their own labor, relied on squeezing their livestock in order to keep down costs.

The SPCA probably garnered support beyond the ranks of those most passionately concerned with the plight of dumb animals. There was a sense in which sympathy for animals was intensified in a kind of colonial identity politics, in which the self-consciously "civilized" emphasized their negative response to the brutal acts of barbarous "natives" in order to reinforce their own putative superiority and claim to rule. Sympathy also came from sections of the colonial bourgeoisie who felt they had had their share of what they saw as ill treatment at the hands of cabbies with whom they had ridden, and who held cabbies in low regard generally. Cabbies were often considered ruffianly, boorish, and incompetent, as well as cruel. A writer in the Egyptian Gazette wrote that "it might be asked why [the police] do not, when issuing licenses to arbaghis, insist on some test of driving and topography. The local Jehu [colonial slang for cabby] has no idea of either, and having also no 'hands,' plies the whip savagely and ceaselessly to cover his defects." The writer continued, "[A]s the arbaghi, so is the donkey boy a class . . . composed chiefly now of hulking loutish men who form a public nuisance to pedestrians and a menace to any defenceless or nervous client."[75] Another wrote, "I have no hesitation in saying that the reckless way in which the Cairo arbaghis drive, their insolent manners, and the condition of their horses, is a disgrace to civilisation."[76]

For much of the local bourgeoisie also, cabbies were hardly interpellated as sons of a rising Egyptian nation. This was not just because of such service workers' long-standing low status among urban professions.[77] It was also a result of new bourgeoise discourses of progress. In comparison with the the science, electricity, and progress encompassed in the tram, cab drivers and carters represented a backward past that had to be transformed as a prelude to, or as part of obtaining independence from colonial rule. Consider the following:

> [T]he tram was the end of a chapter in the history of Cairean society, which was transported through it from the stage of nomadism and backwardness which is represented by the use of the donkey and the mule to the stage of urban civilisation (*al-hadara al-madaniya*) which is represented in the use of electric power . . . the terrible difficulties in transport [stemming] from the tyranny (*istibdad*) of the donkey drivers and coachmen and their power over people, and the cursing that they make people endure.[78]

No matter that trams and cab drivers were both distinctively late-nineteenth-century phenomena in Egypt, and that the latter were multiplying their numbers, and grew out of the modern landscape of the city. This bourgeois discourse of progress placed one behind the other in a largely imaginary progressive time, judged according to mechanization and the development of science and order. Cab drivers were doubly indicted as both backward and to some extent, with their "tyranny" and "cursing," immoral.

Clearly, then, cabbies and carters had a major problem. The SPCA was organized, powerful, and connected, and could count on considerable support among the colonial and local bourgeosie. It was arresting, fining, and imprisoning them, and impounding and confiscating their animals in Cairo at a fierce rate by 1906. The carters and cabbies on the other hand, had few links to those in power and few resources on which to draw. When they initially encountered the SPCA, they were a fragmented and unorganized group. Even in the two or three decades preceding 1890 (when the guilds were tacitly abrogated), it is unlikely that the guilds of coachmen and carters represented much more than units of taxation and regulation. In 1890, carting and cab driving, like the other urban crafts and trades, were declared free, in the sense that anyone was permitted to take up the trades, as long as they registered various details with the governorate and obtained a license and number. Thus after this date, there was no official reason for any cab driver or carter to interact with a guild shaykh or his deputies. Although newspapers occasionally spoke of the *ta'ifa* (or "guild") of coachmen in the 1900s, this word most likely signified little more than the group of all those occupied in that profession. Moreover, these professions were rapidly expanding. New cabbies and carters were obtaining licenses all over the city, which itself had grown to over three quarters of a million souls by 1917. It is unlikely that even rudimentary links were maintained between most in the profession.

On the other hand, one should not push this picture of atomization too far. Mobilizations in the 1870s indicate that groups of crafts and service workers—factions within guilds (whether allied to a guild hierarchy or not), or whether forming links to those outside the trade such as merchants or not—were practiced at banding together, and petitioning to voice their demands. Coffeehouses in certain areas, and various popular hackney stands such as those in 'Ataba al-Khadra or Ezbekiyya, probably supported localized social interaction. Finally, as we recall, the shaykh and other senior members of the profession had not been suppressed in 1890, and likely retained a certain status in the trade. The informalism encountered above could be bent to new purposes. A shaykh, for example, was present— in a new, representative role—among one of the deputations sent by the strikers to the governorate in April 1907, as we shall see.

On these rather uncertain bases, cab drivers and owners, in small groups or individually, turned to petitions, much used as we have seen in the 1860s and 1870s, to protest what they saw, not as a noble crusade, but as a heavy-handed and unjust intervention, involving arbitrary punishments, severe regulations, confiscations, coerced expensive treatments, license withdrawal, police brutality, and prison. In the initial stages, the cabmen blamed each other rather than the strictness of the regulations. For example, when Ahmad 'Ali lost his license because of the ill health of his horse he blamed the owner of the stable, Isma'il Darwish for failing to "follow healthy practices."[79] As the enforcement was intensified, however, cabmen started to blame the police and the regulations themselves. Muhammad Sulayman, who had been dismissed from government service owing to paralysis, had a son who bought a pair of horses so that the family could subsist on income from cab driving. Then the Ezbekiyya police (*qism*) took one of the horses on 2 December 1905 and the second on the sixteenth "and on the first there was a slight injury and on the second a minor lameness." The family only discovered later that the vet had put the horses down. The father requested an investigation and demanded the price of the horses, because he was "very poor and needy." The petition enclosed a certificate from four cabmen stating that the condition of the horses in question had been good for years.[80]

In November 1906, a petition without seals or signatures was sent complaining about the "tyranny (*istibdad*) and injustice" inflicted by the police on the cabmen and the "extraction of large sums of money from them" and the "beating of whoever refuses to cooperate with them," "beating which sometimes leads to the death of who is beaten . . . [whereas] the doctor's statement [stated] that the reason for death was drunkenness." The petition also cited police opposition to "selling [advertising for rides] in the street," and "whoever does not pay what is demanded from him is taken to the station" and the police ensure an unfavourable verdict if the case goes to court.[81] In January 1907, another petition was summarized as follows:

> 'Abd Allah Faqr of Cairo, after finishing his military service, wanted to work as a cabdriver (*'arbaji rukub*) due to his poverty and the size of his family. So his niece bought a carriage to be used [for this] by him. They both benefitted from it. After that he spent a sum on repairing it . . . until it became the best of cabs . . . [but] the inspector of traffic stopped its working without reason. Therefore he petitioned twice about this to the Interior adviser and requests an order [to return the cab to work].[82]

Sometimes women petitioned on behalf of husbands or sons. Perhaps this was thought to be a more effective way of gaining clemency from the powers-that-be (*wilayat al-amur*). For example, Umm 'Abd al-Rahman, the wife of Salih Jawhir, a master cabdriver, petitioned the Khedivial Diwan to forgive (*'afu 'an*) her husband from a prison sentence he had received.[83] Another petition on 17 March 1907 was summarized thus:

> Muhammad Hasan Abu Sitta of Cairo deposes that his trade (*kar*) has been that of cabman since old times. He has been in his trade for around 30 years. [But] the government withdrew the license from him and from some persons on the pretext that they had no permission to work on account of the injuries [of their horses]. However, there are many present like them still in work. And . . . with this family [he is] in the greatest need (*ashadd al-ihtiyaj*) and requests an investigation and their return to their work and that he is prepared to bring the guarantee which is demanded of him.[84]

In a further petition of 21 March 1907, Muhammad Hasan al-Busna, previously a cabman in Cairo, deposed that the governorate took away his license without reason. He was then living off "generosity" for three years until his condition deteriorated, partly because of an illness. His complaints, he said, did not bear any fruit, until finally the governorate permitted him to drive an omnibus owned by the prominent Suarès family. But Muhammad thought this made little sense, given that such coaches involved being in charge of three horses, whereas working on his own account, which was what he wanted, only meant being in charge of two horses. He requested permission for work on his own account, and was ready to offer a guarantee.[85] A few weeks later al-Busna continued to press his case: "[W]hy is it possible for him to run three horses, but it is not possible for him to run two?" Busna claimed this was "tyranny" which "prevented him from making a living," while "he is poor and disabled and has no [criminal] record in the least," and "seeks permission to work his trade directly."[86]

It is difficult to establish empirically to what extent anti-English sentiment or nationalism was either generated by or fed into the sense of grievance felt by cabdrivers in respect of the heavy intervention under which they suffered. The petitions do not give much away on this score: grievances are related to specific instances of tyranny, highhandedness, brutality, and so on. But it was likely that most cabdrivers knew that the English SPCA was behind the enforcement. The petitions make only one or two references to English involvement, but this may well have been a judicious strategy by cabbies who thought it wiser not to trumpet anti-English sentiment. Perhaps cabbies expressed their grievances in actions rather than words. Consider the following account by an English resident of Cairo:

[The cab driver] is . . . a sportsman in his way, and his chief recreation consists in endeavouring to 'run down' well-dressed Europeans. It soothes his racial antipathies and even if he can't bag his man he can splash him with mud or cover him with dust according to local atmospheric conditions, or, if he has a clear street before him and the khawagah does not look like a 'sprinter,' he can slash him over the face with his whip. . . . A month ago an arbaghi came up behind me along the Sharia Kamel and with the whole road to spare hugged the right side and without a word of warning I felt his off horse's shoulder cannon into mine; he had plenty of space but having some experience in 'riding off' I got clear of his hoofs and the wheels, but still it was not a bad attempt.[87]

Both the politics of trade regulation and antiimperial sentiment may have been behind such actions; certainly the timing of this incident, early 1907, is suggestive. Cabdrivers may have been emboldened by ever more vocal nationalist opinion in the wake of Dinshaway, and nationalist thinking provided an apt cultural frame to describe and explain their plight at the hands of the SPCA. However, there is no evidence of organizational links between cabdrivers and nationalists prior to the strike of April 1907.

Far from gaining redress for their grievances, punishments for cabdrivers falling foul of the SPCA were actually increased during the early spring of 1907.[88] The ineffectiveness of petitions was underscored. The regulations, harnessed to a bureaucracy and pushed by a colonial pressure group, were too pervasive and too collective in their impact to be effectively dealt with by the more particularistic means of the petition. Such policies, because of the reach and penetration of the new bureaucracy, now affected the cabdrivers globally: in this sense it equalized their subject positions and threw them together in opposition to the state. Centralization, in this respect, and reactions to it, contributed to the distillation of the people. To complain about the regulations themselves was not to complain to the authorities about a local exploiter of one kind or another, a form of complaint involving the petition that was much used and at least partially effective in the 1870s; instead it was to seek to tackle and change the policies of the authorities themselves. This meant taking on the edifice of the colonial state—a far more ambitious task than taking on a corrupt tax official or a guild shaykh. Arguably, in this case, there was some affinity between this ambitious task and the rising current of nationalism, for the aims and meaning of the two were similar. They both challenged the colonial state in Egypt.[89]

At some point, the idea of a mass strike must have formed among a certain group or groups of cabbies. No direct records exist of cabbies' thinking, but they were almost certainly aware of the handful of strikes that had taken place in Egypt's recent history: to pick two of the most prominent examples, the coal heavers in Port Said had gone on strike en masse on a number of occasions since 1882 and were reported in the press; and the mostly Greek subject cigarette rollers in Cairo had struck for higher wages in 1899 and achieved a settlement in 1900.[90] Meanwhile, strikes in the Ottoman Empire were not unknown prior to the upsurge of 1908 which accompanied the Young Turk constitutional revolution, and the press in Egypt had publicized the workers' demonstrations and protests that had accompanied the Iranian constitutional revolution of 1906.[91] The 1905 revolution in Russia, and the formation of workers' soviets were not unknown in Egypt either. However, it should be stressed that middle-class nationalists, expressing the fears of the propertied against popular disturbances, generally looked unfavorably on strike action prior to 1907: as Muhammad Farid, the leader of the National Party after 1908, commented earlier on hearing of a strike, "This European disease has spread to Egypt."[92]

Nonetheless, cabbies may have been emboldened by their particular position in the city and relationship to its elites. They were in constant proximity with Cairo's well-to-do, despite the social chasm and multiple stigmas that divided driver from passenger. And unlike, say, domestic servants or hotel waiters, they drove clattering vehicles which dominated the new and prestigious streets of the capital, and commanded horses, which until recently were denied all but the ruling class by sumptuary laws. Their loud and regular use of a cracking whip were symbols of this. Under pressure from regulations, what Asef Bayat has called the "passive network," where those occupying similar status positions recognize each other in the street or in other settings, shifted to a more "active network," where such persons start to coordinate and communicate with a view to collective action.[93] Cabbies' mobility and numbers may have facilitated this process. In addition to rising prices and likely static wages, the end of the tourist season in April almost certainly meant that cabbies were no longer getting as many fares, and were charging less for the rides they did give. Finally, Cromer's impending departure, which was generally known by April, may have been construed as a sign of British weakness in the wake of the mishandling of Dinshaway. Certainly the British were preparing to appoint the more conciliatory Eldon Gorst as consul-general in Egypt. It is not impossible that such weakness was sensed as a political opportunity.

My research has not been able to uncover how the cabbies actually organized in the days before the protest, and there may of course have been an unrecorded spark which lit the tinder, but whatever the case, on 18 April

1907, in a development which took all the newspapers by surprise, between two and five thousand Cairean cabdrivers and owners joined a near total strike (*adrabu 'an al-'amal*). *Al-Jarida* reported that "the streets were empty of cabs." The *Egyptian Gazette* concurred: "[N]ot a single cab is to be found in the streets."[94] *Al-Ahram* stated that "a total strike prevailed."[95] In the words of one newsaper,

> The coachmen went this morning in groups to the police stations and the Governorate building . . . [T]hey did not see one of them driving a cab without [ejecting the passenger] . . . in order that their colleague participate with them in the strike against the police and the traffic bureau.[96]

According to *Al-Jarida*, the *hukmdar* of the police, on the arrival of a deputation from the cabmen, "promised them orally that the owners of horses found to be sick would not be imprisoned but a fine would be paid."[97] Some were satisfied; most were not. Therefore, along with their heads (*ru'sa'ahum*) they wrote their complaints and demands down and sent them to the Minister of Justice, with a copy to the *hukmdar*, and then returned to the governorate building at Bab al-Khalq on Khalij Street (not far from the cabbies' central haunts) to await developments. We hear that "[d]uring this time the workers (*al-hudhiyyun al-'ummal*) held a number of meetings in their coffeehouses in areas of the capital and its outskirts and they decided on a general strike until the governorate changed the traffic regulations. They delegated their shaykh and some of their senior persons (*akabir*) to talk with the powers-that-be on the subject."[98]

As the morning wore on, tensions began to rise. "Some joined demonstrations but were arrested and taken forcibly to prison."[99] Large numbers of cabmen, according to *Al-Jarida*, then "called out all of those in sympathy with them to fight to assist them against the injustice (*'asf*) of the police." Then "they met in groups and set about striking private cabs and omnibuses and the tram. Then they surrounded the police stations, clamoring and menacing trouble if those who had been imprisoned were not released."[100] There was a large gathering in 'Abd al-'Aziz Street close to Muski police station, "where they waited for the arrival of the tram cars . . . and prevented the passengers from boarding. . . . After that they smashed [a tram car] to pieces and beat the driver and the passengers, young and old, women and children, as if the strike was directed at everyone and not [simply the] police."[101] There were other similar scenes, where cabdrivers directed attacks not against everyone, but against foreign-owned and competing means of transportation, which as we have seen, were backed in 1900 by the specific directives of the colonial state. Near the Ezbekiyya police station, close to the Abu 'Ala Bridge, for example, "they smashed the windows of around 20 cars and omnibuses carrying school children." *Al-Jarida* reported that "they were assisted . . . by a group of rabble and riff-raff (*al-suqa wa al-ra'a'*) who have no work until most of the coffeehouses in 'Abd al-'Aziz Street as well as [those in] the nearest [streets] of Faggala were closed, and some people hurried to their homes."[102] Al-Ahram wrote that "mixed in with [the cabmen] were fanatics who are considered [mere] street clamorers and who strike one another with cudgels."[103]

These so-called fanatics may well have had more political considerations in mind. Antiimperialist sentiment was apparently abroad during the strike. Consider the following letter written by an Englishman:

When the cab strike was on I . . . noticed a European driving in a cab pursued by a number of low class natives. . . . Several shawishes were in the immediate vicinity making a feeble pretence of protecting the cab and a patrol of mounted police with two officers were galloping to the cab's assistance and at that moment were about eighty yards from the cab. An Arab just then hurled a heavy lump of stone which narrowly missed the head of the European in the cab. It was so big that if it had hit him the blow might easily have proved fatal. Any of the foot police could easily have arrested the man. But on the contrary they flagrantly allowed him to escape up a side street so as to avoid the mounted policemen, who, be it noted, had European officers with them. . . . Ten minutes afterwards when the crowd had dispersed, the man who had thrown the stone was talking and laughing with the two shawishes on the very spot where he had committed the outrage.[104]

The incident indicates popular sentiments, unleashed during a transformative time of disturbance, which must have empowered the strikers, scared the occupiers, and to the extent that they knew about them, suggested possibilities to middle-class nationalists.

Meanwhile, "the tumult at the [police] stations continued until 8 P.M., whereupon they attacked the commissioner of Ezbekiyya police station and wrestled him to the ground, and he was only saved from their hands by the force of the mounted police." But, *Al-Jarida* continued, "the government did not seek to treat them with severity; rather it released those imprisoned in the police stations and then called their leaders and their shaykhs to the governorate to agree with his honor the governor to break up the demonstrations."[105] Indeed, after negotiations in the governorate building, four concessions were made. First, some of the officials about whom complaints had been repeatedly raised were to be sacked. Second, horses and livestock with small injuries were not to be forcibly hospitalized but treated by the owner. Third, serious lameness would lead to hospitalization but not the arrest of the driver or the imprisonment of the owner. Fourth, infractions in traffic regulations would not result in the loss of license, but a fine of fifteen piastres. By the following morning, (Friday) many cabmen had returned to work.[106]

If the cabmen had suspected that they would find some support among certain nationalists, they guessed right. This does not mean that any newspaper supported the actual violence, partly because they saw it as undermining the cause of self-government. As *Al-Ahram* wrote, "[W]e regard [the attacks of the cabmen on people] with sorrow, and perhaps [this] affirmed to us that the powers that be . . . wished for chaos. They take it as a pretext for English government over Egyptians."[107] Nonetheless, both *Al-Ahram*, and most of all *Al-Jarida* were ready to detail what they viewed as the legitimate grievances of the cabdrivers. Here is the latter:

> [The coachmen] have a great many complaints about the police. . . . Scarcely can one of them leave the stable before he is taken by surprise by a policeman and he demands his license and number [saying] that he has too many passengers or some other trivial complaint. [The policemen is then] not satisfied with less than 10 piastres [as a fine/bribe] and [so] withdraws his license and number and takes him to the traffic bureau. This is called "the tomb" from which no license returns.[108]

Al-Jarida went on to say that it would take bribery and "weeks and months" to get the license back, during which time "they and their families do not know how they can eat." The cab drivers, it seems, had found sympathizers among those who found their nationalism stronger than their ideas about boorish and backward cabdrivers.[109] The idea was prompted by the sense that here was an urban constituency which might serve nationalist political ends if it could be properly directed. The cabbies' resistance had provided an impetus to this thinking.

It may have come as a surprise to even the cabdrivers themselves, however, that their strike was something of a success. Not only were reprisals—in terms of fines, prison terms, and police action—relatively mild (as far as one can tell from the relative brevity of the few prison terms meted out), but, more importantly, the concessions made on the evening of 18 April were real and became law. Changes corresponding to the promises given were made to the regulations. In a major sign of the defeat of the SPCA, Major Jarvis resigned in disgust. Witness, furthermore, the subsequent complaints of one SPCA supporter: "For a year past . . . since Major Jarvis left, cruelty has become worse, the police do nothing to check it. . . . The police used to examine the backs and look under the collars of animals. They are not allowed to do so anymore. The order was issued last year because a strike of cabmen . . . was feared by reason of their vigilance. When the order was issued, Jarvis resigned."[110] Subsequent pressure from the SPCA and Grey (the British foreign secretary) to tighten the regulations did not alter Gorst's poststrike policy of noninterference. Gorst had to justify the changes to the regulations as satisfactory to Grey (following a parliamentary question) in April 1908.[111] And he seems to have quietly ignored a letter from Malet in December 1908 urging him, in the wake of another parliamentary question, to take action on the matter.[112]

In an important sense, then, and despite their apparent weakness before the strike, the cabmen had scared the English, defeated the SPCA, and won a major victory. The key to the cabbies' success was almost certainly the connection to nationalist politics. It was not that nationalists had engineered the strike action, although no one could be absolutely sure of this and certainly some of the more hysterical elements in the colonial press claimed that they had. But the seriousness with which the major Arabic dailies took the demands of the strikers was a warning to the occupiers that alliances might be quick in the making. Links between nationalists and popular forces, in particular the unpredictable urban "rabble," were to be avoided by the regime at all costs, especially where the colonial state had been hitherto successful in maintaining urban political quiescence. It seems that such strategic reasons, which went to the heart of the British presence in Egypt, weighed sufficiently with Gorst as to override the counterclaims of the SPCA and their friends in the years following the strike. For this reason above all, victory went to the cabdrivers.

Such success unleashed a cycle of protest among crafts and service workers during the following seven weeks. Now that the cabdrivers had blazed a trail and provided a successful model for action, and now that the regime had been seen to back down in the face of popular action, disaffected workers, self-employed, and small masters across the city glimpsed a political opportunity. Instead of damping the fire, the British response had fanned the flames. It is worth quoting the *Gazette*:

The recent strike of cab-drivers, which occasioned so much inconvenience in Cairo, is, it seems, indirectly responsible for unending disturbances and petty annoyances, inasmuch as they have by their action unwittingly established a precedent, and their lead has been followed by every description of artisan or laborer, both European and native. . . . Daily, one hears of some fresh disturbance among employés, who up to the present time have been perfectly contented with their conditions. One day, we wake up to find the streets crowded with bands of ruffianly silk-weavers, who parade the town and molest innocent pedestrians, or damage valuable property; then again, it is printers, who forceably demonstrate their grievances to uninterested passers-by. So the idea has spread, affecting every kind of trade. To-day we are threatened by a strike of bakers.[113]

And this author could have added a string of other trades to his list, in which during the seven weeks following the cab strike, petitions were sent, wage settlements were agreed on, regulations rolled back or enforced, or strikes joined or threatened. By the end of May, mobilizations of varying intensity and provenance had taken place—starting on the day after the cab strike was settled, and listed here in chronological order—among carters, silk weavers, baker's boys, mat makers, omnibus drivers, domestic servants, survey workers, printers, tramway workers, weavers, fishermen, butchers, and bakers. There was another, lesser series of strikes and petitions in October among employees in commercial houses, the automobile drivers (who struck twice), the butchers, and the cabmen. In November, civil servants sent a petition to Gorst requesting higher salaries.[114] This cycle of protest marked the definite appearance of popular mobilization on the national political stage.

The carters, who had undergone the same intervention as the cabmen, were the first to strike after the cabdrivers, and they took their chance on the day following the cabbies' return to work, Saturday 20 April. The *Egyptian Gazette* gave an account of the events under the title "Troubles in Cairo—Serious Disturbances—Military Demonstration":

A serious state of affairs prevails in Cairo and there is a very uneasy feeling prevalent that troubles of a grave nature may break out. So seriously indeed is the situation regarded by the officials that Mr. Matchell, Adviser to the Minister of the Interior, who had left on a journey to Mariout, has had to be recalled to Cairo. The strike of the cabmen, as we announced on Friday, is over, and on Saturday the cabs were plying as usual. But as soon as this strike had been settled the carters began to rise up and a grave series of outrages took place on Saturday, which has alarmed the inhabitants of the Capital, for the movement is not considered to be solely provoked by economical reasons. At 11 A.M. a large mob, consisting of many hundreds of natives, assembled suddenly at the khalig near Darb el-Gamamy and at once began to savagely attack the trams. The mob broke the windows, maltreated the employes of the Tramway company and the passengers: all traffic was stopped and the street blocked. At the same time another huge mob gathered together in the Gouvernorat square. Mansfield Pasha harangued them in Arabic and the mounted police cleared the square. Twenty employes of the Cairo Tramway Company have been injured and forty-three tram cars have been damaged. It is considered that these outrages have been inspired by some well-known persons who want to encourage disorder for their own purposes. There were other outbursts of the mob and at Abou el Ala bridge a crowd assembled. The manifests, who had a threatening attitude, were prevented from doing any harm and the police made some arrests. . . . Egyptian troops were stationed at the police posts.[115]

The carters, living on the edge of subsistence, and having been harassed for several years by the SPCA and police, demonstrated after the model of the cabdrivers in order to try to obtain a relaxation of invasive regulations. Like the cabbies they directed their grievances in part against the tram, which on the one hand competed with those carters who carried passengers, and on the other was symbol of foreign domination. The colonial press reacted to the protests of the poorest and politically most disempowered of the population with something approaching hysteria. The carters were seen as a threatening and savage mob, "among the roughest elements of the populace." Substituting the opinions of a tiny elite for the majority, the *Gazette* spoke further of "the alarm felt generally at these disorders," and of "extraordinarily disquieting rumours . . . afloat at Alexandria . . . [where it was] announced that the troops of the Army of Occupation had had to be called out. The news exerted a very bad effect in the Bourse and considerable nervousness was the result." Colonial opinion, it is important to note, was under the impression that these "outrages" were "not considered to be solely provoked by economical reasons." In other words, the idea was quite widely circulated that someone somewhere was organizing these "ruffians," who otherwise, or so the reasoning probably went, would surely have no capacity for independent action. In many cases, the suspicion fell on nationalists. In some sense this thinking was in part a self-fulfilling prediction. Once the idea was circulated that nationalists were involved, this must have influenced nationalist thinking towards future involvement. This might contribute towards explaining the deepening links between nationalists and cabbies (not to mention other urban trades) in the after-math of the strike. Nationalist involvement can only have inspired more artisans and wageworkers to action when they realized they had support from the middle classes, regardless of whether the original initiative of the cabbies and now the carters, although partially inspired by nationalist sen-timent, had come without direct organizational links to middle-class nationalists.

Other trades which had attracted intervention in recent years on ac-count of health or environmental concerns now glimpsed a chance to alle-viate the resulting burdens. In late 1906, fishermen on various lakes in the delta had been banned from using fine-mesh fishing nets. The ban, which diminished their catch and thus their income, had come at a particularly difficult time for the several hundred fishermen in Matariyya, because, as 138 of them claimed in a mass petition of May 1907, their "possessions in-cluding houses and jewellery and documents and fishing equipment and some boats have been burned" in a recent fire.[116] To make matters worse, they were supposed to continue to pay a fixed monthly tax on their boats. This left fishermen in "intense need" and with "no recourse except mercy and generosity."[117] In May 1907, when various fishermen tried to continue using fine-mesh nets against police directives, clashes erupted between the fishermen and a military detachment that the local police had brought in from Dakrus.[118] In consequence, the commissioner called upon the provin-cial authorities to send out another force, which duly went up by the eve-ning train.[119] At this point, divisions broke out among the fishermen. Those who wanted to obey the regulations were "threatened with capsizing their boats" by those who wanted to use the fine-mesh nets. Those who had been threatened then complained to the police in Matariyya and to the coast-guard. A whole battery of officials then turned up at the scene: the deputy of the province, the commissioner of Dakranis, the bashkatib of the coast guard, various police, and twenty-five soldiers. The deputy "met the strik-ers and gave them a lecture." They were told to return to work and not to prevent others from doing so. Anyone who attacked another would be punished. *Al-Ahram* reported that "the strikers went and discussed the matter and then returned to work."[120]

The strike had been broken because of the disunity of the fishermen and the force with which they had to contend, but the issue remained un-resolved. A few days later the fishermen sent a delegation, forty strong, to Alexandria to seek clemency from the authorities. They requested permis-sion to fish with the fine-mesh nets. They argued that the small fish would not be destroyed because they only sought permission to fish with the fine-mesh nets in a restricted area, and they asserted that they would throw back the small fish which they could not buy or sell.[121] The deputation's requests were rejected. The fishermen, however, did not give up. Another petition of 4 June "under the signatures of the people of Matariyya" complained about the ongoing ban on the use of fine-mesh nets "for [the people are] without means of subsistence."[122] This time some concessions were forthcoming. A Khedivial grant of some 5,000 LE was made to the fishermen in distress, although there was no movement on the regulations. A petition from twenty-five fishermen thanking the government for its "compassion" and "assistance" was quickly sent, although the government was reminded that "a petition had previously [been sent] by them seeking mercy regarding the complaints about what the government decided in 1906 when it made the fishermen [use] wide-mesh nets instead of fine [mesh nets] and requested the examination of their complaints, but until now nothing has been done." This state of affairs now left them in "intense poverty." They argued that wide-mesh nets did not yield enough for them to live; that they had been taxed heavily; that the fire had destroyed the wide-mesh nets; and that they had small-mesh nets, but that these were lying unused because of the regulation. They requested an order permitting the use of fine-mesh nets.[123] When no action was forthcoming, another mass petition was organized. It was stated that "101 Matariyya fishermen . . . say that they did not receive any of the money which his Highness had granted them."[124] They continued as follows:

[B]ecause of their losses and that they now live, along with their families, in shacks of reed which do not protect them from heat or cold and they do not have any money for building from their families. . . . And they complain about the continuation of fishing by the method that the government decided. They request freedom in fishing (*atlaq hurriyatahum fi al-sayyada*) with the [fine] mesh [nets] suitable to their interests. [They also request] that the support money be distributed among all the fishermen equally, each receiving what each deserves for the sake of repairing the necessary [wide-mesh] nets.[125]

The authorities would not be moved and continued to enforce the regulations on fine mesh nets. Those who broke the law were fined or imprisoned or had their licenses withdrawn and equipment confiscated, or all of the above. In the case of Hussayn al-Adib and four others from Daqhaliyya who were caught by the coastal police, they were imprisoned, and fined 22 LE and had their licenses suspended and boats confiscated.[126] Arguably, the key to the fishermen's weakness was their lack of the power of institutional disruption on the one hand, and the absence of links, potential or actual, to middle-class nationalists, on the other.

In the city, the butchers were to enjoy more success in the matter of challenging unwanted government regulations. On 30 May 1907 they went on strike. They opposed an order of the Health Board which meant that livestock stomachs would have to be scraped clean of all skin. This, argued the butchers, reduced the weight of the stomach and therefore the price. It was an unacceptable regulation. The authorities were quick to climb down. "It appeared to the director of the Health Board that their demands were just and he annulled that order and did what they wanted."[127] After this success, the butchers felt sufficiently empowered to threaten a strike to open recently closed livestock markets in early October. They backed up their petition to the interior minister with a deputation to the governorate, a deputation which included a shaykh who may well have been the old shaykh of the *ta'ifa*.[128] The petition is worth printing at length:

> Many of the papers have opposed the rise in the price of meat and all other foodstuffs, and it appears that they lay the blame for this rise on the guild of butchers. But we take issue with such words and [hope] that the proofs that we offer to Your Honor might allow you to judge the truth of our request. We do not doubt that you will afterwards affirm the falseness of the criticisms directed at us.
>
> The livestock market in Upper Egypt has closed following the appearance of the cattle plague, and there are no more than four or five markets open. So it appears from this that demand outstrips supply. There are still just as many purchasers as there were in the past, but the prices of livestock have risen very greatly due to the small number of sellers. It has become impossible for us to acquire meat for 10 piastres. Nonetheless, many of us have contracted to sell to our agents for 9 piastres.
>
> So, we request from your honor a reopening of the old markets, and especially the Upper Egypt [market], without which one cannot provision a big city like Cairo. And if the health agency considers such an opening to constitute general harm then we request that you grant livestock to be transported from Alexandria to Cairo as occurred in past years. And if the livestock is sent in this way under supervision to the capital, following a medical inspection and a report [declaring] it healthy [and free] from disease [then it may be] immediately slaughtered and offered to the public (*jumhur*). In such a way, public health is maintained, and the interests of the *ta'ifa* of butchers with them. For a major injury is now being done to these interests by the special regulations which prevent the import of livestock to Cairo

and by the system of import of foreign livestock, insofar as these livestock are not acceptable unless they are from Serbia and are transported by steamship. Impermissible [at the present time are imports]
from Ottoman ports or the remainder of the Eastern ports.

The butchers explained that such regulations made it easy for those selling
meat in Alexandria, and for a group of small traders who bought meat from
Alexandria and carried it in bags to Cairo, "which damages us and makes
competition with these traders impossible." The butchers went on: "And it
is known that the high prices of the meat—for the reasons we present—
damage the poor of the community (*umma*), and meat more or less becomes only for the rich." If the state of affairs did not change, the butchers
went on, they would have to close their shops, which were under threat of
bankruptcy. The butchers requested the following measures. First, to open
the markets in Upper Egypt. Second, to allow the transport of imported
meat from Alexandria to Cairo. Third, to review the import regulation (into
Alexandria from Ottoman other ports) to make them easier and wider. And
fourth, to prevent individuals from transporting meat from Alexandria to
Cairo.[129] One notes in these demands how a genuinely national politics—
attempts to influence government policy which affected the whole of the
territory of Egypt—was at play in part because of how the end of the guilds
and state building had transformed state/trade relations.

The deputation, petition, and threatened strike were effective. Unlike the fishermen, the butchers were more successful, probably because of
their more strategic urban location. *Al-Ahram* reported that the governor
promised that markets in Upper Egypt would be opened.[130] And al-Fayyum
market was opened within a week of the petition.[131] After less than a month,
new regulations were issued by the Health Board regarding the import of
livestock from outside the land. The import of cattle, sheep, and goats
from healthy countries was permitted after the necessary health checks.
Balkan livestock was now allowed transport to Cairo by train from Alexandria after twenty-four hours under inspection in the port. Syrian and other
livestock was likewise permitted, except that it required forty-eight hours
under supervision.[132]

Strikes and demonstrations were not restricted to those battling unwanted government regulations. During the cycle of protest of spring 1907,
a number of strikes were joined by wageworkers in larger workshops against
masters and employers. As Vatter has shown for late-nineteenth-century
Damascus, such strikes were not restricted to the emerging industrial
proletariat,[133] and Martin's view that relations between journeymen and

masters were still excellent may have been somewhat misleading. Martin himself mentioned the "distant attitude" and superior "external bearing" of the larger masters, and reported that Cairo's silk spinners had attempted to form a syndicate in 1905, "but without success," and without support from middle-class nationalists.[134] But on 20 April 1907, inspired by the success of the mass strike of the cabdrivers just two days before and the success of the carters, several hundred Cairean silk weavers struck work. *Al-Jarida* reported that "the spirit of the strike has spread from the coachmen to the silk weavers and a group of them met yesterday afternoon [20 April], rounded up their colleagues, and roused them to stop work." The *Gazette* reported that "[a]fter the agitation of the cabmen and carters, the weavers have begun to move and on Sunday about 300 of them went on strike. They did not, however, commit any outrages. . . . These men demand an increase in wages."[135] Such weavers were at a greater social distance from their employers because of the nature of the relations of production, and as a large group they could probably coordinate and communicate more effectively than those fragmented into smaller workshops. But the weavers soon confronted a police detachment sent from Bab Sha'riyya police station. According to *Al-Jarida*, it was likely that the owners (*ashab al-mal*) would answer their demands.[136] Whatever the outcome, the authorities meted out major punishments: fourteen silk-weavers were sentenced to ten days in prison, and each paid a massive fine of 12 LE, equivalent to four to eight months pay.[137]

Within a week, another strike had broken out, this time among Cairo's mat makers. *Al-Jarida* reported a "New Strike" (*i'tisab jadid*) on 27 April 1907: "This morning many of the workers (*'ummal*) of the mat makers (*ta'ifat al-husriyya*) struck work and met in Manshiyya Square." It soon became known that the workers were planning to attack the owners of some of the mat-making workshops, who must have taken such a possibility seriously, as they then "sent a petition to his honor the *hukmdar* today, demanding that he take the necessary precautionary measures to prevent the strikers from attacking them tomorrow."[138] Unfortunately, it is unclear whether punishments or wage increases (or both) resulted. Another strike attempt among weavers about a month later was crushed by police coercion. *Al-Ahram* reported on 22 May that "14 weavers met and went to the workshop of Hassan 'Ali al-Sawwaf in Bulaq and they assaulted him and his workers with the intention of forcing them to agree with them on a strike. So policemen arrested them and sent them for a summary hearing for sentencing."[139] It would appear that journeymen and workers were less successful against their masters than cabdrivers and carters had been in attempting to change government regulations. Even though there was no formal law on strikes, strikers found themselves punished, sometimes heavily. Perhaps the colonial state was so sensitive toward labor unrest, which took on the appearance of working-class protest in the modular Marxist sense, that moves against it were made without concessions of any kind. Workers were heavily constrained by their pressing need for a livelihood to survive, and the existence of a reserve army of underemployed ready to take their jobs. Probably just as important was that such workers had few powers of institutional disruption—at least in comparison with carters, cabbies, and butchers—for weavers and mat makers could only paralyze workshops which provided goods mostly in small quantities and primarily for subaltern groups.

The Making of an Alliance

Middle-class nationalists, although often (but not always) sympathetic, were not involved in organizing the strikes and demonstrations of spring 1907. Indeed, even the radical nationalist leadership, in the shape of Mustafa Kamil (1874–1908), educated in Cairo Law School and one of the first prominent patriotic Egyptians to demand an immediate end to the British occupation, was not particularly interested in forging an alliance with popular groups prior to 1907. But just as Trotsky was heavily influenced by the more or less autonomous actions of the workers' soviets in Russia in 1905, so were nationalist intellectuals, searching for some part of the people to represent in their struggle against the British, impressed by the possibilities of crafts and service workers' activism in Egypt in 1907. Thus it was only in the autumn of 1907, after the cycle of protest, that middle-class nationalists formed political parties, a new vehicle of political engagement, of course, which sought support among a potentially popular membership of one kind or another. And it was precisely during 1907 and afterwards, as Zachary Lockman has persuasively argued, that various intelligentsia shifted from accusing the masses of being a backward and unhealthy rabble, and treating them at least in some measure as if they had a political role to play in the new Egyptian nation—albeit under middle-class leadership and tutelage.[140] These ideological and political changes were given heavy impetus by the bust of the second half of 1907, when the nationalist camp in the ruling class reaped support from those who lost out.

It did not take long for direct organizational links to be made between nationalists and urban workers, in spite of British concessions which had been designed precisely to avoid this eventuality. The cabdrivers at least, themselves empowered by their own energizing political education in how to lobby the state and mobilize their grievances en masse, appear to have been linked to middle-class nationalists by the autumn of 1907. For, in early October 1907, with direct nationalist support, they moved proactively to engage with the threat posed by the arrival of licensed motor taxis in Cairo. The petition they now sent to the Khedivial Diwan proudly listed all their names and was stamped with their seals. A certain Badawi Shafa'i led the protest, "complaining about the arrival of about 500 automobiles by the Companies and the operation of nearly half of them now in Cairo," which would mean a loss of work for the cabmen.[141] Whether or not one writer in the *Egyptian Gazette* thought that he had "seldom hear[d] anything more absurd" than the cabmen's proposal,[142] the authorities could not be so dismissive, particularly when the initiative was then taken up by nationalist supporters of Mustafa Kamil. It was said in the florid language of the *Gazette* that "the agitators and opponents of the Occupation are encouraging the arbaghis to make a demonstration [regarding the issue of motor taxis] on November 9, the anniversary of King Edward's birthday."[143] A more explicit nationalist signal could hardly be sent. Meetings were then held between the heads and owners of the cabs and the *hukmdar*. The authorities again conceded ground even in this case, stating that it was "impossible not to licence automobiles as cabs," "but it was possible to license a limited number in order that their presence did not damage the cabmen."[144] This apparently persuaded the carriage drivers, who left the negotiations agreeing that they would not strike. They must have been impressed by their own political clout, particularly because as far as is known, this was the very first time that any craft or service trade had attempted to change the terms of restructuring by limiting competition directly in a way which clashed openly with the interests of expansionist capitalism. It was a dramatic demand and was successful because it threatened the British with an alliance between middle and lower classes.

Political mobilization and nationalist politics then moved hand in hand. It was said that "innumerable" cabs followed the funeral procession of Mustafa Kamil in February 1908.[145] More suggestive was the participation of the cabdrivers in a memorial procession held for Mustafa Kamil that March:

> A huge procession in honour of the memory of the late Mustapha Pasha Kamel left the offices of the "Lewa" yesterday at 1 PM. . . . It would appear that the cab drivers of Cairo are among those most smitten by the loss of the Nationalistic leader, for the majority of

them shrouded their lamps in crape and flew streamers of the same material from their whips. . . . The sight of arabeahs turned into mourning coaches, not only those in the procession, but those also plying for trade in the streets, did much we admit, to foster the idea, strive how one might against it, of a well-engineered display. The amount of material allotted to each driver was so unmistakeably the same, the very manner in which the material had been utilized was so evidently as "per orders received" that it was hard to keep one's thoughts from wandering into fields of speculation regarding the formation of the procession itself.[146]

If the cabdrivers were now involved somewhat more closely with the nationalists, this made sense in as much as this procession took place almost directly after Muhammad Farid had taken over leadership of the National Party (al-Hizb al-Watani), and thus this may have been one of Farid's earliest moves to build a base among the urban masses.

A syndicate (a mutual protection society) for coachmen appears to have been formed in the autumn of 1909, but may only have been short-lived. The extent of nationalist involvement is unclear. The syndicate mixed wageworkers with small employers and masters. Its goals were apparently above all to revise tariffs, limit fines, and reduce the level of bakhshish paid to the police. From the barest outline which Vallet gives, it would seem that the syndicate achieved its goals and then dissolved. Apparently, tariffs were revised favorably on the one hand, and the chief of the Cairo police, against whom many complaints had been raised, was replaced.[147] If such facts can be trusted, it would seem that again the cabbies got their way.

It was during and after 1907, furthermore, that artisanal education with nationalist involvement really got underway. By 1910 there were eight "people's night schools" in Cairo, set up by members of the Nationalist Party, which taught literacy, numeracy, history, geography, and one or two other subjects. As Beinin and Lockman noted, party activists gave lectures which "exalted the virtues of the Arab race and the advantages of free government."[148] Industrial schools in al-Fayum and Bani Suwaif were completed from 1907 to 1909 and were teaching 540 pupils between them by 1911. The Coptic school in Faggala was provided with machines and completely reorganized after 1907. The school founded on the initiative of the Coptic Patriarchate in Qulali, Bulaq, was completed and fitted by 1908 and trained 120 boys in its industrial section. In February 1908 a fairly large private industrial school (for 300 pupils), the Muhammad Ali school, was inaugurated by his His Highness the Khedive, with much pomp and ceremony and a certain amount of newspaper coverage. The school was not only patronized by the khedive but had obtained a government grant of 6,900 LE. Private industrial and agricultural schools were founded, built, and started operations in Damanhur, Luxor, and Tukh between 1908 and 1910 and two other similar schools in Suhaj and Nag Hammadi were completed before 1914.

Government support following the establishment of the Department for Industrial Education was also forthcoming. Direct government funding of around 100,000 LE a year was made available after 1907, while 5 percent of one of the provincial land taxes was earmarked for education, some of which was supposed to be used for funding and subsidizing industrial education. The government industrial school in Mansura doubled in size between 1907 and 1910, some model workshops being added along with further teaching in ironwork, painting, and weaving. Both the Asyut and the Bulaq government model workshops admitted more pupils during these years and evening classes for artisans were founded at Bulaq. By 1910 there were about one thousand pupils being taught in the government schools. The government also supported private intitiatives by providing land and occasional subsidies grants of around 1,000 LE per year to those private schools which agreed to inspection, and by putting the "services of the administration at the disposal of local committees," choosing sites, studying conditions, making plans, preparing designs for machines, overseeing their installation, choosing personnel, and furnishing detailed teaching programs.[149] In October 1909, furthermore, a bureau started translating teaching manuals from French and English into Arabic and printing them for the use of the new institutions.

However, the greater part of the funding, organization, and actual training came from private intervention colored by nationalism. As Wells wrote, "Of all the characteristics of this rapid development of technical instruction, one of the most striking is the willingness that has led the people of the provinces to respond by voluntary subscriptions, to the call that had been made in view of aiding the movement." Wells mentioned 58,500 LE donated for industrial and schools in Qena, Bani Suwaif, Qaliubiya, Girga, and Bahira and numerous land donations producing an annual revenue of 3,700 LE. From Damanhur alone, came 20,000 LE, a "magnificient gift" from Prince Hussain. Interestingly enough, not all such contributions came from on high. The donkey drivers apparently contributed their own "humble offering" to the 2,500 LE raised in Luxor.[150] As a result, by 1910, there were over two thousand pupils taught in private industrial schools, and thus more than three thousand overall, in about seventeen schools up and down the country. This compared to the several hundred under instruction in early 1906. Around five hundred artisans were graduating every year by 1911.

Such artisanal education did not leave the terms of crafts restructuring untouched. An article published in *Al-Muqtataf* in 1912 noted that "comparing previous agricultural and industrial exhibitions—or [at least] last February's and this one—one sees great progress in industry due to the greater spread of industrial schools and their progress and the general success of this country in increasing wealth."[151] Certainly, as noted in the previous chapter, Sidney Wells and his team in 1910 related the use of more developed machinery in various locations to the existence of industrial schools there, notably among weavers in Abu Tij, where the industrial school of Sulayman Pasha taught weaving, among other things.[152] "If we think to what has been done in a very short space of time," wrote Wells, "there is reason to hope that the development . . . will contribute much to increase the prosperity of the country, and the happiness and well-being of its inhabitants."[153] Modest "factor accumulation" among certain artisans in various trades in various parts of the country was one result of such projects, as outside investment in training, by providing a surplus which would not otherwise have been available within the terms of the self-exploitation and cheap labor predicament. Another was that crafts workers, at one level, were being interpellated as nationals with a real role to play in the economy.

Finally, in addition to seeking a constituency amongst the cabdrivers and organizing artisanal education, in early 1909, middle-class nationalists now sponsored the establishment of the first trade union in Egypt for Egyptians, the Manual Trades Workers' Union (*Niqabat 'Ummal al-Sana'i' al-Yadawiyya*), based in Bulaq. "Most [of its members]," wrote Beinin and Lockman, "were employed in small workshops or were independent artisans."[154] Such crafts and service workers, alongside others from cigarette factories and the railway, more than three thousand strong by 1912, paid regular monthly dues in order to belong to what was above all a mutual aid society providing cash assistance to the sick and unemployed, but also medical care, legal advice, libraries, and lectures. Thus, almost twenty years after the official abandonment of the guilds, and closer to a century after guilds had been co-opted and undermined by dynasty building, crafts and service workers in alliance with middle-class nationalists, and in the wake of strike action under new conditions, started to forge new forms of mutual protection and organization.

Conclusion

The protests, strikes and demonstrations of spring 1907, expressing the predicament of thousands of crafts and service workers forced to restructure, marked the definitive appearance of popular mobilization on the stage of national politics in Egypt. The capture of the state by colonialism, the concentration and centralization of state power which accompanied the end of the guilds, the challenge of the nationalist middle classes and their alliance with the people, and the acute pressures of restructuring combined to make mass action by popular groups a new, if still tentative, feature of the emerging political field prior to the First World War.

But how far had crafts and service workers really changed the terms of restructuring by their activism? New forms of organization—unions and syndicates—remained few and far between, relatively weak, and subject to the vagaries of middle-class nationalist support. Collective action remained risky, frequently unsuccessful, and vulnerable in the face of colonial repression. Crafts and service workers scored one or two notable successes where they threatened an alliance with middle-class nationalism: at these points the colonial state was forced to make some adjustments in order to neutralize an emerging threat to its position. Further, the establishment of political parties did mean an institutionalization, albeit still tentative and subject to reversal, of a connection between subaltern interests and elite politicians. But a link to nationalist political activism did not institutionalize anything close to citizenship or democracy within the autocratic colonial state—no binding consultation, no definition of subjects as citizens (either in breadth or depth), no clear protections against the arbitrary actions of the state, and still less any gains regarding redistribution or welfare. There was no guarantee that slight gains made would not be rolled back with the changing times, particularly as economic inequality continued to grow with world economic integration. Indeed, tax cuts in the 1880s and early 1890s, albeit partially achieved by mobilization and although benefitting crafts workers in the short term, came at the political cost of undermining claims to citizenship by colonial subjects.

Further, the impact of artisanal education should not be exaggerated. Wells's prewar optimism was tinged with colonial self-congratulation. Schools were in fact educating only a tiny fraction of the expanding artisanal population, almost half a million strong according to the 1917 census. Training remained patchy by region and by trade. Wells himself, perhaps disillusioned by the war, appears to have changed his views by 1917, and wrote a fairly damning report in that year on the state of artisanal education. He argued that four of the five biggest provinces had no trades school at all; that the governorate of Damietta, which was "almost wholly industrial, . . . is without any form of industrial education." He claimed that many large and important manual trades had "not yet been touched by Trades Schools."

For example, the building trades, he claimed, which consisted of ninety to one hundred thousand workers had no means of industrial training. As for weaving, he wrote that Cairo and Qaliub were the centers of large and important weaving work, "yet there is no provision for school training in the trade." Further, "the bazaars of Cairo are full of workers in jewellery, precious metals, ornamental metal work, etc., all of which could be materially developed by the technical training of Trades Schools." And, "the same is true of the important manual industries of basket-making, mat-making, pottery and Assiut shawls."[155] William Stewart, a British teacher in the Cairo School of Arts and Crafts from 1912 onwards, suggested that even of those who were trained, many did not go into business themselves, but sought posts in teaching or in government service. This was because some of the trainees in the higher schools were members of the *afandiya* who "disliked handwork" and "felt that they had been raised above the workman's standard, and it was beneath their dignity to handle tools." He went on to say, "I have long since come to the conclusion that it is useless to train youths of this class as craftsmen."[156] In the light of this, it would appear that a government report of 1917 was too sanguine, not to mention ambiguous on the meaning of the word "industry," where it declared that "considerable attention has recently been given [by the government] to the question of Egyptian industries and a good deal has been done by the Department of Technical, Industrial and Commercial Education to prepare the way for industrial developments."[157] In fact, there were drastic limits on artisanal education in Egypt until (and after) the First World War. Most crafts workers, not to mention service workers, remained untouched, and thus remained without the means to transform themselves into the particular kind of modern, literate, numerate, trained artisans sought by the nationalist bourgeoisie. In other words, and apparently paradoxically, this nationalist project defined actually existing artisans as backward and unmodern (rather than as modern national subjects), a powerful form of exclusion in an age seeking progress, strength, and independence.

Further, it seems unlikely that labor, protesting for higher wages in the larger workshops, changed the terms of its exploitation through collective action in a significant way during these years. It was unable to raise its price and protect itself in a way which might have forced employers to find more productivity-raising, as opposed to labor-squeezing, strategies of production. Workers continued to work for what were most likely ever cheaper wages in real terms. Small proprietors, masters, and the self-employed continued to both self-exploit and to squeeze their factors of production, from horses to humans, where collective protective institutions could not be forged.

The fragility of gains was made clear when martial law was imposed by the British at the outbreak of the First World War, and the door of political opportunity was slammed shut. Under such conditions, nationalist activism was drastically curtailed, as were worker protest, collective organization, and protest. Even numbers enrolled in the MTWU were dramatically reduced between 1912 and 1919.[158] Once again, in the face of an autonomous colonial state, crafts and service workers were left to survive through restructuring with few resources and allies, and little in the way of collective institutions to defend and mobilize their interests. Here subaltern groups had little chance and almost no formal mechanism for influencing government policy, whether to modify heavy-handed intervention, or to induce intervention to modify the terms of restructuring, or to regulate local exploiters—from contractors to larger masters, and from creditors to merchants. Under such conditions, crafts and service workers had little choice but to compete, self-exploit, and squeeze their labor, for in spite of the efforts of workers, these were the harsh terms of survival in the social order that had emerged by 1914.

Conclusion

This book has attempted to give the first systematic treatment of political and economic transformation among crafts and service workers in Egypt during the half-century or so preceding the First World War. In search of a popular history outside the factory gates and in pursuit of puzzles surrounding unevenness under capitalism, the preceding pages have examined restructuring, the disaggregation of the guilds, forms of collective assertion, and the growth of new kinds of formal and informal organization in Egypt during years of world economic integration, local state building, and colonial rule.

Restructuring

Contrary to a persistent conventional wisdom in which traditional crafts are perpetually in decline or stagnant, I have argued that crafts and service workers increasingly engaged in forms of restructuring in order to pursue their livelihoods as the nineteenth century lengthened, particularly after the cotton boom of the early 1860s, and with growing intensity during the investment boom of 1897 to 1907. The impact of imports, investment, and changing consumption tastes put tremendous pressure on crafts and service workers, eroding and often rendering impossible older ways of making of a living. Crafts and service workers were neither simply destroyed nor passive, but actively restructured their work, effecting a far-reaching transformation in trades, products, and relations and means of production in order to survive. In contrast to the emphasis of authors such as Martin on stasis and continuity, there was hardly a trade in Egypt by 1914 which had not been affected by restructuring. For example, one of the commonest urban occupations of midcentury, water carrying, was either transformed or largely nonexistent by the First World War. In Cairo, water carriers from the Nile either became local distributors from public fountains using not

191

water skins but tanks on wheels, adapted to sell water, sherbet, or tamarind on the streets, or found entirely new occupations. Likewise, fewer and fewer shoemakers made slippers in older styles, and where such production continued, it was on the basis of new tourist demands for the faux traditional, and cobblers substituted cheaper imports, such as plastic, for more expensive leather. More importantly, where imported shoes remained expensive, shoemakers diversified in their thousands to produce and repair shoes in European styles, customized to taste. Tailors, seamstresses, furniture makers, and construction workers in the tens of thousands thoroughly transformed their products in order to tap new demands for European styles. Masons, for example, started to dress stones in the Italian fashion and tailors now sewed European-style suits and shirts. Moreover, some of the commonest urban trades in Egypt by 1914, such as cabdriving and carting, were completely new. These trades, which were ubiquitous in the newly paved streets of Egypt's cities by 1914, did not exist at all during the first decades of the nineteenth century. Crafts and service workers tapped markets where demand was weak, fluctuating, and unstandardized, a market structure which protected them to some extent from large-scale and capital intensive investment and production, which was unprofitable under these conditions.

Crafts and service workers not only took up new occupations or provided new or adapted goods and services. In the context of world economic integration and the spread of market relations, as competition intensified, and as small masters and others sought ways to reduce costs, new inputs were used, tools were transformed, and relations of production constructed anew. Larger workshops were put together by those seeking to rationalize production, such as in silk weaving. Where employers or clients sought the completion of large or complex tasks and attempted to rid themselves of the costs of direct control of the workforce, such as in construction, contracting and subcontracting became far more extensive. Overheads and labor costs were driven down through the extension of putting-out networks in rural areas and the widespread employment of women and children, especially in the textile trades. Masters and self-employed migrated to find cheaper premises in poorer and low-rent parts of cities. Crafts workers also obtained cheaper working capital by seeking out inexpensive raw materials, often produced by large-scale industry: dyers started to use German synthetic indigo after the turn of the century; metal workers imported sheet metal from Birmingham; weavers, Manchester yarns; cab makers, British varnish and so on. As I have demonstrated, almost every crafts and service trade in Egypt relied on one cheap import or another to lower production costs by 1914. A measure of this can be taken from how much such enterprises suffered when raw material supplies from abroad were diminished with the advent of World War One. In a number of cases, productivity was raised by the piecemeal introduction of new tools and equipment. The hand looms of Cairo were more developed than those used elsewhere in Egypt, metal workers introduced new kinds of lathes, and so on.

The drive for cheap production also involved reductions in the costs of skilled and unskilled labor. I have argued that in the case of those own-ing some means of production—skills in a trade, tools and equipment, or premises—competition was such that self-exploitation, whereby masters lowered rates to the extent that little profit accrued, was the result. Where the guilds were no longer acting in a systematic way to protect the monopo-lies or customary privileges of masters, and where local subjects encountered competition from migrant southern Europeans, cutthroat competition forced many masters to lower rates such that they were only able to reproduce their existing capital and earn a minimum income. Likewise, masters and others squeezed the labor they controlled, lengthening hours, lowering wages, and diminishing health and safety at work in order to extract ab-solute surplus value from exploited workers—men, women, and children. Where labor was cheap and abundant because of population expansion and unequal world economic integration, and largely unprotected by social legislation, guilds, unions, or syndicates, workers, scattered in multiple sites, were unable to robustly or consistently protect themselves against these employment practices. Contrary to Marxian theory, then, exploitation was not about the accumulation of relative surplus value by capitalists at the ex-pense of wage labour, but, under conditions of authoritarian colonial rule, involved self-exploitation and labor squeezing.

Restructuring meant that crafts and service workers were not marginal to Egypt's economy by the early 1900s. Instead they continued to deliver a considerable range of cheap goods and services to Egypt's population, rich and poor: European-style suits and shoes, furniture, painting and decorat-ing, construction work, cloth making, dyeing, butchery, patisserie, bakery, milling, machining, jewellery, tourist trinkets, cab rides, goods transport, ironing, and so on. Indeed the number and variety of goods and services delivered by crafts and service workers appears to have been expanding over time. Such trades continued to provide employment to the majority of the urban population. As we have seen, the overwhelming majority of those listed in the 1907 census as employed in industry—perhaps 97 to 98 percent—worked in small units of production. There were more carters and cabdrivers in Egypt in 1907 than there were employees of the entire national railway system. The proportion of the population employed in small-scale production appears to have increased in the early twentieth century. Adaptation to changing times meant that by 1914, the Egyptian economy, although dominated by large-scale capital accumulation, could hardly function without its numerous small-scale and largely unmechanized producers, as the paralysis of Cairo following the cab strike of 1907 showed. Indeed, those who could not afford European products, because of asymmetrical world economic integration made more unequal by imperialism, had little choice but to purchase the products and services of restructured crafts and service trades.

Lastly, there is no satisfactory basis for the notion that crafts and service trades, for all their vulnerability, were inefficient or wasteful. On the contrary, restructuring stretched meagre resources—equipment, skills, livestock, and hands—to the limit.

The Guilds

This book has presented an original account of the disaggregation and disappearance of the guilds in Egypt. Against older conventional views, I have rejected the idea that the end of the guilds was a simple matter of the decline and destruction of traditional crafts and trades. Instead, guild demise had far more to do with a restructuring which involved the growth of new trades and the transformation of old. Against more recent work, I have shown that state centralization, an important feature of guild demise, was partly driven by protests and petitions emanating from the guilds themselves and was not simply the top-down creation of modernizing elites. And against revisionism, which claims that the guilds wielded substantial corporate autonomy, protected livelihoods, and acted as important vehicles for popular protest as late as the 1880s, I have argued that the corporate guilds were disaggregated and undermined throughout the century. During the eighteenth century it is probable that guilds protected livelihoods, formed meaningful communities, and acted as vehicles for collective protest. However, by the 1870s, guilds did not strongly protect the livelihoods of their members through meaningful monopolies, and nor did they act as significant vehicles for collective protest. Their leaderships were coopted for fiscal and regulatory purposes by Mehmet Ali and Isma'il's dynasty-building projects. Their local autonomies based on customary law were eroded by bureaucratization. Their monopolies and privileges were ignored by the government, except in fiscal matters, and undermined by restructuring, growing competition associated with world economic integration, new patterns of investment, and the presence of nonguild migrant labor from southern Europe.

Collective assertion tended to emerge in spite of the transformed guilds, not because of them. Restructuring and state building set guild leaderships, stronger masters, and contractors against self-employed and journeymen in matters of taxation, dues, contracting, links to merchants, and wage rates. The growth of new trades, the employment of women, putting-out systems, and the admission of numerous new members, often rural-urban migrants, fragmented and in many cases undermined guild communities. Petitions and protests, therefore, were not signed or joined by guilds acting collectively as corporate units. Such petitions are practically nonexistent. Instead, guild members, whether groups drawn from the rank and file, or groups drawn from the leadership, petitioned the state, often against one another. New avenues of participation represented by state regulations and intervention, electoral practices, and discourses of citizenship, far from helping to cement the guilds, operated to blow these venerable institutions apart. Petitions came from subguild groups, or from those within the guild building extraguild networks, including allies from outside the guild. These new informal networks crosscut and undermined the guilds from within and without. This explains why there were no protests when the guilds were abandoned by the government in 1890. According to Martin, indeed, guild members in the early 1900s tended to remember the guilds negatively. Once the guilds were officially abandoned as units of taxation and regulation, ongoing processes of restructuring worked to break down older guild boundaries and submerge guild practices. New organizations now appeared in place of the guilds. On the one hand there were new informal networks, cobbled together without official sanction and often in subversion of state regulation. On the other hand, the first syndicates and unions in Egypt were forged in 1908 and 1909 after the protests of 1907. In my analysis, these new organizations, both informal and formal, were not only the creation of nationalist middle classes, or indeed of a new wage-earning working class, but were also the extension of informal organizing and collective assertion by crafts and service workers which had been developing since the 1860s.

Collective Assertion

With the exception of the important work of Juan Cole, very little has been written about petitions, protests, and strikes in Egypt by crafts and service workers, who are too often relegated to an inert mire of backwardness and tradition. By taking up this subject, this book has aimed to show that this lacuna in the historiography is not justified by the reality of widespread and diverse forms of collective assertion by artisans and others throughout the period. Building on Cole's study, and in support of his claim that the social origins of the constitutionalist and patriotic Urabi rebellion ran surprisingly deep, I have attempted to show that constitutionalism and citizenship in practice and discourse had a real presence among lowly urban workers by the 1870s. In petitions from the 1860s and 1870s, appeals to custom or the mercy of a just ruler were often overlaid or supplanted by appeals to bureaucratic regulations, the rule of law, the rights and dues of subjects, and democratic electoral practices within the guilds. In these ways crafts workers and others, forging new networks, collectively asserted themselves against the pressures of restructuring, taxation, forced labor, and unwanted regulations. They were pushing at the door of the constitutional concessions made by Ismail to a rising group of Egyptian-born provincial notables and newly educated elites, and appropriating recently authorized discourses for their own struggles. Crafts workers and others also made effective use of older discourses, appealing to the mercy and justice of the compassionate ruler. Perhaps their single strongest weapon prior to the British invasion, however, was not a matter of claim making at all, but one of quietly forging local alliances with guild shaykhs-cum-tax collectors, alliances which sheltered thousands of crafts workers from Ismail and the European debt commission's extortionate tax raising.

As I have argued, the British abandoned the guilds and the electoral practices associated with them and diminished urban workers' political mobilization with tax remission. After the British invasion of 1882, the provincial notables shed their fragile nationalism and constitutionalism and allied themselves with the new colonial state which ploughed tax revenue into irrigation. These changes demobilized the urban workforce during the 1890s. The subsequent intensification of the pressures of restructuring during the investment boom of 1897 to 1907 and various heavy-handed regulative interventions by the colonial state in the early 1900s worked to change this situation, particularly as a rising middle class, the *afandiya*, started to mount a nationalist challenge to the colonial state. After the Dinshaway incident of 1906, nationalist middle classes began to make common cause with popular groups for the first time. The resulting political opportunity was seized by crafts and service workers in spring 1907, when they joined a hitherto historiographically invisible six weeks of strikes, demonstrations, and protests. This round of collective assertion, which went ahead with some ideological but little direct organizational support from middle-class nationalism, drew certain regulative and remunerative gains for a number of trades. It also drove middle-class nationalists to take the people seriously in their struggle against the British, and inspired nationalists to try to forge more extensive organizational links with popular groups, who in turn were inspired by some early gains. Bourgeoise nationalists, who were just as likely to disparage cabdrivers as representing a more primitive stage of civilisation as to support their cause as legitimate national political subjects, now had reason to rethink the former position as a result of the self-organised mobilization of the cabdrivers themselves. The formation of political parties followed in autumn 1907 and after, as did further nationalist support for artisanal night schools and education and the first syndicates and unions. Thus 1907 marked the beginnings of a real, if still tentative, alliance between middle-classes and urban workers. Nationalism was thus impacted and tranformed to some extent by popular protest; it was not simply bourgeois or elite based, as so many have averred.

This treatment of collective assertion among crafts and service workers is intended, finally, to put into perspective the growth of a labor movement joined by wageworkers in large, usually foreign-owned units of production, in the context of a historiography which has rarely seen beyond it. I have shown that protests by workers in factories did not have some special role in the vanguard of popular protest and the emergence of mass politics in Egypt. Crafts and service workers were not somehow tied to a backward social consciousness which prevented them from mobilizing and protesting in support of their interests. Instead, as this work has argued, they were heavily involved in popular protest. The point is not to disparage the important protests of factory workers, but to argue that the collective actions of those inside and outside of factories were of complementary importance, reinforced each other, and responded to similar political opportunities. Crafts and service workers were partly inspired by the collective action of wageworkers in large-scale industry, who had struck prior to the spring of 1907. Yet, the mass strikes (outside of Port Said), by Egyptian wageworkers generally took place after spring 1907, coming among tram and railway workers in 1908 and later,[1] and thus may have been inspired to some extent by the protests of crafts and service workers. The idea, then, is to try to link artisanal protests in a coeval, nondevelopmentalist, and noneconomistic way to protests by other popular groups. Both industrial workers and crafts and service workers inhabited similar social and political universes and played important roles in the emergence of popular mobilization and the rise of nationalism in the early 1900s in Egypt.

Unevenness under Capitalism

Addressing larger debates about the uneven distribution of relations of production and exchange under capitalism and forms of work and struggle outside the factory gates, this book is written against the thesis that modernization or the growth of capitalism is linear or unidirectional. Restructuring did not involve a simple progression towards either a factory model of production or the establishment of purely capitalist relations of production and exchange, narrowly defined. The book has also given what I hope is a convincing rejection of dual-economy thinking, or of models which depend on the articulation of modes of production. Crafts and service workers were not in some fundamentally Other ontological, epistemological, or evolutionary space, whether Oriental, backward, traditional, or precapitalist. Orientalism tried to capture what was presumed to be ancient and about to be destroyed: the phantasmagorical Cairo of the "Thousand and One Nights." Linear modernization theorists and developmentalists assigned crafts and guilds to a previous era and assumed their torpor and collapse. Dual-economy thinkers and modes of production theorists merely permitted largely unchanged traditional or precapitalist crafts and guilds a role in modern times while working out ways to link them to modernity, which deprived them of all agency, in order to preserve preestablished Eurocentric principles regarding the functioning of modernity or capitalism. All these models fail to capture the far-reaching transformation, the broad swathe of adaptation, and the seizing of opportunities which crafts and service workers undertook on their own account in order to forge livelihoods in dense interaction with changing conditions. These models also fail to take account of the fact that the unfolding shape and dynamics of the Egyptian economy, polity, and even the world economy at large owed something to the political and economic relations of the majority of its economically active population. Crafts and service workers were not just a residuum, something left over on the margins of modern times, outside of history. Instead they worked and protested within a larger political economy; they were integral to the construction of the modern. They were part of the making of a broader unevenness under capitalism.

The ongoing riddle of how capitalism can be so diverse, both among the colonizer and the colonized, and yet retain an overall unity is not solved here. Nonetheless I have argued that in order to understand the reproduction and distribution of the particular relations of production and exchange involved in this study—restructuring, self-exploitation, labor squeezing, and labor-intensive accumulation—distinct and partially contingent political, economic, and social factors have to be taken into account. In other words, transformation and change is not decided in advance, and does not proceed according to a telos. The idea is emphatically not that there is a universal or essential capitalism, for which various exceptions are made, say, in the periphery. On the contrary, my assumption is that capitalism as a whole is heavily inflected by political and social factors. In Egypt, the growth of market relations in general was important, as well as a specific market structure, related to the form of world economic integration, in which large areas of demand were fluctuating, weak, and unstandardized. The relatively high price of machines and technology, especially as compared to relatively cheap price of labor, were also important. I have also put special emphasis on the politics of the labor process, which helped produce self-exploitation and labor squeezing. The lack of robust collective institutions such as guilds, syndicates, or unions, the absence of social legislation by the colonial state, and the difficulties attendant on successful collective assertion where relatively weak alliances were made with middle classes who were relatively weak themselves, enfeebled masters in their search for inputs and markets, and weakened journeymen in their attempts to escape the exploitative effects of labor squeezing. The prevalence of self-exploitation left little capital over for productivity-raising mechanization, and the predominance of labor squeezing meant that where accumulation did take place, the cheap price of labor made mechanization less likely, and labor-intensive accumulation, rather than productivity-raising mechanization, was selected. The upshot was that significant factor accumulation did not take place among crafts and service workers, while low wages contributed to the ongoing weakness of the mass market, which in turn diminished opportunities for large-scale investment. All these factors went into the making of the particular relations of production and exchange encountered here, and helped forge the overall structure of the Egyptian economy. The most striking element in all this is the way in which workers' political weakness, linked ultimately to colonial rule, reproduced forms of economic weakness and vulnerability.

Popular History

I return in closing to the question of the popular history of the colonized world. The idea has been to demonstrate the possibility of a post-Marxist popular history which neither reduces social lives to language games, nor entangles colonial subjects in a seamless Foucauldian web of dispersed and internalized power relations. I have therefore tried to give concentrations and asymmetries of power and resources their due. Livelihoods were constantly destroyed by world economic integration. Self-strengthening represented an assault on the bodies and economic surplus of the urban working population. Colonial rule intensified world economic integration, wiped away constitutionalist gains, ignored emerging pressures for social reform, and unleashed selective and heavy-handed regulative interventions among, in particular, service workers. Further, in spite of vigorous restructuring, there is little evidence of the economic trickle-down championed by neo-classical economic theory, even at a time when Egypt was regarded by colonial elites as an "El Dorado." Macrological transformation flung crafts and service workers into an insecure and largely unprotected battle for survival against debt and poverty. The workers' political weakness meant there was to be no substantial escape from self-exploitation and labor squeezing.

Contrary to the claims of modernization theory and elitist strands in poststructuralism, however, this study has attempted to demonstrate the recoverability and the irreducibility of popular agency, even in this harsh context. The popular was by no means monolithic. Instead it was fractured, divided, and complex. Yet at no point in this recounting of guild demise, restructuring, and new forms of craft organization has it been possible to dispense with grassroots adaptation and protest in the analysis of historical outcomes. Power was never uncontested where it tried to reshape the social relations of the mass of the population. This contestation had an impact. The guilds, for example, were not abolished simply because elites sought this outcome, but because petitioning from within the guilds had both dragged the state into previously more autonomous guild affairs, and because resistance to taxation from below led elites to seek to abolish an institution that from their point of view had become fiscally ineffective. The guilds were further broken and bypassed by new forms of restructuring, collective assertion, and informal organization. New entrants and participants changed the overall system by their action. Even where elites thought up elaborate ways to circumscribe and overcome it, popular agency—contestation, accommodation, and appropriation—mattered.

Unlike in the Marxist scheme, however, there was no teleology of resistance or progressive social change, no preordained route to salvation, and no master category of class to describe the workings of the system. Resistance and accommodation were no automatic response to assault; nor were they a matter of simply realizing one's true interests in the context of predefined exploitation and on the basis of a predefined ideology. Instead resistance was constituted and transformed within a highly variable political, economic, and social terrain. The languages of protest available to crafts and service workers varied with the discourses adopted by challenging classes, whether provincial notables in the 1860s and 1870s, or the nationalist *afandiya* in the early 1900s. These languages were thus not simply the authentic voice of the people, automatically and transparently articulating objectively given interests. Rather, they were shifting constructions which worked to some extent to specify the content of interests and to define how things could be said and not said. Such languages articulated the limits of the possible for relatively powerless protestors. But language was only part of the story. It was often outrun, made irrelevant, or transformed by power and resources. As we have seen, the structure of demand in the market, the relative strength of local organization, whether in guilds or informal networks, the existence or absence of alliances with middle classes, the relative openness of the state to contestation, and transnational structures of power were all important. Together these factors heavily mediated the clash between power and popular agency, impacted forms of restructuring, and strengthened and diminished political opportunities for effective collective resistance.

Appendix
A Boatman's Petition

A petition ('*ardhala*) to the Minister of the Interior from Ahmad 'Ali, a senior member of the boatman's guild in Alexandria (DWQ ND MA, M26,
1295 AH/1878 AD). It is a copy of the original petition, one of the several
hundred existing in this box series in the Egyptian National Archives. The
writing in the top right-hand corner is the note by Alexandria Governorate
introducing the petition to the minister. The petition is presented on official paper, and was written by a professional petition writer. Ahmad 'Ali's
seal signs the bottom of the petition. The petition appeals to the "known"
and "famous" (and very recently issued) decrees which stipulated that the
shaykh be elected by those with the right to choose him from the guild. It
hints at the protocitizenship of the 1870s.

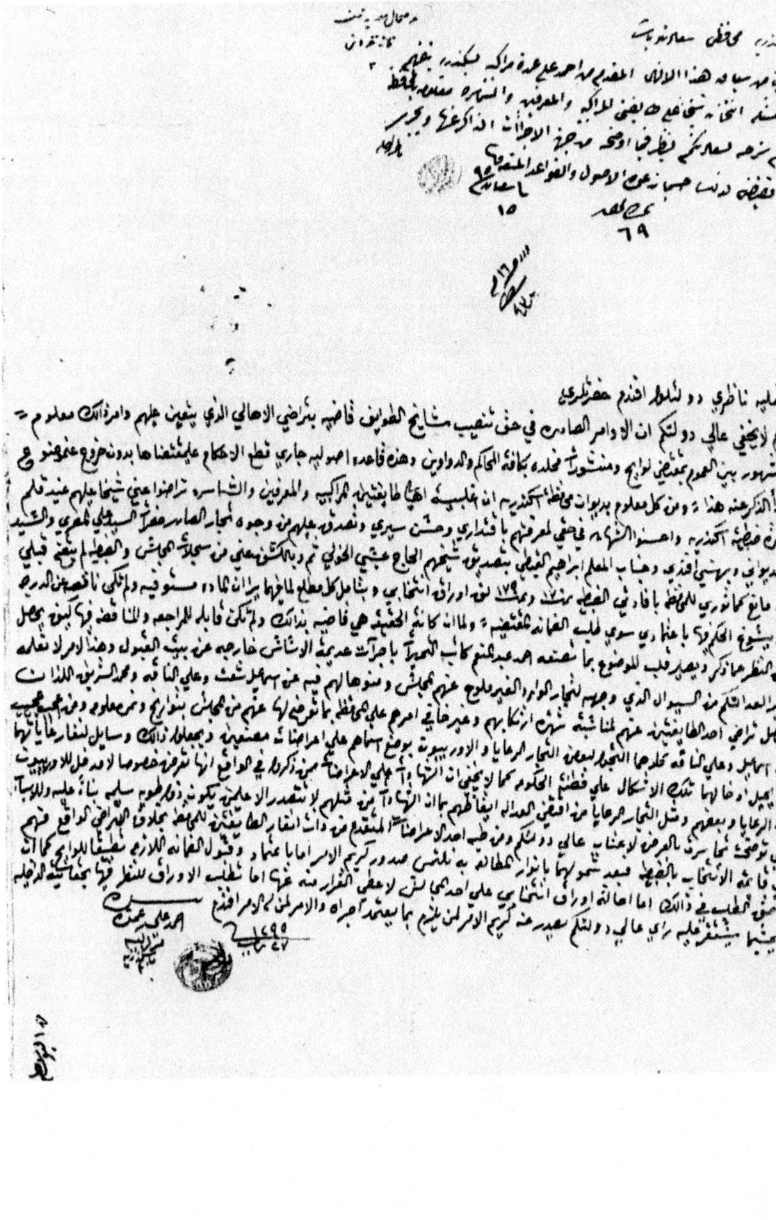

~Notes~

Introduction

1. Cited in Richard J. Evans, *In Defence of History* (London: Granta Books, 1997), 178. Trevor Roper was writing as Regius Professor of Modern History at the University of Oxford (in 1965).

2. To pick two of the most successful examples in the case of Egypt, P. J. Vatikiotis, *The Modern History of Egypt* (London: Weidenfield and Nicolson, 1969); and P. M. Holt, *Egypt and the Fertile Crescent, 1516–1922: A Political History* (Ithaca: Cornell University Press, 1966).

3. E. P. Thompson, *The Making of the English Working Class* (London: Gollancz, 1963).

4. Eric Hobsbawm, *On History* (London: Weidenfield and Nicolson, 1997), 143.

5. Regarding Egypt, landmark studies were Gabriel Baer, *Studies in the Social History of Modern Egypt* (Chicago: University of Chicago Press, 1969); André Raymond, *Artisans et Commerçants au Caire au XVIIIe Siècle*, 2 vols. (Damas: Institut Français de Damas, 1973); Roger Owen, *The Middle East in the World Economy 1800–1914* (London: Methuen, 1981); Joel Beinin and Zachary Lockman, *Workers on the Nile: Nationalism, Communism, Islam, and the Egyptian Working Class, 1882–1954* (Princeton, N.J.: Princeton University Press, 1987); and Kenneth Cuno, *The Pasha's Peasants: Land, Society, and Economy in Lower Egypt, 1740–1858* (Cambridge: Cambridge University Press, 1992). For the most valuable recent survey see Joel Beinin, *Workers and Peasants in the Modern Middle East* (Cambridge: Cambridge University Press, 2001).

6. Edward Said, *Orientalism* (London: Routledge, Kegan & Paul, 1978); Ranajit Guha, "On Some Aspects of the Historiography of Colonial India," in *Mapping Subaltern Studies and the Postcolonial*, ed. Vinayak Chaturvedi (London: Verso, 2000); Timothy Mitchell, *Colonising Egypt* (Cambridge: Cambridge University Press, 1988); Gyan Prakash, *Bonded Histories: Genealogies of Labor Servitude in Colonial India* (Cambridge: Cambridge University Press, 1990).

7. John Tosh, ed., *Historians on History* (Harlow: Pearson Education, 2000), 1.

8. Important contributions from Ranajit Guha (119–125) and Catherine Hall (159–166).

205

9. Eric Hobsbawm, *The Age of Extremes: The Short Twentieth Century 1914–1991* (London: Abacus Books, 1994), 202.

10. Emphasis in original. Guha, "Aspects of Colonial India," 2.

11. From Raymond Williams's essay "Culture is Ordinary" (1958), in *The Raymond Williams Reader*, ed. John Higgins (Oxford: Blackwell, 2001), 24.

12. For example, Robert Young, *White Mythologies: Writing History and the West* (London and New York: Routledge, 1990), 1–27.

13. Mitchell, *Colonising Egypt.*

14. This is Rajnarayan Chandavarkar's criticism in " 'The Making of the Working Class': E. P. Thompson and Indian History," in *Mapping Subaltern Studies*, 65.

15. Gyan Prakash, "Can the Subaltern Ride?" in *Comparative Studies in Society and History* 34, no. 1 (1992): 168–184.

16. See Rosalind O'Hanlon and D. Washbrook, "After Orientalism: Culture, Criticism and Politics in the Third World," in *Comparative Studies in Society and History* 34, no. 1 (1992): 141–167.

17. Gayatri Chakravorty Spivak, "Can the Subaltern Speak?" in *Marxism and the Interpretation of Culture*, ed. and with an introduction by Cary Nelson and Lawrence Grossberg (Basingstoke: Macmillan Education, 1988). The question of "voice" by no means exhausts this issue in any case.

18. Popular pressure, economic activity, or culture have been operative in the making of, say, nation or revolution, in the useful work of Juan R. I. Cole, *Colonialism and Revolution in the Middle East* (Princeton, N.J.: Princeton University Press, 1993); Lockman and Beinin, *Workers on the Nile*; and James L. Gelvin, *Divided Loyalties: Nationalism and Mass Politics in Syria at the Close of Empire* (Berkeley: University of California Press, 1998).

19. James C. Scott, *Domination and the Arts of Resistance: Hidden Transcripts* (New Haven and London: Yale University Press, 1990).

20. Charles Tilly, *Popular Contention in Great Britain, 1758–1834* (Cambridge: Harvard University Press, 1995), 18–19. Wolf spoke in a similar vein of outcomes resulting from the "complex orchestration of antagonistic forces" in Eric R. Wolf, *Europe and the People Without History* (Berkeley: University of California Press, 1982), 5. As Poulantzas suggestively noted, "[T]he State is a strategic field ploughed from one end to the other by working-class and popular struggle and resistance" in Nicos Poulantzas, *State, Power, Socialism*, trans. Patrick Camiller (London: Verso, 1980), 119.

21. Issawi argued that the development of the transport sector and the consequent import of European manufactures in the second half of the nineteenth century "eliminated most handicrafts" in Charles Issawi, "Asymmetrical Development and Transport in Egypt, 1800–1914," in *Beginnings of Modernisation in the Middle East: The Nineteenth Century*, ed. William R. Polk and Richard L. Chambers (Chicago: Chicago University Press, 1968), 397. See also Charles Issawi, "Middle

East Economic Development, 1815–1914," in *The Modern Middle East: A reader*, ed. A. Hourani, P. S. Khoury, and M. C. Wilson (Berkeley: University of California Press, 1993), 177–194.

22. Donald Quataert's pioneering research focusing on rural and household industry has convincingly argued against the simple "decline" thesis, finding busy, complex, and changing forms of rural industry in the Ottoman Empire in the nineteenth century. Among many other works, see Donald Quataert, *Ottoman Manufacturing in the Age of the Industrial Revolution* (Cambridge: Cambridge University Press, 1993), 1–2; and Donald Quataert, *Manufacturing and Technology Transfer in the Ottoman Empire 1800–1914* (Istanbul: Isis Press, 1992). The notion of undifferentiated handicraft decline in the Middle East was challenged as early as the 1960s. Dominique Chevallier led the way with "Un Exemple de résistance technique de l'artisanat syrien aux XIXe et XXe siècles: Les Tissus Ikates d'Alep et de Damas," in *Syria: Revue d'Art Oriental et d'Archéologie* 39 (1962): 300–324; Roger Owen then argued that Egypt's building industry (much of it small scale), was a "major recipient of the great increase in agricultural incomes which took place between 1897 and 1907," in "The Cairo Building Industry and the Building Boom of 1897–1907," *Colloque International sur l'Histoire du Caire* (Cairo: Deutsche Demokratische Republik and Ministry of Culture of ARE, 1969), 347; see also Roger Owen, "The Study of Middle Eastern Industrial History: Notes on the Interrelationship between Factories and Small-Scale Manufacturing with Special References to Lebanese Silk and Egyptian Sugar, 1900–1930," in *International Journal of Middle Eastern Studies* 16 (1984): 475–487. Marxist articulation of modes of production analysis also started to be applied in the Middle East. For an interesting variant of such analysis, see Kristin Koptiuch, *A Poetics of Political Economy in Egypt* (Minneapolis: University of Minnesota Press, 1999); other Marxist-inspired work found protocapitalism rather than simple decline in Syrian textile industries: James A. Reilly, "Damascus Merchants and Trade in the Transition to Capitalism," *Canadian Journal of History* 27, no. 1 (April 1992): 1–27. See also John T. Chalcraft, "The Striking Cabbies of Cairo and Other Stories: Crafts and Guilds in Egypt, 1863–1914" (Ph.D. Dissertation, New York University, 2001).

23. Ra'uf 'Abbas, *Al-Haraka al-'Ummaliyya fi Misr*, 1899–1952 (Cairo: General Egyptian Book Organization, 1967); Amin 'Izz al-Din, *Ta'rikh al-Tabaqa al-'Amila al-Misriyya mundhu nash'atiha hatta thawrat 1919* (Cairo: Dar al-Sha'b, 1967); Beinin and Lockman, *Workers on the Nile*; Donald Quataert and Eric van Zurcher, eds., *Workers and the Working Class in the Ottoman Empire and the Turkish Republic, 1839–1950* (London: I. B. Tauris, 1995); Ellis Jay Goldberg, ed., *The Social History of Labor in the Middle East* (Boulder, Colo. Westview Press, 1996).

24. Sherry Vatter, "Militant Journeymen in Nineteenth-Century Damascus: Implications for the Middle Eastern Labor History Agenda," in *Workers and Working Classes in the Middle East: Struggles, Histories, Historiographies*, ed. Zachary Lockman (New York: State University of New York Press, 1994), 1–19.

25. Cole, *Colonialism and Revolution*. For later times see the important interrogation of relations between work and politics by Ellis Jay Goldberg, *Tinker, Tailor, and Textile Worker: Class and Politics in Egypt, 1930–1952* (Berkeley: University of California Press, 1986).

26. Gabriel Baer, *Egyptian Guilds in Modern Times* (Jerusalem: Hebrew University Press, 1964), 18. Raymond agreed that "une corporation" was "a group of individuals in a town practicing the same professional activity under the authority of a shaykh." Raymond, *Artisans*, 507.

27. Baer, *Egyptian Guilds*. Goldberg's important discussion of the persistence of "guilds or guild-like structures" in the interwar period should not obscure the far-reaching transformation in craft organization which I will chart in this book. Goldberg, *Tinker and Textile Worker*, 77–92. The craft unions which emerged from 1909 onwards, whether dissimilar from European unions or not, were fundamentally new kinds of organizations.

28. Raymond, *Artisans*, 217, 584; Haim Gerber, "Guilds in Seventeenth Century Anatolian Bursa," in *Asian and African Studies* 11 (summer 1976): 59–86; Haim Gerber, *Economy and Society in an Ottoman City: Bursa, 1600–1700* (Jerusalem: Hebrew University, 1988); Pascale Ghazaleh, *Masters of the Trade: Crafts and Craftspeople in Cairo, 1750–1850*, Cairo Papers in Social Science, vol. 22, no. 3 (Cairo: American University in Cairo Press, 1999).

29. Gabriel Baer, *Egyptian Guilds*, 75; Halil Inalçik, "The Appointment Procedure of a Guild Warden," in *The Middle East and the Balkans under the Ottoman Empire: Essays on Economy and Society*, by Halil Inalcik (Bloomington: Indiana University Press, 1993), 194–197; Eunjeong Yi, "The Seventeenth-Century Istanbul Guilds: Leverage in Changing Times" (Ph.D. Dissertation, Harvard University, 2000), Pascale Ghazaleh, "The Guilds between Tradition and Modernity," in *The State and Its Servants: Administration in Egypt from Ottoman Times to the Present*, ed. Nelly Hanna (Cairo: American University in Cairo Press, 1995).

30. Ehud Toledano, *State and Society in Mid-nineteenth Century Egypt* (Cambridge: Cambridge University Press, 1990), 226ff.

31. Cole, *Colonialism and Revolution*, 164–189.

32. This older and problematic view stems mostly from Gabriel Baer, who argued that the crafts and guilds were largely eliminated by the impact of foreign competition in the later nineteenth century in Baer, *Egyptian Guilds*; Raymond did not significantly demur from this point of view in André Raymond, "Les Transformations des corporations de métiers au Caire du XVIIIe au XIXe Siècle," in *Les Institutions traditionelles dans le monde arabe*, ed. Hervé Blanchot (Paris: Karthala, 1999), 29–40; and Raymond explained how foreign investment in Egypt also eliminated traditional trades as in the case of the water carriers in "Les Porteurs d'eau du Caire," in *Bulletin de l'Institut Français d'Archeologie Orientale* 57 (1958): 183–203. For a recent major restatement of this problematic view, see 'Abd al-Salam 'Abd al-Halim 'Amr, *al-Tawa'if al-Hiraf fi Misr 1805–1914* (Cairo: al-Hay'a al-'Amma li-l-Kitab, 1993).

33. Laclau and Brenner persuasively argued in the 1970s that although capitalist relations of exchange have been universalized across the globe since the sixteenth century and help constitute the modern world system as an analytical unit, capitalist relations of production are much more unevenly distributed within the system, having a far denser presence in the core of the world economy than in the

periphery. Ernesto Laclau, "Feudalism and Capitalism in Latin America," *New Left Review* 67 (May–June 1971): 19–38; R. Brenner, "The origins of Capitalist Development: A Critique of Neo-Smithian Marxism," *New Left Review* 104 (July–August 1977): 25–92. Indeed, within the framework of dependencia, unlike in what Wallerstein has called the "developmentalist paradigms," there was no teleology dictating that capitalist relations of production would eventually encompass all of economic life. André Gunder Frank, *Capitalism and Underdevelopment in Latin America: Historical Studies of Chile and Brazil* (New York: Monthly Review Press, 1967); Immanuel Wallerstein, *The capitalist World-Economy* (Cambridge: Cambridge University Press, 1979), see pp. 153–54 for "developmentalism."

34. Revisions of earlier views regarding economic change in the imperial centers have emphasized, in Samuel's words, "a sub soil of small-scale enterprise," a "whole new world of labour intensive jobs" (7–8), a "vast amount of capitalist enterprise [which] was organized on the basis of hand rather than steam-powered technology" (p. 45). Samuel, echoing Trotsky's descriptions of the complex combinations of old and new called into being by ascendant global capitalism, usefully called this kind of economic change "combined and uneven development." Raphael Samuel, "Workshop of the World: Steam Power and Hand Technology in Mid-Victorian Britain" *History Workshop* 3 (1977): 1–74. Other important revisionist works included Maxine Berg, *The Age of Manufactures: Industry, Innovation and Work in Britain 1700–1820* (Totowa, N.J.: Barnes and Noble, 1985). Patrick O'Brien and Çaglar Keyder's important work on French national income statistics showed that the French economy had grown just as fast as Britain's in the nineteenth century, but with a more vibrant crafts sector and with less emphasis on factory industry. *Economic Growth in Britain and France, 1780–1914: Two Paths to the Twentieth Century* (London: Allen and Unwin, 1978). Crafts' work challenged the "take-off" theory of the industrial revolution, arguing that growth was far more gradual in Britain between 1780 and the 1820s than previous historians (following Deane and Cole) had believed. N. F. R. Crafts, *British Economic Growth during the Industrial Revolution* (Oxford: Clarendon Press, 1985). Mendels popularized the notion of protoindustrialization, thus emphasizing the importance and rural networks and putting-out systems in the growth of capitalism. F. F. Mendels, "Protoindustrialization: The First Phase of the Industrialization Process," *Journal of Economic History* 32 (1972).

35. The older historiography was based on both developmental Marxism and models of industrialization dominant in the 1950s and 1960s, which greatly emphasized capital-intensive and factory-based production. P. Deane and W. A. Cole, *British Economic Growth, 1688–1959: Trends and Structure* (Cambridge: Cambridge University Press, 1962); David S. Landes, *The unbound Prometheus: Technological Change and Industrial Development in Western Europe from 1750 to the Present* (London: Cambridge University Press, 1969). Post–Second World War development theory, partly influenced by successful large-scale Soviet industrialization in the 1930s, saw little utility in nonfactory industry. See for example, W. W. Rostow, *The Process of Economic Growth* (Oxford: Oxford University Press, 1953).

36. Although Marx occasionally indicated that capitalism may not everywhere produce a bourgeoise mode of production in its own image, the possibility of

uneven capitalism was much more thoroughly analysed by Leon Trotsky. Trotsky's "combined and uneven development" involved three key insights. First, the idea that the complex amalgam brought into being in Russia was neither noncapitalism, nor exactly capitalism. Second, that nations outside western Europe would not duplicate the latter's trajectory, because global political economy had been transformed by western Europe. And third, in an unorthodox break with economism, he allowed a significant role for the Russian state—an emphasis strikingly appropriate for the Ottoman empire and Egypt, which also built strong militaries and bureaucracies in attempts to resist the power of western Europe. Trotsky's formulation, however, was developmentalist, relying heavily on unsustainable notions of backwardness. He seems further to have dismissed the "Asiatic despotisms." Baruch Knei-Paz, *The Social and Political Thought of Leon Trotsky* (1978; reprint, Oxford: Clarendon Press, 2001). For a recent analysis of multiple forms of work under capitalism in the West, in which economism and developmentalism are persuasively rejected, see Chris Tilly and Charles Tilly, *Work Under Capitalism* (Boulder, Colo. Westview Press, 1998).

37. One of the most important studies of Egypt is Mahmoud Abdel Fadil, "Informal Sector Employment in Egypt," in *Urban Research Strategies for Egypt*, ed. R. Lobbon (Cairo: American University in Cairo Press, 1983), 16–40. See also Nicholas S. Hopkins, ed., *Informal Sector in Egypt* (Cairo: The American University in Cairo Press, 1991). Mabro and Radwan included a chapter on small-scale industry in their study as early as 1976. *The Industrialization of Egypt 1939-1973: Policy and Performance* (Oxford: Clarendon Press, 1976), 115–33. Diane Singerman found that the great majority of urbanites in a *sha'bi* (popular) quarter of Cairo in the 1980s worked in the informal sector as either primary, secondary, or tertiary employment. *Avenues of Participation: Family, Politics and Networks in Urban Quarters of Cairo* (Princeton, N.J.: Princeton University Press, 1995), 195. The study of informality was very much promoted in the late 1970s by an array of international organizations such as the World Bank and USAID, among others, responding to post-Fordist models of economic development.

38. See, for example, Claude Meillasoux, *Maidens, Meal and Money: Capitalism and the Domestic Community* (Cambridge: Cambridge University Press, 1981); Pierre-Philippe Rey, *Les Alliances des classes* (Paris: François Maspero, 1973).

39. For an important collection see Ray Bromley and Chris Gerry, *Casual Work and Poverty in Third World Cities* (Chichester: John Wiley and Sons, 1979). Also Shahid Amin and Marcel van der Linden, "'Peripheral' Labour? Studies in the History of Partial Proletarianization," *International Review of Social History*, Supplement 4, 41 (1996).

40. William H. Sewell, *Work and Revolution in France: The Language of Labor from the Old Regime to 1848* (Cambridge: Cambridge University Press, 1980), 1.

41. In Anthony Brewer, *Marxist Theories of Imperialism: A Critical Survey*, 2nd ed. (London and New York: Routledge, 1990), 233. Rey ultimately defended "modes of production" analysis on the basis of sociopolitical factors, an important departure from economism.

42. As noted above, Trotsky had made a significant but often unremarked departure from orthodox Marxian economism. He had stressed the role of the Russian state, which, seeking to build itself up militarily and administratively in the face of Western European expansion, had robbed the bourgeoisie of its surplus, and pounced on the peasantry in ways which deepened the contradictions of uneven development. Knei-Paz, *Leon Trotsky*. More generally, noneconomistic writing about the economy ranges far and wide, from, say, Max Weber's *The Protestant Ethic and the Spirit of Capitalism*, trans. Talcott Parsons (1930; London: Routledge, 1992) to Michael Burawoy's suggestive linkages between the labor process, state, class, and the international division of labor in Michael Burawoy and Theda Skocpol, eds., *Marxist Inquiries: Studies of Labor, Class and States* (Chicago: University of Chicago Press, 1982), 1–28.

43. Raymond Williams, "Base and Superstructure in Marxist Cultural Theory" (1973), in *The Raymond Williams Reader*, ed. John Higgins (Oxford: Blackwell, 2001), 165.

44. This does not imply any simplistic cultural turn. Although much of Laclau and Mouffe's devastating criticism of economistic essentialism is well taken, their plunge into political and ideological (over)determination, shorn of economic relationships, simply does not follow from this useful criticism. Ernesto Laclau and Chantal Mouffe, *Hegemony and Socialist Strategy: Towards a Radical Democratic Politics*, 2nd ed. (London: Verso, 2001). Rajnarayan Chandavarkar usefully avoids a cultural turn in his *Imperial Power and Popular politics* (Cambridge: Cambridge University Press, 1998). Chandavarkar is persuasively critical of an Orientalist tendency to see India's capitalist development as a kind of exception to a normal pattern (established by Europe and European Marxism), and then to treat culture in India as the variable that accounts for the deviation from the norm. Chandavarkar's analysis instead weaves together the state, the economy, neighborhood politics, class, and discourse in useful and complex ways. Goldberg also avoids any simplistic cultural turn in *Tinker and Textile Worker*, 9.

45. As Burawoy wrote, "Marx had no place in his theory of the labor process for the organization of consent, for the necessity to elicit a willingness to cooperate in the translation of labor power into labor." *Manufacturing Consent: Changes in the Labor Process under Monopoly Capitalism* (Chicago: Chicago University Press, 1979), 26–7.

46. Laclau and Mouffe put this well: "Labour-power differs from the other necessary elements of production in that the capitalist must do more than simply purchase it; he must also make it produce labour. . . . The evolution of the productive forces becomes unintelligible if this need of the capitalist to exercise his domination at the very heart of the labour process is not understood." *Hegemony and Strategy*, 78. Charles Sabel has given one useful reading of how to make transformations in work organization intelligible in terms of political and shop-floor struggles. *Work and Politics: The Division of Labor in Industry* (Cambridge: Cambridge University Press, 1982).

47. Patrick Heller, *The Labor of Development: Workers and the Transformation of Capitalism in Kerala, India* (Ithaca, N.Y.: Cornell University Press, 1999), 41.

48. The phrase is Sewell's. See William H. Sewell, "Toward a Post-Materialist Rhetoric for Labor History," in *Rethinking Labor History*, ed. Lenard R. Berlanstein (Urbana: University of Illinois Press, 1993).

49. Thompson, *English Working Class;* Jacques Rancière, *La Nuit des prolétaires* (Paris: Fayard, 1981); Gareth Stedman Jones, *Languages of Class: Studies in English Working Class History, 1832–1982* (Cambridge: Cambridge University Press, 1983). Alf Ludtke, ed., *The History of Everyday Life*, trans. William Templer (Princeton, N.J.: Princeton University Press, 1995); Patrick Joyce, *Visions of the People: Industrial England and the Question of Class, 1848–1914* (Cambridge: Cambridge University Press, 1991); Joan W. Scott, *Gender and the Politics of History* (New York: Columbia University Press, 1988); Zachary Lockman, *Comrades and Enemies: Arab and Jewish Workers in Palestine, 1906–1948* (Berkeley: University of California Press, 1996); John T. Chalcraft, "The Coal-Heavers of Port Said: State-Making and Worker Protest, 1869–1914," *International Labor and Working Class History* 60 (fall 2001), 110–124.

50. Michael Gilsenan's outstanding portrait of violence and honor narratives among mechanics, chauffeurs, agricultural workers, and bus drivers (among others) in Lebanon in the 1970s forcefully underlines how making a living is intertwined with the active search for status honor. *Lords of the Lebanese Marches: Violence and Narrative in an Arab Society* (Berkeley: University of California Press, 1996). Scott usefully intertwines material and nonmaterial factors in discussions of resistance. *Weapons of the Weak: Everyday Forms of Peasant Resistance* (New Haven and London: Yale University Press, 1985); Scott, *Arts of Resistance*.

51. "Political contention" is defined by Hanagan, Moch, and Te Brake as the "interaction between those who occupy positions of governmental authority, that is, the rulers of a political domain, and those who are effectively subject to their authority, the subjects or citizens of that domain." These authors are interested in a "fundamentally relational approach to the study of contentious politics" which treats "all actors, subjects and rulers alike, as creative and potent participants in a larger interactive process. To do so is to give them both a past and a future—not only a past that renders them explicable, but a future that reveals them to be consequential." Michael P. Hanagan, Leslie Page Moch, and Wayne Te Brake, eds., *Challenging Authority: The Historical Study of Contentious Politics* (Minneapolis and London: University of Minnesota Press, 1998), ix–x.

52. See for example, the useful synthetic and comparative perspectives taken up in Doug McAdam, John D. McCarthy, and Mayer N. Zald, eds., *Comparative Perspectives on Social Movements: Political Opportunities, Mobilizing Structures, and Cultural Framings* (Cambridge: Cambridge University Press, 1996).

53. I borrow this phrase from Dietrich Rueschmeyer, Evelyne Huber Stephens, and John D. Stephens, *Capitalism, Development and Democracy* (Chicago: Chicago University Press, 1992). "Transnational structures of power" are the forces exerted on a state by international political economy.

54. Marx alludes to something similar where he writes that where the capitalist mode of production was not strongly developed, "the peasants who are in debt are

obliged to produce and sell, even at prices that merely give them the means to survive and to pay off, at least in part, the burden of debt that weighs upon them." Cited in Charles Bettelheim, "Theoretical Comments," in the appendix to *Unequal Exchange: A Study of the Imperialism of Trade* by Arghiri Emmanuel, trans. Brian Pearce (London: Monthly Review Press, 1972), 298–9. In a like vein Sweezy speaks of a "high social rate of exploitation," high rates of extraction of absolute surplus value from small producers in the periphery by "landlords, traders, and usurers, primarily in the countryside but also in the cities and towns." Paul M. Sweezy, "Center, Periphery, and the Crisis of the System," in *Introduction to the Sociology of "Developing Societies,"* ed. Hamza Alavi and Teodor Shanin (London: Macmillan, 1982), 210–217.

55. "Absolute surplus value" is distinguished from "relative surplus value" by Marx. The former refers to surplus extracted from the worker by the capitalist on a zero-sum basis, that is, where the worker's loss is directly the capitalist's gain, as with longer hours or with wage rates. Relative surplus value is instead associated with fully capitalist relations of production, is increased on the basis of productivity raising, and does not necessarily involve longer hours or lower wages.

56. Sweezy, "Center, Periphery," p. 216.

57. Patrick Heller's study of the unorganized sector in Kerala, India, makes a strikingly similar argument and was an important inspiration here. Heller, *The Labor of Development*.

58. Sweezy, "Center, Periphery," p. 214. Sweezy here noted that in the center, union struggles from the 1860s and the bourgeoise realization that higher wages could mean higher profits transformed these forms of social exploitation and accounted for economic development.

59. DWQ (Dar al-Watha'iq al-Qawmiyya) *Sijillat Muhafizat Misr. Ta'dad nufus* (1285 / 1865) 84 / 1 / lam.

60. The 1872 census is drastically incomplete on the macrological level regarding occupations, and 'Ali Mubarak's statistics provide a sketchy summary at best.

61. Cole, *Colonialism and Revolution*.

62. *Nizarat al-Dakhiliyya,* (Interior Ministry) *Mukatibat 'Arabi,* (Arabic Correspondence) *Mahfaza,* (file) 1–40. Hereafter abbreviated to DWQ ND MA M, 1–40. N.B. All translations are by the author unless otherwise stated.

63. The drawback of these registers is that they only summarize the original petitions. Their consequent homogenization and loss of detail and nuance diminishes their value. DWQ *Sijillat 'Abdin 'Arabi wa Turki: Qayyid al-'Ardhalat al-Warida* 27 / 5 / Seen, 1893–4 and *Qayyid al-'Ardhalat* 32 / 5 / Seen, 1902–1914; and, relating to the same series DWQ *'Abdin: Diwan Khidiwi 'Ardhalat* 612–618, 1892–1912. One or two other petition series relating only to the 1860s and 1870s are useful, but more fragmentary. Registers of petitions sent to the Cairo police and to the Cairo governorate have been used. DWQ *Dabtiyyat Misr, Warid al-'Ardhalat* 1274–1287 AH; DWQ *Sijillat Muhafizat Misr: Warid al-'Ardhalat* 31 / 1 / lam, 1275–1296 AH. Both such series are summaries rather than originals.

64. There are ministerial records not listed in the *Majlis al-Wuzara* (MW) index. For example the records found by Alleaume in the mid-1980s, which I have made use of with respect to the construction trades: DWQ *Nizarat al-Ashghal* (NA) 5/1. Ghislaine Alleaume, "Politiques urbaines et contrôle de l'enterprise: Une loi inédite de 'Ali Mubarak sur les corporations du bâtiment," *Annales Islamologiques* 21 (1985): 147–188.

65. These contain the results of miscellaneous government research projects, and the Archive Card Index (*Bitaqat Mawadi'a al-Dar*—BMD), which is no longer an index, but has some useful information such as summarized petitions and notes on government requisitions.

66. Although I consistently tried to get hold of unindexed but surely extensive court records, particulary the Tribunals of First Instance and Appeals Court, the material I obtained was fragmentary, or rich only in bursts. (For instance, one of the volumes of records I consulted was entirely given over to cases involving crafts and trades). DWQ *Majlis Ibtida'i Misr: Qayyid al-Qararat* 529–585. These are scattered between the years 1879 to 1883; DWQ *Majlis Isti'naf Misr* No. 87 [1880]; DWQ *Majlis Tujjar Misr: Khulasat wa Qararat wa Ifadat* 1272–1297 AH. It is not clear what becomes of these records after the reorganization of the courts in 1883.

67. Embassy and Consular Correspondence, FO141; Cairo Consular Court, FO841; The Cromer Papers, FO633; The Milner Mission, FO848; London/Cairo correspondence, FO371.

68. *Al-Nashra al-Sanawiyya li'l-Tijara al-Kharijiyya*, 30 vols. (Cairo: *al-Maktaba al-'Amma*, 1876–1914). Hereafter given as *External Trade Statistics*.

69. I would like to draw attention (with Kristin Koptiuch, *Poetics of Political Economy*) to the utility of the books and articles put out by Egypt's French intelligentsia in the two or three decades prior to the First World War, for example Pierre Arminjon, *La Situation economique et financière de l'Egypte* (Paris: Libraire Generale de Droit et de Jurisprudence, 1911).

70. For example, the informative and substantial *Géographie economique et administrative de l'Egypte: Basse Egypte*, vol. 1 (Cairo: n. p. 1902).

71. This is the same government publication that Gabriel Baer used in *Egyptian Guilds*. There are two sets of volumes. One set contains Khedivial Decrees (*awamir al-'aliya*) and the other Ministerial Decisions and Publications (*al-qararat wa al-manshurat*). Both sets run from around 1876 to 1914 and beyond, one volume from each published yearly. Egyptian Government, *Majmu'a al-'Awamir al-'Aliya al-Sadira fi sanat   *, Cairo; Egyptian Government, *Al-Qararat al-Sadira min Majlis al-Nuzzar wa min al-Nazarat wa al-Manshurat fi sanat   *, Cairo. Hereafter the former series is rendered GP, AA and the latter, GP, QM.

72. For example, an eight-volume, large-scale (1:1000) map of Cairo showing every house, street and alley from the 1922 *Atlas of Cairo* (Cairo: Offices of the Survey of Egypt, Ministry of Finance, 1922). Other useful maps include *Atlas of Egypt* (Cairo: Egyptian Government, Survey of Egypt, 1928); *Atlas of Egypt* (Cairo: Ministry of Finance, Government Press, 1914). This latter atlas (on a scale of 1:50,000)

is an economic and geological digest also, containing information on industry and agriculture.

Chapter 1

1. Raymond's estimate of the proportion of Egyptian trade with Asia and Africa, in *Artisans*, vol. 1, 194.

2. Issawi claimed that Egypt was "ruined by the diversion of trade from the Mediterranean to the Atlantic" and "spent the next three centuries in a stupor." *Egypt in Revolution*, 13–19.

3. Al-Jabarti, the most well-known and prolific Egyptian chronicler of the early nineteenth century used this phrase, among others, to describe crafts and service workers. See, for example, Gabriel Baer, "Popular Revolt in Ottoman Cairo," *Der Islam* 54 (1977): 213–4.

4. Raymond, *Artisans*, vol. 1, 204.

5. Cairo accounted for far more in tax on merchants and crafts and service workers than the rest of Egypt's towns put together in 1800. Cuno, *Pasha's Peasants*, 49–50.

6. Owen, *World Economy*, 45–6.

7. Ibid.

8. Raymond, *Artisans*, vol. 1, 229.

9. Production was also scattered in the smaller towns and villages, most of which contained nonagricultural specialists. Both Haim Gerber and Suraiya Faroqhi argue that in Anatolia putting-out systems of some kind existed but only in particular sectors, and guild production remained the dominant form. Haim Gerber, *Economy and Society*, 64–8; Suraiya Faroqhi, in *An Economic and Social History of the Ottoman Empire*, ed. Halil Inalçik with Donald Quataert (Cambridge: Cambridge University Press, 1994), 452–460

10. Raymond, *Artisans*, vol. 1, 237–9.

11. Raymond, "Les Porteurs d'eau."

12. Baer, "Popular Revolt," 213–4.

13. Although Quataert shows that much rural production and trade was carried on outside of guild organization. See for example, Donald Quataert, *Ottoman Manufacturing*, 8.

14. Massignon, "Pacte d'honneur artisanal."

15. Baer, *Egyptian Guilds*, 18. Goitein, Stern, and Cahen's devastating criticisms of Massignon's massively generalizing vision need not be rehearsed here. S. D. Goitein, "Cairo: An Islamic City in the Light of the Geniza Documents," in *Middle*

Eastern Cities: A Symposium on Ancient, Islamic, and Contemporary Middle Eastern Urbanism, ed. Ira Lapidus (Berkeley: University of California Press, 1969), 80–96, 94; C. Cahen, "Y-a-t-il des corporations professionelles dans le monde Musulman classique? Quelques notes et réflexions," in *The Islamic City: A Colloquium*, ed. A. H. Hourani and S. M. Stern (Oxford: Bruno Cassirer, 1970), 51–63.

16. Ghazaleh has persuasively emphasized the caution necessary in the use of the flexible term *ta'ifa*. Ghazaleh, *Masters of the Trade*, 15–19.

17. Donald Quataert, "The Social History of Labor in the Ottoman Empire," in *The Social History of Labor*, ed. Goldberg, 29.

18. Gabriel Baer, *Egyptian Guilds*, 75.

19. Gerber, "Guilds in Bursa;" Gerber, *Economy and Society*; Inalçik, "Appointment Procedure of a Guild Warden," 194–197; Yi, "Seventeenth-Century Istanbul Guilds;" Ghazaleh "Guilds Between Tradition and Modernity;" Ghazaleh, *Masters of the Trade*; Amnon Cohen, *The Guilds of Ottoman Jerusalem* (Leiden: Brill, 2001), 5.

20. Gerber, *Economy and Society*.

21. Only in discussions of European guilds have authors seen guild control over taxes as a privilege; when it comes to guilds outside Europe, assumptions of despotism appear to have taken over.

22. Bowring, *Report on Egypt*, 117.

23. As Al-Jabarti wrote, in 1786 these practices "weighed heavily on the people of the city." 'Abd al-Rahman al-Jabarti, *Al-Jabarti's History of Egypt*, ed. and trans. Thomas Philipp and Moshe Perlman, 4 vols., vol. 2 (Stuttgart: Franz Steiner, 1994), 193.

24. In July 1709, when the Cairo qadi demanded, on orders from the Porte, that the Janissaries were not to have any relationship with the guilds, "they replied that most of them were either soldiers or sons of soldiers, and that they therefore could not comply. . . . [T]he qadi became afraid . . . and never mentioned it again." Al-Jabarti, *History of Egypt*, vol. 1, 60. As Tomiche argued, this gave the guilds a kind of aggregate power against certain forms of state intervention. Nada Tomiche, "La Situation des artisans et petits commerçants en Egypte de la fin du XVIIIe siècle jusqu'au milieu du XIXe," *Studia Islamica* 12 (1960): 79–98, 85.

25. Al-Jabarti, *History of Egypt*, vol. 3, 306. Baer misinterprets this example as indicating Janissary exploitation of the guilds, a misreading of Jabarti which supports Baer's problematic view that Janissary involvement meant either the degeneration of the guilds or excessive government or military control of these institutions. Baer, *Egyptian Guilds*, 122. This case fits more readily with Quataert's sense that Janissary involvement acted as a bulwark against unwanted state intervention: "[T]he effects of [the Janissaries'] actions served to protect the interests of Ottoman workers as a whole (whether these effects were intended is not clear)." Quataert, "Social History of Labor," 23.

26. Edmund Burke III, "Islam and Social Movements: Methodological Reflections," in *Islam, Politics and Social Movements*, ed. Edmund Burke III and Ira M. Lapidus (Berkeley: University of California Press, 1988), 28.

27. André Raymond, "Quartiers et mouvements populaires au Caire au XVIIIe siècle," in *Political and Social Change in Modern Egypt*, ed. P. M. Holt (London: Oxford University Press, 1968), 115–116. Baer's account adds to the precision of the analysis. Gabriel Baer, "Popular Revolt," 220–21. Eunjeong Yi detailed the guilds' role in the Istanbul rebellion of 1651 in "Seventeenth Century Guilds." Olson's work long ago revealed the guild contribution to the Istanbul rebellions of 1730 and 1740. Robert W. Olson, "The Esnaf and the Patrona Halil Rebellion of 1730: A Realignment in Ottoman Politics?" *Journal of the Economic and Social History of the Orient* 17 (1974): 329–344; and Robert W. Olson, "Jews, Janissaries, Esnaf and the Revolt of 1740 in Istanbul: Social Upheaval and Political Realignment in the Ottoman Empire," *Journal of the Economic and Social History of the Orient* 20 (1977): 185–207. The guilds were also probably involved in the rebellion which brought down Selim III in 1806 in Istanbul after the Sultan had set himself against their monopolistic rights. See Engin Deniz Akarli, "*Gedik*: Implements, Mastership, Shop Usufruct, and Monopoly Among Istanbul Artisans, 1750–1850," *Wissenschaftskolleg Jahrbuch (1985/6)*, (Berlin: n. p. 1987) 228. Marsot mentions some examples from Jabarti of where "guilds rose in protest at a forced loan" in October 1787, and where "there was an uprising in protest at the arrest of the head of the guild of butchers" in September 1790. Afaf Lutfi al-Sayyid, "Review of Gabriel Baer's Egyptian Guilds in Modern Times," *Middle Eastern Studies* 2 (April 1966): 275.

28. "Most of the services offered by modern governments," wrote Yapp, "were supplied in the Near East of 1800 by non-governmental bodies—the family, the tribe, the village, the guild and the religious community." Malcolm E. Yapp, *The Making of the Modern Near East, 1792–1923* (London: Longman, 1987), 36–7.

29. Stanford Shaw, *History of the Ottoman Empire and modern Turkey*, vol. 1 (Cambridge: Cambridge University Press, 1976), 165. "The premodern state," writes James C. Scott, "was, in many crucial respects, partially blind; it knew precious little about its subjects, their wealth, their landholdings and yields, their location, their very identity. It lacked anything like a detailed 'map' of its terrain and its people." *Seeing Like a State: How Certain Schemes to Improve the Human Condition Have Failed* (London and New Haven: Yale University Press, 1998), 2.

30. Todorov has shown the hierarchies involved in the determination of custom from below. His study of the *aba*-making guild of Plovdiv in Ottoman Bulgaria shows how the powerful masters of the guild largely defined the content of customary practice by which the trade was regulated. Nikolai Todorov, *The Balkan City, 1400–1800* (Seattle: University of Washington Press, 1983), 207–237.

31. Gabriel Baer, *Studies in the Social History of Modern Egypt* (Chicago: University of Chicago Press, 1969), 159.

32. Raymond, *Artisans*, 217, 584. Gibb's account of restrictions on initiative by monopolistic practices, although more generous, was not seriously at odds with this

view. H. A. R. Gibb and Harold Bowen, *Islamic Society and the West: A Study of the Impact of Western Civilization on Moslem Culture in the Near East*, vol 1. (Oxford: Oxford University Press, 1950), 281–3.

33. In Istanbul the *gedik* appears to have been an innovation of the eighteenth century, resulting from attempts by masters to shore up their positions in the trade. Akarli, "Implements, Mastership," 223–232.

34. Raymond, *Artisans*, 271.

35. For example, 37 licenses (*gedik*) were available in 1767 for the cloth- beaters of Aleppo. Abraham Marcus, *The Middle East on the Eve of Modernity: Aleppo in the Eighteenth Century* (New York: Columbia University Press, 1989), 178–9.

36. Raymond, *Artisans*, 549.

37. See Raymond, *Artisans*, 271. See also for Aleppo, Marcus, *The Middle East*, 179.

38. Raymond, *Artisans*, 271; Akarli shows that under pressure from landlords artisans used the powers of both judges and the Imperial *diwan* to shore up and recognize their claim that the right to shop space was included in the *gedik* that they held. Akarli, "Implements, Mastership," 227.

39. Raymond, *Artisans*, 549. It is a serious problem with Baer's analysis that he tends to see guild weakness where the qadi increased or decreased the number of positions available, as if the qadi's actions were part of some oppressive state-imposed master plan, rather than a response to pressure from the guild itself. See for example, Gabriel Baer, *Fellah and Townsman in the Middle East: Studies in Social History* (London: Frank Cass, 1982), 227. Nor does Baer attempt to investigate the logic of why it might be beneficial that the number of positions in a guild was "not very flexible," preferring to see it as a kind of negative restriction on trade activity.

40. Raymond, *Artisans*, 549.

41. Baer, *Egyptian Guilds*, 126.

42. For a succinct description, see Raymond, "Corporations de métiers," 31–33.

43. Edwin Lane, *Manners and Customs of the Modern Egyptians* (1836; London: East-West Publications, 1978), 502–3.

44. Bowring, *Report on Egypt*, 117. Lane's extensive description of the cutting of the Khalij is in *Manners and Customs*, 487–492.

45. Raymond, *Artisans*, 567.

46. FO141/73 Borg/Stanton no. 40, "Report upon the Native Guilds and on the Work Wages and Cost of Living of Working Classes at Cairo," 14 October 1870 (hereafter, *Borg Report*). Mahmoud Sedky, "La Corporation des cordonniers: Fabricants de markoubs au Caire," *La Revue Egyptienne* 1, (1912), 1–12, 108–110.

47. Al-Sayyid, "Review of Gabriel Baer's Egyptian Guilds," 275.

48. Ghazaleh, *Masters of the Trade*, 63–64.

49. As Judith Tucker noted, "convincing proof of the rapidity with which the country was harnessed to an international economy." *Women in Nineteenth-Century Egypt* (Cambridge: Cambridge University Press, 1985), 67.

50. Albert Hourani, *A History of the Arab Peoples* (London: Faber and Faber, 1991), 263.

51. Pascale Ghazaleh, "Organizing Labor: Professional Classifications in the Late 18th-/Early 19th-Century Cairo" (MESA, unpublished paper, 2001), 8.

52. Amira el-Azhary Sonbol, *The New Mamluks: Egyptian Society and Modern Feudalism*, foreword by Robert A. Fernea (Syracuse, N.Y.: Syracuse University Press, 2000), 37–38.

53. Ghislaine Alleaume and Philippe Fargues, "Voisinage et Frontière: Résider au Caire en 1846," in *Urbanité Arabe: Homage à Bernard Lepetit*, ed. Jocelyne Dakhlia (Paris: Sindbad, 1998), 101.

54. Recent research has emphasized that the larger Ottoman economy during the eighteenth century, at least until the 1780s, was stable and even expanding. See for example, Mehmet Genç, "L'Economie Ottoman et la guerre au XVIIIe siècle," *Turcica* 27 (1995): 177–96.

55. Owen, *World Economy*, 10.

56. Şevket Pamuk, "The Price Revolution in the Ottoman Empire Reconsidered," *International Journal of Middle East Studies* 33 (2001): 69–89.

57. See especially Dominique Chevallier, *La Société du Mont Liban à l'époque de la révolution industrielle en Europe* (Paris: Librairie Orientaliste Paul Geultner, 1971), 182–3. £E = 100 piasters = £1. 0s 6d.

58. Quataert, *Ottoman Manufacturing*; Reilly, "Damascus Merchants," 1–27.

59. Chevallier argues that there was such a flight of precious metals from the Levant in *Mont Liban*, 184–192, although Owen suggests Chevallier may have exaggerated this, citing the lack of increase in prices and the balancing factor of specie inflow from the East. *World Economy*, 97–98.

60. Quataert, *Ottoman Manufacturing*, 27–40.

61. Cuno, *Pasha's Peasants*, 53; Tucker, *Women in Egypt*, 84.

62. Kenneth M. Cuno, "A Tale of Two Villages: Family, Property, and Economic Activity in Rural Egypt in the 1840s," in *Agriculture in Egypt from Pharaonic to Modern Times*, ed. Alan K. Bowman and Eugene Rogan (Oxford: Oxford University Press, 1999), p. 315.

63. The atrocities of the "Overseer of the Linen," who apparently burned to death weavers who defied Mehmet Ali by operating private looms or selling the produce of such looms privately, were well known and widely condemned in Cairo in the 1820s. Lane, *Manners and Customs*, 129.

64. Baer, *Egyptian Guilds*, 128–29.

65. Clerget, *Le Caire*, vol. 2, 258–59.

66. John Bowring, *Report on Egypt*, 8–10, 59. Bowring also mentions weavers in employment at Esneh and Manshiyya. On Khurunfish see Ghazaleh, *Masters of the Trade*, 131. In addition to the trades mentioned above, there were lathe shop workers (*maghlaq al-makharit*), rope plaiters (*fattalin al-abbal*), tinsmiths (*samkariyya*), card makers (*imshatiyya*), smelters (*sabbakin*), saddle makers (*surujiyya*), local turners (*kharratin baladi*), coal sievers (*mugharbilin al-fahm*), silk-loom turners (*kharratin haririyya*), painters (*naqqashin*), and others.

67. Owen, *World Economy*, 72. Hands and about three thousand animals provided the power.

68. Owen, *World Economy*, 70.

69. Baer, *Egyptian Guilds*, 125ff.

70. Baer, *Egyptian Guilds*, 129–138; See also Toledano, *State and Society*, 226ff. As Lane wrote in the 1830s, "[T]he members of various trades and manufactures in the metropolis and other large towns have also their respective shaykhs, to whom all disputes respecting matters connected with those trades or crafts are submitted for arbitration, and whose sanction is required for the admission of new members." *Manners and Customs*, 130.

71. Nazih Ayubi, *Overstating the Arab State: Politics and Society in the Middle East*, (London: I. B. Tauris, 1995), 104. For a treatment of the *ulama* see Afaf Lutfi al-Sayyid, "The Role of the *"ulama"* in Egypt during the Early Nineteenth Century," in *Social Change*, ed. Holt 264–80.

72. André Raymond, "Mouvements populaires," 116.

73. Quataert wrote, "[O]nce the Janissaries were gone, the state could act with relative disregard for the interests of labor." "The Social History of Labor," 23.

74. Frederik de Jong, *Turuq and Turuq-Linked Institutions in Nineteenth-Century Egypt: A Historical Study in the Organizational Dimensions of Islamic Mysticism* (Leiden: E. J. Brill, 1978).

75. Ghazaleh, "Organizing Labor," 8.

76. Lane, *Manners and Customs*, 136.

77. The *wirku* was sometimes later referred to as the *firda*, but the *firda* was not necessarily specific to merchants, traders, crafts, and service workers, whereas the *wirku* was.

78. Ghazaleh, *Masters of the Trade*, 30–1.

79. Ibid., 29. See also 'Amr, *al-Tawa'if al-Hiraf*, 161–88.

80. As Ghazaleh points out, "[T]he state's overriding concerns are reflected in the frequent use of the expression *dabt wa rabt* (regulating/controlling and binding), which appears almost constantly in documents on guild organization." *Masters*

of the Trade, 31–32. See also Afaf Lutfi al-Sayyid Marsot, *Egypt in the Reign of Muhammad Ali*, (Cambridge: Cambridge University Press, 1984), 100.

81. 'Amr, *al-Tawa'if al-Hiraf*, 161–88; Pascale Ghazaleh, *"Tawa'if hirafiyya*: Crafts and Craftspeople in Cairo, 1750–1850" (American University in Cairo, Master's thesis, 1996), 105–41.

82. As Ghazaleh notes, some guilds had also been more closely identified with the state in the eighteenth century, for example money changing and weighing, but now intervention was widening and became more intrusive. *Masters of the Trade*, 32.

83. Ibid., 30–31.

84. Ibid., 29–31.

85. Lane, *Manners and Customs*, 129.

86. Al-Sayyid, "Review of Gabriel Baer's Egyptian Guilds," 274.

87. As Bowring wrote "Mahomet Ali made an attempt, a few years ago, to ascertain the number of inhabitants in Cairo, his capital. He failed, however, in the effort. Not only did the lower classes combine to resist the authorities, but persons of distinction, even those immediately connected with the court, took a part in opposing the census." Bowring, *Report on Egypt*, 5. This incident recalls Scott's discussion of struggles waged between government and populace in France over censuses, cadastral surveys, and standardization of weights and measures in *Seeing Like a State*, 27–48.

88. Fahmy, *All the Pasha's Men*, 76–112.

89. See Baer, *Studies in Social History*, 96–99.

90. Baer, "Popular Revolt," 220–21.

91. F. Robert Hunter, *Egypt under the Khedives, 1805–1879: From Household Government to Modern Bureaucracy* (Pittsburg: University of Pittsburg Press, 1984), 3.

92. Tilly's analysis of "categorical inequality" shows how classifications based on religious affiliation, ethnic origin, or race "do crucial organizational work" in decision making over resource allocation. Charles Tilly, *Durable Inequality* (Berkeley: University of California Press, 1998), 6–8.

Chapter 2

1. The mean annual value of Egypt's exports from 1853 to 1861 was 2.5 million LE, rising dramatically to 12 million LE during 1863 to 1872. *Statistique de l'Egypte*, 1873 / 1290 (Le Caire, 1873), 164.

2. Only from the 1860s, then, did manufactured imports really have an impact.

3. Cotton productivity gains were slight; output grew due to extensions of the cultivated area, and labor repression. Roger Owen, "The Development of Agricultural Production in Nineteenth Century Egypt: Capitalism of What Type?" in *The Islamic Middle East, 700–1900: Studies in Economic and Social History*, ed. A. L. Udovitch (Princeton, N.J.: Darwin Press, 1981), 521–46.

4. Hunter, *Khedives*, 104.

5. Ibid., 103.

6. This key development was new, as until 1840 "there was no association between office and landholding." Hunter, *Khedives*, 103. In contrast, Ismail granted 876,863 feddans to allies (Ibid., 106).

7. This slightly clumsy sounding formulation refers to either Ottoman subjects or Europeans who had obtained protected status under one or another European consul.

8. Hunter, *Khedives*, 115.

9. Cited in David S. Landes, *Bankers and Pashas: International Finance and Economic Imperialism in Egypt* (Cambridge, Mass.: Harvard University Press, 1958), 66.

10. Ibid., 96.

11. Memorandum by Baring enclosed in Malet/Granville, 5 May 1880, PRO FO633/96, 281.

12. Consul West, *Commercial Report 1872* 114, 60.

13. The achilles heel of self-strengthening was therefore partly made by class formation, which constrained the autonomy and shaped the policies of Ismail's state.

14. Memorandum by Baring enclosed in Malet/Granville, 5 May 1880, PRO FO633/96, 281.

15. Hunter, *Khedives*, 212.

16. DWQ *Muhafiz al-Abhath* 118: *Amwal.* Order / *Mudir* Daqhaliyya, 15 *Rabi'a al-Thani* 1280.

17. GP, AA (1876–1880, part 1, 1879), 124–25. NB. The exact date of this legislation is unclear.

18. Muhammad Mahmud Mawsi to Fayum Province. *Rabi'a al-Akhir* 1289. DWQ ND MA M9.

19. Yacoub Artin Pacha, "Essai sur les causes du renchérissement de la vie matérielle au Caire," in *Mémoires Présentés à l'Institut Egyptien*, vol. 5 (1907), 57–140, 61.

20. GP, AA (part 1, 1876–1880), 157–58.

21. DWQ MW NM 3/1/2 *'Awa'id wa Dara'ib wa Rusum Atayan.*

22. GP, AA (part 1, 1876–1880). Riad Pasha (President, Council of Ministers) / the Khedive: 147–49.

23. DWQ MW NM Alif/2/1/2 *'Awa'id al-Dukhuliyya* G. Antoniadis / Nubar Pasha, 5 May 1886, 10 May 1886, and 11 May 1886.

24. Ibid. 26 local subjects and 5 foreign subjects / Nubar Pasha 12 May 1886.

25. DWQ MW NM Alif / 2 / 1 / 2 *'Awa'id al-Dukhuliyya*. Director General of Indirect Contributions and Octrois / Minister of Finance, 20 January 1886.

26. *Borg Report*.

27. DWQ ND MA M30 Firemen Draftees/Interior 26 *Jumada al-Ula* 1296 [1879].

28. DWQ BMD *Raqam al-Durj* 262: *Sina'a:* 10 *Muharram* 1289–4 Safar 1290.

29. *Borg Report*.

30. DWQ MW NM alif / 1 / 9.

31. Mehmet Ali's conscription had been just as invasive. Fahmy, *All the Pasha's Men*, 99–103.

32. Malet to Granville. Cairo, 2 / 6 / 80: 75, 753.

33. Vallet, *La Grande industrie*, xvii–iii.

34. In search of increasing revenue and control, Isma'il commissioned two population censuses, the first of Cairo governorate, taken in 1868 and the second of Egypt, taken in 1872. The results of the 1872 census are not as detailed and have been published elsewhere, for example, Owen, *World Economy*, 149. The more detailed 1868 census is little known and I am presenting its results here for the first time. I have also used a Mansura tax return, issued in 1863 following a Khedivial order demanding tax increases following from increased prosperity, which records numbers employed in crafts and guilds and levels of tax paid in each. DWQ *Muhafiz al-Abhath: Mawadi'a Mukhtalifa Amwal* 118: Order / Mudir of Daqahliyya 15 *Rabi'a al-Thani* 1280 [1863] (hereafter *Mansura Tax Return*). Also, a partially useful return enumerates "different handicrafts throughout the country" drawn up by Sharif Pasha, the interior minister, in 1870, listed in Consul-General Stanton / Earl Granville, Cairo, 17 November, 1870, *Parliamentary Papers 1871*, vol. 68 (PRO), 119–120.

35. This finding is distant from the older conventional view of dislocation and destruction. Issawi, "Middle East Economic Development," 177.

36. Egypt's trade balance was positive through the 1860s and 1870s, export value almost doubling that of imports. Prior to the time when interest repaid exceeded the capital sums borrowed, the capital account balance was also positive. Owen, *World Economy*, 122–35.

37. According to the census, construction employed 30 percent of the artisanal workforce in Cairo, around 9,426 persons. In Mansura construction and carpentry employed a little less than one-fifth of manufacturers, fewer than food and textiles. Sharif Pasha's incomplete return from 1870 gives 17,110 workers in construction and related trades in Egypt as a whole, this total being roughly equivalent, in the same return, to numbers working in textiles. Stanton / Granville, Cairo, 17 November, 1870 *Parliamentary Papers 1871*, vol. 68 (PRO), 119–20.

38. See Alleaume, "Politiques urbaines et contrôle de l'enterprise," 147–88.

39. The commerce-led growth of Egypt's port cities spearheaded urbanization, as certain cities became hubs of credit, commerce, and communications. Robert Ilbert, *Alexandrie: 1830–1930: Histoire d'une communauté citadine* (Cairo: Institut Français d'Archéologie Orientale, 1996). Zayn al-'Abidin Shams al-Din Najm, *Bur Sa'id: tarikhuha wa tatawwuruha mundhu nasha'iha 1859 hatta 'am 1882* (Cairo: al-Hay'a al-'Amma li-l-kitab, 1987).

40. J. E. Marshall, *The Egyptian Enigma, 1890–1928* (London: John Murray, 1928), 10.

41. See Owen, *World Economy*, 150.

42. *External Trade Statistics*. In the 1860s, large-scale cotton ginning seasonally employing *fallahin* became widespread in the Delta. Sugar refining was also extended in Upper Egypt, especially on royal estates. Such industrial ventures, including the arsenal in the citadel, a shipyard in Alexandria, and the growing railway workshops in Bulaq, had little significant impact on small-scale crafts and services.

43. Even protected subjects suffered on occasion. For example, in February 1874, Michael Naggiar complained to Consul Rogers that his carts delivering sand from 'Abbasiyya to Isma'iliyya, where he was building two houses, were being detained at the octroi station. He claimed that the local authorities had no right to exact such dues from him. In this case, it appears that even the intervention of the consul had not done much to redress the protected subject's complaint. FO 841 / 40 Cairo Consular Court, no. 4, 1874. Michael B. Naggiar / Consul Rogers, 12 February 1874.

44. *Commercial Reports, Accounts and Papers* (1873) 64: Suez "Report by Consul George West on the Trade and Commerce of the Port of Suez for 1872," 50.

45. Census of 1897.

46. *Commercial Reports Accounts and Papers* (1873) 64: Suez "Report by Consul George West on the Trade and Commerce of the Port of Suez for 1872," 50.

47. *Borg Report*, emphasis added.

48. Ralph Borg, "Report on the Hygiene of Cairo and on the Condition and Labour of the Industrial Classes," Borg / Stanton (20 September 1870). PRO 141 / 73. Consuls warned Europeans not to come to Egypt without certain employment commonly enough during the 1880s.

49. *Commercial Reports Accounts and Papers* (1873) 64: Suez "Report by Consul George West on the Trade and Commerce of the Port of Suez for 1872," 48.

50. Consul Stanley / Stanton, 155.

51. DWQ *Ta'dad Nufus 1285 Lam / 1 / 84 / 86* (*Qadim* 742), 246–48.

52. DWQ ND MA M28 17 Safar 1296, and MA M31 12 *Rajab* 1296. Limekiln owners often owned boats for transport in the eighteenth century. Raymond, *Artisans*, 352–53.

53. *Sijill I'alamat* 1890: *Mahkama Misr al-Shar'iyya* no. 51. (1307/8 AH), case 61, p. 48.

54. In this connection, witness Borg: "[T]heir [high quality] toil is seldom appreciated by the purchasing public, the majority of whom look principally to cheapness rather than to quality of work and material," and in fact "thus the skilled artisan has little chance of displaying his abilities and when, from a sense of honour, he attempts to do so, he has to contend aginst serious disadvantages, which may lead him to ruin, unless he be supported by some influential friend." Borg, "Industrial Classes."

55. Daily subsistence for a local subject workman Borg put at 7–10 piastres, and for a European, 12.5–15 piastres. Rent for a local ranged from 10–120 piastres per month, whereas for a European subject from 60–160 piastres per month. A set of working clothes for a local cost 80–100 piastres, whereas a European's would could 125–200 piastres; holiday clothes for a local cost 300–400 piastres, whereas a European's holiday clothes cost 400–600 piastres. Overall, Borg estimated daily maintenance for a working man and his family, including subsistence, rent, and clothing to be 16.5 piastres per day for a local, and 22.5 piastres per day for a European. *Borg Report.*

56. Borg, "Industrial Classes." Borg states that migrant workers had more costly requirements in point of dwelling, clothing, and family maintenance.

57. Those imitating European-style work—carpenters, masons, sculptors, pavers in marble, gilders, plumbers, and shipwrights—were paid 10–20 piastres per day, and paid their assistants 5–10 piastres per day. Those performing "native work"—carpenters, stonecutters, pavers in stone, plasterers, glaziers, cartwrights, calkers, blacksmiths, locksmiths, shoemakers and builders—were paid 9–15 piastres per day, their assistants receiving 2.5–7.5 piastres per day. Further, turners, sawyers, painters, and coopers were paid 6–11 piastres per day, their assistants earning 2.5–5 piastres per day. From Alexandria, Consul Stanley reported that Egyptian carpenters and blacksmiths earned about 10 piastres a day and masons from 15–25 piastres per day. Consul Stanley/Consul-General Stanton, Alexandria, 2 November 1870. *Parliamentary Papers*, vol. 68, 1871 (PRO), 153.

58. Dr. Mackie/Consul-General Stanton, Alexandria, 25 September 1870. *Parliamentary Papers*, vol. 68, 1871 (PRO), 162.

59. Karl Baedeker, ed., *Egypt: Handbook for Travellers, Part First: Lower Egypt with the Fayum and the Peninsula of the Sinai* (Leipsic: Baedeker, 1878), 17–18. Baedeker wrote that Buza was "commonly drunk by the boatmen of the Nile, and by other persons of the lower orders." Baedeker continued, "[N]umerous taverns now exist exclusively for the sale of buzeh, kept chiefly by Nubians." Customers were of "both sexes" and the drink was "very slightly intoxicating."

60. *Al-Tabkit wa al-Tankit*, 2 (19 June 1881), 25–27.

61. The writer linked artisanal characteristics of mutual mistrust and envy to the backwardness of Egyptian industry in general as compared to European. The article described foreigners as clubbing together to avoid mutually ruinous competition. (The author failed to specify that less numerous European workers, along with their

skills and labor, were in heavy demand in Egypt.) The author urged that locals should learn "brotherhood" (*mushaqq*) from Europeans, proposing reform through the founding of guild councils to distribute contracts fairly and administer mutual funds to assist workers in distress. *Al-Tabkit wa al-Tankit*, 2 (19 June 1881), 25–7.

62. DWQ ND MA M5, People of the Guild of Box Makers / Interior Minister *Ramadan*, 1285 / 1868. This petition mentions that some of the apprentices were eight years old. These petitioners may have understated apprentices' rates because the petition claimed that they paid too much tax.

63. For rural-urban migration at midcentury, see Ehud Toledano, *State and Society*, 196–205. Forced labor remained widespread. Thousands were employed, and many hundreds killed, in the construction of the Suez canal, for example.

64. These "unemployed" were probably unskilled construction workers hired by the day. They paid tax at between 15 and 17 piastres per annum. *Mansura Tax Return*.

65. "Report by Consul George West on the Trade and Commerce of the Port of Suez for 1872," in *Commercial Reports: Accounts and Papers*, (1873), 50.

66. These figures seem high. Stanley / Stanton, 153. Stanley also noted that Egyptians who quarried and dug stone for building purposes were paid at about 8 piastres per day. Stanley noted that "Egyptians do this work and ordinary ground labour as well, if not better, than Europeans, and the latter are only paid more owing to the difficulty at certain times in procuring Egyptians. This rarely occurs, and it may be said that Egyptians monopolize all the unskilled out-door labour" (154).

67. DWQ ND MA M30 no. 1698, Firemen Draftees / Interior 26 *Jumada al-Ula* 1296 [1879].

68. Artin Pasha, "Hagg Ahmed le Maçon," *Bulletin de L'Institut Egyptien*, 5th series, vol. 8, 2nd fascicule (1914): 248–251.

69. Masters who employed and trained their sons in the trade were common. Nayl al-Fatatri was a Bulaq upholsterer in 1868. Two of his sons were upholsterers. DWQ *Ta'dad Nufus 1285 Lam / 1 / 84 / 86 (Qadim 742)*, 248. Examples of sons taking different professions from their fathers also abound, such as the baker of Bulaq whose son was a mat maker (350–51).

70. Alexandria's thirty-eight cotton weaving workshops sold 9,747 LE of cloth per annum. Cairo's sixty cotton and linen weaving workshops made a profit of 1,100 LE in 1871. *Statistique de l'Egypte*, 204–20.

71. The exact figure was 1,284,860 LE, which represents an average value per annum for the years 1874–78. Wool manufactures averaged 172,733 LE per annum, and silk and velvet manufactures 72,064 LE. The average per annum value of imported thread was 125,764 LE. *External Trade Statistics*.

72. *Statistique de L'Egypte*, 214–15.

73. *Mansura Tax Return*. (The average tax paid per year by Mansura crafts and service workers was around 40 piastres). Ali Mubarak mentions that Cairo had

eighty-three silk-weaving establishments in 1877, owned by forty-eight people. *Al-Khitat*, vol. 1, 94.

74. Ali Mubarak's statistics are from 1877. These dyehouses were owned by 389 persons. Ali Mubarak, *Al-Khitat*, vol. 1, 94. Most dyers were from Egypt and "from the capital" (*al-mahrusa*).

75. Ali Mubarak, *Al-Khitat*, vol. 1, 102. Over 150 tons of reed used for plaiting mats and 4,000 camel loads of rushes from Upper Egypt and elsewhere are also mentioned.

76. Donald Quataert has already demonstrated how widespread, energetic and adaptable rural textile manufacturing was in Anatolia during the nineteenth century. Quataert, *Ottoman Manufacturing*.

77. Consul-General Stanton/Earl Granville, Cairo, November 17, 1870. *Parliamentary Papers* 1871, vol. 68 (PRO), 119. Enclosing this return, Stanton wrote that the major exceptions to city-based industry in Egypt were in textiles: "The industrial population of Egypt, with the exception of weavers, dyers, and basketmakers, may be said to be confined to Cairo, Alexandria, and a few other large centres of population."

78. *Statistique de l'Egypte*, 213–15.

79. Ali Mubarak, *Al-Khitat*, vol. 1, 102–3. 115,000 mats were also imported in that year.

80. These figures suggest a rural-urban trade on a scale difficult to imagine for previous times, when Cairo's textiles production was extensive, guild monopolies stronger, and transport weak.

81. Tucker, *Women in Egypt*, 84–87.

82. *External Trade Statistics*, 1874–78.

83. *Mansura Tax Return*.

84. *Statistique de L'Egypte*, 212. This statistic, like others, is not to be taken literally, but it may provide some evidence for the pattern described here.

85. "Report by Consul G. West," in *Commercial Reports: Accounts and Papers*, vol. 64 (1873), 50.

86. Stanley/Stanton, 155.

87. I examine below the petitions marking the splintering of the "foreign" shoemakers guild from that of the local shoemakers in the late 1870s. Such "foreigners"—probably migrants from other Ottoman lands—may well have made European-style shoes, as they were called *jazmajiya*, and were likely richer than their local counterparts as they paid more tax. DWQ ND MA M34 1297.

88. *Mansura Tax Return*. Borg noted that a shoemaker doing "native work" in Cairo in 1870 earned from 8 to 15 piastres per day, and their assistants from 2 to 8 piastres. *Borg Report*.

89. According to the 1868 census of Cairo governorate.

90. The 53 water carriers of Mansura paid the lowest annual tax (14 piastres) of any guild in town, indicating extreme poverty. *Mansura Tax Return.*

91. Ali Mubarak mentions the presence of 174 such carts in Cairo in 1887. *Al-Khitat*, vol. 1, 103.

92. André Raymond, "Les Porteurs d'eau," 183–203.

93. Stanley reported that water and coal carriers at cotton gins in the delta were paid 320 piastres per month. Stanley / Stanton 1871, 152.

94. Prior to the nineteenth century, wheeled passenger transport in Egypt, and the Middle East more generally, was largely unknown. See, for example, Michael Winter, *Egyptian Society under Ottoman Rule 1517–1798* (Routledge: London and New York, 1992), 239.

95. Quoted in Toledano, *State and Society*, 166. See his discussion of how various modes of transport marked differing levels of status in Cairo around midcentury, 166–69.

96. Ibid., 167.

97. Hunter, *Khedives*, 100. Transport by litter was becoming steadily becoming obsolete.

98. 'Ali Mubarak, *Al-Khitat*, vol. 1, 95.

99. *Egyptian Gazette*, 4 January 1907, 4.

100. Baedeker, *Egypt* (1878), 230.

101. The term *arbajiya* in the census in the 1860s meant coachman or carter. At this stage the meaning depended on qualifying terms—for example, *arbajiya al-rukub* indicated a cab driver.

102. Ali Mubarak, *Al-Khitat*, vol. 1, 95.

103. Baedeker, *Egypt* (1878), 243.

104. An early usage of this phrase comes in a petition written to the Ministry of the Interior in 1879: DWQ ND MA M33 No. 477 Cairo Local Authority / Ministry of the Interior 27 *Dhu al-Qa'da* 1296.

105. DWQ ND MA M8 19 *Rajab* 1288: Sudanese cab-drivers / Interior. Cole used this group of petitions in *Colonialism and Revolution*, 183–88.

106. This name could of course be Cohen, or Kohane. The Arabic *kahin* is unclear.

107. Especially if such migrants were willing to work hard temporarily and then return to Upper Egypt—a familiar pattern for migrant labor.

108. Baedeker, *Egypt* (1878), 230–31.

109. Carting was practically nonexistent in the Middle East before the nineteenth century. Carts were used in northern Iraq and in certain spots in Anatolia, but riverine valleys and mountainous terrain favored boats, hooves, and feet over wheels. Owen, *World Economy*, 28, and 300, footnote 19. Gerber noted the unusual use of hundreds of wagons for transporting goods between Bursa and the hinterland in the seventeenth century. *Economy and Society*, 75–76.

110. Of the 1,470 carters and cabdrivers (*'arbajiya wa qumashjiya*) in the 1868 census, some were public cabdrivers, but almost certainly not more than about 300 to 400—that is, some figure lower than the total given by 'Ali Mubarak for the 1880s, by which time the trade had probably expanded. Further, private coachmen may have been included in this enumeration, which would have accounted for another three or four hundred persons. The balance was made up by carters.

111. DWQ MA 118: "Health": Report from the *Majlis al-Khasusi* to the *Ma'iyya Saniyya*.

112. *Mansura Tax Return*.

113. Carters were also known in the 1870s as *'arbajiya karu*, the latter word possibly coming from the French *carrosse*, meaning horse-drawn coach. Carts also carried poorer passengers.

114. DWQ ND MA M31 *Rajab & Sha'ban* 1296 *Ma'mur Dabtiyat Misr / Nizarat al-Dakhiliya* 12 *Rajab* 1296.

115. Bulaq was to be the center of unrest during the 1907 carters' strike. More carters lived in Bulaq than any other region of Cairo according to the 1917 census—1,098 persons out of 5,195.

116. See André Raymond, "Problèmes urbains et urbanisme au Caire," in *Colloque International sur l'histoire du Caire*, 353–72. Lane wrote in the 1830s, "Asses are most generally used for riding through the narrow and crowded streets of Cairo, and there are many for hire." *Manners and Customs*, 145. References to similar practices go back many centuries.

117. In 1817, Mustafa Kurd, Mehmet Ali's *muhtasib*, attempted to strip various privileges, including horse and mule riding, from Christian Greeks, Syrians, and Armenians. Kurd's attempts were to fail in the face of the "indignation" of the populace. Raymond, *Artisans*, 597. As Lane wrote in the 1830s, "Wealthy merchants, and the great 'Ulama, usually ride mules." *Manners and Customs*, 145. Riding horses was more elevated still, and in theory restricted to military men. Winter, *Egyptian Society*, 239. Even donkeys or asses could be associated with higher status. For example, in an anecdote related by Lane, a woman planning to launch a law suit went to her opponent's shop "riding on an ass, to give herself consequence." *Manners and Customs*, 126.

118. Baedeker, *Egypt* (1878), 244.

119. Ibid., 11. Lane had agreed in the 1830s that "Egypt has long been famed for its excellent asses." *Manners and Customs*, 145.

120. West recorded in 1872 that to hire a donkey and boy for a short ride at Suez cost about 2 piastres, and for the whole day 20 piastres. "Report by Consul George West," 50.

121. Baedeker, *Egypt* (1878), 231.

Chapter 3

1. West / Stanton, no. 35 (13 July 1870), PRO141 / 72. (Hereafter *West Report*).

2. Ali Mubarak, *Al-Khitat*, vol. 1, 100–1. In some villages in Upper Egypt village shaykhs allocated the artisanal professional tax. See Baer, *Social History*, 41.

3. Girgis Hanayn Bek, *Al-Atiyan wa al-Dara'ib fi al-Qatr al-Misri* (Bulaq: Government Press, 1904), 102–4. Guild shaykhs were supposed to send price data to Octroi stations where a 9 percent tax was levied. DWQ ND MA M10 Suez Governor / Interior. 16 *Safar* 1290.

4. Ahmad Ali (a senior boatman) / Ministry of Interior. *Jumada al-Akhira* 1295. DWQ ND MA M26.

5. GP, AA (1876–80, part 2), 304.

6. *Borg Report.*

7. Martin also claimed that guilds were becoming above all a means of taxation in *Les Bazars*, 27.

8. Hourani's politics of notables homologously involved intermediary figures balancing central demands against the claims of local constituencies. Hourani, "Ottoman Reform and the Politics of the Notables," in *The Middle East*, ed. Hourani et al., 83–111.

9. Cited in Alexander Schölch, *Egypt for the Egyptians! The Socio-Political Crisis in Egypt 1878–1882* (London: Ithaca Press, 1981), 35–36.

10. The Health Board (*Majlis al-Saha*), for example, registered the names of all Egypt's barbers, requiring an examination "in the presence of the shaykh of the guild." Successful barbers paid 10 piastres for a license (*rukhsa*). All guild shaykhs were officially registered by the 1870s. Ali Mubarak, *Al-Khitat*, vol. 1, 100–1.

11. GP, AA (1876–1880, part 2), 304.

12. Ibid.

13. DWQ MA 118: "Health": Report from the *Majlis al-Khasusi* to the *Ma'iyya Saniyya*.

14. DWQ MW NM *'Awa'id al-Dukhuliyya*. Alif / 2 / 1 / 2.

15. Village shaykhs, likewise unpaid by the state, acted similarly. As Schölch remarked, "[F]or an appropriate sum they 'overlooked' certain persons in their choice . . . for the corvée or . . . for the army; they took care that their fields came first when water was distributed, or made the villagers work them without pay;

when assessing and collecting taxes they knew how to line their own pockets; they lent money to the fallahin and took possession of their property if the fallahin were not able to repay them." Schölch, *Egypt for the Egyptians!*, 34–35.

16. DWQ ND MA M33 no. 43 1 *Dhu al-Qa'da* 1296.

17. *Majlis Isti'naf Misr* 1880, *Rabita* 75, *Raqam* 87, 8 *Jumada al-Ula* 1297. The shaykh, when asked to justify his hiding of people from the levy, put the blame on his deputies, who in turn claimed that the 50 members were new in 1294/1877. Police suspicions remained.

18. DWQ ND M34 4 *Jumada al-Ula* 1297 Local authority/Minister of Interior.

19. *Al-Ahram*, 16 January 1890. Martin, referring to these years three decades later, also called this shaykhly practice "abuse." Martin, *Les Bazars*, 27.

20. Schölch wrote similarly of the village shaykhs, "[T]heir position was unenviable, as they had to see to it that full satisfaction was given to the increasingly intolerable and insatiable demands of Isma'il." *Egypt for the Egyptians!*, 34–35.

21. Gabriel Baer, *Social History of Modern Egypt*, 111–12.

22. Ibid., 126.

23. Hunter, *Khedives*, 43. As Hunter explains, this new organization made redundant the long-standing and important urban post of market inspector (*muhtasib*).

24. Hunter, *Khedives*, 46.

25. Hunter, *Khedives*, 47–48. Interior was abolished in late 1859, but reestablished under Ismail.

26. Cole also analyzes what this legislation meant. *Colonialism and Revolution*, 164–89.

27. GP, AA (1876–1880, part 2), 12 *Rajab* 1286, 305.

28. DWQ ND MA M30 3 *Jumada al-Akhira* 1296.

29. DWQ ND MA M26 *Jumada al-Akhira* 1295.

30. GP, AA (1876–1880, part 2), 305.

31. Hunter, *Khedives*, 46.

32. As Cuno's research has shown, the roots of Egypt's "wealthy peasantry" extended back into the eighteenth century at least. *The Pasha's Peasants*.

33. See, for example, Serif Mardin, *The Genesis of Young Ottoman Thought: A study in the Modernization of Turkish Political Ideas* (Syracuse: Syracuse University Press, 2000).

34. Following Schölch's argument, one should note that the constitutionalism of the Consultative Chamber was not to be meaningful until the later 1870s. Schölch, *Egypt for the Egyptians!*, 14–20.

35. Conflict within and among elites provides incentives for resource-poor groups to take the risks of collective action. In particular, they "encourage portions of the elite to seize the role of 'tribune of the people' in order to increase their own political influence." Sidney Tarrow, "States and Opportunities: The Political Structuring of Social Movements," in *Comparative Perspectives on Social Movements*, ed. McAdam et al., 54–55.

36. Morgan argues that when the gentlemen of the seventeenth century Commons, contending with the English King, "affirmed the rights of all the King's subjects," they may not have "intended themselves to be taken literally." Nonetheless, their claims went on the statute books, "where all men could lay claim to its benefits." Edmund S. Morgan, *Inventing the People: The rise of Popular Sovereignty in England and America*, (New York: W.W. Norton and Co, 1988), 24. In Egypt, constitutionalist claims made by aspirant landholders in the 1870s made it onto the statute books in an uneven fashion, providing a basis for subsequent subaltern claim making.

37. Cited in Schölch, *Egypt for the Egyptians!*, 16–17.

38. DWQ ND MA M28 *Muharram-Safar* 1296. Sometimes exemption was a matter of negotiating one's tax status. Thus a metalworker from Suez in the early 1860s claimed he was not a "craftsman of the bandar [town]" but working (presumably temporarily) on "government service" in Suez. DWQ *Muhafiz al-Abhath. Mawadi'a Mukhtalifa* 118. "*Amwal*": Order / Finance 27 *Shawwal* 1280.

39. DWQ *Muhafiz al-Abhath. Mawadi'a Mukhtalifa* 118. "*Amwal*": High Order / Inspector of Bureaux of Upper Egypt, 11 *Shawwal* 1280.

40. European states' search for the means of war after 1750, particularly in conscription and taxation, led to bargaining with a pressured population and the forging of forms of citizenship. Charles Tilly, *Coercion, Capital and European States, AD 990–1990* (Oxford: Blackwell, 1990), 22.

41. Vatter notes similarly that the tax burden was unfairly dumped on lowlier guildsmen by their more powerful colleagues in Damascus. Sherry Vatter, "Journeymen Textile Weavers," 75–90. In Aleppo, such practices could have serious consequences, causing business to stagnate, shops to close and merchants to flee. See for example, Marcus, *The Middle East*, 176–77.

42. DWQ ND MA M5 Box-makers / Interior 9 Ramadan 1285 / December 1868.

43. Nelly Hanna, *Construction Work in Ottoman Cairo (1517–1798)* (Cairo: Institut Français d'Archéologie Orientale, 1984), 8.

44. Ghazaleh gives the best insight into this. *Masters of the Trade*, 87–96.

45. *Borg Report*.

46. Ali Mubarak, *Al-Khitat*, vol. 1, 100–1.

47. DWQ BMD *Raqam al-Durj* 271 2 *Jumada al-Ula* 1294 [1877] *Tawa'if. Majlis al-Khususi* / Diwan of Public Works.

48. DWQ *Majlis Isti'naf Misr* 1880, 8 *Jumada al-Ula* 1297.

49. DWQ ND MA M30, no. 1698 Firemen Draftees / Interior, 26 *Jumada al-Ula* 1296 [1879].

50. DWQ *Warid 'Ardhalat Dabityyat Misr* 40 / 2 / lam. (1286–87), p. 1, no. 70 *Muharram* 1286.

51. DWQ ND MA M26 no. 2382 14 *Jumada al-Akhira* 1295.

52. I have not seen evidence to suggest that guilds in Egypt distributed raw materials among members, as guilds did elsewhere such as in Aleppo. Marcus, *Eve of Modernity*, 175.

53. DWQ ND MA M10, al-Shafa'i / Interior Minister, *Rabi'a al-Awwali* 1290/ April 1873.

54. DWQ ND MA M10, Deputy of Alexandria Police, Deputy of Ministry of Interior, 5 *Rabi'a al-Akhir*, 1 June 1873.

55. DWQ ND MA, M8, 19 Rajab 1288.

56. Gentlemen in the English Commons in the seventeenth century did not say, "The King is wise and good. Therefore let us do what he wants." Instead, they said, "The king is wise and good. Therefore he must want what we want." Morgan, *Inventing the People*, 29–30.

57. "The basis of a claim to privilege and power creates, as it were, the groundwork for a blistering critique of domination on the terms invoked by the elite." Scott, *Domination and Resistance*, 103.

58. Certainly to impute mercy and justice to the leadership was a form of approbation and thus legitimated the control of the ruling group. But subalterns had very little choice. Even slight deviations from the sanctioned script could mean severe penalties. This kind of subaltern strategy should not therefore be understood simply as consent, or as implying a seamless hegemony.

59. Cole was equally impressed by guildsmen's assertiveness in *Colonialism and Revolution*, 188.

60. DWQ ND MA M15, Ahmad Muhammad / Interior Minister, *Muharram* 1292 / 1875.

61. A later judgement from the Cairo Tribunal of the First Instance did not dispute these claims.

62. DWQ ND MA M15, Ahmad Muhammad / Interior Minister, *Muharram* 1292 / 1875. Juan Cole examined this petition in *Colonialism and Revolution*, 181–3.

63. DWQ ND MA M15, President of the Cairo Tribunal of the First Instance / Interior Minister 7 *Muharram* 1292 / 14 February 1875.

64. Ibid.

65. DWQ ND MA M26, no. 2368 *Jumada al-Akhira* 1295.

66. DWQ ND MA M32, Cairo Police Commissioner / Interior, 5 *Ramadan* 1296.

67. The shaykh himself had previously used legal channels to go on the offensive against another candidate for the deputyship. In other words, much depended on whether or not official procedures were enforced. DWQ ND MA M32, *Ramadan—Shawwal* 1296: Cairo Police Commissioner/Minister of Interior, 5 *Ramadan* 1296.

68. DWQ ND MA M26, no. 2404 *Rajab* 1295.

69. DWQ ND MA M26, no. 2368 Alexandria Governor/Interior Ministry. *Jumada al-Akhira* 1295.

70. DWQ ND MA M27, no. 3270. *Dhu al-Qaʻda* 1295.

71. See Chalcraft, "The Coal Heavers of Port Saʻid," 110–24.

72. This virtuous or viscious circle was one of the multitudinous levers of state building in nineteenth-century Egypt.

73. DWQ ND MA M32, Mudir of Giza / Minister of Interior, 14 *Shawwal* 1296.

74. DWQ ND MA M33, 4 *Dhu al-Hijja* 1296.

75. Cole, *Colonialism and Revolution*, 164–89.

76. Such movements were present during the *Tanzimat* elsewhere in Ottoman lands. Doumani writes that peasants in petitions and lawsuits "also openly adopted the government's public interpretation of the *Tanzimat* and used it as a weapon against the authority and privileges of their traditional leaders." *Rediscovering Palestine*, 180.

77. This was the governor of Alexandria's summary of the porters' claim. DWQ ND MA M8, Alexandria Governor/Interior Minister, 11 January 1872 / 29 *Shawwal* 1288.

78. DWQ ND MA M8, Police/Alexandria Governor, 2 October 1871 / 17 *Rajab* 1288.

79. Ibid.

80. Raymond does not mention the *rukiyya* and found little evidence for mutual assistance in the previous century. *Artisans*, vol. 2, 567. Ghazaleh reported no mention of the term *rukiyya*, but documented a case where the porters of sugar implemented a communal division of income in 1720. *Masters of the Trade*, 63. Cole discovered a number of references to *al-rukiyya* in the 1870s related to porters, weighers, and measurers in Alexandria—essentially the same set of disputes and practices to which I am referring here. Cole, *Colonialism*, 71–75. Lowly guild members in eighteenth-century Aleppo took their more successful colleagues to court for refusing to share their business but in these cases the judges showed little sympathy, deferring to rules established within the guild. On the other hand there were agreements among guild members over due shares of raw materials, and occasionally over set prices and levels of production, which were fair to all members. Marcus, *Eve of Modernity*, 167. The *rukiyya* existed in seventeenth-century Aleppo. Bruce Masters, *The Origins of Western*

Economic Dominance in the Middle East: Mercantilism and the Islamic Economy in Aleppo, 1600–1750 (New York: New York University Press, 1988), 54.

81. *Borg Report.*

82. *Borg Report.*

83. Martin, *Les Bazars du Caire,* 66–67.

84. Martin, *Les Bazars du Caire,* 67. Baer took most of his evidence on Egypt from the nineteenth century, and arguably back-projected this state of affairs into the eighteenth century and before.

85. DWQ ND MA M8, Alexandria Governor/Interior Minister, 11 January 1872/29 *Shawwal* 1288.

86. DWQ ND MA M8, Police/Alexandria Governor, 2 October 1871/17 *Rajab* 1288.

87. This quotation is taken from a short note written by the police to the Alexandria governor above a porters' petition, the great bulk of which is missing from the file and the date of which is unknown. DWQ ND MA M8, Police/Alexandria Governor.

88. DWQ ND MA M8, Alexandria Governor/Interior Minister, 11 January 1872/29 *Shawwal* 1288.

89. Ibid.

Chapter 4

1. One of the strongest political accounts remains that of Schölch, *Egypt for the Egyptians!,* while Juan Cole has done most in English to investigate the social origins of the rebellion. Cole, *Colonialism and Revolution.* See also Latifa Salim, *Al-Quwa al-Ijtima'iyya fi-l-Thawra al-'Urabiyya* (Cairo: General Egyptian Book Organization, 1981).

2. Lord Cromer, *Report on the Administrative and Financial Condition of Egypt and the Progress of Reform [for 1891],* 11, emphasis added. Indeed, Cromer's reports in the 1880s were suggestively entitled "Financial Reports." After 1891 the term "administration" appeared alongside "finance" in the titles of Cromer's reports, as the colonial state multiplied its functions.

3. This was a kind of colonial Keynesianism, well before Keynes.

4. Vast sums were readily signed over for agricultural works in the 1880s and 1890s, while relatively tiny sums for education were haggled over intensely—a reminder of the force of this political economy. The only other area where the British were willing to add to Egypt's debt was in indemnifying European subjects whose property had been damaged during 'Urabi's rebellion.

5. "The provincial notables were anything but revolutionaries, and the majority of them also were no firm patriots. They were concerned about the protection of the socio-economic positions they had acquired in the context of the emergence of a dependent agrarian capitalism. When they were not able to secure their positions *against* the European control, they were prepared to consolidate and to improve them *with* the European control. . . . In the face of military intervention they deserted the 'Urabiyin." Schölch, *Egypt for the Egyptians!*, 314, emphasis in original.

6. Owen, *World Economy*, 135–48. Valued at around 50 million LE per annum in the years immediately preceding the First World War, the value of Egypt's external trade had advanced dramatically on that of the previous twenty years, when it was worth less than 20 million LE.

7. See Owen, "Capitalism of What Type?" 521–46. Legislation affording at least some measure of protection to small holders suffering from usury did not appear until 1912.

8. Owen, *World Economy*, 234.

9. Arminjon, *Situation Economique*, 590–91.

10. Around 5,000 worked in the cigarette industry, a few hundred in the Filature Nationale in Alexandria, and several hundred in the production and transmission of power (including gas workers and electric power suppliers). Beyond this a few thousand worked in factories, such as those for fertilizer, chemical products, and aerated drinks, a large-scale brick, pipe and pottery works, a *tarbush* factory, and one or two other establishments such as the Egyptian Salt and Soda company, or the cement works at al-Ma'asara. Overall, an estimate of 10–15,000 workers in large-scale industrial manufacturing prior to 1914 is fairly liberal. Of the almost half a million workers listed, this comes to just 2–3% of those employed. Thus, 97–98% of those employed in industry in Egypt in the 1900s were employed in the nonfactory sector. The census figures only include a few hundred cotton ginners and sugar refiners, probably because such employment was seasonal. Likewise railway and tramway employees are listed under transport.

11. This position is spelled out by a writer in 1889 under the title "The Future of Industry in our Country." The author takes issue with "extremists" who "only want industry" and argues that "business is not successful in a country that is not prepared for it," that Egypt's God-given agricultural fertility was highly profitable, and above all that industry would draw off workers "required to serve the land." "*Mustaqbal al-Sina'a 'Indana,*" in *Al-Muqtataf* (1889), 182–84.

12. As Cromer wrote, "Egypt being essentially an agricultural country, agriculture must of necessity be its first care. Any education, technical or general, which tended to leave the fields untilled, or to lessen the fitness or disposition of the people for agricultural employment, would be a national evil." Lord Cromer, *Annual Report of 1905*, 89. Such was Britain's civilizing mission in Egypt.

13. Cromer's excise duty of 8 percent on the Anglo-Egyptian Spinning and Weaving Company imposed in 1901 is the best known example of this. Owen has argued that British policy towards local industry was more complex, but his example

of favorable British intervention in the sugar industry is problematic, because seasonal sugar production was bound closely to an export economy which the British sought to encourage, and was no threat to colonial capitalism. Roger Owen, "Lord Cromer and the Development of Egyptian Industry," *Middle Eastern Studies* 2 (July 1966): 282–301.

14. The nominal value of imports roughly tripled between the early 1890s and the period from 1905 to 1909 to reach a value of about 23 million LE. In per capita terms import value doubled from 1 LE to 2 LE. Price inflation may have accounted for a reduction in the value of this increase in real terms of perhaps between 20 percent and 50 percent.

15. These figures are only rough indicators. The census was vague respecting women and domestic and seasonal work, and categories were reconstructed each census and were thus highly variable.

16. Moreover, if one looks ahead to 1927, the first industrial census tells the same story regarding the small size of units of production. Even in Cairo, where permanent units of production and trade were probably the largest in the country, 85 percent of manufacturing establishments involved five persons or less, and 93 percent employed 10 persons or less. Trading enterprises were even smaller: 95 percent of Cairo establishments employed five persons or less, and almost 99 percent ten persons or less. In the rest of the country, barring Alexandria, units were even smaller on average. In 1927, Cairo had about 40,000 commercial and manufacturing establishments—thus for every 20 men, women, and children living in Cairo, there was a workshop or shop.

17. "Le Dévelopment de l'industrie en Egypte," part 3 of the Report, 12–16. DWQ NM 19 *Lajnat al-Tijara*. As Levi, a long-time French subject and Jewish resident of Egypt and supporter of industrialization in Egypt, remarked a few years later, "[O]ne essential notion becomes clear, which is that Egypt, a country of small agriculture, is also a country of small industry." I. G. Levi, "Le Commerce et L'Industrie," in *L'Egypte*, 284–85, 296.

18. As the commissioners noted, "[S]mall industry . . . has a niche especially for objects adapted to taste, personal convenience or for objects difficult to conserve, or, finally, [which] work for small local demand." Thus works of "art, luxury and fantasy," it was said, remained suited to small-scale production. As long as small workshops did not compete exactly with big European industry, argued the report, they could continue to be a viable form of production in Egypt. "Le Dévelopment de l'industrie en Egypte," part 3 of the Report, 12–16. DWQ NM 19 *Lajnat al-Tijara*.

19. See, for example, the comments in *Egyptian Government Almanac 1917* (Cairo: Government Press, 1919), 185. FO848/16 PRO. The statistics noted above are derived from the censuses of Egypt. For more detail see Chalcraft, "Striking Cabbies," 229–31 and 237–38.

20. DWQ MW NM 19 *Lajnat al-Tijara wa al-Sana'a*, part 2, 4–5.

21. Ablett, "Asyut industries," *L'Egypte Contemporaine* (1910): 330.

22. *"Nubdha Sina'iyya,"* in *Sahifa al-Tijara* 3 (April 1925), 64. This "Industrial Sketch" was the result of the first systematic review of all Egyptian industry.

23. Lane, *Manners and Customs,* 38–40.

24. *External Trade Statistics.*

25. *Egyptian Gazette,* 12 December 1907, 4.

26. Tailors' wages in government service varied from 10 to 23 piasters. PRO FO 848/17 *Government Budget 1919,* 121–81.

27. In 1868, production had still been overwhelmingly of older-style products as shown above.

28. Karl Baedeker, *Egypt and the Sudan: Handbook for Travellers* (Leipzig: Baedeker, 1908), 49–50.

29. Along with saddlers, shoemakers reportedly obtained a large proportion of their fresh leather from Europe, where it was tanned cheaply. According to the author of the same article, their other raw materials were "mostly from Europe." *"Al-Sina'a fi Misr,"* in *Al-Muqtataf* (1912), 278–80.

30. Lord Cromer, *Annual Report for 1905,* 89.

31. In spite of the fact that Arabs were now for the most part wearing European-style shoes, sandals, or went barefoot.

32. Martin, *Les Bazars,* 54. Shoemakers used little more than a paring knife and a stool of hard wood on which the raw materials were cut.

33. PRO FO848/17 *Government Budget 1919,* 121–81.

34. Cotton imports, already enormously valuable, tripled to a value of over 3 million LE by 1914.

35. Sidney Wells and his team from the Department of Industrial, Technical and Commercial Education conducted fieldwork on the weaving trades up and down the country in 1909 and 1910. Their research was published in *L'Egypte Contemporaine* between 1909 and 1911.

36. J. Langley, "Note on the Native Mat Industry," *Journal of the Khedivial Agricultural Society and the School of Agriculture* 3 (Jan. and Feb. 1901): 83–85.

37. DWQ MW NM 19 *Lajnat al-Tijara,* part 2, 8.

38. DWQ MW NM 19 *Lajnat al-Tijara,* part 3, 31.

39. W. V. Shearer, "Report on the Weaving Industry in Asyut," in *L'Egypte Contemporaine* (1910): 183–86, 183. Qalyub was dubbed "very famous" for its weaving, and it was said that two thousand looms were at work largely making "colorful and cheap" cotton goods, *"Nubdha Sina'iyya,"* in *Sahifa al-Tijara* 3 (April 1925), 2–4.

40. Idku near Rosetta had four hundred looms for producing "quality silk cloth" in 1925. *"Nubdha Sina'iyya,"* in *Sahifa al-Tijara* 3 (April 1925), 9.

41. Sidney Wells, "The Weaving Industry in Egypt," in *L'Egypte Contemporaine* (1911): 52–73, 65.

42. Ibid., 69.

43. Ibid., 62.

44. Demand for mats remained high throughout these years. As Langley noted, "[T]hese mats are used in all native houses from the poorest to the richest." Langley, "Mat Industry," 83–85.

45. Wells, "Weaving Industry," 71.

46. As does the later industrial survey of 1925, *"Nubdha Sina'iyya."*

47. F. Moore Gordon, "Notes on the Weaving Industry at Mehalla-Kebir," *L'Egypte Contemporaine* (1910): 334–39, 335.

48. J. J. V. Wilson, "Textile Industry in Kalioubieh," *L'Egypte Contemporaine* (1911): 53. As the surveys of 1910 and 1925 make clear, the picture was not entirely dissimilar up and down the Nile.

49. Shearer in *L'Egypte Contemporaine* (1910): 185.

50. Attya Chenouda in *L'Egypte Contemporaine* (1910): 187.

51. Wells, "Weaving Industry," 72. In 1925, Abu Qurqas was still a major producer, mainly of woollen cloaks. By then, however, "most of the raw materials are brought from outside." *"Nubdha Sina'iyya," Sahifa al-Tijara* 4 (July 1925): 3–4.

52. Raw Egyptian cotton was expensive (owing to strong foreign demand), and of too fine a type for the heavy cloth in demand amongst the *fallahin*. Imported cotton yarn was therefore purchased from local merchants. Silk cocoons and silk yarn also had to be purchased from or provided by merchants, as sericulture was little developed locally.

53. *"Nubdha Sina'iyya," Sahifa al-Tijara* 1 (October 1925): 15–18. The industrial survey of 1925 noted that wool weaving in Giza and Damanhur and carpet making in Upper Egypt all benefited from abundant local supplies of raw wool. *"Nubdha Sina'iyya," Sahifa al-Tijara* 4 (July 1925): 2–3, 41–42; and no. 3 (April 1925): 9. This factor probably mattered before 1914 as well as after.

54. Ablett in *L'Egypte Contemporaine* (1910): 329.

55. Ibid.

56. Gordon, "Weaving," 334–39.

57. Wells, "Weaving Industry," 52–73.

58. DWQ MW NM 19 *Lajnat al-Tijara*, part 2, 10–11.

59. Ablett, "Asyut industries," 328.

60. Wells, "Weaving Industry," 68.

61. Ibid.

62. Gordon, "Weaving," 336. Cotton weavers in al-Fayyum and Abu Qurqas made 5 piasters per diem. The highest rural wage in the survey belonged to master wool weavers in Qalyubiyya, who could make 6–8 piasters profit per day. Wells, "Weaving Industry," 52–73. Shearer reported that a cotton weaver in Asyut could earn 6 piasters per day in "Weaving Industry," 183–86.

63. "*Al-Sina'a al-Baytiyya* [Household Industry]," in *Al-Muqtataf* (1911), 78–79.

64. Wells, "Weaving Industry," 61.

65. "*Al-Sina'a al-Baytiyya*," 78.

66. Wells expressed doubt about the large size of this figure. "Weaving Industry," 59.

67. Ibid., 63. (1 oke in Egypt = 1.248 kg). If al-Manzala's produce was comparable in price to imported Chinese silk yarn at 120 to 130 piastres per oke, then its production was worth something in the region of 60,000 LE per annum.

68. See, for example, Tucker, *Women in Egypt*.

69. "*Nubdha Sina'iyya*," *Sahifa al-Tijara* 3 (April 1925): 8. Such threads were used in the clothes of the *fellahin*. In 1925 it was reported in carpet making areas, "[Y]ou can scarcely pass by the fellahin . . . without seeing them spinning wool of sheep and goats and camels on hand spindles." "*Nubdha Sina'iyya*," *Sahifa al-Tijara* 4 (July 1925): 41–42.

70. In 1910, indigenous wool in wads was said to cost 2–3 piastres per *ratl*, whereas foreign wool, spun and dyed cost 11 piasters per *ratl*. Wells, "Weaving Industry," 60.

71. Ibid., 70.

72. Wilson, "Textile Industry in Kalioubieh," *L'Egypte Contemporaine* (1911): 66.

73. Ibid.

74. Shearer, "Weaving Industry," in *L'Egypte Contemporaine* (1910): 183–86.

75. Gordon, "Weaving at Mehalla-Kebir," in *L'Egypte Contemporaine* (1910): 334–39.

76. GP, AA (1901), 127. Such a tax would be difficult to collect and, more importantly, politically sensitive, where landowners and British sought to keep the *fallahin* quiescent.

77. Wells in *L'Egypte Contemporaine* (1911): 52–73. Weavers in Qalyubiya and Daqahliyya bought loom parts such as the cards in Cairo and made the rest locally. The old-established wooden looms made in Egypt were extremely inexpensive, as Metayer-Masselin was quick to point out in the late 1860s. Le Metayer-Masselin, *L'Egypte et l'Industrie Rubaniere* (Paris: Alcan-Levy, 1870), 49.

78. *"Nubdha Sina'iyya," Sahifa al-Tijara* 1 (October 1925): 15–18.

79. Gordon, "Weaving Industry," 334–39. In 1925 most cotton was woven by hand, as well as being "backward," antique, and low profit. *"Nubdha Sina'iyya," Sahifa al-Tijara* 3 (April 1925): 2–4.

80. A cotton loom in Asyut cost 80 piastres. Shearer, *L'Egypte Contemporaine* (1910): 184–86.

81. FO848/16 *Egyptian Government Almanac 1917* (Cairo: Government Press, 1919), 184–85.

82. Martin, *Les Bazars*, 52–53.

83. Wells, "Weaving Industry," 63.

84. Martin, *Les Bazars*, 52–53.

85. DWQ MW NM 19 *Lajnat al-Tijara*, part 3, 14.

86. Ibid.

87. 920 looms worked in Kirdasa in 1925. *"Nubdha Sina'iyya," Sahifa al-Tijara* 4 (July 1925): 2.

88. Martin, *Les Bazars*, 83.

89. Ibid., 61–62.

90. Ibid. Pierre Arminjon emphasized worker's endurance in the face of heat, long hours, and hunger, noting their "physical strength, stamina, sobriety, derisorily small wages, surprising skill of hands and feet, instinct for rhythm, and facility for adaptation and assimilation that one rarely finds in Europe." Arminjon, *La Situation Economique*, 153, 186–87.

91. Sidney Wells, "Preliminary Note on Weaving," *L'Egypte Contemporaine* (1910): 578–84.

92. Chenouda, "Asyut weaving industry," *L'Egypte Contemporaine* (1910): 187–88.

93. Sidney Wells, "Preliminary Note," 578–84.

94. Sidney Wells, *L'Egypte Contemporaine* (1911): 52–73. There were machines among the string makers in Benha in Qalyubiya. *"Nubdha Sina'iyya," Sahifa al-Tijara* 3 (April 1925), 2.

95. Wright and Cartwright, *Twentieth Century Impressions*, 230.

96. The paid-up capital and debentures of agricultural and urban land companies in Egypt increased from about half a million LE in 1892 to over 19 million LE in 1907, dropping back slightly after the slump of 1907 to around 18 million by 1914. Roger Owen, *World Economy*, 234.

97. See especially the research on a grand scale of Ilbert, *Alexandrie 1830–1930*. See Janet Abu Lughod's *Cairo: 1001 years of the City Victorious* (Princeton: Princeton University Press, 1971).

98. Gabriel Baer, "Urbanization in Egypt, 1820–1907," in *Beginnings of Modernization in the Middle East*, ed. W. R. Polk and R. L. Chambers (Chicago: University of Chicago Press, 1968), 158.

99. One travel guide of 1905 noted of Mansura that "several of the streets are wide and the houses are well built according to the French pattern." E. A. Wallis Budge, *Cooks Handbook for Egypt and the Sudan* (London: Thos. Cook and Son, 1905), 472.

100. As a confident promoter wrote in 1907, At the present moment throughout Egypt . . . buildings are rapidly springing up in increasing numbers. . . . [A]t Alexandria alone it is estimated that no less than 75 million bricks are used annually, and this number is continually increasing." *Egyptian Gazette*, 25 March 1907, 3.

101. Clerget, *Le Caire*, vol. 2, 200.

102. Ibid., 201. As one author wrote, "Those who knew Cairo ten or fifteen years ago cannot recognize it now, with its crowded streets, fine shops, high white houses, huge hotels, and expansion on all sides." A. O. Lamplough, *Egypt and How to See It*, (London: Ballantyne, 1908), 26.

103. *External Trade Statistics*. See also Arminjon, *La Situation economique*, 342.

104. In Qalyubiya, Sharqiya, Daqahliya, and Damietta Governorate, 21,245 tons of wood for construction, and 12,092 tons of stone and marble arrived by rail in 1899. Only coal, cereals, and cotton were greater in quantity and value. In 1898, 2,864 river boat loads arrived carrying stone. *Geographie Economique*, xvi–xvii. (1 boat load = 140 ardebbs; 1 ardebb = 198 litres).

105. For the derivation of these figures see Chalcraft, *Striking Cabbies of Cairo* (dissertation) 310–14.

106. Clerget, *Le Caire*, vol. 2, 281.

107. Ibid., 283.

108. Ibid., 268. The value of imports of construction materials was not particularly great in the early 1900s (about 1 / 2 million LE per annum) relative to the amount of construction, indicating significant local production.

109. See Raymond, *Artisans*, 353.

110. Ablett, "Asyut industries," 331.

111. Rayond, *Artisans*, 352–53.

112. In 1934, Clerget mentioned that such ovens had started to use either oil and coke or a mixture of oil and cinders for heat. Clerget, *Le Caire*, 280–82.

113. These figures are rounded off. The numbers in the censuses for furniture makers are unusable because they fluctuate wildly due to reclassification.

114. The average furniture import between 1909 and 1912 was only 59 percent of what it had been between 1904 and 1907, whereas imports of wood for

cabinetmakers rose four-fold from 7,793 LE in 1904 to 32,200 LE in 1912. *External Trade Statistics.*

115. Marshall, *The Egyptian Enigma*, 10.

116. Clerget, *Le Caire*, vol. 2, 287. During and after World War One furniture making expanded considerably, and went on to become one of Egypt's major workshop industries by the 1960s. See Joseph Cattaui Pasha, "L'Industrie," in *L' Egypte: Aperçu historique et géographique, Gouvernement et Institutions, Vie économique et sociale* (Cairo: L'Institut Français d'Archéologie Orientale, 1926), 291, and Mabro and Radwan, *Industrialization of Egypt*, 128.

117. See, for example, the following advertisement, published after the war: "Muhammad Sa'id Shintinawy, Upholsterer to his Majesty the King Gold Medal and First Place in Egypt Agricultural and Industrial exhibition 1907, 1909, 1912. Ready to make furnishings and furniture, 'Abdin Street, Cairo Telephone 26–36." *"Nubdha Sina'iyya," Sahifa al-Tijara* 1 (October 1925): 79.

118. Douglas Sladen, *Oriental Cairo: The City of the "Arabian Nights"* (London: Hurst and Blackett, 1911), 47.

119. Ablett, "Asyut Industries," 329.

120. *"Ittqan al-Sina'a" Al-Muqtataf* (1911), 595–96.

121. Marshall "was compelled" to make use of "country-made armchairs" in the 1890s and noted the ubiquity of a "type of divan stuffed with cotton or vegetable hair" in homes, and the use of roughly made wardrobes in government rest houses. *Egyptian Enigma*, 10, 88.

122. *Egyptian Gazette*, 18 December 1907.

123. Vallet, *Condition des ouvriers*, 6. The term "local subject" conceals the ethnic variety of builders who fell under Egyptian and Ottoman jurisdiction. In the 1868 census, under "carpenters, box and bed makers," admittedly a more multiethnic category than most, one finds 49 Turks, 25 Greek Orthodox, 9 Syrians, 8 North Africans, 1 Indian, and 1 Armenian.

124. In Cairo such occupations accounted for about 5,000 jobs in 1907, or almost a fifth of all those employed in construction and related trades.

125. Vallet suggested that about 70% of the indigenous construction workforce had been trained on site rather than by their fathers or small masters in workshops. Vallet, *Industrie au Caire*, 118.

126. Cromer, *Annual Report for 1905* (Accounts and Papers 137), 571–75.

127. Clerget, *Le Caire*, vol. 2, 284. Meanwhile, Cromer was asserting falsely that all plumbing and electric fitting was "done by Europeans." Cromer, *Annual Report for 1905*, 571–74.

128. Vallet, *Industrie au Caire*, 116.

129. Ibid., 123–25.

130. Martin, *Les Bazars*, 78.

131. Ibid. Masons in Cairo kept costs down by foregoing premises and living close to the stone quarries south of the citadel. According to the censuses of 1868 and 1917 most stone masons lived in Old Cairo and al-Khalifa. In 1917, of the 1,676 "stone and marble cutters, manufacturers of flat stones" in Cairo Governorate, most (1,028) lived in al-Khalifa, and of the remainder, over a third (252) lived in Old Cairo. As one observer noted in 1903, near the dusty tombs of the Khalifs "are built the little houses of the quarrymen and labourers from Cairo." R. Talbot Kelly, *Egypt Painted and Described* (London: Adam and Charles Black, 1903), 72.

132. Vallet, *Industrie au Caire*, 26–27.

133. Vallet also noted a major fall since 1907 in women on building sites, *Industrie au Caire*, 119.

134. Martin, *Les Bazars*, 83.

135. Vallet, *Industrie au Caire*, 123–25.

136. Ibid., 118.

137. Ibid., 125.

138. Ibid., 116–17.

139. A 1903 law regulated the commodiousness, danger, and hygiene of commercial and industrial establishments and some articles in the civil code related to contracts, but that was all.

140. Edoardo D. Bigiavi, "Des Accidents du travail et de la protection des ouvriers en Egypte," in *L'Egypte Contemporaine* (1910), 630–42, 630.

141. Vallet, *Industrie au Caire*, 119–22. Vallet also criticised the *kholi*, a subcontractor of often child labor to cotton gins and sugar refineries. Vallet, *Industrie en Egypte*, 23–24.

142. Clerget, *Le Caire* vol. 2, 157.

143. DWQ *'Abdin Diwan Khidiwi 'Ardhalat* 615, 1906–7, 12 June 1907.

144. Vallet, *Industrie au Caire*, 121.

145. *Egyptian Gazette*, 13 September, 1907. These kinds of stories were fairly frequent.

146. The census of 1897 lists just 1,052 and that of 1917 just 1,571 foreign subjects in construction; that is, less than 3 percent of the total.

147. A song reportedly sung by Upper Egyptian construction workers. In Legrain, "Chansons," 353.

148. Many cabdrivers lived in Bulaq according to the 1897 census.

149. Urban transport livestock collected at Qasr al-Nil bridge. *Egyptian Gazette*, 7 April 1908.

150. Where many cabdrivers also lived in 1897 according to the census.

151. The 1897 and 1917 censuses indicate that cabbies were increasingly living in Shubra, Wayly, and 'Abbasiyya.

152. 1917 census.

153. All the drivers were men, and they were largely local subjects born in Egypt, often, as we have seen, from Upper Egypt. Copts took up the profession: one Hanna al-Qubti signed a petition in 1879. DWQ ND MA M33, no. 477, Cairo Local Authority/Ministry of the Interior 27 Dhu al-Qa'da 1296. The censuses suggest that very few foreign subjects worked as cabdrivers.

154. Ali Mubarak, *Al-Khitat* 7: 185–86.

155. Census of 1917.

156. Ilbert, *Alexandrie*, 832.

157. Lamplough, *Egypt*, 16.

158. 15,851 to be exact. Census of 1917. Cabbies had replaced water carriers (who had been around 16,000 strong in 1897) as the commonest transport occupation in the city.

159. Baedeker, *Egypt* (1908), 172.

160. Ibid., 189.

161. Lamplough, *Egypt*, 82.

162. Census of 1917.

163. Marshall, *Egyptian Enigma*, 87. Colonial memoirs as well as fictional accounts indicate the quotidien usage of these cabs by rich foreign subjects, civil servants, and others. For example, Edward Cecil, *The Leisure of an Egyptian Official* (London: Hodder and Stoughton, 1921), 16; Lawrence Durrell, *The Alexandria Quartet* (London: Faber & Faber, 1986), 22, 618–22.

164. Baedeker estimated that "hire of donkeys and carriages and the inevitable 'pourboires'" added at least 5 francs to daily tourist expenditures. Baedeker, *Egypt* (1878), 3.

165. Baedeker, *Egypt* (1908), xvi. Tourists were informed that in Cairo "generally good victorias . . . are always abundant in . . . quarters . . . frequented by strangers." Baedeker, *Egypt* (1908), 34.

166. Lamplough, *Egypt*, 12. Cabs were recommended for numerous excursions, such as to the Antoniadis gardens outside of Rosetta. Baedeker, *Egypt* (1908), 22. Ladies were recommended to take cabs to "Muhammadan festivals." Ibid., 38.

167. As Berque noted in a footnote, "[T]his was the period of the *'araba* (cart)." Jacques Berque, *Egypt: Imperialism and Revolution*, trans. Jean Stewart (London: Faber and Faber, 1972), 98.

168. To give the exact figures: carters in Egypt, 1917: 11,943; in Cairo 5,195; and in Alexandria 1,728. The highest proportion of carters lived in Bulaq, and after that, Old Cairo.

169. Accordingly, in the rural areas, carts were much slower to appear. In parts of the Delta in 1899 "cart transport was unknown." *Géographie Economique*, xvi–xvii.

170. Nevertheless, Baedeker still insisted on their value: *Egypt* (1908), 34–35.

171. Martin, *Les Bazars*, 74. Two and three horse "omnibuses" for public hire with space for six to ten passengers started to be organized in Cairo and Alexandria in the 1890s and 1900s (*suwwaq al-awmnibus*).

172. Automobiles started to be licensed as "motorized taxis" and hired out to passengers during and after 1907. The census of 1917 records 435 so employed (*suwwaq al-sayyarat al-'umumiya*).

173. Baedeker, *Egypt* (1908), xvi.

174. GP, QM 1900, 198. The regulation banned carts, cabs, or camels from Khalij Street.

175. Hence the large numbers of cabbies in Midan 'Ataba al-Khadra, where the trams converged, or outside the Gare Centrale in Alexandria.

176. As Marshall noted, "[T]he only way to reach [Mena house before the early 1900s] was by carriage or donkey from Cairo." *Egyptian Enigma*, 10.

177. Ibid. 11.

178. Lamplough, *Egypt*, 12.

179. DWQ *'Abdin Diwan Khidiwi 'Ardhalat* 615 1906–7, 28 January 1907.

180. These are Sladen's observations. *Oriental Cairo*, 58–59. Saddlers, harness makers, and whip and lash makers in Cairo increased their numbers by half between 1897 and 1907.

181. Piles of fodder were observed in 'Ataba al-Khadra. The 1903 abolition of the octroi duty on goods entering Cairo probably had a favorable impact on this particular supply line.

182. There were 793 dealers and hirers of donkeys, horses, and camels in Cairo in 1907 according to the census. There are several examples of cabdrivers who, along with their families, owned or purchased horses. In one case, Muhammad Suleyman's son purchased two horses to pull his cab. DWQ *'Abdin Diwan Khidiwi 'Ardhalat* 615 1906–7, no. 46, 10 January 1906.

183. A certain Ahmad 'Ali was renting a stable from Isma'il Darwish. In this case, the latter was responsible, at least according to Ahmad 'Ali, for the upkeep and hygiene of the stable. DWQ *'Abdin Diwan Khidiwi* 613, 1902–3, 3 March 1902.

184. Vallet claimed in 1911 that coachdriving included both salaried employees and a large number of small employers or masters. Vallet, *Industrie au Caire*, 143–44.

185. DWQ *'Abdin Diwan Khidiwi 'Ardhalat* 615, 1906–7, 28 January 1907.

186. PRO FO848/17 *Government Budget 1919*, 121–81.

187. Baedeker alluded to this as early as 1878: "[T]he hotel commissionaires with their omnibuses or carriages await the arrival of each train." Baedeker, *Egypt* (1878), 229.

188. PRO FO841/55, case no. 3, 19 May 1893.

189. DWQ MW NM 19 *Lajnat al-Tijara wa al-Sina'a* 1916, part 3, 10.

190. Heller, *Labor of Development*, 42.

191. Martin, *Les Bazars*, 61.

Chapter 5

1. Cole, *Colonialism and Revolution*, 190–234.

2. Even Cromer later apologized for the often arbitrary and brutal behavior of these commissions.

3. DWQ MW NM 11, *Taqarir* 1879–1923, File 17/2/1887. Report from Mustafa Fahmy/President of Council of Ministers dated 26/1/1887 enclosing Alexandria weighers' petitions.

4. DWQ MW NM, Alif/2/1/2, *'Awa'id al-Dukhuliyya*. Note to the Ministry of Finance, May 1886.

5. Ibid.

6. GP, AA (1890), 17–33.

7. DWQ MW NM, Zal/1/9, *Mayzaniyya 'Amma* 1890–92: Finance Committee/Council of Ministers.

8. GP, AA (1892), 9–10; DWQ MW NM, h/1/9, *Mayzaniyya 'Amma* 1892–94. Finance Committee/Council of Ministers.

9. Even this small tax caused oil-pressing establishments to close. DWQ MW NM, alif/2/1/2, Note/Ministry of Finance, May 1886.

10. Artin Pasha, "Essai sur renchérissement," 63–65.

11. Some have mistakenly argued that taxes on crafts and service workers were increasing at this time. See for example 'Amr, *Al-Tawa'if Al-Hiraf*, 286.

12. Apart from significant intervention in agriculture to raise revenue for debt repayment.

13. GP, AA (1876–80, part 1), 124–25.

14. Artin Pasha, "Essai sur renchérissement," 63.

15. Hence the Prime Minister's memorandum to the new Khedive in 1879 condemning the "current tax regime" as "pernicious (*say'a*)". GP, AA (1876–80, part 1) Riad Pasha (President of the Council of Ministers)/Khedive, 147–49.

16. *Al-Ahram*, 26 November 1889.

17. Ibid.

18. GP, AA (1892), 9–10.

19. Corruption in taxation in general, and regarding the octroi in particular was the subject of a great many reports, petitions, and complaints. DWQ MW NM, box no. 11 *Taqarir* 1879–1923 Inspector General of Octroi/Minister of Finance 7 August 1881; and DWQ MW NM, alif/2/1/2, *'Awa'id al-Dukhuliyya* G. Antoniadis/Nubar Pasha 5 May 1886.

20. Martin, *Les Bazars*, 85.

21. Tilly's remarks are strikingly appropriate: "Any system of indirect rule set serious limits on the quantity of resources rulers could extract from the ambient economy. Beyond that limit, intermediaries acquired an interest in impeding extracting, even in allying themselves with ordinary people's resistance to state demands. In the same circumstances, however, rulers developed an interest both in undermining the autonomous powers of intermediaries and in making coalitions with major segments of the subject population." Tilly, *Coercion Capital*, 104.

22. Contrary to Baer's claim this decree only annulled collection, not assessment.

23. GP, QM (1880) Publication from Ministry Finance, 15 Jan 1881, 294.

24. GP, QM (1880). From Ministry of Finance, 4 January 1882.

25. DWQ NA 1/5, 6 June 1888.

26. GP, QM (1886). Publication from Ministry of Finance 25 September 1886, 589–90.

27. GP, AA (1890), 19.

28. DWQ MW NM h/4 *Mawadi'a Mukhtalifa* 1888–1894.

29. GP, AA (1892), 9–10.

30. GP, AA (1890), 17.

31. Arminjon, *La Situation*, 176–77.

32. Martin, *Les Bazars*, 27–28.

33. *'Abdin Diwan Khidiwi* 613 1902–03, 4 January 1902.

34. DWQ *'Abdin Diwan Khidiwi 'Ardhalat* 615 1906–1907, 30 March 1907, no. 360.

35. DWQ *'Abdin Diwan Khidiwi* 613 1/1902–12/1903, 15 April 1902.

36. Albert Metin, *La Transformation de l'Egypte* (Paris: Felix Alcan, 1903), 291–92.

37. Arminjon, *Situation Economique*, 176–78.

38. Martin, *Les bazars*, 28.

39. *Egyptian Gazette*, 15 January 1907, 4. Cf. similar complaints by West (1872) and 'Ali Mubarak in the 1880s.

40. G. Martin and I. G. Levi, "The Egyptian Market and the Usefulness of Publishing Market Price Lists," in *L'Egypte Contemporaine* (1910): 441–89, 475–79.

41. Ibid.

42. Practice and discourse among fishermen escaped at one level what Mitchell has called "modern microphysical methods of order," the "meticulous organization of space, movement, sequence, and position," "methods of enclosing and partitioning space, systematizing surveillance and inspection, breaking down complex tasks into carefully drilled movements, and coordinating separate functions into larger combinations." Timothy Mitchell, "The Limits of the State: Beyond Statist Approaches and Their Critics," *American Political Science Review* 85 (March 1991): 77–96, 92. Nonetheless, the unofficial activity of the fishermen was interpellated by the coming of these new forms of order.

43. "Informalism" is defined here as activity associated with state functioning in official discourse—coercion, tax raising, making binding rules, regulation—and yet carried out by members of society who have no official connection to or sanction by the state. Because official discourse changes so does activity dubbed "informal." This is precisely what was happening in the 1880s and 1890s, when activities long sanctioned by the state—that is, the levying of customary dues by shaykhs—became illegal and thus in this case "informal."

44. Such informalism was later married to another new practice, the organization of craft unions after 1909. As Goldberg's nuanced discussion shows, the terms *ta'ifa* and *shaykh* persisted for decades in this context, as did personalism and patronage. But I argue that these continuities meant something entirely new in a society now transformed by world economic integration, restructuring, state building and colonial rule, and discontinuity with the guilds of the eighteenth century is more salient than any traditional continuity. Goldberg, *Tinker and Textile Worker*, 77–92.

45. Tilly, *Coercion Capital*, 106.

46. PRO FO848/16. Documents presented to the Milner Mission. *Code Administratif Egyptien*, (Paris: Libraire de la Société du Recueil Sirey, 1911). For details see Amir, *Tawa'if al-Hiraf*, 235–45.

47. Vallet, *La Grande Industrie*, 139–40.

48. Arminjon, *La Situation*, 177.

49. Metin, *Transformation*, 291.

50. DWQ NA 1/5, 6 June 1888.

51. GP, AA (1883). Regulations for the Organisation of the National Courts, 115.

52. The cry "no taxation without representation" had, of course, been writ large in popular demands for political inclusion since the third quarter of the eighteenth century in Europe and its settler colonies. The logic of constitutionalism in the 1860s and 1870s in Egypt itself had in some measure followed this pattern, as I argued in chapter 3.

53. To put the numbers of this class into perspective, there were fewer magistrates, advocates, clerks, doctors, surgeons, midwives, pharmacists, architects, engineers, and other liberal professions listed in the 1907 census (about 37,000 altogether) than there were food producers (butchers, bakers, patisserie makers, millers, and so on), who numbered over 40,000.

54. Yaseen Noorani, "A Nation Born in Mourning: The Neo-classical Funeral Elegy in Egypt," *Journal of Arabic Literature* 28 (1997): 38–67, 49.

55. Jacques Berque, *Egypt: Imperialism and Revolution*, 238.

56. As a writer in al-Muqtataf put it in 1889, "Nothing weighs more heavily on the East than the ruin of its industry." "Household Industry," *Al-Muqtataf*, 1 December 1889, 145.

57. "Reasons for the Backwardness (*ta'akhkhur*) of Industry in Syria," in *Al-Muqtataf* (1884), 85.

58. Artisans were praised for being hard working and possessed of remarkable skills of eyes, hands and feet. Martin mentions the skill and rapidity of glance that denoted a great sangfroid among all the metal beaters. He spoke of children of eight to ten years beating copper discs distinctly and successively with "unbelievable speed": "[O]ne hammer never hits its neighbour's even though most of the hits are on the same point," Martin, *Les Bazars du Caire*, 61–64. Vallet noted laborers' "endurance," and "great resistance to fatigue." Vallet, *Condition des ouvriers*, 9–10.

59. Georges Laplange, who directed l'Ecole des Beaux Arts in Cairo before 1914, was very positive about the special aptitudes of Egyptian artisans who turned their skills to artistic work in cabinetmaking, carving, fine metal work, and goldsmithery. G. Laplange, "L'Avenir des industries d'art en Egypte," in *Bulletin de L'Institut Egyptien*, vol. 7, part 1 (1913), 38–42.

60. Some claimed that various Egyptian artisans remained highly skilled in the production of artistic or luxury objects (such as inlay work, lamp making, and fine weaving), and thus such areas should be preserved and developed. 'Al-Sina'a al-'Arabiyya,' [Arabic Industry] in *Al-Muqtataf* (1909), 7–9.

61. Hand industry and domestic production, it was said, was a vital presence in Egypt as in Europe, and should therefore be encouraged. "Al-Sina'a al-Baytiyya," *al-Muqtataf* (1 December 1889): 146.

62. "Al-Sina'a al-Baytiyya," *al-Muqtataf* (1911), 78–79.

63. Until this time, except for an industrial school for training artisans in Mansura founded in 1889, and a small government-run industrial school founded in Alexandria in 1901, the only government provision for artisanal education was the School of Arts and Crafts in Bulaq, founded by Mehmet Ali, but which by the 1890s and 1900s was mainly turning out clerks and telegraphists for the Railway and Telegraph Administration.

64. Sidney H. Wells, "L'Organisation et le développement de l'enseignement agricole industriel et Commercial en Egypte," in *L'Egypte Contemporaine* (1911): 345.

65. Wells, "Enseignement industriel," 345–46.

66. Cromer mentioned wheelwrights, blacksmiths, printers, bookbinders, masons, plasterers, carpenters, plumbers, and electricians, as well as "platelayers, moulders, mechanics . . . carriage builders, painters, upholsterers, [and] glaziers" for the railways. *Annual Report for 1905*, 89.

67. The SPCA was founded in England in 1824 and became the Royal SPCA in 1840. In Egypt it was referred to simply as the SPCA.

68. Marshall, *The Egyptian Enigma*, 34.

69. Baedeker referred to the hospital in 1908 as the "Clinical hospital of the Society for the Prevention of Cruelty to Animals." *Egypt* (1908), 74.

70. FO 371/450, enclosure to a PQ 12378, 10 April 1908.

71. Some published their passionate allegiance to the cause. *Egyptian Gazette*, 6 July 1907.

72. It provoked questions in parliament in England, and later secured letters from the Foreign Office to Gorst. FO 371/450 PQ 12378, 10 April 1908; FO 371/450 43520 Malet/Gorst, 15 December 1908.

73. A raft of regulations affecting cabbies across Egypt (from Gharbiyya province in the Delta, to Asyut in Upper Egypt) had been promulgated in the early 1890s, probably in view of the public and visible nature of a trade patronized by the elite. Licenses were to be issued by the governorate or provincial offices in return for the registration of the applicant's name, title, nationality, address, and description of his cab. Livestock were to be kept healthy, able, and adequately fed. Cabs were restricted to certain areas, and tariffs were drawn up. Daqhaliyya Province, April 1893: GP, QM (1893), 194–197; Gharbiyya, Sharqiyya, Asyut, May-June 1893: GP, QM (1893), 275–95; Cairo governorate: GP, QM (1894), 166; Alexandria and Suez Governorate: GP, QM (1894), 400–5 and elsewhere. In 1901, regulations on passenger cabs were tightened, GP, QM (1901), 170–3.

74. The figures make clear that a considerable proportion of Cairo's very numerous cabdrivers and carters were directly affected. *Egyptian Gazette*, 5 September 1907.

75. *Egyptian Gazette*, 27 February 1907, 3.

76. *Egyptian Gazette*, 18 October 1907.

77. Before 1800 the "basse classe" (*al-nas al-dun*) included stablemen. Raymond, *Artisans*, 381.

78. Jamal Badawi, "'Afrit," in *Misr min Nafidhat al-Tarikh* (Cairo: Dar al-Shuruq, 1994), 196–98. Al-Badawi is here summarizing Kitani's account from the early 1900s. At some point, further, the word *'arbagi* became an insult in popular idiom, meaning "low life" or "scum."

79. DWQ *'Abdin Diwan Khidiwi* 613, 1902–3, 3 March 1902.

80. DWQ *'Abdin Diwan Khidiwi 'Ardhalat* 615, 1906–7, no. 46, 10 January 1906.

81. DWQ *'Abdin Diwan Khidiwi 'Ardhalat* 615, 1906–7, 24 November 1906.

82. DWQ *'Abdin Diwan Khidiwi 'Ardhalat* 615, 1906–7, 28 January 1907.

83. DWQ *Sijillat 'Abdin Qayyid al-'Ardhalat al-Warida*, 1 / 27 / 5 / S, 1893–94, 16 March 1893.

84. DWQ *'Abdin Diwan Khidiwi 'Ardhalat* 615, 1906–7, no. 288, 17 March 1907.

85. DWQ *'Abdin Diwan Khidiwi 'Ardhalat* 615, 1906–7, no. 309, 21 March 1907.

86. DWQ *'Abdin Diwan Khidiwi 'Ardhalat* 615, 1906–7, no. 386, 2 April 1907. The third person is used here because this is the scribe's summary of al-Busna's petition.

87. *Egyptian Gazette*, 27 February 1907, 3. Such incidents would have further ingrained the colonial prejudice (which mistook politics for nature), that cabbies were naturally boorish.

88. Seven days in prison and a 100-piastre fine decreed for emaciation. *Al-Jarida*, 18 April 1907, 3.

89. As Tilly has suggested, although in a noncolonial context, "[d]irect rule and mass national politics grew up together, and reinforced each other mightily." *Coercion Capital*, 115.

90. Smaller strikes included the Alexandria coal heavers in 1900, the Alexandria tramwaymen in 1900, the Alexandria telegraphists in 1903, and another cigarette rollers' strike in 1903–4. See Beinin and Lockman, *Workers on the Nile*, 48–59.

91. Quataert and Zürcher, eds., *Workers in the Ottoman Empire*; Quataert, *Social Disintegration and Popular Resistance*; Lockman, ed., *Workers and Working Classes*; Habib Ladjevardi, *Labor Unions and Autocracy in Iran* (Syracuse, N.Y.: Syracuse University Press, 1985).

92. Beinin and Lockman, *Workers on the Nile*, 55.

93. Asef Bayat, *Street Politics: Poor People's Movements in Iran* (New York: Columbia University Press, 1997), 16–19.

94. *Egyptian Gazette*, 18 April 1907.

95. *Al-Ahram*, 18 April 1907. *Al-Jarida* estimated that there were more than two-thousand strikers, and that the number at work under police supervision remained very small. *Al-Jarida*, 18 April 1907, 3. *Al-Ahram* estimated that as many as twelve-thousand cabmen had struck work—surely an exaggeration.

96. *Al-Jarida*, 18 April 1907, 3.

97. Ibid.

98. Ibid.

99. Ibid.

100. *Al-Jarida*, 24 April 1907, 4.

101. Ibid.

102. Ibid.

103. *Al-Ahram*, 19 April 1907.

104. *Egyptian Gazette*, 26 April 1907.

105. *Al-Jarida*, 1 May 1907, 4.

106. Twenty-three cabmen were ultimately accused of attacking police, tramway workers, or passengers during the strike. Eighteen of these went to prison for between seven and thirty-one days. *Al-Jarida*, 1 May 1907, 4.

107. *Al-Ahram*, 20 April 1907.

108. *Al-Jarida*, 18 April 1907, 3.

109. The colonial press tended to dismiss the cabmen as a brutish urban rabble without purpose or legitimate cause. Here is the *Journal du Caire:* "These recent events clearly show that at the present time there is a large number of people in Cairo without any occupation, whose pleasure it is to utilise their leisure in the refined amusement of maltreating the passengers and the staff of the tramways. In such a case the police in every country in the world sweeps them away and clears the town of this disagreeable class. When are we to have a clearance at Cairo?" Quoted in *Egyptian Gazette*, 22 April 1907. *Les Pyramides* hinted that "the whole affair was engineered for a political object by the Anglo-Egyptian authorities." Quoted in *Egyptian Gazette*, 23 April 1907.

110. FO371/450 12378, 10 April 1908.

111. FO371/450, no. 14076, 18 April 1908, Gorst/Sir Edward Grey.

112. FO371/450, no. 43520, PQ John Robertson MP.

113. *Egyptian Gazette*, 8 June 1907.

114. The strikes were the cabmen (18 April), Carters (20 April) silk weavers (21 April), bakers' boys (25 April), mat makers (27 April), omnibus drivers (29 April), domestic servants (30 April), survey workers (2 May), printers (May), tramway

workers (petition but no strike, 7 May), weavers (22 May), fishermen of Matariya (24 May), butchers (30 May), bakers (8 June), automobile drivers (5 October), employees in commercial houses (agreement 13 October), automobile drivers (14 October), butchers (15 October), cabmen (31 October), and civil servants (13 November).

115. *Egyptian Gazette*, 22 April 1907.

116. DWQ *'Abdin Diwan Khidiwi 'Ardhalat* 615, 1906–7, no. 556, 5 May 1907.

117. Ibid.

118. *Al-Ahram*, 21 May 1907.

119. *Al-Ahram*, 23 May 1907.

120. *Al-Ahram*, 25 May 1907.

121. *Al-Ahram*, 1 June 1907.

122. DWQ *'Abdin Diwan Khidiwi 'Ardhalat* 615, 1906–7, 4 June 1907.

123. DWQ *'Abdin Diwan Khidiwi 'Ardhalat* 615, 1906–7, 12 June 1907.

124. DWQ *'Abdin Diwan Khidiwi 'Ardhalat* 615, 1906–7, 15 June 1907.

125. DWQ *'Abdin Diwan Khidiwi 'Ardhalat* 615, 1906–7, 15 June 1907.

126. DWQ *'Abdin Diwan Khidiwi 'Ardhalat* 615, 1906–7, 22 July 1907.

127. *Al-Ahram*, 1 June 1907.

128. *Al-Ahram*, " 'Azmat al-Jazzarin," 11 October 1907.

129. *Al-Jarida*, 15 October 1907, 4.

130. *Al-Ahram*, 11 October 1907.

131. *Al-Jarida*, 24 October 1907, 3.

132. *Al-Jarida*, 24 October 1907, 3.

133. Vatter, "Militant Journeymen," 1–21.

134. Martin, *Les Bazars*, 86. This is to follow Lockman's powerful analysis of the importance of the nationalist movement in the making of labor protest in the early twentieth century. Zachary Lockman, "Imagining the Working Class: Culture, Nationalism, and Class Formation in Egypt, 1899–1914," *Poetics Today* 15 (summer 1994): 157–90.

135. *Egyptian Gazette*, 23 April 1907.

136. *Al-Jarida*, 21 April 1907, 4.

137. *Al-Jarida*, 1 May 1907, 4.

138. *Al-Jarida*, 27 April 1907, 4.

139. *Al-Ahram*, 22 May 1907.

140. Lockman, "Imagining," 157–90.

141. DWQ *'Abdin Diwan Khidiwi 'Ardhalat* 615, 1906–7, 6 October 1907.

142. *Egyptian Gazette*, 18 October 1907.

143. *Egyptian Gazette*, 21 October 1907.

144. *Al-Jarida*, 27 October 1907, 3.

145. *Egyptian Gazette*, 12 February 1908.

146. *Egyptian Gazette*, 21 March 1908.

147. Vallet, *Industrie au Caire*, 143–44.

148. Beinin and Lockman, *Workers*, 67.

149. Wells, "Enseignement Industriel," 349.

150. Ibid.

151. "*Al-Sina'a fi Misr*," in *al-Muqtataf* (1912), 278–80.

152. Sidney Wells, "Weaving Industry," 52–73.

153. Wells, "Enseignement Industriel," 369.

154. Beinin and Lockman, *Workers*, 69.

155. PRO FO848/7, "Note from the Director-General (Mr. S.H. Wells) on the present position and needs of Technical Industrial Commercial Education—March 1917."

156. This criticism did not apply to the model workshops and almost all the other industrial schools which trained artisans with a *kuttab* education who could not aspire to office work or teaching. PRO FO/848/8, no. 7a, Jan–March 1920, William A. Stewart, "Memo on Egyptian Education".

157. *The Egyptian Government Almanac 1917* (Cairo: Government Press, 1917), 182. (FO848/16)

158. Beinin and Lockman, *Workers*, 69.

Conclusion

1. In October 1908, for example, 1,600 tramway workers struck work in Cairo. In the summer of 1908 the railway workers in the Bulaq depots threatened a strike, and subsequently struck in their thousands in October 1910. Beinin and Lockman, *Workers*, 57–76.

Bibliography

ARCHIVES

The Egyptian National Archives, Cairo (Dar al-Watha'iq al-Qawmiyya)

Cairo Appeals Court: *Majlis Isti'naf Misr*, no. 87 [1880]

Cairo Commercial Court: *Majlis Tujjar Misr: Khulasat wa Qararat wa Ifadat* 1272–1297 AH

Cairo Governorate: *Sijillat Muhafizat Misr: Warid al-'Ardhalat* 31/1/lam 1275–1296 AH; *Sijillat Muhafizat Misr: Ta'dad nufus* 1285 84/1/lam [Cairo Census, 1868]

Cairo Tribunal of the First Instance: *Majlis Ibtida'i Misr: Qayyid al-Qararat*, nos. 529–585 [1879–1883]

Card Index: *Bitaqat Mawadi'a al-Dar*

Council of Ministers (Majlis al-Wuzara'): *Nizarat al-Maliyya* [Finance]; *Nizarat al-Dakhiliyya*; [Interior]; *Nizarat al-Ashghal* [Public Works]; *Majlis al-Nuzzar* [Council of Ministers]

Interior Ministry: *Nizarat al-Dakhiliyya: Mukatibat 'Arabi, Mahfaza*, nos. 1–40.

Khedivial Council: *Sijillat 'Abdin 'Arabi wa Turki: Qayyid al-'Ardhalat al-Warida* 27/5/Seen 1893–1894 and *Qayyid al-'Ardhalat* 32/5/Seen 1902–1914 and *'Abdin: Diwan Khidiwi 'Ardhalat*, nos. 612–618, 1892–1912

Police: *Dabtiyyat Misr, Warid al-'Ardhalat*, 1274–1287 AH

Research Files: *Muhafiz al-Abhath*

The Public Record Office, London

Cairo Consular Court, 1889–1902: FO841

Cromer Papers: FO633

Documents submitted to the Milner Mission: FO848

Embassy and Consular Correspondence: FO141

Foreign Office Correspondence: FO371

GOVERNMENT PUBLICATIONS

Annuaire Statistique. Cairo: Ministry of Finance, 1910–1917.

Atlas of Cairo. Cairo: Offices of the Survey of Egypt, Ministry of Finance, 1922.

Atlas of Egypt. Vol. 1, Lower Egypt, Cairo: Ministry of Finance, Government Press, 1914.

Atlas of Egypt. Cairo: Egyptian Government, Survey of Egypt, 1928.

Budget Provisoire à Compte Général. Cairo: Ministry of Finance, 1876–1914.

Census of Egypt. 1872, 1882, 1897, 1907, 1917, and 1927.

Géographie Economique et Administrative de L'Egypte (Basse Egypt I). Cairo: n. p., 1902.

Majmu'a al-Awamir al-'Aliyya. Bulaq: Government Press, 1876–1914.

Al-Nashra al-Sanawiyya li-l-Tijara al-Kharijiyya. Cairo: Government Press, 1876–1914.

Al-Qararat wa-l-Manshurat al-Sadira min al-Nizarat. Bulaq: Government Press, 1876–1914.

Statistique de l'Egypte. Cairo: Ministry of the Interior, 1873.

BOOKS AND ARTICLES

Abbas, Ra'uf. *Al-Haraka al-'Ummaliyya fi Misr 1899–1952.* Cairo, 1967.

Abu Lughod, Janet. *Cairo: 1001 years of the City Victorious.* Princeton: Princeton University Press, 1971.

Abdel Fadil, Mahmud. "Informal Sector Employment in Egypt." In *Urban Research Strategies for Egypt,* ed. R. Lobbon. Cairo: American University Press, June 1983, 16–40.

Ablett, N. L. "Notes on the Industries of Assiut." *L'Egypte Contemporaine* 1(1910): 328–33.

Akarlı, Engin. "Gedik: Implements, Mastership, Shop Usufruct and Monopoly Among Istanbul Artisans, 1750–1850," *Wissenschaftskolleg Jahrbuch (1985/6):* Berlin: n. p., 1987: 357–69.

Alleaume, Ghislaine. "Politiques urbaines et contrôle de l'enterprise: Une Loi in-édite de 'Ali Mubarak sur les Corporations du Bâtiment." *Annales Islam-ologiques* 21 (1985): 147–88.

Alleaume, Ghislaine, and Philippe Fargues, "Voisinage et frontière: Résider au Caire en 1846." In *Urbanité arabe: Homage à Bernard Lepetit,* ed. Jocelyne Dakhlia Paris: Sindbad, 1998.

Allouche, Adel. *Mamluk Economics: A Study and Translation of Al-Maqrizi's Ighathah.* Salt Lake City: University of Utah Press, 1994.

Aminzade, Ronald. "Reinterpreting Capitalist Industrialization: A Study of Nineteenth Century France." In *Work in France*, ed. Steven Laurence Knapp and Cynthia Koepp, 393–417 Ithaca: Cornell University Press, 1986.

'Amr, 'Abd al-Salam 'Abd al-Halim. *al-Tawa'if al-Hiraf fi Misr 1805–1914*. Cairo: Al-Hay'a al-'Amma li-l-Kitab, 1993.

Arminjon, Pierre. *La Situation economique et financière de l'Egypte*. Paris: Libraire jerirale de Droit & le jurisprudence, 1911.

Artin Pacha, Yacoub. *Contes populaires de la vallée du Nil traduits de l'Arabe parlé*. Paris, 1895.

———. "Essai sur les causes du renchérissement de la vie matérielle au Caire." *Mémoires Presentés a l'Institut Egyptien*. 57–140 vol. 5. 1907.

———. "Hagg Ahmed Le Maçon." *Bulletin de l'institut Egyptien* 8, no. 2 (1914): 247–59.

Association des Industries en Egypte. *Notes et Rapports*. Cairo: n. p., 1925.

Ayubi, Nazih. *Overstating the Arab State: Politics and Society in the Middle East*. London: I. B. Tauris, 1995.

Badaoui, Zaki *Les Problèmes du travail et les organisations ouvrières en Egypte*. Alexandria: 1948.

Badawi, Jamal. " '*Afrit*," in *Misr min Nafidhat al-Tarikh*. Cairo: Dar al-Shuruq, 1994.

Baedeker, Karl, *Egypt: Handbook for Travellers. Part First: Lower Egypt with the Fayum and the Peninsula of the Sinai*. Leipzig: Baedeker, 1878.

———. *Egypt and the Sudan: Handbook for Travellers*. Leipzig: Baedeker, 1908.

Baer, Gabriel. *Egyptian Guilds in Modern Times*. Jerusalem: Israel Oriental Society, 1964.

———. "Correspondence." *Middle Eastern Studies* 3 (October 1966): 106–7.

———. "Urbanization in Egypt, 1820–1907," in *Beginnings of Modernization in the Middle East*, ed. W. R. Polk and R. L. Chambers. Chicago: University of Chicago Press, 1968.

———. *Studies in the Social History of Modern Egypt*. Chicago: University of Chicago Press, 1969.

———. The Administrative, Economic and Social Functions of Turkish Guilds. *International Journal of Middle East Studies* 1 (January 1970): 28–50.

———. "Monopolies and Restrictive Practices of Turkish Guilds." *Journal of the Economic and Social History of the Orient*, 13 (April, 1970): 145–65.

———. "The Organization of Labour." *Wirtschaftsgeschichte des Vorderen Orients in Islamischer Zeit*. Leiden: E. J. Brill, 1977.

———. "Popular Revolt in Ottoman Cairo." *Der Islam*, 54 (1977): 213–242.

————. "Ottoman Guilds: A Reassessment." In *The Social and Economic History of Turkey (1071–1920)*, ed. O. Okyar and H. Inalcik. Ankara: 1980.

————. *Fellah and Townsman in the Middle East: Studies in Social History*. London: Frank Cass, 1982.

Bayat, Asef. *Street Politics: Poor People's Movements in Iran*. New York: Columbia University Press, 1997.

Beinin, Joel. "Class and Politics in Middle Eastern Societies." *Comparative studies in Society and History* 28 (July 1986): 552–57.

Beinin, Joel, and Zachary Lockman. *Workers on the Nile: Nationalism, Communism, Islam and the Egyptian Working Class*. Princeton, N.J.: Princeton University Press 1987.

————. *Workers and Peasants in the Modern Middle East*. Cambridge: Cambridge University Press, 2001.

Berg, Maxine. *The Age of Manufactures: Industry, Innovation and Work in Britain, 1700–1820*. Totowa, N.J.: Barnes and Noble, 1985.

Berg, Maxine, Pat Hudson, and Michael Sonenscher, eds. *Manufacture in Town and Country before the Factory*. Cambridge: Cambridge University Press, 1983.

Bernal, Victoria. *Cultivating Workers: Peasants and Capitalism in a Sudanese Village*. New York: Columbia University Press, 1991.

Berque, Jacques. *Egypt: Imperialism and Revolution*. Trans. Jean Stewart. London: Faber, 1972.

Bigiavi, Edoardo D. "Des Accidents du travail et de la protection des ouvriers en Egypte." *L'Egypte Contemporaine* 1 (1910): 630–42.

Blunt, Wilfred Scawen. *Secret History of the English Occupation of Egypt*. London: Martin Secker, 1907.

Boinet Bey, A. "L'Accroissement de la population en Egypte." *Bulletin de L'Institut Egyptien* 2nd series, no. 7 (1886): 272–305.

————. *Dictionnaire géographique de l'Egypte*. Cairo, 1899.

Bourgeois, François. "L'Industrie céramique en Egypte." *L'Egypte Contemporaine* (1916): 467–84.

Bouriant, U. *Chansons populaire arabes en dialecte du Caire*. Paris, 1893.

Bowring, John. *Report on Egypt and Candia*. London: n. p., 1840.

Brinner, William M. "The Significance of the Harafish and Their 'Sultan.'" *Journal of Economic and Social History of the Orient*, 6 (1963).

Burawoy, Michael. *Manufacturing Consent: Changes in the Labor Process under Monopoly Capitalism*. Chicago: University of Chicago Press, 1979.

Burawoy, Michael, and Theda Skocpol, eds. *Marxist Inquiries: Studies of Labor, Class and States*. Chicago: University of Chicago Press, 1982.

Burek, Gunseli. "Women Carpet Weavers in Rural Turkey: Patterns of Employ-ment Earnings and Status." *Women, Work and Development Series*, no. 15. Geneva, 1987.

Burke, Edmund III. "Islam and Social Movements: Methodological Reflections." In *Islam, Politics and Social Movements*, ed. Edmund Burke III and Ira M. Lapidus. Berkeley: University of California Press, 1988.

———, ed. *Global Crises and Social Movements: Artisans, Peasants, Populists and the World Economy*. Boulder, Colo.: Westview Press, 1988.

———. *Struggle and Survival in the Modern Middle East*. Berkeley: University of California Press, 1993.

Cahen, Claude. "Y a-t-il des corporations professionelles dans le monde musulman classique? Quelques notes et réflexions." In *The Islamic City: A Collo-quium*, ed. A. H. Hourani and S. M. Stern. Oxford: Bruno Cassirer, 1970.

Caron, François. *An Economic History of Modern France*. Trans. Barbara Bray. New York: Columbia University Press, 1979.

Cattaui Pasha, Joseph. *L'Egypte: Aperçu historique et géographique*. Cairo: L'Institut Français d'Archéologie Orientale, 1926.

Cecil, Edward. *The Leisure of an Egyptian Official*. London: Hodder and Stoughton, 1921.

Chakrabarty, Dipesh. *Rethinking Working Class History: Bengal 1890–1940*. Prince-ton, N.J.: Princeton University Press, 1989.

Chalcraft, John. *The Striking Cabbies of Cairo and Other Stories: Crafts and Guilds in Egypt, 1863–1914*. Ph.D. diss., New York University, 2001.

———. "The Coal-Heavers of Port Sa'id: State-Making and Worker Protest, 1869–1914." *International Labor and Working Class History* 60 (fall 2001): 110–24.

———. "The Cairo Cab-Strike of 1907." In *Arab Provincial Capitals in the Late Ottoman Empire*, ed. Jens Hanssen and Thomas Philipp. Beirut: Orient Institut, 2002.

Chandavarkar, Rajnarayan. *Imperial Power and Popular politics*. Cambridge: Cam-bridge University Press, 1998.

Chaturvedi, Vinayak. *Mapping Subaltern Studies and the Postcolonial*. London: Verso, 2000.

Chenouda, Attya. "Notes on the Weaving Industry." *L'Egypte Contemporaine* 1 (1910): 187–93.

Chevallier, Dominique. "Un éxemple de résistance technique de l'artisanat syrien aux XIXe et XXe siècles: Les tissues ikâtes d'Alep et de Damas." *Syria* 30 (1962): 300–24.

———. *La Société du Mont Liban à l'epoque de la révolution industrielle en Europe*. Paris: Librairie Orientaliste Paul Geultner, 1971.

Chevallier, Dominique, and Jacques Berque. *Les Arabes par les archives.* Paris, 1976.

Cinar, E. Mine. "Labour Market Opportunities for Home Working Women in Istanbul." Working Paper no. 2 Los Angeles: von Grunebaum Center for Near Eastern Studies, 1992.

Clerget, Marcel. *Le Caire.* 2 Vols. Cairo, 1934.

Cohen, Amnon. *The Guilds of Ottoman Jerusalem.* Leiden: Brill, 2001.

Cole, Juan R. I. *Colonialism and Revolution in the Middle East.* Princeton, N.J.: Princeton University Press, 1993.

Couland, Jacques. *Le Mouvement Syndical au Liban, 1919–1946.* Paris: Editions Anthropos, 1969.

Crafts, N. F. R. *British Economic Growth during the Industrial Revolution.* Oxford: Clarendon Press, 1985.

Crossick, Geoffrey ed. *The Artisan and the European Town, 1500–1800.* Aldershot: Scolar Press, 1997.

Cuno, Kenneth. *The Pasha's Peasants: Land, Society, and Economy in Lower Egypt, 1740–1858.* Cambridge: Cambridge University Press, 1992.

David, Jean-Claude. "Alep, dégradation et tentatives actuelles de réadaptation des structures urbaines traditionelles." *Bulletin d'Etudes Orientales* 28 (1975): 19–50.

Davis, Eric. "Political Development or Political Economy?" *Review of Middle Eastern Studies* 1 (1975): 41–61.

———. *Challenging Colonialism: Bank Misr and Egyptian Industrialization, 1920–1941.* Princeton, N.J.: Princeton University Press, 1983.

Deane, Phyllis, and William Alan Cole. *British Economic Growth, 1688–1959: Trends and Structure.* Cambridge: Cambridge University Press, 1962.

De Jong, Frederik. *Turuq and Turuq-Linked Institutions in Nineteenth Century Egypt: A historical Study in the Organizational Dimensions of Islamic Mysticism.* Leiden: E. J. Brill, 1978.

Diyab, al-Sayyid Ahmad Tawfiq. *Al-Siyaha fi Misr khilal al-Qarn al-Tasi'a 'Ashr.* Cairo: General Egyptian Book Organization, 1994.

Doumani, Beshara. *Rediscovering Palestine: Merchants and Peasants in Jabal Nablus, 1700–1900.* Berkeley: University of California Press, 1995.

Dumont, Paul. "A propos de la classe ouvrière ottomane à la veille de la révolution jeune turque." *Turcica* vol. 9 (1977).

Elyachar, Julia. "Mappings of Power: The State and International Organizations of the 'Informal Economy' of Cairo. "Paper presented to American Anthropological Association, 2000.

Encyclopaedia of Islam, 1st ed., s.v. "sinf."

Evans, Richard J. *In Defence of History*. London: Granta Books, 1997.

Fahmy, Khaled. *All the Pasha's Men: Mehmed Ali, His Army and the Making of Modern Egypt*. Cambridge: Cambridge University Press, 1997.

Fisher, Sydney Nettleton, ed. *Social Forces in the Middle East*. Ithaca, N.Y.: Cornell University Press, 1955.

Gelvin, James L. *Divided Loyalties: Nationalism and Mass Politics in Syria at the Close of Empire*. Berkeley: University of California Press, 1998.

Genç, Mehmet. "Ottoman Industry in the Eighteenth Century: General Framework, Characteristics and Main Trends." In *Manufacturing in the Ottoman Empire and Turkey, 1500–1950*, ed. Donald Quataert, 59–86. Albany: State University of New York Press, 1994.

———. "L'Economie ottoman et la guerre au XVIIIe siècle." *Turcica* 27 (1995): 177–96.

Gerber, Haim. "Guilds in Seventeenth Century Anatolian Bursa." *Asian and African Studies* 11 (1976).

———. Gerber, Haim. *Economy and Society in an Ottoman City: Bursa, 1600–1700*. Jerusalem: Hebrew University, 1988.

———. *State, Society and Law in Islam: Ottoman Law in Comparative Perspective*. Albany: State University of New York Press, 1994.

Ghazaleh, Pascale. "The Guilds between Tradition and Modernity." In *The State and Its Servants: Administration in Egypt from Ottoman Times to the Present*, ed. Nelly Hanna. Cairo: American University in Cairo Press, 1995.

———. "*Tawa'if hirafiyya*: Crafts and Craftspeople in Cairo, 1750–1850." (Master's thesis, American University in Cairo, 1996.

———. *Masters of the Trade: Crafts and Craftspeople in Cairo, 1750–1850*. Cairo: American University in Cairo Press, 1999.

———. "Organizing Labor: Professional Classifications in the Late 18th-/early 19th Century Cairo." Unpublished paper.

Gibb, Hamilton, A.R., and Harold Bowen. *Islamic Society and the West: A Study of the Impact of Western Civilization on Moslem Culture in the Near East*. Vol. 1. Oxford: Oxford University Press, 1950.

Gilsenan, Michael. *Lords of the Lebanese Marches: Violence and Narrative in an Arab Society*. Berkeley: University of California Press, 1996.

Goitein, Shelomo D. "Cairo: An Islamic City in the Light of the Geniza Documents." In *Middle Eastern Cities: A Symposium on Ancient, Islamic, and Contemporary Middle Eastern Urbanism*, ed. Ira M. Lapidus. Berkeley: University of California Press, 1969.

Goldberg, Ellis Jay. *Tinker, Tailor, Textile Worker: Class and Politics in Egypt, 1930–1952*. Berkeley: University of California Press, 1986.

————, ed. *The Social History of Labor in the Middle East*. Boulder, Colo.: Westview Press, 1996

Gordon, F. Moore. "Beni Adi, Beni Souef, Abou Kerkas." *L'Egypte Contemporaine* (1911): 69–75:

Gran, Peter. *Islamic Roots of Capitalism: Egypt 1760–1840*. With a foreword by Afaf Lutfi al-Sayyid Marsot. Austin: University of Texas Press, 1979.

————. "Political Economy as a Paradigm for the Study of Islamic History." *International Journal of Middle East Studies* 11 (1980): 511–26

————. Gran, Peter. *Beyond Eurocentrism: A New View of Modern World History*. Syracuse, N.Y.: Syracuse University Press, 1996.

al-Gritli, 'Ali. *Tarikh al-Sina'a fi Misr*. Cairo: Dar al Ma'arif Press, 1953.

Guha, Ranajit, and Gayatri C. Spivak, eds. *Selected Subaltern Studies*. New York: Oxford University Press, 1988.

Hanafi, Sahar Ali. *Al-'Alaqat al-Tijariyya bayn Misr wa Bilad al-Sham al-Kubra fi-l-Qarn al-Thamin 'Ashr*. Cairo: General Egyptian Book Organization, 2000.

Hanagan, Michael P., Leslie Page Moch, and Wayne Te Brake, eds. *Challenging Authority: The Historical Study of Contentious Politics*. Minneapolis and London: University of Minnesota Press, 1998.

Hanayn Bek, Girgis. *al-Atiyan wa al-Dara'ib fi al-Qatr al-Misri*. Bulaq, al-Matba' al-Kubra al-Amiriyya, 1904.

Hanna, Nelly. *Construction Work in Ottoman Cairo (1517–1798)*. Cairo: Institut Français d'Archéologie Orientale, 1984.

Heller, Patrick. *The Labor of Development: Workers and the Transformation of Capitalism in Kerala, India*. Ithaca, N.Y.: Cornell University Press, 1999.

Higgins, John ed. *The Raymond Williams Reader*. Oxford: Blackwell, 2001.

Hobsbawm, Eric. *The Age of Extremes: The Short Twentieth Century, 1914–1991*. London: Abacus Books, 1994.

————. *On History*. London: Weidenfield and Nicolson, 1997.

Holt, P. M. *Egypt and the Fertile Crescent, 1516–1922: A Political History*. Ithaca, N.Y.: Cornell University Press, 1966.

Hopkins, Nicholas S., ed. *Informal Sector in Egypt*, Cairo: American University in Cairo Press, 1991.

Hourani, Albert. *Arabic Thought in the Liberal Age, 1798–1939*. Cambridge: Cambridge University Press, 1962.

————. *A History of the Arab Peoples*. London: Faber and Faber, 1991.

————. "Ottoman Reform and the Politics of the Notables." In *The Modern Middle East: A reader*, ed. A. Hourani, P. S. Khoury, and M. C. Wilson Berkeley: University of California Press, 1993.

Hunter, F. Robert. *Egypt under the Khedives, 1805–1879: From Household Government to Modern Bureaucracy.* Pittsburg: University of Pittsburg Press, 1984.

Ilbert, Robert. *Alexandrie, 1830–1930: Histoire d'une communauté citadine.* Cairo: Institut Français d'Archéologie Orientale, 1996.

Inalcik, Halil. *The Ottoman Empire: The Classical Age, 1300–1600.* New York: 1973.

———. *The Middle East and the Balkans under the Ottoman Empire: Essays on Economy and Society.* Indiana University Turkish Studies and Turkish Ministry of Culture Joint Series, vol. 9. Bloomington, 1993.

Inalcik, Halil, and Donald Quataert, eds. *An Economic and Social History of the Ottoman Empire, 1300–1914.* Cambridge, Cambridge University Press, 1994.

Islamoglu-Inan, Huri ed. *The Ottoman Empire and the World-Economy.* Cambridge University Press, 1987.

Issawi, Charles. *Egypt in Revolution: An Economic Analysis.* London: Oxford University Press, 1963.

———, ed. *The Economic History of the Middle East, 1800–1914.* Chicago: University of Chicago Press, 1966.

———. "Asymmetrical Development and Transport in Egypt, 1800–1914." In *Beginnings of Modernisation in the Middle East: The Nineteenth Century,* ed. William R. Polk and Richard L. Chambers. Chicago: University of Chicago Press, 1968.

———. "Middle East Economic Development, 1815–1914." In *The Modern Middle East: A Reader,* ed. A. Hourani, P. S. Khoury, and M. C. Wilson Berkeley: University of California Press, 1993.

'Izz al-Din, Amin. *Ta'rikh al-Tabaqa al-'Amila al-Misriyya.* 3 vols. Cairo Dar al-Sha'b, 1967–1971.

al-Jabarti, 'Abd al-Rahman. *Al-Jabarti's History of Egypt.* Ed. and trans. Thomas Philipp and Moshe Perlmann. 4 vols. Stuttgart: Franz Steiner, 1994.

Joyce, Patrick. *Visions of the People: Industrial England and the Question of Class, 1848–1914.* Cambridge: Cambridge University Press, 1991.

———, ed. *Class.* Oxford: Oxford University Press, 1995.

Kasaba, Resat. *The Ottoman Empire and the World Economy: The Nineteenth Century.* Albany, N.Y.: State University of New York Press, 1988.

Kelly, R. Talbot. *Egypt Painted and Described.* London: Adam and Charles Black, 1903.

al-Khadem, Saad. "Quelques récus de commerçants et d'artisans du Caire des XVIIe et XVIIIe siècles." In *Colloque International sur l'Histoire du Caire,* 269–276. Cairo: Deutsche Demokratische Republik and Ministry of Culture of the Arab Republic of Egypt, 1969.

Klunzinger, C. B. *Upper Egypt: Its People and its Products.* London: Blackie & Son, 1879.

Koptiuch, Kristin. *A Poetics of Political Economy in Egypt.* Minneapolis, University of Minnesota Press, 1999.

Laclau, Ernesto, and Chantal Mouffe. *Hegemony and Socialist Strategy: Towards a Radical Democratic Politics.* London: Verso, 1985.

Ladjevardi, Habib. *Labor Unions and Autocracy in Iran.* Syracuse, N.Y.: Syracuse University Press, 1985.

"La Filature en Egypte." *L'Egypte Industrielle* (February 1930).

Lamplough, A. O. *Egypt and How to See It.* London: Ballantyne, 1908.

Landes, David S. *Bankers and Pashas: International Finance and Economic Imperialism in Egypt.* Cambridge: Harvard University Press, 1958.

———. *The Unbound Prometheus: Technological Change and Industrial Development in Western Europe from 1750 to the Present.* London: Cambridge University Press, 1969.

Lane, Edward William. *An Account of the Manners and Customs of the Modern Egyptians.* 1836. East West Publications, 1978.

Langley, J. "Note on the Native Mat Industry." *Journal of the Khedivial Agricultural Society and the School of Agriculture* 3 (January & February 1901): 83–85.

Lapidus, Ira M. *Muslim Cities in the Later Middle Ages.* Cambridge: Cambridge University Press, 1984.

———. *A History of Islamic Societies.* Cambridge: Cambridge University Press, 1988.

Laplange, G. "L'Avenir des industries d'art en Egypte." *Bulletin de l'Institut Egyptien* 7, part 1 (1913): 38–42.

Legrain, Georges. "Chansons dans les Ruines." *La Révue Egyptienne* 1, 1–12 (1912): 307–10.

———. "Chants des manoeuvriers." *La Révue Egyptienne* 1, 1–12 (1912): 348–55.

"Les Industries agricoles an Egypte." *Bulletin de la Chambre de Commerce International* 1, no. 5 (November 1903): 1–5.

Levi, I. G. "Le Commerce et l'Industrie." In *L'Egypte: Aperçu historique et géographique,* 261–97. Cairo: L'Institut Francais d'Archéologie Orientale, 1926.

Lewis, Bernard. "The Islamic Guilds." *Economic History Review* 8 (1937–38): 20–37.

Lockman, Zachary, ed. *Workers and Working Classes in the Middle East: Struggles, Histories, Historiographies.* Albany: State University of New York Press, 1994.

———. "Imagining the Working Class: Culture, Nationalism, and Class Formation in Egypt, 1899–1914." *Poetics Today* 15 (summer 1994): 157–90.

Longuesse, Elizabeth. "La Classe ouvrière dans les payes arabes: La Syrie." *La Pensée* 20 (1978): 120–32.

Low, S. *Egypt in Transition*. London, 1914.

Mabro, Robert, and Samir Radwan, *The Industrialization of Egypt, 1939–1973: Policy and Performance*. Oxford: Clarendon Press, 1976.

Mann, Michael. *The sources of social power*. Vol. 1, *A History of Power from the Beginning to A.D. 1760*. Cambridge: Cambridge University Press, 1986.

Marcus, Abraham. *The Middle East on the Eve of Modernity: Aleppo in the Eighteenth Century*. New York: Columbia University Press, 1989.

Mardin, Serif. *The Genesis of Young Ottoman Thought: A study in the Modernization of Turkish Political Ideas*. Syracuse, N.Y.: Syracuse University Press, 2000.

Marshall, J. E. *The Egyptian Enigma, 1890–1928*. London: John Murray, 1928.

Marsot, Afaf Lutfi al-Sayyid. *Egypt in the Reign of Muhammad Ali*. Cambridge: Cambridge University Press, 1984.

Masters, Bruce. *The Origins of Western Economic Dominance in the Middle East: Mercantilism and the Islamic economy in Aleppo, 1600–1750*. New York: New York University Press, 1988.

Martin, Germain. *Les Bazars du Caire et les petits métiers arabes*. Cairo: Université Egyptienne, 1910.

Martin, Germain, and I. G. Levi. "Le Marché egyptien et l'utilité de la publication des mercuriales." *L'Egypte Contemporaine* 1 (1910): 441–89.

Marx, Karl. "The Eighteenth Brumaire of Louis Bonaparte." In *Karl Marx: Selected Writings*, ed. David McLellan. Oxford: Oxford University Press, 1977.

Massignon, Louis. "La 'Futuwwa,' ou 'Pacte d'honneur artisanal' entre les travailleurs musulmans aú moyen age." In *Opera Minora*, ed. Y. Moubarac. Vol 1. Beirut: Dar al-Ma'arif, 1963.

Maunier, Réné. "L'Apprentissage dans la petite industrie en Egypte: L'Organisation actuelle les réformes possibles." *L'Egypte Contemporaine* (1912): 341–69.

———. "L'Exposition des industries Egyptiennes." *L'Egypte Contemporaine* (1916): 433–43.

Mavris, N. G. *Contribution à l'etude de la chanson populaire egyptienne*. Alexandria: P. Castrounis and Z. Halkiadis, 1932.

McAdam, Doug, John D. McCarthy, and Mayer N. Zald, eds. *Comparative Perspectives on Social Movements: Political Opportunities, Mobilizing Structures, and Cultural Framings*. Cambridge: Cambridge University Press, 1996.

McCoan, J. C. *Egypt As It Is*. London 1877.

Mendels, F. F. "Proto-Industrialization: The First Phase of the Industrialization Process." *Journal of Economic History* 32 (1972).

Metayer-Masselin, Le. *L'Egypte et l'industrie rubanière*. Paris: Alcan-Levy, 1870.

Metin, Albert. *La Transformation de l'Egypte*. Paris: Felix Alcan, 1903.

Mitchell, Timothy. *Colonising Egypt*. Cambridge: Cambridge University Press, 1988.

———. "The Limits of the State: Beyond Statist Approaches and Their Critics." *American Political Science Review* 85 (March 1991): 77–96.

Moore, Barrington. *Social Origins of Dictatorship and Democracy: Lord and Peasant in the Making of the Modern World*. London: Penguin, 1967.

Moore Gordon, F. "Notes on the Weaving Industry at Mehalla-Kebir." *L'Egypte Contemporaine* 1 (1910): 334–39.

———. "Notes on the Industries of Assiut." *L'Egypte Contemporaine* 1 (1910): 337–39.

Morgan, Edmund S. *Inventing the People: The Rise of Popular Sovereignty in England and America*. New York: W. W. Norton, 1988.

Mubarak, 'Ali. *al-Khitat al-Tawfiqiyah al-Jadida li-Misr al-Qahira wa-Muduniha wa Biladiha*. Cairo: al-Hay'a al-Misriyya al-'Amma li-l-Kitab, 1980.

Najm, Zayn al-'Abidin Shams al-Din. *Bur Sa'id: tarikhuha wa tatawwuruha mundhu nasha'iha 1859 hatta 'am 1882*. Cairo: Al-Hay'a Al-Misriyya Al-'Amma li-l-kitab, 1987.

Naus Bey, H. "L'Industrie egyptienne." *L'Egypte Contemporaine* 21 (1930): 1–16.

Noorani, Yaseen. "A Nation Born in Mourning: The Neo-Classical Funeral Elegy in Egypt." *Journal of Arabic Literature* 28 (1997): 38–67.

O'Brien Patrick, and Çaglar Keyder. *Economic Growth in Britain and France, 1780–1914: Two Paths to the Twentieth Century*. London: Allen and Unwin, 1978.

O'Hanlon, Rosalind, and D. Washbrook. "After Orientalism: Culture, Criticism and Politics in the Third World." *Comparative Studies in Society and History* 34 (1992): 141–67.

Olson, Robert W. "The Esnaf and the Patrona Halil Rebellion of 1730: A Realignment in Ottoman Politics?" *Journal of the Economic and Social History of the Orient* 17 (1974): 329–44.

———. "Jews, Janissaries, Esnaf and the Revolt of 1740 in Istanbul: Social Upheaval and Political Realignment in the Ottoman Empire." *Journal of the Economic and Social History of the Orient* 20 (1977): 185–207.

Owen, Roger. "Lord Cromer and the Development of Egyptian Industry." *Middle Eastern Studies* 2 (July 1966): 282–301.

———. *Cotton and the Egyptian Economy, 1820–1914: A Study in Trade and Development*. Oxford: Clarendon Press, 1969.

———. *The Middle East in the World Economy, 1800–1914*. London: Methuen, 1981.

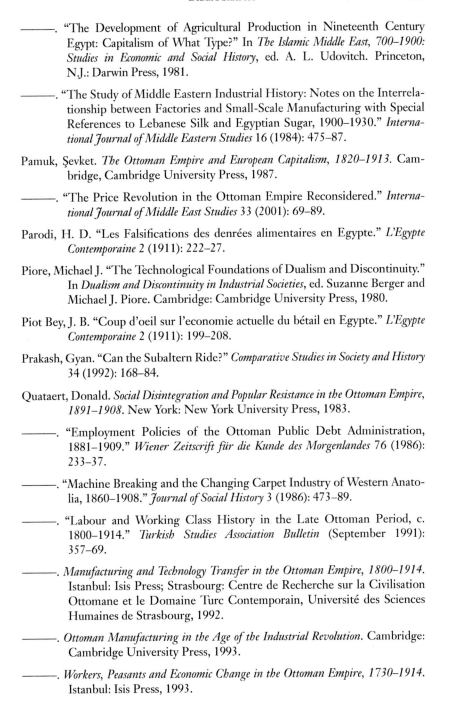

———. "The Development of Agricultural Production in Nineteenth Century Egypt: Capitalism of What Type?" In *The Islamic Middle East, 700–1900: Studies in Economic and Social History*, ed. A. L. Udovitch. Princeton, N.J.: Darwin Press, 1981.

———. "The Study of Middle Eastern Industrial History: Notes on the Interrelationship between Factories and Small-Scale Manufacturing with Special References to Lebanese Silk and Egyptian Sugar, 1900–1930." *International Journal of Middle Eastern Studies* 16 (1984): 475–87.

Pamuk, Şevket. *The Ottoman Empire and European Capitalism, 1820–1913.* Cambridge, Cambridge University Press, 1987.

———. "The Price Revolution in the Ottoman Empire Reconsidered." *International Journal of Middle East Studies* 33 (2001): 69–89.

Parodi, H. D. "Les Falsifications des denrées alimentaires en Egypte." *L'Egypte Contemporaine* 2 (1911): 222–27.

Piore, Michael J. "The Technological Foundations of Dualism and Discontinuity." In *Dualism and Discontinuity in Industrial Societies*, ed. Suzanne Berger and Michael J. Piore. Cambridge: Cambridge University Press, 1980.

Piot Bey, J. B. "Coup d'oeil sur l'economie actuelle du bétail en Egypte." *L'Egypte Contemporaine* 2 (1911): 199–208.

Prakash, Gyan. "Can the Subaltern Ride?" *Comparative Studies in Society and History* 34 (1992): 168–84.

Quataert, Donald. *Social Disintegration and Popular Resistance in the Ottoman Empire, 1891–1908.* New York: New York University Press, 1983.

———. "Employment Policies of the Ottoman Public Debt Administration, 1881–1909." *Wiener Zeitscrift für die Kunde des Morgenlandes* 76 (1986): 233–37.

———. "Machine Breaking and the Changing Carpet Industry of Western Anatolia, 1860–1908." *Journal of Social History* 3 (1986): 473–89.

———. "Labour and Working Class History in the Late Ottoman Period, c. 1800–1914." *Turkish Studies Association Bulletin* (September 1991): 357–69.

———. *Manufacturing and Technology Transfer in the Ottoman Empire, 1800–1914.* Istanbul: Isis Press; Strasbourg: Centre de Recherche sur la Civilisation Ottomane et le Domaine Turc Contemporain, Université des Sciences Humaines de Strasbourg, 1992.

———. *Ottoman Manufacturing in the Age of the Industrial Revolution.* Cambridge: Cambridge University Press, 1993.

———. *Workers, Peasants and Economic Change in the Ottoman Empire, 1730–1914.* Istanbul: Isis Press, 1993.

Quataert, Donald, and Eric van Zurcher, eds. *Workers and the Working Class in the Ottoman Empire and the Turkish Republic, 1839–1950.* London: I. B. Tauris, 1995.

Qudsi, Ilyas 'Abduh. *Elias Qudsi's Sketch of the Guilds of Damascus in the Nineteenth Century.* Trans. Yusuf Ibish. Al-Hamra, 1992.

Rafeq, Abdel Karim. "The Law Court Registers of Damascus with Special Reference to Craft-Corporations during the First Half of the Eighteenth Century." *In Les Arabes par leurs archives (XVIe–XXe siecles),* ed. Jacques Berque and Dominique Chevallier, 141–59. Paris: Centre National de la Recherche Scientifique, 1976.

———. "Craft Organizations, Work Ethics and the Strains of Change in Ottoman Syria." *Journal of the American Oriental Society* 111 (1991): 495–511.

Rancière, Jacques. *The Nights of Labor: The Workers' Dream in Nineteenth Century France.* Trans. John Drury. Philadelphia: Temple University Press, 1989.

Raymond, André. "Une Liste des corporations de métiers au Caire en 1801." *Arabica* 4 (1957): 150–63.

———. "Les Porteurs d'eau du Caire." *Bulletin de l'Institut Francais d'Archéologie Orientale* 57 (1958): 183–203.

———. "Quartiers et mouvements populaires au Caire au XVIIIe Siècle." In *Political and Social Change in Modern Egypt,* ed. P. M. Holt London: Oxford University Press, 1968.

———. "Problèmes urbains et urbanisme au Caire." *Colloque International sur l'Histoire du Caire.* Cairo: Deutsche Demokratische Republik and Ministry of Culture of Arab Republic of Egypt, 1969.

———. *Artisans et commerçants au Caire au XVIIIe siècle.* 2 vols. Damas: Institut Français de Damas, 1973.

———. *The Oxford Encyclopaedia of the Modern Islamic World.* Vol. 2. New York: Oxford University Press, 1995.

———. "Les Transformations des corporations de métiers au Caire du XVIIIe au XIXe Siècle." In *Les Institutions traditionelles dans le monde arabe,* ed., Hervé Blanchot. 29–40. Paris: Karthala, 1999.

Reilly, James A. "Origins of Peripheral Capitalism in the Damascus Region, 1830–1914." Ph.D. dissertation, Georgetown University, 1987.

———. "Damascus Merchants and Trade in the Transition to Capitalism." *Canadian Journal of History* 27 (April 1992): 1–27.

———. "From Workshops to Sweatshops: Damascus Textiles and the World-Economy in the last Ottoman century." *Review* 16 (spring 1993): 199–213.

Richards, Alan, and John Waterbury. *A Political Economy of the Middle East: State, Class and Economic Development.* Boulder, Colo.: Westview Press, 1990.

Rifa'i, Husayn 'Ali. *Al-Sina'a fi Misr*. Cairo, 1935.

Rostow, Walt Whitman. *The Process of Economic Growth*. Oxford: Oxford University Press, 1953.

Roux, François Charles. "Le Capital français en Egypte." *L'Egypte Contemporaine* 2 (1911): 465–502.

Rueschmeyer, Dietrich, Evelyne Huber Stephens, and John D. Stephens. *Capitalism, Development and Democracy*. Chicago: University of Chicago Press, 1992.

Russell Pasha, Thomas. *Egyptian Service, 1902–1946*. London: John Murray, 1949.

Sabel, Charles F. *Work and Politics: The Division of Labor in Industry*. Cambridge: Cambridge University Press, 1982.

Sabel, Charles F., and Jonathan Zeitlin. "Historical Alternatives to Mass Production: Politics, Markets and Technology in Nineteenth Century Industrialisation." *Past and Present* 108 (1985): 133–76.

Sa'id, Rifa't. *Al-Asas al-Ijtima'i li-l-Thawra al-'Urabiyya*. Cairo: General Egyptian Book Organization, 1994.

Salim, Latifa. *Al-Quwa al-Ijtima'iyya fi-l-Thawra al-'Urabiyya*. Cairo: General Egyptian Book Organization, 1981.

Sami, Amin. *Taqwim al-Nil. 3*, 2 Vols. Cairo, 1936.

Samuel, Raphael. "Workshop of the World: Steam Power and Hand Technology in Mid-Victorian Britain." *History Workshop* 3 (1977).

Sartre, Jean-Paul. *Search for a Method*. Translated and with an introduction by Hazel E. Barnes. New York: Vintage Books, 1963.

al-Sayyid, Afaf Lutfi. Review of "Egyptian Guilds in Modern Times," by Gabriel Baer. *Middle Eastern Studies*. 3 (1966): 272–276.

Schölch, Alexander. *Egypt for the Egyptians! The Socio-Political Crisis in Egypt 1878–1882*. London: Ithaca Press, 1981.

Scott, James C. *Arts of Domination and Resistance: Hidden Transcripts*. New Haven and London: Yale University Press, 1990.

———. *Seeing Like a State: How Certain Schemes to Improve the Human Condition have Failed*. London and New Haven: Yale University Press, 1998.

Sedky, Mahmoud. "La Corporation des cordonniers: Fabricants de markoubs au Caire." *La Révue Egyptienne* 1 nos. 1–12 (1912): 108–10.

Sewell, William H. *Work and Revolution in France: The Language of Labor from the Old Regime to 1848*. Cambridge: Cambridge University Press, 1980.

———. "Towards a Post-materialist Rhetoric for Labor History." In *Rethinking Labor History: Essays on Discourse and Class Analysis*, ed. Lenard R. Berlanstein. Urbana: University of Illinois Press, 1993.

Shatzmiller, Maya. *Labour in the Medieval Islamic World*. Leiden: E. J. Brill, 1994.

Shaw, Stanford. *History of the Ottoman Empire and Modern Turkey*. Cambridge: Cambridge University Press, 1976.

Shearer, W. V. "Report on the Weaving Industry in Assiout." *L'Egypte Contemporaine* 1 (1910): 184–46.

Shechter, Relli. "Selling Luxury: The Rise of the Egyptian Cigarette and the Transformation of the Egyptian Tobacco Market, 1850–1914." *International Journal of Middle East Studies* 35 (2003), 51–75.

Singerman, Diane. *Avenues of Participation: Family, Politics and Networks in Urban Quarters of Cairo*. Princeton, N.J.: Princeton University Press, 1995.

Sladen, Douglas. *Oriental Cairo: The City of the "Arabian Nights."* London: Hurst and Blackett, 1911.

Sonbol, Amira el-Azhary. *The New Mamluks: Egyptian Society and Modern Feudalism*. Syracuse, N.Y.: Syracuse University Press, 2000.

Sonenscher, Michael. *Work and Wages: Natural Law, Politics and the Eighteenth Century French Trades*. Cambridge, Cambridge University Press, 1989.

Sornaga, S. *L'Industrie en Egypte*. Cairo: Poditi, 1916.

Soucail, Bernard. "Commercial Education in Egypt. Its economic Importance, and the Surest Method of Dissemination." *L'Egypte Contemporaine* 1 (1910): 559–68.

Swanson, Heather. *Medieval Artisans: An Urban Class in Late Medieval England*. Oxford: Blackwell, 1989.

Thompson, E. P. *The Making of the English Working Class*. Harmondsworth, England: Penguin Books, 1963.

Tilly, Charles. *Coercion, Capital and European States, AD 990–1990*. Oxford: Blackwell, 1990.

———. *Popular Contention in Great Britain, 1758–1834*. Cambridge: Harvard University Press, 1995.

———. *Durable Inequality*. Berkeley, University of California Press, 1998.

Todorov, Nikolai. *The Balkan City, 1400–1800*. Seattle: University of Washington Press, 1983.

Toledano, Ehud. *State and Society in Mid-Nineteenth Century Egypt*. Cambridge: Cambridge University Press, 1990.

Tomiche, Nada. "La Situation des artisans et petits commerçants en Egypte de la fin du XVIIIe siècle jusqu'au milieu du XIXe." *Studia Islamica* 12 (1960): 79–98.

Tosh, John. Ed. *Historians on History*. Harlow: Pearson Education, 2000.

Tribier, Paul. "La Fête de la Rouya." *La Révue Egyptienne* 1, nos. 1–12 (1912): 236–39.

Tucker, Judith. *Women in Nineteenth Century Egypt*. Cambridge: Cambridge University Press, 1985.

Vallet, Jean. *Contribution à l'étude de la condition des ouvriers de la grande industrie au Caire*. Valence: Imprimerie Valentinoise, 1911.

Vatikiotis, P. J. *The Modern History of Egypt*. London: Weidenfield and Nicolson, 1969.

Vatter, Sherry. "A City Divided: A Socioeconomic Study of Damascus, Syria, 1840–1870." Ph.D. Dissertation, UCLA.

de Vaujany, H. *Alexandrie et la Basse Egypte*. Paris, 1885.

Wallis Budge, E. A. *Cook's Handbook for Egypt and the Sudan*. London: Thos. Cook and Son, 1905.

Weber, Max. *Economy and Society*. Ed. Guenther Roth and Claus Wittich. 2 vols. Berkeley: University of California Press, 1968.

Wells, Sidney H. "Preliminary Note on the Weaving Industry in Egypt." *L'Egypte Contemporaine* 1 (1910): 578–84.

———. "L'Industrie du tissage en Egypte." *L'Egypte Contemporaine* 2 (1911): 52–73.

———. "L'Organisation et le développement de l'Enseignement Agricole Industriel et Commercial en Egypte." *L'Egypte Contemporaine* 2 (1911): 344–69.

Williams, Raymond. "Base and Superstructure in Marxist Cultural Theory." In *The Raymond Williams Reader*, ed. John Higgins. Oxford: Blackwell, 2001.

Winter, Michael. *Egyptian Society under Ottoman Rule, 1517–1798*. London and New York: Routledge, 1992.

Wright, A., and Cartwright H. A. *Twentieth Century Impressions of Egypt*. London: 1909.

Wuthnow, Robert. *Communities of Discourse: Ideology and Social Structure in the Reformation, the Enlightenment, and European Socialism*. Cambridge: Harvard University Press, 1989.

Yapp, Malcolm E. *The Making of the Modern Near East, 1792–1923*. London: Longman, 1987.

Yi, Eunjeong. "The Seventeenth-Century Istanbul Guilds: Leverage in Changing Times." Ph.D. Dissertation, Harvard University, 2000.

Index